Irene C. Fountas & Gay Su Pinnell

The Writing Minilessons Book

Your Every Day Guide for Literacy Teaching

KINDERGARTEN

HEINEMANN
Portsmouth, NH

Heinemann
145 Maplewood Avenue, Suite 300
Portsmouth, NH 03801
www.heinemann.com

Offices and agents throughout the world

The authors and publisher wish to thank those who have generously given permission to reprint borrowed material: Please see the Credits section beginning on page 501.

Photography: Photo of apple on page 343 by Anthony Riso Photography www.anthonyriso.photo

Library of Congress Cataloging in Publication data is on file at the Library of Congress.
Library of Congress Control Number: 2021935850
ISBN: 978-0-325-11866-6

Editors: Kerry Crosby and Sue Paro
Production: Cindy Strowman
Production Assistant: Anthony Riso
Cover and interior designs: Ellery Harvey and Kelsey Roy
Illustrators: Sarah Snow and Will Sweeney
Typesetter: Sharon Burkhardt
Manufacturing: Erin St. Hilaire

Printed in the United States of America on acid-free paper

1 2 3 4 5 6   MP   25 24 23 22 21
April 2021 Printing

CONTENTS

Introductory Chapters

1 Interactive Writing

2 Management

3 Telling Stories

4 Making Books

5 Drawing

6 Exploring Early Writing

7 Writing Process

Planning and Rehearsing

Drafting and Revising

Editing and Proofreading

Publishing

Introduction

Welcome to *The Writing Minilessons Book, Kindergarten*

To young children, drawing and writing are new ways to play. To you, they provide an opportunity to see children grow in amazing ways as they explore written language. You are the one who best knows your young students, and the lessons in this book will help you meet them where they are. Enjoy helping them use their imaginations to discover more about their world and watching them emerge as young artists and writers. And now, the journey begins.

Organization of Lessons

You will find two kinds of lessons in this book:

- ▶ 25 interactive writing lessons
- ▶ 125 writing minilessons

In the interactive writing lessons, you and the children write together as you provide a high level of support. In the writing minilessons, you help children expand what they know about drawing and writing so they can feel like artists and writers. The 25 interactive writing lessons are presented together in Section 1. The 125 writing minilessons are organized across Sections 2–7:

- ▶ Section 1: Interactive Writing (IW)
- ▶ Section 2: Management (MGT)
- ▶ Section 3: Telling Stories (STR)
- ▶ Section 4: Making Books (MBK)
- ▶ Section 5: Drawing (DRW)
- ▶ Section 6: Exploring Early Writing (EWR)
- ▶ Section 7: Writing Process (WPS)

Sections 2–7 contain groups of minilessons, or "umbrellas." Within each umbrella, the minilessons are all related to the same big idea so you can work with it for several days. The umbrellas are numbered sequentially within each section, and the minilessons are numbered sequentially within each umbrella. Each writing minilesson is identified by section, umbrella, and minilesson. For example, MBK.U1.WML1 indicates the first minilesson in the first umbrella of the Making Books section.

Content of Lessons: The Literacy Continuum

All of the lessons in this book are based on the behaviors and understandings presented in *The Fountas & Pinnell Literacy Continuum: A Tool for Assessment, Planning, and Teaching* (Fountas and Pinnell 2017). This volume presents detailed behaviors and understandings to notice, teach for, and support for prekindergarten through middle school, across eight instructional reading, writing, and language contexts. In sum, *The Literacy Continuum* describes proficiency in reading, writing, and language as it changes over grades and over levels. When you teach the lessons in this book, you are teaching for the behaviors and understandings that kindergartners need to become proficient readers and writers over time.

Organized for Your Children's Needs

We have provided a suggested sequence of lessons for you to try out and adjust based on your observations of the children. The sequence in Figure I-1 provides one path through the lessons. If this is your first time teaching minilessons, you may want to stick to it. However, once you become familiar with this book and the children's needs, choose the lessons that meet those needs. You will be able to locate the lessons easily because they are organized into sections. We organized the lessons into sections for these reasons:

1. The children in any given kindergarten class will vary greatly in their literacy experiences and development. Lessons organized by topic allow you to dip into the sections to select specific umbrellas or lessons that respond to your students' needs. You can find lessons easily by section and topic through the table of contents.

2. You can teach the lessons that make sense for the children in your class and omit any lessons that would be too advanced or too easy.

3. Writing is a complex learning process and involves many levels of learning—from figuring out the idea to communicate, to thinking about what to draw and write, to the mechanics of getting it on paper. Having the lessons organized by section enables you to focus on the areas that might be most helpful to the children at a specific point in time.

Key Words Used in Minilessons

The following is a list of key terms that we will use as we describe minilessons in the next chapters. Keep them in mind so that together we can develop a common language to talk about the minilessons.

▶ **Umbrella** A group of minilessons, all of which are directed at different aspects of the same larger understanding.

▶ **Minilesson** A short, interactive lesson to invite children to think about one idea.

▶ **Principle** A concise statement of the concept children will learn and be invited to apply.

▶ **Writing** All the kinds of "writing" that kindergarten children will do, including drawings, scribbles, approximated writing, and making letters they know.

▶ **Mentor Text** A fiction or nonfiction text in which the author or illustrator offers a clear example of the minilesson principle. Children will have heard the text read aloud and talked about it. Mentor texts can be books you have read to them as well as simple texts that you have written or ones you and the children have written together.

- **Text Set** A group of either fiction or nonfiction books or a combination of both that, taken together, help children explore an idea or a type of book (genre). You will have already read the books to them before a lesson. Children will have also made important connections between them.

- **Anchor Chart** A visual representation of the lesson concept using a combination of words and images. You create it as you talk with the children. It summarizes the learning and can be used by the children as a reference tool.

The chapters at the beginning of this book help you think about the role of talking, drawing, and writing in kindergarten, how the lessons are designed and structured, the materials and resources you will need to teach the lessons, and how to integrate drawing and writing into the play-based activities happening within your classroom.

Suggested Sequence of Lessons

If you are new to kindergarten minilessons, you may want to use the Suggested Sequence of Lessons (Figure I-1) for teaching the interactive writing lessons and writing minilessons across the year. This sequence weaves in lessons from the different sections so that children receive instruction in all aspects of writing and drawing throughout the school year. Lessons are sequenced in a way we think will support most kindergarten children, but you need to observe what most of your young students are doing as talkers, artists, and writers. Then choose lessons that will lead them forward.

The lessons in this book are sequenced in a way that builds on the sequence of mentor texts used in *Fountas & Pinnell Classroom™ Interactive Read-Aloud Collection* (2018) and *Shared Reading Collection* (2018). It is our intention that whenever possible children will have already seen and heard the mentor texts by the time they are used in a lesson.

Every kindergarten class is different, so it is impossible to prescribe an exact sequence of lessons. However, this sequence will give you a good starting place as you begin to teach the lessons in *The Writing Minilessons Book, Kindergarten*.

- The number of days assigned to each umbrella suggests how many days you will spend on teaching the minilessons in an umbrella. You may want to give children time in between lessons to apply the lesson during independent writing.

- You do not have to teach a writing minilesson every day. We have left room in the sequence for you to repeat or revisit lessons as needed or to spend more time exploring certain kinds of writing depending on the children's interests.

- You want to expose children to writing early in the year, so you teach quite a few lessons in the first few months. It's also a good idea to revisit and repeat umbrellas. Children will apply the lessons in different ways as they develop their abilities to write and draw across the school year.

Figure I-1: The complete Suggested Sequence of Lessons is on pages 481–494 in this book and in the online resources.

Suggested Sequence of Lessons

Months	Texts from *Fountas & Pinnell Classroom™ Shared Reading Collection*	Text Sets from *Fountas & Pinnell Classroom™ Interactive Read-Aloud Collection*	Reading Minilessons (RML) Sequence from *The Reading Minilessons Book, Kindergarten*	Interactive Writing (IW) Lessons* •	Writing Minilesson (WML) Umbrellas	Teaching Suggestions for Extending Learning
Months 1 & 2	The Itsy Bitsy Spider Wiggles: Poems to Make You Wiggle Your Fingers and Toes School Days	Sharing Stories and Songs: Nursery Rhymes Learning and Playing Together: School	MGT.U1: Working Together in the Classroom MGT.U2: Using the Classroom Library for Independent Reading (RML1–RML5)	**IW.1: Making a Name Chart (1 day)** **IW.2: Writing About Our Classroom (1 day)** **IW.3: Creating a Job Chart (1–2 days)**	**MGT.U1: Working Together in the Classroom (8 days)**	If you are using *The Reading Minilessons Book, Kindergarten*, you do not need to teach MGT.U1. Both RML and WML establish the same routines. However, be sure to take time to build community in your classroom by asking children to draw and write about themselves as they practice these new routines. The opening page of the writing minilessons umbrella MGT.U1 provides specific suggestions. IW.2 can be taught as a culminating activity.
	City ABCs Country ABCs The Sleepover	Letters at Work: The Alphabet	LA.U1: Thinking and Talking About Books	**IW.4: Making a Menu (1 day)**	**EWR.U7 Learning to Draw and Write Through Play, WML1 (1 day)**	Teach IW.4 shortly before EWR.U7. Together IW.4 and ERW.U7.WML1 show children how writing can be part of their daily play. Invite them to write for the play corner during both choice time and independent writing.
				IW.5: Making ABC Book		After reading several ABC books together, teach IW.5. Children can ⸺rk on finishing the clas⸺BC book ⸺ ⸺ ⸺

You do not need *Fountas & Pinnell Classroom™ Shared Reading Collection*, *Interactive Read-Aloud Collection*, or *The Reading Minilessons Book, Kindergarten* to teach these lessons. We have included them in this sequence for teachers who use these resources so they can connect and organize reading and writing across the year. If you do not have the texts that appear in the lessons as mentor texts, simply pick similar books and examples from your own classroom library or school library. Characteristics of the books used in the lessons are described in the active learning experience of interactive writing lessons and on the opening page of the umbrellas for the writing minilessons. To read more about using the Suggested Sequence of Lessons to plan your teaching, see chapter 8.

Chapter 1 : The Role of Writing in Early Literacy Learning

*Writing can contribute to the building of almost every kind of inner control
of literacy learning that is needed by the successful reader.*

—Marie Clay

LOOK AROUND A KINDERGARTEN CLASSROOM, bustling with the energy of
young children. Some children are busily playing with blocks or drawing with
crayons. Other children are pretending to be firefighters, store clerks, chefs,
and scientists. As children play, you might see them planning skyscrapers
in the block area, making books in the writing center, making menus in the
play corner restaurant, or making discoveries and observations in the science
center. All this active play can be connected to writing and reading because
children naturally take on the role of writer as easily as they take on the role
of firefighter, store clerk, chef, or scientist. Together they play, explore, imagine,
create, talk, write, and wonder. The classroom is filled not only with play but
with the tools of literacy (Figure 1-1).

Children in your kindergarten classroom are learning to be part of a community of talkers, scientists, mathematicians, artists, readers, and writers. The interactive writing lessons and writing minilessons in this book play an important role in this process. In these lessons, children will draw and write in many different ways for many different purposes across the curriculum (Figure 1-2), both together and on their own. Pieces of writing that the children create as a class will become familiar texts for reading and rereading. Writing and drawing done by individual children can be shared with one another.

Kindergartners live in a literate world, a world filled with print in all sizes, shapes, and colors for different purposes. They notice print all around them—from road signs and store names to cereal boxes and text messages. These noticings lead them to understand that the marks on paper or screens mean something, and they want to try to do their own writing.

When we talk about a kindergartner's writing, what do we mean? At the beginning of kindergarten, writing involves mostly talking and giving a try with a pencil or a marker to communicate meaning through marks on a page, mostly in the form of scribbles, lines, and drawings. You might think these initial marks look like scribbles, but letterforms will gradually come out of these early scribbles. When a child writes a squiggly letter, it's not an accident. It might be an attempt at the letter *s*. A few kindergartners will already be forming recognizable letters and demonstrating a beginning understanding that letters represent sounds, but many will be expressing their messages solely through drawing and scribbling. As the year progresses, talk continues to be an important part of the writing process, scribbles begin to take the form of letters, and children start to use these letters to form temporary spellings of words.

Figure 1-1: As children explore new concepts, they expand their learning by talking, drawing, writing, and reading about their new learning.

The circle shows:
Surveys, All-About Books, Question-and-Answer Books, How-to Books, Memory Stories, Menus, Poems, Labels, Story Maps, Letters, Cards, Invitations, Science Observations, Signs, ABC Books, Counting Books, Class Big Books, Charts

Center: Kinds of Writing in *The Writing Minilessons Book, Kindergarten*

Figure 1-2: Children will have opportunities to write in many ways.

Whether they are drawing, making marks on a page, or writing letterforms, children see themselves as artists and writers. It's the beginning of a learning process they'll use throughout their lives. If children have daily opportunities to write, as guided by the lessons, you will see enormous change in them across the school year. We have been astounded at young children's ability to grow in writing over time.

Children Grow as Writers over Time

Some children have had more experience with or opportunities for drawing or writing than others, but with your support they can all grow as writers. Figure 1-3 shows a rough progression of early writing that you might see in your classroom. (We don't use the word *stages* because writing development is complex and writers can show more than one element at a time in their approximations.) Although the examples move from left to right, forward progress is not linear. Not every child will exhibit the same sequence, and most children will move back and forth. Use Figure 1-3 to look at Hallock's writing in Figure 1-4 and when you look to see how your own students' writing is developing. Look for evidence that children are noticing written language and trying it out for themselves.

Children Emerge as Artists, Writers, and Readers

In a kindergarten classroom, expect to see a range of emergent writing behaviors from children who can barely hold a pencil or marker to those who are experimenting with writing their names and to those who are writing a few words. Clay (1975) points out that when we see these early attempts at writing, "the child is reaching out towards the principles of written language and any instruction should encourage him to continue to do this" (15). In chapter 7, we explore these writing principles in more depth.

Children learn differently from one another, but all make progress toward the kind of writing they see in books. Watching kindergartners write and looking at their writing will show you what they know. Notice whether they can

- ◗ hold a writing tool,
- ◗ write any letters,
- ◗ write any words,

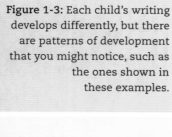

Figure 1-3: Each child's writing develops differently, but there are patterns of development that you might notice, such as the ones shown in these examples.

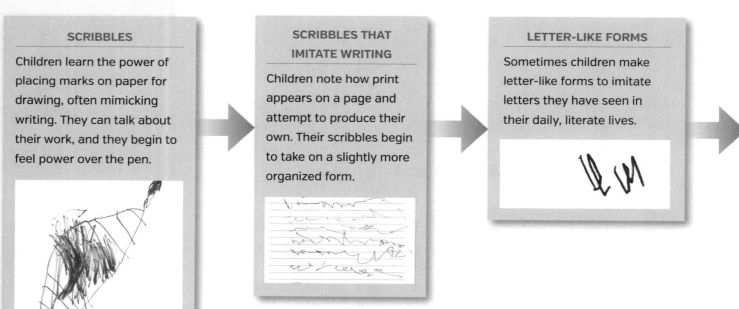

SCRIBBLES

Children learn the power of placing marks on paper for drawing, often mimicking writing. They can talk about their work, and they begin to feel power over the pen.

SCRIBBLES THAT IMITATE WRITING

Children note how print appears on a page and attempt to produce their own. Their scribbles begin to take on a slightly more organized form.

LETTER-LIKE FORMS

Sometimes children make letter-like forms to imitate letters they have seen in their daily, literate lives.

The Writing Minilessons Book, Kindergarten

- ◗ write their names,
- ◗ talk about their pictures and messages,
- ◗ write words in sentences,
- ◗ leave spaces between words,
- ◗ write from left to right, or
- ◗ read what they have written.

Children Connect What They Hear, Say, and Write

A child's journey to becoming literate begins at birth. As caregivers engage the child in language interactions, the child learns to communicate, and this oral language foundation paves the way for learning about written language—reading and writing. All aspects of children's oral and written language—listening, speaking, reading, and writing—develop together and support each other as the young child emerges into literacy. Any time you and the children write together—whether labels, descriptions, observations, or stories—thinking and talking come first. Children learn that their thoughts and ideas can be put into language and language can be put into writing and it can be read (Figure 1-5).

STRINGS OF LETTERS

Children often begin writing random strings of letters, showing that they understand that letters are written together in a word. They don't yet understand that the letters relate to the sounds in a word, but they have begun to notice how words look.

APPROXIMATED (TEMPORARY) SPELLING

As children have more experiences with reading and writing, they begin to write words with some standard letter-sound representation. This shows what they know about letters and sounds. They are hearing the predominant sounds in a word, as in the example that says *Bella comes back*.

BLLA ✳M BC

BEGINNING WORD AND SENTENCE WRITING

As children begin to form sentences, they combine approximated spelling with the standard spelling of some high-frequency words. This can be seen in the example that reads *I like when you play with me*.

I like wn you PY wf me

Hallock tells a story about her friend Marianna and how they like to play outside together. They are holding hands and smiling in the picture. Though she is not yet writing words to go with her story, Hallock understands that she can use drawing to communicate an idea to her readers. She clearly shows that she enjoys playing outside with her friend.

In this card to her mom, Hallock demonstrates her understanding that people write messages in cards. She uses the letters she knows to write strings of letters to represent words. She also attempts to write *mom* at the top of the card.

Hallock is beginning to control some high-frequency words that appear on her classroom word wall and is experimenting with upper- and lowercase letters. She is easily able to spell the word *drew* because it is her brother's name. Notice her reversal of the letter *a* in *fall*—a common occurrence in early writing.

Figure 1-4: Use Figure 1-3 to note the change in Hallock's writing over time.

One section of this book is dedicated to telling stories, because for children to be able to write their stories, they first need to be able to tell their stories. By listening to stories read to them and by telling stories themselves (stories from their own lives or retellings of stories from books), children begin to develop an understanding of story structure. They develop the ability to use the patterns of language and build strong vocabularies as they listen to and talk about books, ask questions about their classmates' stories, and clarify their own stories for an audience. As they begin to draw and write their oral stories, they have conversations about their writing that deepen their ability to explain their thinking. They learn to put ideas in time order, to elaborate with story details, to develop vocabulary, and to more accurately describe what they want to say.

Children Have Opportunities to Write All Day

In the kindergarten classroom, it is important to carve out a dedicated time for writing as well as embed writing opportunities into a variety of daily classroom activities. From the time they enter the literacy-rich classroom, children are engaged in writing. They sign in on attendance sheets, answer survey questions on charts, create writing pieces with their class, make labels for their block creations, and create signs for the latest play corner. They talk about what authors do in their books, and they make their own

Hallock uses her knowledge of letters and sounds to write more detailed and complicated sentences: *I made a noise maker and I liked it*. Notice some of her early attempts at editing as she crosses out letters and words and tries writing them again.

Hallock uses the name chart to help her spell names in her classroom. Here she writes *I liked Jackson's birthday. I liked the cookies*. She labels her teacher Ms. Mastroianni and Jackson in her picture. She is also starting to consistently use the past tense in her writing.

Hallock writes more than one sentence as she describes her experience parading as a butterfly at the end of a butterfly science unit: *I flied all around and we flied in line. We went flying in every classroom*. Hallock is beginning to pay attention to the way words look. She writes *-ing* in *flying* and knows that *room* has a double letter though she doubles the wrong one. She also writes the same way she talks, pronouncing *Ls* like *Ws* in her oral speech.

books. Providing kindergartners with a predictable time to write each day allows them the opportunity to experiment with writing, to make books over time, and to apply the new things they learn from interactive writing and writing minilessons. Consider carving out the following times in your day for writing, and think about how you might build writing into other established routines (e.g., independent work time and choice time) in your classroom.

The Contributions of Writing to Language, Literacy, and Learning

As children take on literacy in a playful way, they grow in oral language, reading, and writing. As they write, they

- Move from thoughts to ideas to language to written representation in images or words
- Link spoken language to written language
- Work on communicating meaningful messages
- Say words slowly to hear the individual sounds in words
- Learn about letters—how they look and their individual features
- Connect a sound with a letter
- Learn how print works
- Read their writing attempts

Figure 1-5: Contributions of writing to literacy learning

Shared/Interactive Writing Time During interactive writing, children have the chance to collaborate on a piece of writing as a whole class. You can read in depth about interactive writing lessons in chapter 3.

Independent Writing Time During Writers' Workshop Independent writing time is typically bookended by a writing minilesson and a chance for children to share their writing (Figure 1-6). Children learn about an aspect of writing during a writing minilesson and then have a chance to apply what they learned in that lesson as they write independently for a short period of time. The teacher has the opportunity to confer with individual writers or to work with small groups in guided writing (see page 28 for information about guided writing). Children engage in a variety of writing, especially in making books, which is described in more detail on pages 20–22. The writers' workshop ends with a whole-group meeting in which children share their writing and, if applicable, the ways they applied new learning from the writing minilesson. Chapter 4 describes how the writing minilessons in this book follow and support this structure. Using the Management minilessons will help you establish a productive and engaging independent writing time with your kindergartners.

Independent Work Time After engaging in an inquiry-based reading minilesson, children participate in a variety of independent literacy activities. They listen to books in the listening center, act out stories with puppets in the drama area, independently read from book boxes, play phonics and word games in the word study center, and/or write in the writing center. During this literacy work time, teachers often confer with individual readers as they apply the reading minilesson to their independent reading, or work with small groups in a guided reading lesson. As children engage in these different literacy activities, they have many opportunities to write. They write about their reading in the listening center, respond to poems in the poetry center, write in response to books in guided reading, and continue their bookmaking in the writing center. Children also use the writing center to write notes or letters to their classmates, make signs or props for the play corner, or create in ways you might never have imagined. Teachers often manage this time with a work board or with a simple lists of tasks. We provide details for

Figure 1-6: A writers' workshop structure allows for whole-class learning, individual and small-group guidance from the teacher, independent writing, and whole-class sharing.

Structure of Writers' Workshop		
Whole Class	Writing Minilesson	5–10 Minutes
Individuals and Small Groups	Independent Writing Individual Conferences Guided Writing Groups	15–30 minutes (The time will expand as children learn to build stamina across the year.)
Whole Class	Group Share	5–10 Minutes

establishing and managing this time in both *Guided Reading: Responsive Teaching Across the Grades* (Fountas and Pinnell 2017) and *The Reading Minilessons Book, Kindergarten* (Fountas and Pinnell 2019).

Choice Time Many kindergarten classrooms include an active choice time in which children engage in playful activities infused with writing opportunities. Children should be invited and encouraged, not required, to draw and write during choice time. Drawing and writing can be a choice just like playing with blocks or making art (Figure 1-7). To children it's all play, so it makes sense to weave some writing into choice time activities as shown in Figure 1-8. Choice time is an important part of the joyful kindergarten learning experience. You can read more about how to manage choice time in chapter 5.

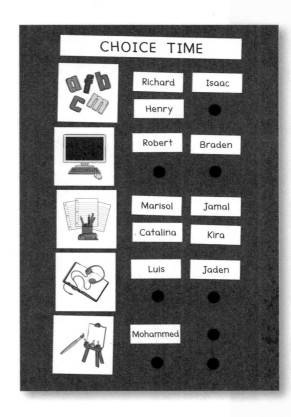

Figure 1-7: A choice time board allows children to make decisions about their activities during choice time.

Children Make Connections Between Reading, Writing, and Phonics/Word Study

Besides having dedicated times for writing, kindergartners are immersed in a variety of literacy experiences throughout the day so they can make important connections between reading, writing, and word study. From the time children enter a literacy-rich classroom, they are immersed in a literacy-building environment. Children see print everywhere in the classroom. They talk and listen to others. They hear books read aloud, learn to read their own books, experience phonics lessons, and write and draw about their reading. They learn about and play with language. They make their own books. All of this supports children's writing development.

Print All Around the Classroom Children live in a world full of print. Just as they see print in their neighborhoods, they walk into a classroom with labels and signs that are meaningful to them. They even participate in making these labels and signs. When you work with children to label parts of the classroom or materials (e.g., window, door, chair, stapler, paper), you provide a chance for them to produce print that is meaningful and helpful.

Ways to Explore Writing Across the Curriculum During Choice Time

Choice Time Activity	Ways to Write
Writing Center	• Make books • Write letters, invitations, notes • Make cards (thank you, birthday, etc.) • Draw or write in response to stories
Block Center	• Label buildings • Make signs (e.g., store signs, road signs) • Make a plan or "blueprint" on graph paper • Draw what you built • Make a how-to book for building a structure • Write a story about what you have built • Take a photograph of a structure or scene and label the photograph • Write up work orders and receipts
Sand/Water Table	• Draw about what you made (e.g., boat that floats, sand pies/cakes, volcanoes) • Draw about your discoveries (e.g., water and sand experiments) • Draw and write about making a boat • Write name in sand with finger • Write letters in sand with finger • Write stories about an experience at the sand/water table • Make a how-to book about how to do an experiment
Play Corner	• Make signs that go with the theme • Take orders, make appointments, etc. • Make receipts • Make labels • Write letters • Make maps • Take a phone message • Write lists • Create magazines, newspapers • Make a book about what you played in play corner *[See chapter 7 for more ideas for specific types of writing based on play corner themes.]*

Figure 1-8: Writing is integrated into all choice time activities.

The Writing Minilessons Book, Kindergarten

Ways to Explore Writing Across the Curriculum During Choice Time (cont.)

Choice Time Activity	Ways to Write
Art Center	• Label drawings • Label 3D creations • Use collage to illustrate books • Make pop-ups, flaps, tabs, cut-outs to add to books • Illustrate interactive/shared writing
Word Work Center	• Trace names on textured surfaces • Practice writing names • Build names with magnetic letters • Sort letters • Play letter games and word games • Make names in salt/sand
Creation Station	• Draw and write a how-to book based on a creation • Draw and write a story about a creation/invention • Make directions for how to use an invention • Make signs for a creation • Take a photo of the creation and write about it
Science Center	• Draw and write a how-to book for an experiment • Draw and write about observations of nature (e.g., plants growing, terrarium, classroom pet, pumpkin decaying) • Make plans for an experiment • Ask questions and note wonderings

A word wall that includes children's names provides a helpful resource for the writers in your class. As you introduce high-frequency words (e.g., *the*, *and*, *is*, *I*, *am*, *here*), add them to your word wall. In some cases, teachers even include examples of familiar environmental print—words from cereal boxes, ads, logos, and so forth, that children bring into the classroom—on a word wall (Figure 1-9).

The Most Important Word Is Your Name Children will likely learn to read and write their names before they learn other words. In a kindergarten classroom, children see their names all around the classroom—on attendance or sign-in charts, on the name chart, on cubbies, on the choice time board, and on a bulletin board display. Their names are displayed on cards that they

Figure 1-9: A word wall in kindergarten starts with children's names and is built over time as you introduce simple, commonly used words.

use to express their opinions on class survey questions, which they create together during interactive writing. They play matching games with name cards. In some classrooms, a wall has been dedicated to framed self-portraits with children's names written clearly below and to drawings of children's families, inviting all who visit to get to know the children in this special community of learners.

Interactive Read-Aloud and Shared Reading Reading aloud to children is essential for joyful early literacy. We call it "interactive" because it is so important for children to talk with each other about the books they hear. They also love shared reading with enlarged print books and charts, reading together from the same book, song, or poem (Figure 1-10). Books they read many times become "theirs." Interactive read-aloud and shared reading expose children to a variety of stories, informational books, nursery rhymes, songs, and poems. As children listen to and discuss these books and poems, they hear the way written language sounds and start to notice what other writers and illustrators do in their books. When you spend time pointing out how the illustrator designed the cover, the colors used in the illustrations, an interesting choice of words, or the rhythm of a repeating line, children become aware of the author's or illustrator's craft in a simple and authentic way.

Reading Minilessons, Guided Reading, and Independent Reading Reading minilessons build on the literary understandings developed during interactive read-aloud and shared reading. Children learn more about what illustrators and writers do, how written language sounds, and how stories and information are organized. They learn about the author's message, how print and words work, and about different kinds of writing. They participate in shared writing as they work with you to create anchor charts for reading minilessons and learn how to write and draw about their reading. Children grow in all of these understandings as they participate in brief, small-group guided reading lessons in which they read books at their instructional level. Children are also given opportunities throughout the day to read independently. (In the beginning of kindergarten, this might simply mean telling a familiar story using the pictures and thinking about what happens in the story.) As children engage with a variety of texts independently, they not only apply what they have learned during reading minilessons and guided reading but also make their own discoveries about print, writer's and illustrator's craft, and other literary elements. We have written extensively about reading minilessons and guided reading in *The Reading Minilessons Book, Kindergarten* (2019) and in *Guided Reading* (2017). Good teaching in reading is essential to the teaching of writing and vice versa. Interactive writing lessons and writing minilessons help children transfer what they have learned in reading to their own writing. In turn, what they learn about writing will make them stronger readers. It is a deeply reciprocal process.

Writing About Reading Kindergarten children love to draw to show what they are thinking about a book and can begin to write simple responses to their reading after you have modeled how through reading minilessons and interactive writing. You will find several examples of writing about reading in the interactive writing lessons in this book. Some kindergarten teachers use a reader's notebook as a place to collect their children's writing about

Figure 1-10: Children develop an understanding of story structure, knowledge of how books work, and familiarity with early print concepts through interactive read-aloud and shared reading (shown here).

reading. The writing minilessons in this book focus on having children write their own original pieces, but writing about reading is still an important part of becoming a writer. For minilessons on writing about reading and how to use a reader's notebook with kindergartners, see *The Reading Minilessons Book, Kindergarten*.

Phonics and Phonemic Awareness Through interactive writing and writing minilessons, children have several opportunities to begin noticing individual sounds in words (phonemic awareness) and distinctive features of letters in their names (letter work). They also begin to understand the relationship between the letters and sounds (phonics). To further support this learning, many kindergarten teachers also provide a specific time for phonics, spelling, and word study lessons (see *Fountas & Pinnell Phonics, Spelling, and Word Study System, Kindergarten*, 2017). Through inquiry, children learn key principles about the way words work. Additionally, children need lots of opportunities to learn the sounds in words through songs, finger plays, and rhymes. The following list has a few simple ways you can help children develop in these areas. Many of these suggested activities could be done in the word work center, during morning meeting or circle time, or during choice time.

- Play oral games (e.g. rhyming).
- Incorporate songs, poems, rhymes, and finger plays to help children hear sounds in words.
- Connect sounds and letters to children's own names.
- Help children explore letter features by using magnetic letters.
- Demonstrate sorting magnetic letters by features (tails, tall sticks, circles, etc.).
- Demonstrate making words (including names) with magnetic letters.
- Use alphabet and letter puzzles.
- Make ABC books accessible.
- Provide games (e.g., picture lotto with letter sounds or rhymes or concepts) and teach children how to play.

Children Love to Make Books

Bookmaking is a powerful way for children to enter into drawing and writing and bring together all of these important literacy experiences. Glover (2009) said it well:

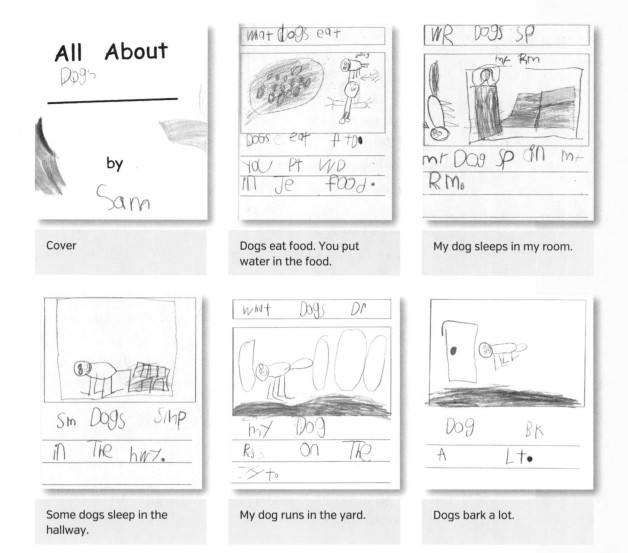

Figure 1-11: Sam showed her understanding of books with her own nonfiction book about a topic she cares about—dogs. She included a cover, facts she knows about dogs, and headings to group similar information together: what dogs eat, where dogs sleep, and what dogs do.

The reason for making books is simple. Books are what children have the greatest vision for, and having a clear vision for what you are making is important in any act of composition. Young children have the clearest vision for making picture books because that is the type of writing that they have seen most. (13)

Kindergartners can "make books" by telling a story through drawings even before they can read and write. You can then invite them to make their own books, just like the authors of the books they love (Figure 1-11). Children enjoy using blank books (even as simple as a piece of paper folded in half), but you can also offer any of the variety of optional templates for writing from the online resources. The act of making books—we use the term *making* instead of *writing* because some children will protest that they can't write—benefits you and the children in lots of ways.

- Children see themselves as authors, illustrators, and readers.
- Children develop feelings of independence and accomplishment at having created something that is uniquely theirs.
- Children begin to take in and try out concepts of writing, such as holding a marker, moving left-to-right across a page, and making letterforms.
- Children build stamina by working on a book over several days.
- Writing and reading reinforce one another, so as children make their own books, they become more aware of the decisions that authors and illustrators make in their books.
- Children learn that reading and writing are similar in many ways (left to right direction, top to bottom progression, space between words, letterforms, letter-sound relationships).
- Children expand their understanding about print, illustrations, and text structure.
- In children's books, you can look for evidence of what they know about drawing and writing and use that information to decide what they need to learn next.
- Children see themselves as authors, illustrators, and readers.

Some minilessons in Section 4: Making Books get children started in the basics of making books. Other minilessons provide opportunities for children to try making different kinds of books, including how-to books, all-about books (informational books), and memory books.

> Once you treat children as authors and illustrators, and engage them in conversations about how authors and illustrators do things, they notice more and more of those things and wonder how and why authors do them. (Johnston et al. 2020, 14)

In your classroom, offer writing support through shared and interactive writing and writing minilessons so that children can continue to grow as they engage and play with the writing process throughout the day. You'll be amazed at what they discover and learn through their explorations.

Chapter 2 Inviting Young Children into the Writing Process

The key is that regardless of whether there are words on the page or not, or how approximated the writing appears, the child is conveying a thought through symbols and pictures on a page and is therefore writing.

—Matt Glover

CHILDREN WANT TO BE WRITERS because they become aware of writing in their environment at a very young age. They see others writing, learn its purpose, and start trying to do it on their own. Even a simple grocery list communicates something important to the young child: writing is a useful tool. Take advantage of children's natural curiosity! How do you plan classroom instruction, use language, and provide drawing and writing opportunities in ways that invite these curious young learners into the world of writing?

Young Children Engage in the Writing Process

All writers, regardless of age or experience, engage in the same aspects of the writing process every time they write. Although components of the writing process are usually listed in a sequence, writers can and will use any or all of the components at any point while writing.

- ▶ Planning and Rehearsing (Talk about it.)
- ▶ Drafting and Revising (Get it down.)
- ▶ Editing and Proofreading (Make it better.)
- ▶ Publishing (Share it with friends.)

Of course, drawing and reading are fundamental parts of this process as well and are especially important for kindergarten children.

Planning and Rehearsing

For children, talk is an important part of planning and rehearsing their writing. They need to be able to form their ideas into oral language before they can attempt to put those ideas on paper. Some of the talk is about children's ideas—*what* they are writing. Some of the talk is about *why* children are writing and for *whom*—the purpose and the audience. When children begin to think about who will read their writing, they are able to ask themselves and each other, "What will the reader need to know? What else should I put in my story to help my reader enjoy and understand it?"

Knowing the purpose for writing often leads to discussions about what type of writing to do and what kind of paper is best for that purpose. For example, if children want to

- ▶ say thank you, they might choose to write a note or a letter;
- ▶ teach others how to do something, they might write a how-to book;
- ▶ let people know when the restaurant in the play corner is open, they might make a sign; or
- ▶ remember an experience or entertain their audience, they might write a story.

In all of these cases, the writer thinks about the purpose, determines what kind of writing will serve that purpose, and then begins to write a message. As you write together as a class with shared and interactive writing, children gradually learn all these connections.

From listening to many books read aloud to them, children learn that writers get their ideas from their own experiences and from what they have learned. When children write personal stories, they discover that they can write about what they have done, what they know or care about, a place they want to remember, or a special object. The possibilities are endless.

Drafting and Revising

At the beginning of the year, most kindergarten writing is just getting something down on the paper. We do not expect standard spelling, and drawing is an important way for children to express what they want to say. Young children are pleased to celebrate their marks on paper, and it is important for them to feel this power. Talk is especially important for those students whose first language is not English. They need opportunities to rehearse their ideas by telling stories or talking about their ideas before they write. Minilessons in Section 3: Telling Stories invite children to talk in ways that support the process of getting ideas down on paper.

As you guide children in constructing texts, they learn that part of the process of getting something down involves rereading and thinking about each word as part of a larger idea. You can show them how to think what they want to say before they draw or write.

Over the course of the year, children learn more about the way words work, talk about the decisions authors make, and begin to make their own decisions about how to get their ideas down on paper. As children learn more about sounds, letters, and words, they begin to use approximated spelling and include names and high-frequency words in their writing. They start to capture their ideas and messages in both drawing and words.

Children get excited about learning new ways to add to their writing so they can make it more interesting. They learn to reread their writing to make sure it makes sense and to add or cross out when it doesn't. The minilessons in Section 7: Writing Process will help you offer guidance in drafting and revising.

Proofreading and Editing

Kindergartners are rapid learners, but most of what they produce early in the year will not be conventional writing. Often, you can't read what they write, but they can usually tell you what their writing says or means. For now, your goal in guiding children to reread and revisit their work is to help them notice what they can do to make their writing and drawings interesting and easy to read. At this point, editing is best demonstrated during interactive writing, as you and the children read and revisit a piece of writing to check whether it makes sense and uses particular aspects of print (e.g., upper- and lowercase letters, punctuation).

As kindergartners become more familiar with print, you can teach them how to check their own writing for things like spacing between words, correctly spelled known words, and proper letter formation. They learn the importance of proofreading and editing in making their writing accessible to their readers.

EL CONNECTION

When you teach English learners, you can adjust your teaching—not more teaching, but different teaching—to assure effective learning. Look for the symbol above to see ways to support English learners.

Publishing

When we say "publish" in kindergarten, we really mean "show it to others." Kindergartners publish or celebrate their writing all the time as they produce group writing with illustrations. Children are invited to share their independent drawing and writing daily as they experiment with new ideas taught through the lessons in this book. Publishing can also take the form of framing a piece of writing or drawing, displaying it, posting it on a bulletin board, or holding informal writing celebrations. For example, you can have children share their books with another class or with a teacher or administrator, or you can invite families and guests to look at published books. Children have the opportunity not only to celebrate finished pieces but also to celebrate risks taken and new techniques tried.

Children Learn About Writing by Seeing and Doing

Children benefit from seeing examples and demonstrations of drawing and writing before they try drawing and writing on their own. Use modeled, shared, interactive, or guided writing so that children see writing happen and participate in the process. Let's look at these supportive instructional contexts, all of which lead young children toward independent writing.

Modeled Writing

Modeled writing, which in kindergarten includes drawing, has the highest amount of teacher support (Figure 2-1). Children see what it looks like to produce a piece of writing as you demonstrate creating a particular type of

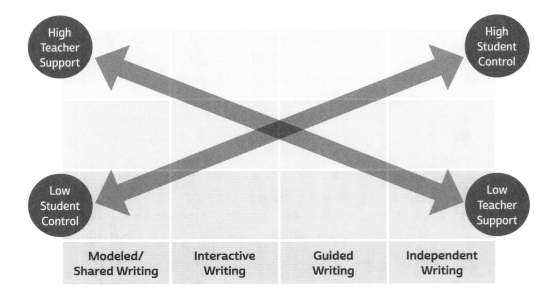

Figure 2-1: Each instructional context for writing has a different amount of teacher support and student control (from *The Literacy Quick Guide* by Irene C. Fountas and Gay Su Pinnell, 2018).

writing. As you draw and write, talk through the decisions you are making as an artist or writer. Sometimes, you will have prepared the writing before class, but you will still talk about your thought process for the children. Modeled writing or drawing is often used within a writing minilesson to demonstrate what a particular kind of writing looks like and how it is produced.

Shared Writing

In shared writing, use the children's experiences and language to create writing that they can read. Shared writing is used for most of the charts in the writing minilessons. Although you are the scribe who writes the text on chart paper displayed on an easel or whiteboard, children participate by contributing ideas. First, children talk about their experiences and ideas. Then, you and the children decide together what to say and how to say it. Moving from thoughts or ideas to saying the words to putting the ideas in print (perhaps with a drawing) is a process children need to engage in over and over. The process begins with a plan you make together, and then you move to writing the message word by word as the children observe and talk about the process.

Sometimes you will ask the children to say a word slowly to listen for the sounds and to think about the letters that go with those sounds. It is important for the children to say the word for themselves. Other times, you (with the children's input) will write the word, sentence, or phrase on the chart quickly to keep the lesson moving. Reread what you have written as you go along so that children can rehearse the language structure, anticipate the next word, and check what has been written. The chart then becomes a model, example, or reference for future reading, writing, and discussion (Figure 2-2).

Figure 2-2: This name chart is an example of shared writing. The teacher did all the writing to make the letters easy to recognize.

Interactive Writing

Interactive writing and shared writing are very similar. The only difference is that in interactive writing the children "share the pen" by writing letters, word parts, or words (Figure 2-3). Occasionally, while making teaching points that help children attend to various features of letters and words as well as punctuation, invite a child to the easel to contribute a letter, a word, a part of a word, or a type of punctuation. This process is especially helpful to beginning readers and writers because their contributions have high instructional value. Children also participate by helping you add illustrations, though this can be done at a later time.

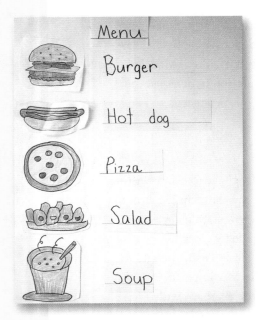

Figure 2-3: In this example of interactive writing, the teacher did most of the writing but children wrote the letters B, P, and S. The teacher chose letters that stand for sounds that are easy for children to hear and/or appear in one of their names. Eventually, children will be able to contribute parts of words and whole words.

Because interactive writing is such a powerful way to learn about writing across the curriculum, we have dedicated a whole section of this book (twenty-five lessons) to support this learning context. These lessons will help you and your students become familiar with the process and use it for a variety of purposes throughout the day. Note that shared writing is recommended for the first interactive writing lesson (IW.1: Making a Name Chart), but any of the interactive writing lessons in this book can be converted to shared writing lessons if you choose to do all of the writing yourself instead of sharing the pen.

Guided Writing

Guided writing allows for differentiated learning in order to address the common needs of a small group of students. By conducting conferences with children and examining their writing, you will determine which students would benefit from small-group teaching. For example, you have introduced a new kind of writing to the whole group but notice that there are a few students who need more support to take on the new learning. Or, you have noticed a few students experimenting with writing poetry and you want to support their new interest. In each case, you can pull a guided writing group together to deepen and expand children's understandings. When the new learning is accomplished, the group is disbanded. Whether you are reviewing or teaching something new that the whole class is not quite ready for, the small-group setting of guided writing allows you to closely observe childrens' writing behaviors and provide specific guidance. Guided writing lessons are brief and focused. Typically a guided writing lesson lasts only ten to fifteen minutes and can take place while the rest of the class is engaged in independent writing (Figure 2-4).

Independent Writing

When children draw and write for themselves, all of their understandings about drawing and writing—literacy concepts, word solving, purpose, audience—come together in a way that is visible. Sometimes they will write about their reading. Sometimes they will write about their creations. Sometimes they will write from their personal experiences, and other times they will write about what they know or have learned about a topic through their observations. Through their participation in interactive writing lessons and writing minilessons, children take on new understandings. Through independent writing, they try them out. As they happily make books, they

Structure of a Guided Writing Lesson

Teach a Minilesson	Teach a single principle that is useful for a small group of writers at a particular point in time. Keep the lesson brief, and allow student inquiry to drive the learning.
Students Have a Try	Provide a piece of writing, and invite students to apply the new thinking. Support students' learning with additional teaching, as needed. Point out effective applications of the principle by group members.
Students Apply the Principle to Their Own Writing	Invite students to try out the principle using an existing piece of writing or, as appropriate, by beginning a new piece of writing. Students continue to work at the small table as you observe and provide guidance that deepens individual students' understanding of the principle.
Students Share	Invite students to share what they noticed and learned during the lesson. Reinforce the principle, and encourage students to share the next steps they will take in their writing.

learn more about writing and language, which leads to richer talk and discussion in all writing contexts.

The chart in Figure 2-5 summarizes the features of modeled writing, shared writing, interactive writing, guided writing, and independent writing. Interactive writing lessons obviously use interactive writing, while writing minilessons might use any one or more levels of support: modeled, shared, and interactive writing. The ultimate goal of both interactive writing lessons and writing minilessons is to support children in developing their own independent drawing and writing.

Figure 2-4: Structure of a guided writing lesson from *The Literacy Quick Guide* (Fountas and Pinnell 2018)

Figure 2-5: Choose the level of support that helps you reach your goals for the children. These supports apply to both writing and drawing.

Levels of Support for Writing

Type of Writing	Characteristics
Modeled	• Whole class or small group • Teacher composes the text (creates and says the sentences) • Teacher writes the print and/or draws images • Used to demonstrate ideas and refer to • Used as a resource to read
Shared	• Whole class or small group • Teacher and children compose the text (create and say the sentences) • Teacher writes what the children decide together • Used to record ideas to read or refer to • Often included in writing minilessons to show something about writing or drawing

Type of Writing	Characteristics
Interactive	• Whole class or small group • Teacher and children plan what to write and/or draw • Teacher and children share the pen to write and illustrate the text • Slows down the writing/drawing and allows focus on specific drawing and writing concepts (e.g., spaces between words, left-right directionality, features of letters and words, techniques for drawing) • The writing/drawing can be used as a mentor text during writing minilessons and as a reference for independent writing • Often used as a shared reading text later
Guided Writing	• Small group • Teacher provides a brief lesson on a single writing principle that children apply to their own writing • Allows for close observation and guidance • Used to differentiate instruction • Teaching might involve modeled, shared, or interactive writing • Similar to a writing minilesson but in a small group setting
Independent	• Individuals • Children decide what to say or draw and then write or illustrate their own texts (mostly through making books) • Supported by side-by-side talk with the teacher • Engages children in all aspects of the drawing and writing processes

Once you get to know the children in your class and understand what they can do on their own and what they can do with your support, you will be able to decide which level of support is most appropriate for a particular purpose. When the processes for each kind of writing are established, you can use them as needed throughout the day.

Chapter 3 | What Is an Interactive Writing Lesson?

Interactive writing is an instructional context in which a teacher shares a pen—literally and figuratively—with a group of children as they collaboratively compose and construct a written message.

—Andrea McCarrier, Irene C. Fountas, and Gay Su Pinnell

IN AN INTERACTIVE WRITING LESSON, the teacher and children play active roles in producing a common piece of writing. Everyone participates in planning what to write and how to say it. Several children help write the planned text by "sharing the pen" at a few selected points.

Children Learn About the Writing Process

Interactive writing lessons are designed to ease children into part or all of the writing process in a highly supported way. McCarrier, Fountas, and Pinnell (2000) describe what goes on when children participate in interactive writing in the following passage:

When children compose [plan] a text, they work on several levels of language at once. They place letters within words, words within phrases, phrases within sentences, and sentences within a longer text. They must first think of meaning in a larger sense and then compose the language. They shift down to put the message into words.

The construction [writing] of the text requires further shifts down the levels of language to attend to specific words, sounds in words, parts of words, and letters.

After using details to write a word, the composer/constructor has to go right back up to the meaning of the larger text to think of the next word to write. The composer/constructor is always climbing up and down the levels of language, from meaning down to the details and then back up to the meaning. (96)

The interactive writing lessons in this book are carefully planned to guide children through the details of writing the text while always thinking about the meaning. It all happens in a very short time. You need only five to ten minutes to write a message or other type of writing with the children. Don't let the lesson go on and on! You can always go back to longer pieces (e.g., class big books), which might be extended across two or three days (Figure 3-1).

Figure 3-1: The children and their teacher planned and wrote the labels for a mural about animals in winter.

Children Participate in Real Writing for Real Reasons

The purpose of interactive writing is not simply to practice writing. Children write about their discoveries and the ideas they care about. Interactive writing lessons are richest when they are rooted in real experiences during which children explore, think, and talk. Children who are actively involved in a meaningful experience—reading and talking about books, making something, going somewhere—will have ideas to contribute.

Here's an example of how an active learning experience led to interactive writing. Students in Mrs. Halves's class had read books about different types of homes and houses and had talked about what makes a home. They had read *A House Is a House for Me* by Mary Ann Hoberman, *Houses and Homes* by Ann Morris, and *Two Homes* by Claire Masurel (Figure 3-2). Mrs. Halves invited them to make their own houses (imaginary or real) out of cardboard and other materials in the classroom creation station (maker space).

Figure 3-2: Books used for interactive read-aloud can inspire interactive writing.

Together, the class used interactive writing to write about each of their classmates' creations (Figure 3-3). The children also decided that the class should make a gallery displaying their houses and writing. They used interactive writing to create an invitation to their families and other classes to come view the gallery. Later, the class might write a how-to book to teach others how to make a house out of cardboard and boxes. Eventually, children might write thank you notes to families or even a memory book about the showing. Each experience immerses children in the writing process and the mechanics of writing, moving them forward in their own thinking and language.

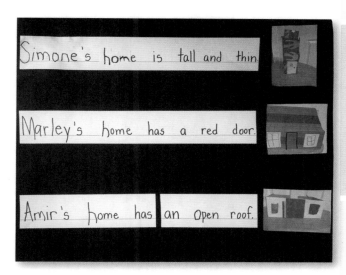

Figure 3-3: In this example of interactive writing, the teacher chose a few easy-to-hear consonants (*h, m*) and a vowel (*o*) for children to contribute. A few children also were invited to write the letters of their names that they know how to write quickly.

A Few Things to Know About Interactive Writing Lessons

Before we take a close look at the individual parts of an interactive writing lesson, here are a few general things to know:

▶ The interactive writing lessons are stand-alone lessons. They are not grouped in umbrellas like writing minilessons; however, they do build in complexity from the first to the twenty-fifth.

▶ Lessons can easily be taught out of sequence according to the needs of the class by using shared writing (teacher does all of the writing).

▶ The twenty-five lessons in this book are models for you to use to learn more about the process and structure. Use what you learn about interactive writing to actively involve children in any type of writing in any subject across the day. These twenty-five lessons are a starting point.

▶ Each lesson is two pages. All lessons follow the structure and routines of an interactive writing lesson (Figure 3-4).

▶ To help you locate the lesson you are looking for, each interactive writing lesson is identified with IW plus a number and the lesson name, for example, IW.1: Making a Name Chart.

▶ The lesson name indicates the type of writing that will be produced in the lesson. The kinds of writing that kindergartners can be expected to try can be found in the Grade K writing section of *The Literacy Continuum* (Fountas and Pinnell 2017).

Each lesson is carefully designed to promote oral language and talk before any text is written. Children need to learn that they can say what they are going to write. As you move from talking to writing, children might be invited up to the easel or chart to do any of the following:

▶ Write a known letter (sometimes the first letter of the child's name).

▶ Place two fingers on the chart to "hold" a space while the next word is being written.

▶ Write a letter that is connected to a sound the children hear in the word.

▶ Write a known word.

▶ Write a word part.

▶ Add punctuation.

▶ Sign their names.

▶ Create a quick sketch.

Be intentional about whom you invite to share the pen. Asking too many children to write something or having them write more than they are able to do quickly will slow everything down. Not every child needs a turn to write something in every lesson. Work to keep the writing moving along.

Structure of an Interactive Writing Lesson	
Establish Purpose	Talk together with the children to decide what to write.
Talk About What to Write	Talk together about what to say and how to say it.
Write Together	Invite several children to help you do the writing by contributing a letter, a word, or a part of a word.
Read and Revisit	Invite children to notice details, like specific letters, spaces between words, or words that begin with the same letter.
Summarize and Invite/Extend	Review the lesson and offer a way to extend the learning.

Figure 3-4: Once you learn the structure of an interactive writing lesson, children become used to the routine, making the lesson run smoothly and keeping it short.

A Closer Look at the Interactive Writing Lessons

While the content of each interactive writing experience will vary, the structure of each lesson is the same. Children will learn the routines, and that means the lesson will be smoother and shorter.

Before the Lesson

Each interactive writing lesson in this book begins with information to help you make the most of the lesson. There are four types of information here:

The Active Learning Experience is the foundation of every interactive writing lesson. Shared classroom experiences provide real opportunities for children to explore, talk, and write. You and the children can take a field trip, conduct a scientific experiment, paint a mural, make something in the creation station (maker space), read a book, or bake a cake. An example of how an active learning experience can lead to a meaningful interactive writing lesson follows.

Active Learning Experience: Take a field trip.

Interactive Writing Possibilities:

- ▶ Write a thank you note to the field trip host.
- ▶ Write a memory story about the trip.
- ▶ Make and label a map of the place you visited.
- ▶ Make a book about the trip.

The topics of these active learning experiences will vary widely depending on your school curriculum and the interests of the children in your class, but we have tried to provide ideas for common activities and experiences for kindergartners. In many cases, these experiences are also linked to the books in the text sets from *Fountas & Pinnell Classroom™ Interactive Read-Aloud Collection* (2018). These sets of books are grouped by ideas, topics, or type of book. They help children build rich knowledge and language because they have themes that are familiar to kindergartners, such as animals, nursery rhymes, and family. If you don't have this collection, we have offered ideas for the kinds of books you might choose to read aloud ahead of the interactive writing lessons.

The active learning experience provides the opportunity to build a shared vocabulary about the hands-on activity. These active experiences are especially good for children who are learning English. Having already had an opportunity to think and talk about the topic, children will find it easier to contribute ideas during the interactive writing lesson.

Goals are based on behaviors from the Grade K sections of *The Literacy Continuum*. Interactive writing mirrors the writing process:

- ▶ Composing (planning what to write)
- ▶ Constructing (writing the print)
- ▶ Rereading

So, in interactive writing, you can get a lot done in one lesson. You can address several goals. (A writing minilesson, on the other hand, has one focused goal.)

Why It's Important describes how the lesson will support children in their journey as writers.

Assess Learning is a list of behaviors to look for as you observe children during the lesson and when they attempt to apply what they have learned to their own writing. Your observations will inform your decisions about what to teach next.

EL CONNECTION

Interactive Writing Lesson

Under the heading **Interactive Writing Lesson**, you will find a sample lesson. The example includes suggestions for teaching with precise language and open-ended questions that help children think of what to write and then get it down on paper. Each part of the lesson is described below and shown in an annotated lesson in Figure 3-5 (pp. 40–41).

Establish Purpose

Interactive writing lessons begin by talking about the active learning experience, which is the purpose for writing, and about why it is important to write about it. Thinking about your purpose helps in choosing the form of writing, such as a memory story about a class trip.

Talk About What to Write

After deciding on a purpose, spend a short time talking about what to write. Together, think about the message and how it could be said in words. Remember, young children will be thinking about a lot during the short time of the lesson, so don't plan to write too much. A few words, a phrase, or a sentence can be enough to communicate an idea: labels for a picture, the names of a few items on a menu, or one or two sentences in a thank you note. After you have decided what to write, say it and ask the children to repeat after you. (A writer has to remember the message while writing.) To help children learn about word boundaries and that words are made up of letters, take a moment sometimes to count the number of words you are going to write.

Write Together

The next part of the lesson provides an example of how you might write the message—sentence by sentence, word by word, letter by letter. When children have the opportunity to plan and write the text with the teacher, they learn much about early concepts of print, such as the following:

- You read print left to right and top to bottom.
- Words are made up of letters.
- Words have boundaries (space before and after).

As you write the words in the message, keep the following in mind:

- Help the children connect letters to sounds and make connections to familiar words, particularly to the names of children in the class.
- Have children watch your mouth as you say each word slowly.

- Emphasize sounds but avoid artificially segmenting a word, distorting it so much that children are listening only to the individual sounds instead of the smooth sequence of sounds in a word. (They will have opportunities to segment words in phonics lessons.)

- Say the word slowly and then have children say the word out loud slowly with you and then for themselves. (It is important for them to enunciate the words and listen for the sounds.)

- Always write the letters of a word in sequence from left to right.

- Keep the lesson moving quickly so it will not bog down.

- In one lesson, invite only a few children to do some writing.

Keeping everyone engaged is a challenge! Moving the writing along quickly is the most effective practice, but here are some ways to keep children focused while one child is sharing the pen:

- Have the rest of the children practice writing the letters in the air, on the rug, or in their hands.

- Give the children individual bags with whiteboards and markers so that they can make the letter or word along with the child at the easel.

Many kindergartners are just beginning to distinguish between letters and to connect letters to sounds, so select teaching points for easy-to-hear sounds. Use the following guidelines to be selective and thoughtful about the letters you ask children to contribute particularly at the beginning of the year:

- Initial and ending sounds are often the easiest to hear, and consonant sounds are generally easier to hear than vowel sounds.

- Avoid asking children to write letters in words that may lead to confusion (e.g., the o in the word one could be confused with the letter w).

- Quickly write harder words that are beyond children's experience.

As children contribute letters, they make connections between the sounds and letters. They also think about the directional movements needed to mechanically write each letter. The Verbal Path for Letter Formation (Figure 7-3) lists the movements a writer uses to make letters. It is referenced throughout this book and is available in the online resources.

While children are focused on making the movements to form letters, they need to keep in mind the purpose they have set and the message they are communicating. That's a lot for kindergartners to coordinate at once, so your guidance during the interactive writing process is highly valuable.

The process of writing the text is particularly powerful for English learners because in a sense it makes language "stand still." After you have written a word, children are free to reread the sentence to help them remember the next word. It "slows down" processing and makes it easier to focus on the details.

Read and Revisit

Keep reading the writing in a shared way so children can think about the word to write next. When the writing is finished, reread it together to make sure it makes sense and sounds right. This step provides a model for how to reread for revision.

Rereading also gives you the opportunity to revisit or look back at the text for important teaching about phonics, spelling, and word study. You can have children revisit the text multiple times for different purposes. Here are a few ideas for rereading and revisiting a text:

- Find letters with distinctive features (e.g., letters with sticks or rounded parts).
- Point to upper- and lowercase letters.
- Point to the spaces between words.
- Point to the beginning or end of a word.
- Find a letter you know.
- Find a word you know.
- Find a word that begins like your name or a classmate's name.
- Find words that begin (end) with a certain letter.
- Find the vowel(s) in a word.

This part of the lesson reinforces some of the teaching you did while writing the text and perhaps even outside of the lesson. The suggestions provided for revisiting the text get more sophisticated over time as children learn more about letters and words. Keep in mind what the children in your class know as you make decisions for how you will have them revisit the text. Use the Writing and Phonics, Spelling, and Word Study continua in *The Literacy Continuum* to consider other behaviors you might reinforce through this part of the lesson.

Summarize and Invite/Extend

This part of the lesson includes two parts: summarizing the learning and extending the learning. First, help children remember what they learned during the lesson. In IW.7: Writing a Thank You Card, we remind children that they learned how to write a thank you card and invite them to try writing their own. In addition to this invitation, children will later experience writing minilessons that further extend this lesson by explicitly teaching why people write letters, what to include in a letter, and where to write the recipient's and sender's names.

A Closer Look at an Interactive Writing Lesson

This code identifies this lesson as the eighteenth interactive writing lesson.

Involve children in an **active learning experience** to provide a purpose and some content for writing.

The **goals** of the lesson are clearly identified to support your understanding of what this particular lesson is and why it is important for the children in your classroom.

Important vocabulary used in the lesson is listed.

Look for these specific behaviors and understandings as you **assess** children's learning after presenting the lesson.

Precise language is suggested for teaching the lesson.

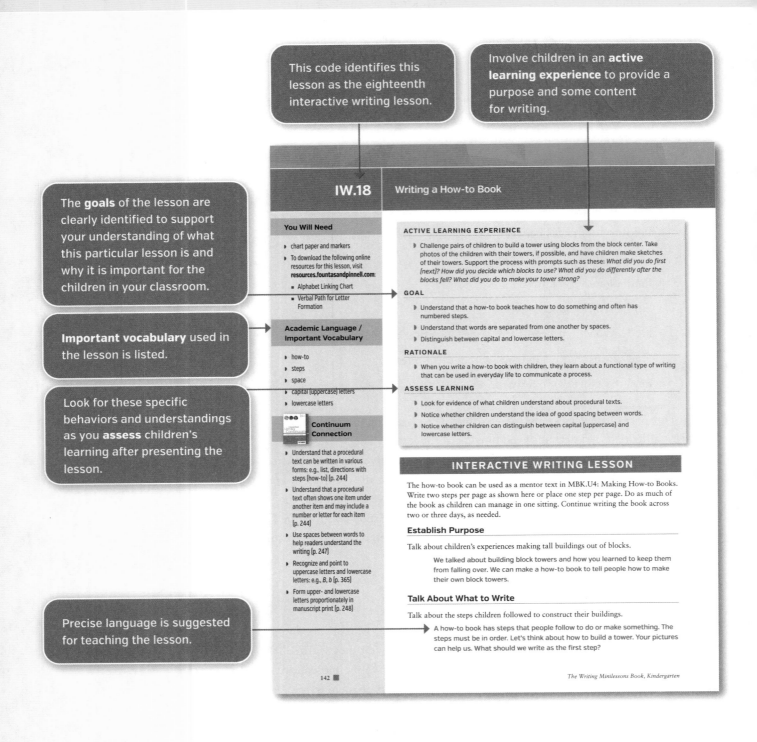

IW.18 — Writing a How-to Book

You Will Need

- chart paper and markers
- To download the following online resources for this lesson, visit **resources.fountasandpinnell.com**:
  - Alphabet Linking Chart
  - Verbal Path for Letter Formation

Academic Language / Important Vocabulary

- how-to
- steps
- space
- capital (uppercase) letters
- lowercase letters

Continuum Connection

- Understand that a procedural text can be written in various forms: e.g., list, directions with steps (how-to) [p. 244]
- Understand that a procedural text often shows one item under another item and may include a number or letter for each item [p. 244]
- Use spaces between words to help readers understand the writing [p. 247]
- Recognize and point to uppercase letters and lowercase letters: e.g., *B, b* [p. 365]
- Form upper- and lowercase letters proportionately in manuscript print [p. 248]

ACTIVE LEARNING EXPERIENCE

- Challenge pairs of children to build a tower using blocks from the block center. Take photos of the children with their towers, if possible, and have children make sketches of their towers. Support the process with prompts such as these: *What did you do first (next)? How did you decide which blocks to use? What did you do differently after the blocks fell? What did you do to make your tower strong?*

GOAL

- Understand that a how-to book teaches how to do something and often has numbered steps.
- Understand that words are separated from one another by spaces.
- Distinguish between capital and lowercase letters.

RATIONALE

- When you write a how-to book with children, they learn about a functional type of writing that can be used in everyday life to communicate a process.

ASSESS LEARNING

- Look for evidence of what children understand about procedural texts.
- Notice whether children understand the idea of good spacing between words.
- Notice whether children can distinguish between capital (uppercase) and lowercase letters.

INTERACTIVE WRITING LESSON

The how-to book can be used as a mentor text in MBK.U4: Making How-to Books. Write two steps per page as shown here or place one step per page. Do as much of the book as children can manage in one sitting. Continue writing the book across two or three days, as needed.

Establish Purpose

Talk about children's experiences making tall buildings out of blocks.

> We talked about building block towers and how you learned to keep them from falling over. We can make a how-to book to tell people how to make their own block towers.

Talk About What to Write

Talk about the steps children followed to construct their buildings.

> A how-to book has steps that people follow to do or make something. The steps must be in order. Let's think about how to build a tower. Your pictures can help us. What should we write as the first step?

142

The Writing Minilessons Book, Kindergarten

These suggestions provide guidance for constructing a piece of writing with the children.

Each lesson has an example of how the interactive writing piece might look.

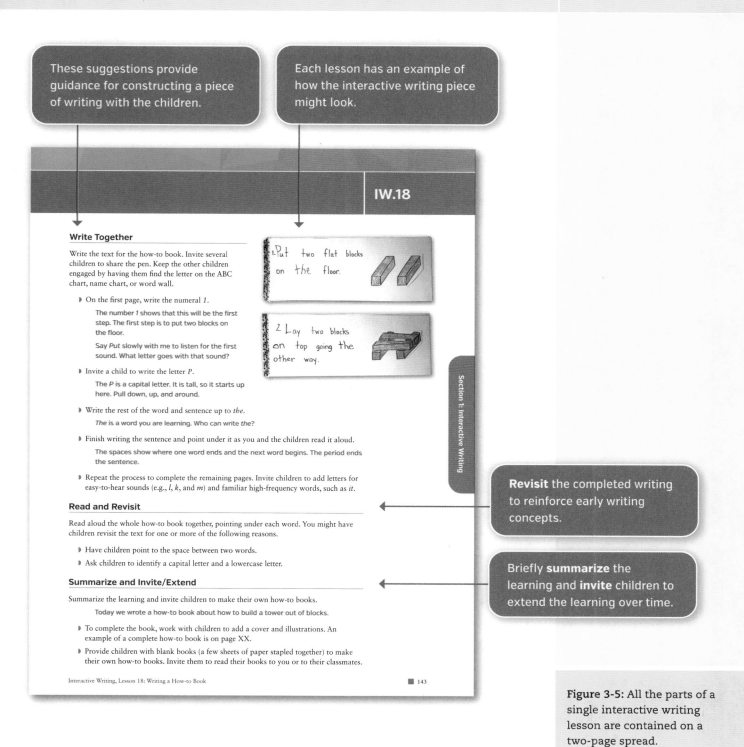

IW.18

Write Together

Write the text for the how-to book. Invite several children to share the pen. Keep the other children engaged by having them find the letter on the ABC chart, name chart, or word wall.

▶ On the first page, write the numeral *1*.

The number *1* shows that this will be the first step. The first step is to put two blocks on the floor.

Say *Put* slowly with me to listen for the first sound. What letter goes with that sound?

▶ Invite a child to write the letter *P*.

The *P* is a capital letter. It is tall, so it starts up here. Pull down, up, and around.

▶ Write the rest of the word and sentence up to *the*.

The is a word you are learning. Who can write *the*?

▶ Finish writing the sentence and point under it as you and the children read it aloud.

The spaces show where one word ends and the next word begins. The period ends the sentence.

▶ Repeat the process to complete the remaining pages. Invite children to add letters for easy-to-hear sounds (e.g., *l*, *k*, and *m*) and familiar high-frequency words, such as *it*.

Read and Revisit

Read aloud the whole how-to book together, pointing under each word. You might have children revisit the text for one or more of the following reasons.

▶ Have children point to the space between two words.
▶ Ask children to identify a capital letter and a lowercase letter.

Summarize and Invite/Extend

Summarize the learning and invite children to make their own how-to books.

Today we wrote a how-to book about how to build a tower out of blocks.

▶ To complete the book, work with children to add a cover and illustrations. An example of a complete how-to book is on page XX.
▶ Provide children with blank books (a few sheets of paper stapled together) to make their own how-to books. Invite them to read their books to you or to their classmates.

Interactive Writing, Lesson 18: Writing a How-to Book ■ 143

Section 1: Interactive Writing

Revisit the completed writing to reinforce early writing concepts.

Briefly **summarize** the learning and **invite** children to extend the learning over time.

Figure 3-5: All the parts of a single interactive writing lesson are contained on a two-page spread.

Effective Interactive Writing Lessons

The goal of interactive writing lessons is to provide a context in which the children experience what it feels like to create a written piece of text. The activities move them closer to trying writing for themselves. Interactive writing lessons are flexible so that you and the children can create any kind of writing. But no matter what you compose and construct together, the characteristics of an interactive writing lesson, listed in Figure 3-6, apply.

Effective Interactive Writing Lessons . . .

- are **based on a common active, meaningful experience** (e.g., cooking, attending a field trip, reading a book)
- create **a community of learners** who think, explore, play, talk, read, write, and draw together
- establish a **purpose and real reason** for writing
- use drawing and writing for a **variety of purposes** across the curriculum
- are very **brief** and use **explicit** teaching
- use **focused, concise language**
- use **conversation** to support the process
- create a **common text** that can be used for shared reading or as a mentor text for writing
- raise awareness of the writer's and illustrator's **craft**
- develop children's understanding of the **conventions** of writing (capitals, punctuation)
- make **letter-sound connections**
- connect **reading and writing**
- develop young children's **oral vocabulary**
- develop **phonological awareness** (the sounds of language)
- reinforce **how letters and words look**
- are taught at the **cutting-edge of what children can learn** with your assistance
- are **selective** about when the pen is shared
- model **rereading the message** each time a word is added
- make **connections to classroom resources** such as the ABC chart and the name chart
- summarize **new learning**
- invite children to try **drawing and writing on their own**
- provide **documentation** of the understandings of a group of learners
- **differentiate instruction** to meet individual students' needs

Figure 3-6: Characteristics of effective interactive writing lessons

The Writing Minilessons Book, Kindergarten

Organize for Interactive Writing Lessons

Interactive writing typically takes place with the whole class in the group meeting area, though there are times you may decide to use it with a small group to address a specific need or to provide more intensive support. These small-group lessons can take place in the large-group meeting area or at tables or small-group areas elsewhere in the room. Be sure the children have enough space to sit comfortably. You will need to plan space for children to walk up to the chart, so be sure it is visible and accessible.

Resources

Take some time to think about the materials and resources that will support effective learning opportunities. Make resources such as those listed below available near the meeting area. When limited display space is available, consider using hangers to place charts on a rack. Resources in or near the meeting area might include the following:

- name chart (Figure 2-2)
- Alphabet Linking Chart (Figure 3-7)
- poems or stories for shared reading
- a word wall (with children's names and some high-frequency words) (Figure 1-9)
- classroom labels
- completed or in-progress pieces of interactive writing
- children's independent writing

Figure 3-7: The Alphabet Linking Chart (Fountas and Pinnell 2017) is just one of the helpful resources for shared and interactive writing. An 8 ½" x 11" version is available from online resources.

Materials and Equipment

The chart in Figure 3-8 and the text that follows describe materials to help you make the most of an interactive writing lesson.

Easel An easel that children can reach easily will help them contribute to the writing (Figure 3-9). The slanted surface of an easel is easier to write on than a flat surface. Easels also make it easier for teachers or children to stand to one side to use a pointer with the written text.

Materials and Equipment for Interactive Writing

Materials and Equipment	Description
Easel	• Sturdy, slanted surface • Accessible height for children
Paper	• White or light-colored unlined chart paper (about 25" x 30"; avoid dark colors) • Light-brown wrapping paper or butcher paper (with a dark black marker) • Large-size construction paper in white or light colors • Sentence strips or card stock cut into word-sized cards
Markers	• Broad-tipped markers that do not bleed through the paper • Dark colors
Correction tape	• One-inch white correction tape • White peel-off mailing labels • Small pieces of paper (matching the color of the chart) applied with a glue stick
Magnetic letters	• Brightly colored plastic magnetic letters organized on a cookie sheet or in a plastic case with compartments
Magnetic drawing board or small whiteboard	• Magnetic or dry-erase board for demonstrating how to write a letter or word
Pointers	• A 48" dowel rod cut in half • Bright or dark color on the tip
Art materials	• Crayons, washable markers, glue sticks, scissors, a variety of paper

Figure 3-8: Materials and equipment for interactive writing

Paper Paper selection is surprisingly important. Having a choice of paper affects how children organize their writing and encourages them to be flexible and creative during the writing process. For the easel, chart paper that is wider than it is long works best. A measurement of 30" x 25" is appropriate. Wider paper provides space for more words in each line of print, which allows for more practice of left-to-right movement and spacing of words. Unlined paper is preferable because it allows young children to organize space with greater flexibility of letter size. Keep children's focus on producing the features of letters that they can control rather than on trying to fit them into the lines. Horizontal lines can interfere with the child's perception of letterforms in the early stages, especially if there is an overemphasis on staying within lines.

Figure 3-9: Place an easel similar to this one in the meeting area to use for interactive writing and shared writing.

Writing on cut-up sentence strips or word cards is beneficial early in the year. After you and the children have composed the message orally and repeated it several times, count the number of words in the sentence and then either attach a card for each word on the chart paper or add a card for each new word as you write it. Writing words on individual cards demonstrates word boundaries and helps children begin to understand word-for-word matching. Cut the sentence strip to the length of the word to reinforce children's visual memory of words as long or short.

Use word cards and cut-up sentence strips only temporarily. Once children have a good idea of how individual words are defined by space, move away from them so children have the opportunity to write and read words in continuous text on the entire blank surface of the paper.

Markers To make the print easy to read, especially from a distance, use markers in dark colors (e.g., black, blue) on a white or very light background. It is important to write the piece in one uniform color so that the final product looks like a unified text. Using many different colors for the print breaks up the continuous flow and can distract children's attention away from the visual features of the letters and words. Use highlighter tape to draw attention to a particular word or phrase or word part.

Correction Tape Use one-inch correction tape or white mailing labels to cover mistakes—a wrong letter, an uppercase letter instead of a lowercase letter, too little space between words—instead of crossing out or erasing. White tape also allows for quick error correction, which encourages children to take risks because they know how easily a letter or word can be altered. We sometimes call it "magic tape" (Figure 3-10)!

Figure 3-10: Keep correction tape near the easel to use during interactive writing lessons.

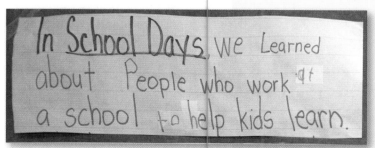

Magnetic Letters Magnetic letters can be used to show how a letter looks or to demonstrate how to spell a word. Organize magnetic letters so that you can find letters that you want quickly and not bog down the lesson. Store the letters alphabetically on a cookie sheet or in a box that has separate compartments for each of the letters. Children can use the letters on a cookie sheet or magnetic whiteboard (Figure 3-11).

Magnetic Drawing Board or Whiteboard A magnetic drawing board has a plastic board with magnetic filings under the surface that can be written on with magnets. Both magnetic drawing boards and dry-erase whiteboards allow you to quickly produce an image for the children—a letter or a word—to help them notice distinctive features. The whiteboard allows you to easily erase a word part, in any location of the word, and you can also underline or circle parts of words.

Figure 3-11: A cookie sheet keeps the magnetic letters in place while children practice making words.

Pointers Pointer sticks allow you to point crisply under each word and to emphasize left-to-right motion. A pointer is better than your finger because it doesn't block children's view of the print in the same way that your arm or hand does. A helpful suggestion is to color the tip of your pointer to draw children's attention to the part that is placed under the print. We advise against pointers that have embellishments on them such as hands, apples, etc., because such objects can block the view of the print. Teach children where to stand and how to point to the words so as not to block the print.

Art Materials for Children and Downloadable Art Children love the opportunity to illustrate the writing that you have produced together during an interactive writing lesson. Assign children to make the art in the art center during choice time and then attach it to the chart. In some cases, downloadable art is available from online resources. Use downloadable art judiciously. We have provided this art as a time saver for you, but the choices you and the children make will be different. But when it is particularly important for the children to have clear pictures to understand the writing you may decide to use the art provided.

To read more about interactive writing, see *Interactive Writing: How Language and Literacy Come Together, K–2* (McCarrier, Fountas, and Pinnell 2000).

The Writing Minilessons Book, Kindergarten

Connect Reading and Writing

Reading books with the children is a shared experience that can be the active learning experience of an interactive writing lesson. The interactive read-aloud lessons in *Fountas & Pinnell Classroom™ Interactive Read-Aloud Collection* (2018) offer suggestions for shared and interactive writing. Many of these suggestions are examples of how you can make strong connections between reading and writing. Figure 3-12 shows how the text sets (collections of books grouped thematically) align with the interactive writing lessons. If you do not have these text sets, there are suggestions for the kinds of books you might want to read to the children prior to the interactive writing lessons so they can be the foundation for the writing.

Use the Finished Pieces from Interactive Writing Lessons

Children love to revisit the illustrated pieces you have created together and read them again and again. You'll find that children can identify just about every letter or word they have personally contributed! That kind of ownership and engagement is why completed interactive writing texts are so good for shared reading and independent reading. Consider making small copies of some for children to take home to share with their families.

Interactive writing pieces also are useful as mentor texts (examples) for writing minilessons and independent writing. Use an interactive writing lesson to demonstrate a particular type of writing before children try it on their own. Here are some important things to consider as you create interactive writing pieces:

▶ Keep interactive writing pieces simple and legible.

▶ Invite children to add illustrations after the lesson to add support to the meaning. You can have children make illustrations in the art center on separate pieces of paper and glue them onto the chart. This process avoids the crowding and space issues that can occur if children try to draw directly on the chart.

▶ With clear pictures, children can understand the message even if they can't yet read the words.

▶ Limit the amount of print and drawings that you include on the chart. Too much print and other details can clutter up the piece and make it difficult to read.

▶ Use the same dark color marker for all of the printing so children see words rather than separate letters. Use correction tape or blank address labels to cover errors so children are reading accurate words.

Aligning *Interactive Read-Aloud Collection* Text Sets with Interactive Writing	
	IW.1: Making a Name Chart
Sharing Stories and Songs: Nursery Rhymes	
Learning and Playing Together: School	IW.2: Writing About Our Classroom IW.3: Creating a Job Chart
Letters at Work: The Alphabet	IW.4: Making a Menu IW.5: Making an ABC Book
	IW.6: Making Labels for the Classroom
Taking Care of Each Other: Family	IW.7: Writing a Thank You Note
The Importance of Friendship	IW.8: Making a Class Big Book
Noticing the Way the World Looks: Colors	IW.9: Making a Color Chart IW.10: Writing a Color Poem
Exploring Pictures: Wordless Books	IW.11: Writing from a Picture
Numbers at Work: Counting	IW.12: Making a Counting Book IW.13: Taking a Survey
	IW.14: Writing About a Class Memory
The Importance of Kindness	
Eric Carle: Exploring the Natural World	
The Place You Call Home	IW.15: Writing About Our Creations
Living and Working Together: Community	IW.16: Making Signs IW.17: Labeling a Map
Exploring Fiction and Nonfiction	IW.18: Writing a How-to Book
Having Fun with Language	
Exploring Animal Tales	IW.19: Making a Story Map Mural
Sharing Stories: Folktales	IW.20: Writing an Alternative Ending
Sharing the Earth: Animals	IW.21: Writing a Question-and-Answer Book
	IW.22: Writing Scientific Observations
Lois Ehlert: Bringing Color and Texture to Life	

Figure 3-12: Alignment of *Fountas & Pinnell Classroom™ Interactive Read-Aloud Collection* text sets with interactive writing lessons in *The Writing Minilessons Book, Kindergarten.*

Learning How to Be Yourself	IW.23: Writing a Letter About a Book
Understanding Feelings	
Exploring Nonfiction	IW.24: Writing an All-About Book
Rhythm and Rhyme: Joyful Language	IW.25: Innovating on a Text
Grace Lin: Exploring Family and Culture	
Celebrating Differences	
Using Patterns: Cumulative Tales	

▶ Though we value the use of approximated spelling in children's own independent writing, we strongly recommend that the print on the interactive writing pieces reflect conventional spelling and grammar so children have a clear model for their own writing and can read and reread the writing easily.

Turn Interactive Writing Lessons into Shared Writing Lessons

You might choose to change an interactive writing lesson into a shared writing lesson by doing the writing yourself if you are short on time, if you want children to focus more on the content and/or routines of writing together, or if you are creating an important classroom resource that needs to be very clearly legible. In fact, the first lesson in the interactive writing section (IW.1: Making a Name Chart) is actually a shared writing lesson.

Likewise, any shared writing activity becomes interactive writing if children contribute by writing a letter or a word. The writing minilessons in this book rely heavily on shared writing.

Interactive writing lessons allow children the opportunity to participate in the writing process before they try writing on their own. Writing minilessons build on what children have learned through interactive writing lessons, as you will see in the next chapter.

Chapter 4 | What Is a Writing Minilesson?

Every minilesson should end with students envisioning a new possibility for their work, and the key to successful minilessons is helping the group of students sitting in front of us to envision the difference this lesson might make in their work.

—Katie Wood Ray and Lisa Cleaveland

A WRITING MINILESSON IS BRIEF. It focuses on a single writing concept to help children write successfully. A writing minilesson uses inquiry, which leads children to discovering an important understanding that they can try out immediately.

Writing minilessons are about ways to make the classroom a community of learners. They are about telling stories and drawing, both of which are foundations of writing. They are also about making books, learning important early writing concepts, and guiding children through the writing process. Writing minilessons help children emerge as readers and writers by thinking about one small understanding at a time.

> In an **inquiry lesson**, children engage in the thinking and develop the thinking for themselves. They learn from the inside, instead of simply being told what to understand. *Telling* is not the same as teaching.

Six Types of Writing Minilessons

This book has 150 lessons—25 interactive writing lessons and 125 writing minilessons—in seven color-coded sections. The 25 interactive writing lessons are in Section 1, and the 125 writing minilessons are organized within the next six sections (Figure 4-1):

Figure 4-1: The writing minilessons are organized within six sections.

Minilessons in the Management section help children become a strong community of diverse learners who play and learn together peacefully and respectfully. Most of your minilessons at the beginning of the school year will focus on organizing the classroom and building a community in which children feel safe to share ideas and learn about one another. Repeat any of the lessons as needed across the year. A guiding principle: teach a minilesson on anything that prevents the classroom from running smoothly. In these lessons, children will learn

- routines that will help them work well with their classmates,

- ways they can participate,

- the importance of listening, taking turns, and looking at the speaker when in a group, and

- how to gain an ability to work independently as they learn the structures and routines for playing and writing together in the classroom (including learning about independent writing time, choice time, and the tools of writing).

Minilessons in the Telling Stories section support the oral language component of writing, which is the first step for kindergarten children as they move from their thoughts to oral language to drawing and writing their ideas on paper. Listening to stories and telling stories are rehearsals for writing stories. These writing minilessons help children learn that

The Writing Minilessons Book, Kindergarten

- they have stories to tell,

- stories can be about things in everyday life, and

- it is important to consider your audience when you tell stories.

These lessons also give children the opportunity to learn how to use storytelling to act out familiar stories that they have heard. By acting out and retelling stories with puppets or other props, children begin to develop a broader understanding of the elements of a story.

Minilessons in the Making Books section support children by helping them see that they can make their own books like the authors of the books that they read. The first umbrella, Getting Started with Making Books, is designed to get bookmaking up and running in your classroom. As the year progresses, children begin to explore different types of books they can make. They learn how to

- teach others something they know how to do in a how-to book,

- share stories they have told in a memory book, and

- tell what they know about a topic in an all-about book.

Each time children are exposed to a new kind of book, they expand their understanding of ways they can write and learn more about the way illustrators and authors craft their books.

Minilessons in the Drawing section are used to teach children how to draw and use color to represent real life. Drawing is one of the primary ways kindergartners tell their stories on paper. The minilessons in this section also help children use a variety of materials and techniques to create interesting illustrations for the books they make.

Minilessons in the Exploring Early Writing section help children develop early concepts of print. There are generative lessons that help children learn "how print works," for example, that

- print is read left to right,

- words have space on either side, and,

- letters and sounds are connected.

> A **generative lesson** is one that can be used over and over to teach ideas that are alike. For example, the structure of a lesson on how to form the letter *c* could be used to teach how to form a different letter.

Other umbrellas in this section touch on how to use classroom resources to write words, use simple punctuation and capitalization, and write for a practical task (e.g., writing a letter or writing for the play corner).

Minilessons in the Writing Process section provide ideas for how to introduce children in very basic and concrete ways to the parts of the writing process.

Writing Minilessons Are Grouped into Umbrella Concepts

EL CONNECTION

Within each of the six major sections, lessons are grouped in what we call "umbrellas." Each umbrella is made up of several minilessons that are related to the larger idea of the umbrella. Within an umbrella, the lessons build on each other. When you teach several minilessons about the same idea, children deepen their understandings and develop shared vocabulary. These connections are especially helpful to English learners.

In most cases, it makes sense to teach the minilessons in an umbrella in order. But for some umbrellas, it makes sense to spread the minilessons over time so that children gain more experience with the first idea before moving on to the next. In this book, lessons are placed together in an umbrella to show you how the lessons build the concept over time.

Anchor Charts Support Writing Minilessons

Anchor charts are an essential part of each writing minilesson (Figure 4-2). They capture children's thinking during the lesson and hold it for reflection at the end of the lesson. The chart is a visual reminder of the big, important ideas and the language used in the minilesson. Each writing minilesson features one sample chart, but use it only as a guideline. Your charts will be unique because they are built from ideas offered by the children in your class.

Each minilesson provides guidance for adding information to the chart. Read through lessons carefully to know whether any parts of the chart should be prepared ahead or whether the chart is constructed during the lesson or left until the end. After the lesson, the charts become a resource for the children to refer to throughout the day and on following days. They are a visual resource for children who need to not only hear but also see the information. Children can revisit these charts as they apply the key understandings to their writing or as they try out new routines in the classroom. You can refer to them during interactive writing and shared writing lessons and when you confer with children about their independent writing.

Figure 4-2: Constructing anchor charts with and in front of your class provides verbal and visual support for all learners.

Some of the art you see on the sample charts is available from the online resources to represent concepts that are likely to come up as you construct the charts with children. The downloadable chart art is provided for your convenience. Use it when it applies to the children's responses, but do not let it determine or limit children's responses. Valuing the ideas of the class should be your primary concern.

When you create charts with kindergartners, consider the following:

Make your charts simple, clear, and organized. Keep the charts simple without a lot of dense text. Provide white space and print neatly in dark, easy-to-read colors.

Make your charts visually appealing and useful. All of the minilesson charts contain visual support, which will be helpful for all kindergartners, especially English learners. Children will benefit from the visuals to help them in understanding the concept and maybe even reading some of the words. The drawings are intentionally simple to give you a quick model to draw yourself. You might find it helpful to prepare these drawings on separate pieces of paper or sticky notes ahead of the lesson and tape or glue them on the chart as the children construct their understandings. This time-saving tip can also make the charts look more interesting and colorful, because certain parts will stand out for the children.

Make your charts colorful. The sample minilesson charts are colorful for the purpose of engagement or organization. Color can be useful, but be careful about the amount and type you choose. Color can support English learners by providing a visual link to certain words or ideas. However, color can also be distracting if overused. Be thoughtful about when you choose to use color to highlight an idea or a word on a chart so that children are supported in reading continuous text. Text that is broken up by a lot of different colors can be very distracting for readers who are still becoming accustomed to using the visual information in print. You will notice that the minilesson principle is usually written in black or a dark color across the top of the chart so that it stands out and is easily recognized as the focus of the lesson. In most cases, the minilesson principle is added at the end of the lesson after children have constructed their own understanding of the concept.

Use the charts to support language growth. Anchor charts support language growth in all children, especially English learners. Conversation about the minilesson develops oral language and then connects oral language to print when you write words on the chart and provide picture support. By constructing an anchor chart with the children, you provide print that is immediately accessible to them because they helped create it and have ownership of the language. After a chart is finished, revisit it as

EL CONNECTION

often as needed to reinforce not only the ideas but also the printed words (Figure 4-3).

Umbrellas and Minilessons Have Predictable Structures

Understanding how the umbrellas are designed and how the minilessons fit together will help you keep your lessons focused and brief. Each umbrella is set up the same way, and each writing minilesson follows the same predictable structure (Figure 4-4). **Use mentor texts that you have previously read and enjoyed with the children** to streamline the lessons. You will not need to spend a lot of time rereading large sections of the text because the children already know the texts well.

Figure 4-3: Characteristics of an effective anchor chart

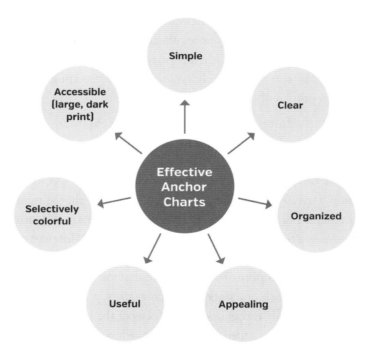

Structure of a Writing Minilesson	
Minilesson	• Show examples/provide demonstration. • Invite children to talk. • Make an anchor chart.
Have a Try	• Have children try doing what they are learning.
Summarize and Apply	• Summarize the learning. • Invite children to apply the learning during independent writing time. • Write the minilesson principle on the chart.
Confer	• Move around the room to confer briefly with children.
Share	• Gather children together and invite them to talk about their writing.

Figure 4-4: Once you learn the structure of a writing minilesson, you can create your own minilessons with different examples.

A Closer Look at the Umbrella Overview

All umbrellas are set up the same way. They begin with an overview and end with questions to guide your evaluation of children's understanding of the umbrella concepts plus several extension ideas. In between are the writing minilessons.

At the beginning of each umbrella (Figure 4-5), the minilessons are listed and directions are provided to help you prepare to teach them. There are suggestions for books from *Fountas & Pinnell Classroom™ Interactive Read-Aloud Collection* (2018) and *Shared Reading Collection* (2018) to use as mentor texts. There are also suggestions for the kinds of books you might select if you do not have these books.

A list of minilessons is organized under the umbrella title.

Prepare for teaching the minilessons in this umbrella with these suggestions.

Use these suggested mentor texts as examples in the minilessons in this umbrella or use books that have similar characteristics.

Figure 4-5: Each umbrella is introduced by a page that offers an overview of the umbrella.

Getting Ideas for Writing

Umbrella 1

Minilessons in This Umbrella

WML1 Get ideas from things you collect.

WML2 Look at the class story charts.

WML3 Get ideas from other writers.

WML4 Go back to ideas you love.

Before Teaching Umbrella 1 Minilessons

We recommend teaching STR.U1: Storytelling before teaching these minilessons. You do not need to teach the minilessons in this umbrella consecutively. Rather, they can be used whenever you feel the children need some writing inspiration.

Give children plenty of opportunities to write and draw freely and without constraints. Read and discuss simple books from a variety of genres that the children will enjoy. Use the following texts from *Fountas & Pinnell Classroom™ Interactive Read-Aloud Collection*, or choose books from your classroom library.

Interactive Read-Aloud Collection
Eric Carle: Exploring the Natural World

From Head to Toe

Does a Kangaroo Have a Mother, Too?

"Slowly, Slowly, Slowly," said the Sloth

Have You Seen My Cat?

The Mixed-Up Chameleon

Interactive Writing Lessons

IW.20: Writing an Alternative Ending

As you read and enjoy books together, help children

- discuss, whenever possible, how the author got the idea for the book (using the author's note, if applicable),

- notice when an author writes repeatedly about the same topic, idea, or characters, and

- talk about their own ideas for writing about a similar topic or theme.

Interactive Read-Aloud
Eric Carle

Interactive Writing

Section 7: Writing Process

Umbrella 1: Getting Ideas for Writing

■ 429

A Closer Look at the Writing Minilessons

The 125 writing minilessons in this book help you teach specific aspects of writing. An annotated writing minilesson is shown in Figure 4-6. Each section is described in the text that follows.

Before the Lesson

Each writing minilesson begins with information to help you make the most of the lesson. There are four types of information here:

The Writing Minilesson Principle describes the key idea the children will learn and be invited to apply. The idea for the minilesson principle is based on the behaviors in the Grade K sections of *The Literacy Continuum* (Fountas and Pinnell 2017), but the language has been carefully crafted to be accessible and memorable for children.

The minilesson principle gives you a clear idea of the concept you will help children construct. The lessons are designed to be inquiry-based because we want the children to build to this understanding instead of hearing it stated at the beginning.

Although we have crafted the language to make it appropriate for the age group, you can shape the language to fit the way your children use language. When you summarize the lesson, be sure to state the principle simply and clearly so that children are certain to understand what it means. State the minilesson principle the same way every time you refer to it.

The Goal of the minilesson is based on a behavior in *The Literacy Continuum*. Each minilesson is focused on one single goal that leads to a deeeper understanding of the larger umbrella concept.

The Rationale is the reason the minilesson is important. It is a brief explanation of how this new learning leads children forward in their writing journey.

Assess Learning is a list of suggestions of specific behaviors and understandings to look for as evidence that children have absorbed the minilesson concept. Keep this list in mind as you teach.

A Closer Look at a Writing Minilesson

The **Writing Minilesson Principle** is a brief statement that describes what children will be invited to learn and apply.

This code identifies this lesson as the third writing minilesson in the first umbrella of the Writing Process section.

Look for these specific behaviors and understandings as you **assess** children's learning after presenting the lesson.

Important vocabulary used in the minilesson is listed.

Precise language is suggested for teaching the lesson.

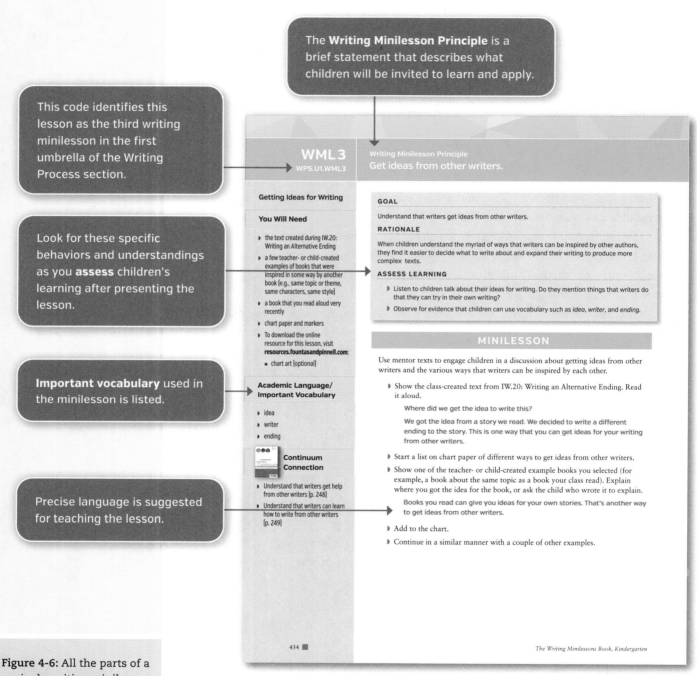

WML 3
WPS.U1.WML3

Writing Minilesson Principle
Get ideas from other writers.

Getting Ideas for Writing

You Will Need

- the text created during IW.20: Writing an Alternative Ending
- a few teacher- or child-created examples of books that were inspired in some way by another book (e.g., same topic or theme, same characters, same style)
- a book that you read aloud very recently
- chart paper and markers
- To download the online resource for this lesson, visit **resources.fountasandpinnell.com**:
  - chart art (optional)

Academic Language/ Important Vocabulary

- idea
- writer
- ending

Continuum Connection

- Understand that writers get help from other writers (p. 248)
- Understand that writers can learn how to write from other writers (p. 249)

GOAL
Understand that writers get ideas from other writers.

RATIONALE
When children understand the myriad of ways that writers can be inspired by other authors, they find it easier to decide what to write about and expand their writing to produce more complex texts.

ASSESS LEARNING
- Listen to children talk about their ideas for writing. Do they mention things that writers do that they can try in their own writing?
- Observe for evidence that children can use vocabulary such as *idea*, *writer*, and *ending*.

MINILESSON

Use mentor texts to engage children in a discussion about getting ideas from other writers and the various ways that writers can be inspired by each other.

- Show the class-created text from IW.20: Writing an Alternative Ending. Read it aloud.

  Where did we get the idea to write this?

  We got the idea from a story we read. We decided to write a different ending to the story. This is one way that you can get ideas for your writing from other writers.

- Start a list on chart paper of different ways to get ideas from other writers.
- Show one of the teacher- or child-created example books you selected (for example, a book about the same topic as a book your class read). Explain where you got the idea for the book, or ask the child who wrote it to explain.

  Books you read can give you ideas for your own stories. That's another way to get ideas from other writers.

- Add to the chart.
- Continue in a similar manner with a couple of other examples.

434 ■

The Writing Minilessons Book, Kindergarten

Figure 4-6: All the parts of a single writing minilesson are contained on a two-page spread.

Children try out the new thinking from the minilesson, usually with a partner.

Create **anchor charts** as a useful reference tool and reinforcement of the minilesson principle for children during independent writing.

WML 3
WPS.U1.WML3

Have a Try

Invite children to talk to a partner about their ideas for writing.

- Show a book that you read aloud very recently. Briefly review the pages.

    What ideas does this book give you for your own writing? Turn and talk to your partner about your ideas.

- After children turn and talk, ask several children to share their ideas. Add to the chart if they suggest new ways of being inspired by an author.

Summarize and Apply

Write the principle at the top of the chart. Read it to children. Summarize the learning and remind them to think about books they have read when they are deciding what to write about.

    Today you noticed that you can get ideas from other writers in lots of different ways. When you are deciding what to write about today, think about books you have read. What ideas can you get from those books?

Get ideas from other writers.

- Write a different ending.
- Write about the same topic.
- Write about the same characters.
- Write in the same way.
- Make the pictures the same way.

Summarize the learning that has taken place and ask children to **apply** what they have learned during independent writing.

Confer

- During independent writing, move around the room to confer briefly with as many individual children as time allows. Sit side by side with them and invite them to talk about their ideas for writing. Use prompts such as the following as needed.

    - *What are you going to write about?*
    - *What ideas does your favorite book give you for your own writing?*
    - *Could you write a story that has the same characters doing something different?*
    - *Is there something on the chart that makes you think of something in your own life?*

Helpful prompts focus the conversation when you **confer** with children about their drawing and writing.

Share

Following independent writing, gather children in the meeting area.

    Did anyone get an idea for your writing from another writer?

    What did you write about? Where did you get that idea?

After independent writing, it is important for children to have a chance to **share** their learning, which gives you feedback on the learning children took on.

Umbrella 1: Getting Ideas for Writing

■ 435

Minilesson

The **Minilesson** section provides an example of a lesson for teaching the writing minilesson principle. We suggest some precise language and open-ended questions that will keep children engaged and the lesson brief and focused. Effective minilessons, when possible, involve inquiry. That means children actively think about the idea and notice examples in a familiar piece of writing. They begin to construct their understanding from concrete examples.

Create experiences that help children notice things and make their own discoveries. You might, for example, invite children to look at several nonfiction information books, carefully chosen to illustrate the minilesson principle. Children will know these books because they have heard them read aloud and have talked about them. Often, you can use the same books in several writing minilessons to make your teaching efficient. Invite children to talk about what they notice across all the books.

As kindergartners explore the mentor text examples using your questions and supportive comments as a guide, make the anchor chart with children's input. From this exploration and the discussion, children come to the minilesson principle. Learning is more powerful and enjoyable for kindergartners when they actively search for the meaning, find patterns, talk about their understandings, and share in making the charts. Children need to form networks of understanding around the concepts related to literacy and to be constantly looking for connections for themselves.

EL CONNECTION

Children learn more about language when they have opportunities to talk. Writing minilessons provide many opportunities for them to express their thoughts in language, both oral and written, and to communicate with others. The inquiry approach found in these lessons invites more child talk than teacher talk, and that can be both a challenge and an opportunity for you as you work with English learners. However, building talk routines, such as turn and talk, into your writing minilessons can be very helpful in providing opportunities for English learners to talk in a safe and supportive way.

When you ask children to think about the minilesson principle across several stories or informational books that they have previously heard read aloud and discussed, they are more engaged and able to participate because they know the stories and informational books and begin to notice important things about writing through them. Using familiar texts, including some writing that you and the children have created together, is particularly important for English learners. When you select examples for a writing minilesson, choose books and other examples that you know were particularly engaging for the English learners in your classroom. Besides choosing accessible, familiar texts, it is important to provide plenty of wait-and-think time. For example, you might say, "Let's think about that for a minute" before calling for responses.

When working with English learners, look for what the child knows about the concept instead of focusing on faulty grammar or language errors. Model appropriate language use in your responses but do not correct a child who is attempting to use language to learn it. You might also provide an oral sentence frame to get the student response started, for example, *I like the story because* _____. Accept variety in pronunciation and intonation, remembering that the more children speak, read, and write, the more they will take on the understanding of grammatical patterns and the complex intonation patterns that reflect meaning in English.

Have a Try

Before children leave the whole group to apply the new thinking during independent writing, give them a chance to try it with a partner or a small group. **Have a Try** is designed to be brief, but it offers you an opportunity to gather information on how well children understand the minilesson goal. In Management lessons, children might quickly practice the new routine that they will be asked to do independently. In the other lessons, children might verbalize how it might be possible to apply the new understanding to their writing. Add further thinking to the chart after the children have had the chance to try out or talk about their new learning. Have a Try is an important step in reinforcing the minilesson principle and moving the children toward independence.

The Have a Try part of the writing minilesson is particularly important for English learners. Besides providing repetition, it gives English learners a safe place to try out the new idea before sharing it with the whole group. These are a few suggestions for how you might support children during the Have a Try portion of the lesson:

- ❯ Pair children with partners that you know will take turns talking.

- ❯ Spend time teaching children how to turn and talk. (See MGT.U1: Working Together in the Classroom.) Teach children how to provide wait time for one another, invite the other partner into the conversation, and take turns.

- ❯ Provide concrete examples to discuss so that children are clear about what they need to think and talk about. English learners will feel more confident if they are able to talk about a mentor text that they know very well.

- ❯ When necessary, provide the oral language structure or language stem for how you want the children to share their ideas. For example, ask them to start with the sentence frame *I noticed the writer* _____ and to rehearse the language structure a few times before turning and talking.

- Imagine aloud how something might sound in a child's writing. Provide children with some examples of how something might sound if they were to try something out in their own writing. For example, you might say something like this: "Marco, you are writing about when you fell off your bike. You could start by drawing yourself on the ground. You could write a speech bubble that says, 'OW!!'"

- Observe partnerships involving English learners and provide support as needed.

Summarize and Apply

This part of the lesson includes two parts: summarizing the learning and applying the learning to independent writing.

The **summary** is a brief but essential part of the lesson. It brings together the learning that has taken place through the inquiry and helps children think about its application and relevance to their own learning. Ask children to think about the anchor chart and talk about what they have learned. Involve them in stating the minilesson principle. Then write it on the chart. Use simple, clear language to shape the suggestions. Sometimes, you may decide to summarize the new learning to keep the lesson short and allow enough time for the children to apply it independently. Whether you state the principle or share the construction with the children, summarize the learning in a way that children understand and can remember.

After the summary, the children apply their new understandings to their independent writing. The invitation to try out the new idea must be clear enough for children but "light" enough to allow room for them to have their own ideas for their writing. The application of the minilesson principle should not be thought of as an exercise or task that needs to be forced to fit their writing but instead as an invitation for deeper, more meaningful writing.

We know that when children first take on new learning, they often want to try out the new learning to the exclusion of some of the other things they have learned. When you teach about speech bubbles, for example, expect to see lots of speech bubbles. Encourage children to try out new techniques while reminding them about the other things they have learned.

Before children begin independent writing, let them know that they can apply the new understanding to any writing they do and will have an opportunity to share what they have done with the class after independent writing. Kindergartners love to share!

Confer

While children are busy independently making books and writing, move around the room to observe and confer briefly with individual children. Sit side by side with them and invite them to talk about what they are doing. In each minilesson, we offer prompts focused on the umbrella concept and worded in clear, direct language. Using direct language can be particularly supportive for English learners because it allows them to focus on the meaning without having to work through the extra talk that we often use in our everyday conversations. Occasionally you will see sentence frames to support English learners in both their talk and their writing.

If a child is working on something that does not fit with the minilesson principle, do not feel limited to the language in this section. Respond to the child in a sincere and enthusiastic way. Remember that the invitation to apply the new learning can be extended another time. This will not be the only opportunity.

General prompts, such as the following, are provided to get children talking so that you can listen carefully to the thinking behind the writing (in using the word *writing* we include *drawing*). Be sure to let children do most of the talking. The one who does the talking does the learning!

- *How is your writing going?*
- *How can I help you with your writing?*
- *What do you think about this piece of writing?*
- *What do you want to do next in your writing?*
- *What is the best part of your writing (book) so far?*
- *Is any part of your writing (book) still confusing for the reader?*
- *What would you like to do with this writing (book) when it is finished?*

Observational notes will help you understand how each writer is progressing and provide purposeful, customized instruction every time you talk with children about their writing (Figure 4-7). You can use your notes to plan the content of future minilessons. You can also take pictures, scan, or make copies of key pieces to discuss with families.

Share

At the end of independent writing, gather children together for the opportunity to **share** their learning with the entire group. During group share, you can revisit, expand, and deepen understanding of the minilesson's goal as well as assess learning. Often, children are invited to bring their drawing and writing to share with the class and to explain how they tried

| Teacher | Ms. Sanchez | Grade | K | Week of | Jan. 6–Jan. 10 |

Conferring Record 1

Minilesson Focus MBK.U3: Making Memory Books

Student	Monday	Tuesday	Wednesday	Thursday	Friday
Tarika		1/7 Not sure what to write about. Looked at Stories We Have Told chart for ideas. Will write about losing her tooth.			1/10 Checked back in. Still on first page. Had her tell the story across the pages while pointing to each page.
Lorenzo	1/6 Making a memory book about his birthday party. Drawing across pages and labeling pictures.				
Jamison				1/8 Need... with se... Worked... transitio... words: f... next, th...	
Charlotte					
Kendall					

| Teacher | Ms. Goldberg | Grade | K | Week of | Feb. 8–12 |

Conferring Record 2

Minilesson Focus WPS.U2: Adding to Writing

Student	Comments/Observations
NahJee	2/9 Experimenting with speech bubbles. Talked about writing first and then making the bubble.
Alma	2/8 Talked about how to draw facial expressions to show feelings.
Myka	2/11 Used a caret to add words to give more details.
Anh	2/10 Labeling pictures with approximated spelling.
Sarah	2/12 Writing about playing mermaid at recess with her friends. Talked about how she could also write a book about how to play mermaid.
Jenna	2/9 Making a book of her favorite foods. Worked on how to say pizza slowly and write the letters for the sounds she hears.
Chris	2/8 Brainstormed ideas for his next book—maybe about riding go-carts.
Eric	2/11 Added a page because he remembered a detail he wanted to include in his story about visiting his cousins.
Jamie	2/10 Writing a book about going to his hip-hop class. Adding speech bubbles.
Marnique	2/12 Asked how to put talking into her story. Showed her how to use quotation marks.
Beth	2/10 Struggling to get started making a book. Talked about what she did at choice time. She will write about the play corner.
Tricia	2/12 Talked about adding a background to her drawings. She will try drawing her kitchen.

The Writing Minilessons Book, Kindergarten

out the new understanding. As you observe and talk to children during independent writing, plan how to share by assessing how many children tried the new learning in their writing. If only a few children were able to apply the minilesson principle to their writing, you might ask those children to share with the whole group. However, if you observe most of the class applying the principle, you might have them share in pairs or small groups.

You might also consider inviting children to choose what to share about their writing instead of connecting back to the minilesson principle. For example, one child might share a detail added to make a drawing clearer. Another might share the sign she made for the play corner. Another might read his story to the class.

The Writing Minilessons Book, Kindergarten

Share time is a wonderful way to bring the community of learners back together to expand their understandings of writing and of each other as well as to celebrate their new attempts at writing. There are some particular accommodations to support English learners during the time for sharing:

▶ Ask English learners to share in pairs before sharing with the group.

▶ While conferring, help children rehearse the language structure they might use to share their drawing and writing with the class.

Teach the entire class respectful ways to listen to peers and model how to give their peers time to express their thoughts. Many of the minilessons in the Management section will be useful for developing a peaceful, safe, and supportive community of writers.

A Closer Look at the Umbrella Wrap-Up

Following the minilessons in each umbrella, you will see the final umbrella page, which includes a section for assessing what children have learned and a section for extending the learning.

Assessment

The last page of each umbrella, shown in Figure 4-8, provides questions to help you **assess** the learning that has taken place through the entire umbrella. The information you gain from observing what the children can already do, almost do, and not yet do will help inform the selection of the next umbrella you teach. (See chapter 8 for more information about assessment and the selection of umbrellas.)

Extensions for the Umbrella

Each umbrella ends with several suggestions for **extending** the learning of the umbrella. Sometimes the suggestion is to repeat a minilesson with different examples. Kindergartners will need to experience some of the concepts more than once before they are able to transfer actions to their independent writing. Other times, children will be able to extend the learning beyond the scope of the umbrella.

A Closer Look at the Umbrella Wrap-Up

Gain important information by **assessing** what children have learned as they apply and share their learning of the minilesson principles. Observe and then follow up with individuals in conferences or in small groups in guided writing.

Optional suggestions are provided for **extending** the learning of the umbrella over time or in other contexts.

Figure 4-8: The final page of each umbrella offers suggestions for assessing the learning and ideas for extending the learning.

| Umbrella 1 | Getting Ideas for Writing |

Assessment

After you have taught the minilessons in this umbrella, observe children as they draw and write. Use the behaviors and understandings in *The Literacy Continuum* (Fountas and Pinnell 2017) to notice, teach for, and support children's learning as you observe their attempts at reading and writing.

▶ What evidence do you have of new understandings children have developed related to getting ideas for writing?

  • Can children independently think of ideas for writing?

  • Do they get ideas from things they collect?

  • Do they look at the class story charts to get ideas for writing?

  • Do they get ideas from other writers?

  • Do they return to their favorite ideas or topics?

  • What evidence is there that children can use vocabulary such as *idea, writing,* and *story*?

▶ In what other ways, beyond the scope of this umbrella, are children ready to expand their writing and illustrating skills?

  • Are they ready to learn about revising (adding, reorganizing) their writing?

  • Do they need support in drawing pictures?

Use your observations to determine the next umbrella you will teach. You may also consult Suggested Sequence of Lessons (pp. 483–494) for guidance.

EXTENSIONS FOR GETTING IDEAS FOR WRITING

▶ In the books you read aloud, look to see if the authors reveal where they got their ideas (for example, in an author's note). If so, share this information with the children.

▶ Invite children to bring in objects from home and use them as inspiration for writing.

▶ After reading aloud a book, invite children to write their own text that is inspired in some way by the book, for example, the same story with a different ending, the same characters in a different situation, or the same writing or illustration style.

438   *The Writing Minilessons Book, Kindergarten*

Effective Writing Minilessons

The goal of all writing minilessons is to help children think and act like writers and illustrators as they build their capacity for independent writing and drawing across the year. Whether you are teaching lessons about drawing or telling stories or teaching any of the other minilessons, the characteristics of effective minilessons, listed in Figure 4-9, apply.

Figure 4-9: Characteristics of effective minilessons

Effective Writing Minilessons . . .

- are based on a **writing principle** that is important to teach to kindergartners
- are based on a **goal** that makes the teaching meaningful
- are **relevant to the specific needs of children** so that your teaching connects with the learners
- are very **brief, concise, and to the point**
- use **clear and specific language** to avoid talk that clutters learning
- stay **focused on a single idea** so children can apply the learning and build on it day after day
- use an **inquiry approach** whenever possible to support active, constructive learning
- often include **shared, high-quality mentor texts** that can be used as examples
- are **well paced** to engage and hold children's interest
- are **grouped into umbrellas** to foster depth in thinking and coherence across lessons
- **build one understanding on another** across several days instead of single isolated lessons
- provide time for children to **"try out" the new concept** before they are invited to try it independently
- engage children in **summarizing the new learning and applying it to their own writing**
- build **important vocabulary** appropriate for children in kindergarten
- help children **become better artists and writers**
- **foster community** through the development of shared language
- **can be assessed** as you observe children engaged in authentic writing
- **help children understand what they are learning** how to do as artists and writers

Writing minilessons can be used to teach anything from telling stories to drawing pictures to making books and more. Teach a writing minilesson whenever you see an opportunity to nudge the children forward as writers and illustrators.

Chapter 5 | Management Minilessons

> *We need a caring classroom community in which multiple perspectives*
> *are developed and used to think critically and expand learning.*
> *We need a community in which children come to appreciate the*
> *value of different perspectives for their own development, in which*
> *they recognize changes in their own and others' thinking and*
> *that that difference is the source for the change.*
>
> —Peter Johnston

INDIVIDUALS LEARN BETTER AND HAVE more fun when they have some routines for working safely and responsibly. The lessons in Section 2: Management establish these routines. Children learn how to

- listen,
- take turns,
- show kindness to one another,
- draw and write independently,
- share their writing,
- work in the classroom centers,

- make choices during choice time, and
- use and return materials.

They become independent problem solvers who can work and play as members of a community.

Building a Community of Writers

Writers need to feel valued and included in a community whose members have learned to trust one another with their stories. The minilessons in the Management section are designed to help children build this trust and learn to include one another in discussions and play. The first lesson in MGT.U1: Working Together in the Classroom (WML1: Get to know your classmates) sets the tone for building this community. As children share who they are, where their families come from, what languages they speak, what foods they eat, and what activities they enjoy, they begin to explore their identities and learn about the identities of others. A person's identity influences the way one reads and writes; it impacts the perspective one brings to these literacy experiences. We see this even with our youngest readers and writers. When we celebrate children's unique identities and perspectives, we teach children to value and include one another. This is one of the reasons the share time at the end of independent writing is so important. This time of sharing inspires writing ideas, but it does so much more. It provides a time to celebrate writing and more importantly carves out space to celebrate each writer in the classroom community.

Create a Peaceful Atmosphere

The minilessons in this section will help you establish a classroom environment in which children are confident, self-determined, and kind and in which every child's identity is valued. The lessons are designed to contribute to peaceful activity and shared responsibility. Through the Management minilessons, children learn how to modulate their voices to suit various purposes (silent to outdoor). They also learn to keep supplies in order, help others, listen to and look at a speaker, and clean up quickly and quietly (Figure 5-1).

All of these minilessons contribute to an overall tone of respect in every classroom activity. Kindergartners who enter your classroom for the first time have learned ways of interacting that are appropriate for home and neighborhood, but many do not know how to work with other children in a small room day after day. These minilessons are designed to help you establish the atmosphere you want. Everything in the classroom reflects the children who work there; it is their home for the year.

Figure 5-1: Characteristics of a peaceful atmosphere for the community of readers and writers

Teach the minilessons in this section in the order that fits your class needs, or consult the Suggested Sequence of Lessons (pp. 483–494). You may need to reteach some of these lessons because as the year goes on you will be working in a more complex way. A schedule change or other disruption in classroom operations might prompt a refresher minilesson. Any problem in your classroom should be addressed through minilessons that focus on building a community of learners.

Design the Physical Space

In addition to creating a peaceful atmosphere, prepare the physical space in a way to provide the best support for learning (Figure 5-2). Each umbrella in Section 2: Management will help your kindergartners become acquainted with the routines of the classroom and help them feel secure and at home. Make sure that the classroom has the following qualities.

▶ **Welcoming and Inviting.** Pleasing colors and a variety of furniture will help. There is no need for commercially published posters or slogans, except for standard references such as the Alphabet Linking Chart (Figure 3-7) or colorful poetry posters. The room can be filled with the work that the children have produced beginning on day one, some of it in languages other than English. They should see signs of their learning everywhere—shared and interactive writing, charts, drawings of various

Figure 5-2: Layout of a kindergarten classroom

kinds, and their names. Be sure that children's names are at various places in the room—on tables, on cubbies, on a helper's or "jobs" chart, and on some of the charts that you will make in the minilessons. A framed wall of children's photographs and self-portraits sends the clear message that this classroom belongs to them and celebrates their unique identities. The classroom library should be as inviting as a bookstore or a library. Place books in baskets and tubs on shelves to make the front covers of books visible and accessible for easy browsing. Clearly label the supplies in the writing center so children can see the materials that are available and can access them and return them independently (Figure 5-3). Better yet, have children make labels with you during shared or interactive writing. Children also love to be involved in the naming of the different classroom areas so they truly feel like they have ownership of the classroom. We have seen some classrooms that create space on a low bulletin board with each child's name so that children can choose items to display.

▶ **Organized for Easy Use.** The first thing you might want to do is to take out everything you do not need. Clutter increases stress and noise. Using scattered and hard-to-find materials increases the children's dependence on you. Consider keeping supplies for bookmaking and writing in clearly labeled areas. For example, some teachers organize a writing area where they keep paper, highlighters, staplers, etc. Provide paper and booklets in a variety of different sizes so children can choose the kind of paper they want to use. For example, a simple four-page booklet (two pieces of paper folded in half) or a stapled book folded horizontally can be made and placed in a tray. You might also provide a selection of templates for writing (available from online resources). Some teachers choose to have children keep the books or other writing projects they are making in writing folders that are stored in the writing center. Others have them in bins located throughout the room so children can easily access their writing without causing traffic jams.

In the first few days of school, children learn how to get supplies and return supplies. Children who choose to make books can get what they need independently and work at their tables. Some teachers choose to have caddies at tables instead of keeping supplies on a shelf in the writing center so that children can spread out and get started right away.

Work and play areas are clearly organized with necessary, labeled materials and nothing else. Labels with pictures and words as well as an arrow pointing to where the items belong show children exactly what goes where. Some teachers stick a shape on the shelf that matches the bottom of the container (Figure 5-4). Over the course of the year, introduce different kinds of media into the art center and creation station (maker space) so children can experiment with collage, 3D materials, and materials that have different textures.

Arrange furniture to create traffic patterns that discourage running, promote safe movement around the room for all children, and allow for easy access to emergency exits. Be sure that all furniture is appropriate for the children's size/height and that children's work is displayed at their eye level so they can appreciate it.

Figure 5-3: All the materials in the writing center are organized. Each kind of material is kept in a separate, labeled container.

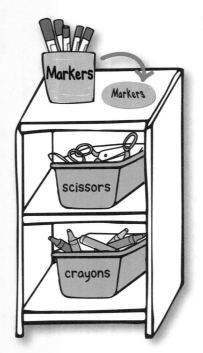

▶ **Designed for Whole-Group, Small-Group, and Individual Instruction.** Interactive writing lessons and writing minilessons are generally provided as whole-class instruction and typically take place at an easel in a meeting space. The space is comfortable and large enough for all children to sit as a group or in a circle. It will be helpful to have a colorful rug. Create some way of helping children find an individual space to sit without crowding one another. (For example, the rug often has squares of different colors.) The meeting space is next to the classroom library so that books are displayed and handy. The teacher usually has a larger chair or seat next to an easel or two so that he can display the mentor texts, make anchor charts, do shared or interactive writing, or place big books for shared reading. This space is available for all whole-group instruction; for example, the children come back to it for group share. In addition to the group meeting space, assign tables and spaces in the classroom for small-group writing instruction. Use low shelving and furniture to define and separate learning areas and to create storage opportunities. Kindergartners need tables and spaces throughout the classroom where they can play and work independently and where you can easily set a chair next to a child for a brief writing conference.

Establish Independent Writing

The second umbrella in the Management section helps you establish independent writing time with your kindergartners. Through the minilessons in this umbrella, children will learn the routines needed to be independent and productive. They learn to get started with their writing quickly and quietly. They increase in stamina and become efficient in storing their writing and materials at the end of writing time. Children will learn that writers are never finished. When they finish making a book, they can start another. At the beginning of the year, keep the writing time short (you may even start with just five minutes of independent time) so they can feel successful right away. Add a few minutes every day until they are able to sustain writing for twenty to thirty minutes. Involve the children in setting goals for stretching their writing time and celebrate each time you reach them as a class. You will soon have children begging for more time to do this important work. Kindergartners also begin to see the value of working on a piece of writing over time. They establish important routines like rereading their writing to think what to do next. Through this umbrella, children also learn that writers receive feedback and guidance from other writers. They learn the routines for conferring with a teacher and how to productively share their writing with an audience at the end of independent writing.

Manage Choice Time

The third Management umbrella (U3: Learning About Choice Time) introduces routines for centers for imaginative play, such as the play corner, block center, and science center. **Besides providing an opportunity for more active play, choice time allows children the choice to revisit some of the centers that they might have been assigned to during other parts of the day.** For example, some classrooms have an independent literacy work time. Children are assigned to literacy centers like the listening center, writing center, and the word work center while the teacher meets with individual readers and small groups for guided reading. This time for centers often takes place after a reading minilesson and before a share time in the same way that independent writing is framed by a writing minilesson and share time. During choice time, children enjoy the option of continuing the work they may have started in one of these literacy centers as well as the opportunity to try some of the more active play centers like the creation station (maker space), the block center, the sand or water table, and the play corner. For any of these choices, writing can play a role when you help children imagine the possibilities (Figure 1-8). Figure 5-5 offers suggestions for stocking the activity centers, including writing materials to encourage writing during play.

Figure 5-5: Suggestions for stocking the activity areas of the classroom to encourage writing

Stocking the Activity Centers

Yearlong Activity Center	Materials
Classroom Library	• books in labeled tubs organized by topic, author, illustrator, and kind of book (genre) • covers facing out for easy browsing • labels for the tubs written using shared or interactive writing
Writing Center	• pencils, markers, crayons • a variety of paper–different sizes, colors, formats (see online resources) • textured paper for covers • staplers • scissors • glue • premade blank books for bookmaking • sticky notes • white correction tape • name chart and Alphabet Linking Chart • tub of favorite books to help stimulate ideas • additional writing tools: letter stamps and pads, letter tiles, letter sponges, whiteboards, notebooks, notepads, traceable letters, sandpaper letters, stencils

Stocking the Activity Centers (cont.)

Yearlong Activity Centers	Materials
Art Center (This can be adjacent to the writing center in order to share supplies.)	• paper • paints, markers, colored pencils, crayons (in a variety of colors to provide options for different skin tones and hair colors) • glue • scissors • textured materials (e.g., cloth, ribbed paper, tissue paper) • craft sticks • yarn • tub of books with a variety of interesting art (e.g., collage, found objects, paintings)
Word Work (ABCs)	• blank word cards • very simple wall of words nearby (mostly with children's names and a few high-frequency words) • Alphabet Linking Chart and name chart • magnetic letters • games • word cards to sort • cookie trays • index cards with textured names; names with dots indicating where to begin tracing
Listening Center	• listening device • clear set of directions with picture clues • multiple copies of books organized in boxes or plastic bags • clipboards and paper to draw responses to books
Block Center	• a variety of blocks organized on shelves (e.g., wooden blocks in a variety of shapes, foam blocks, colorful blocks, cube blocks, cardboard blocks, waffle blocks) • straws and connectors • pictures, magazines and/or picture books of structures (e.g., buildings, bridges) • small toy figures (e.g., animals, people), vehicles, and signs • clipboards with paper for drawing plans • tape • craft sticks and index cards for signs • graph paper • mailing labels • rulers

Stocking the Activity Centers (cont.)

Yearlong Activity Centers	Materials
Sand/Water Table	• a variety of materials that can pour and that change throughout the year (e.g., sand, water, dry pasta, rice) • funnels • shovels • containers of different sizes and shapes • colanders • clipboards • paper • colored pencils • name chart • photographs of sand and water • poems about sand and water hung near the sand/water table • small toy animals, dinosaurs, trucks, etc., that generate scene making and storytelling
Play Corner	• fabric or costumes for dressing up • familiar objects from home/parent workplaces • different types and sizes of paper (e.g., poster board, construction paper, plain paper, colored paper) for signs, menus, receipts, bills • labels • index cards • sticky notes • clipboards • markers • See comprehensive list for different themes in Figure 7-4.
Creation Station (Maker Space)	• cardboard boxes (e.g., shoeboxes, cereal boxes, tissue boxes) • cones • toilet paper and paper towel rolls • string • clean egg cartons or food containers • clean craft sticks, paint stirrers • nuts and bolts • variety of recycled materials for inventions • tape • glue • different types of paper • writing tools

Stocking the Activity Centers (cont.)

Yearlong Activity Centers	Materials
Science Center	• a range of natural items gathered from outside of school (e.g., rocks, shells, leaves, abandoned bird's nest/beehive, snake's skin) • magnifying glasses • writing tools • paper • rulers • pastels and tracing paper for rubbings • nonfiction books with colorful photographs and drawings of subjects such as animals, foods, families, communities • booklet or notebook labeled *Lab Book*

We recommend introducing a choice board to help manage the number of children using a particular area of the classroom. Some choice boards have Velcro® dots that allow children to place their name cards on the board next to their choices (Figure 1-7). Another style of choice board uses clothespins. A child simply clips a clothespin with her name on it next to an activity. Consider using a random selection method (e.g., pulling craft sticks with names) so that different children get a chance to choose first or devising a regular schedule for who gets to select first. Limit the choices when you first introduce the centers to allow children time to get used to each one. Once children understand the rules and routines, you can have several activities running at once. You may want to consider rotating activities every couple of weeks. If you do choose to rotate the centers, keep the center choices consistent for the week so that everyone has a chance to visit the center and build on a project over time.

Chapter 6

Minilessons for Telling Stories, Making Books, and Drawing

Through their talk, children let us into their worlds, so we listen, pay attention, and continue to carve out space where they can talk their way into stories in the company of an audience who values what they have to say.

—Martha Horn and Mary Ellen Giacobbe

TALK IS WHERE THE WRITING process begins and the way it expands. One section in this book is called Telling Stories and is dedicated to minilessons that "carve out space" for children to talk, share stories, and learn the value of their own storytelling. Once children can tell their stories, they can make a book about them. Because many kindergartners are not yet writing, it is through drawing that they will first put their stories on paper. It is through bookmaking that oral language and drawing come together.

Children need to learn that their everyday lives are a great source for telling and writing stories. Kindergartners have a lot to say, so it is important to give them many chances to be part of meaningful conversation. Providing time to share stories builds a community in which children get to know and respect one another. And children receive an important message: their personal and varied life experiences are unique and highly valued.

Telling Stories

All children have stories to tell. The minilessons in the first umbrella of Section 3: Telling Stories focus on different ways children can find the stories in their lives—by thinking about places, people, and things that are meaningful to them. Capture these stories on a chart (Figure 6-1) that children can return to as they move from telling to drawing their stories.

Storytelling is rooted in an individual's family and community, and that might be particularly important to remember when working with African American children (Gardner-Neblett 2015). Several studies have demonstrated that from early on African American children have a wide variety of storytelling styles and tell high-quality stories. It is important to both value and engage a variety of storytelling styles in the classroom. Gardner-Neblett points out that when children are encouraged to engage in storytelling, they have the opportunity to use orally the language that they usually hear and see only in written texts.

When you embrace and celebrate children's storytelling, you support children's development of important literacy understandings that can be applied to both reading and writing. Schools have traditionally taught a familiar European story structure: a beginning, a revelation of the story problem, a series of events, a problem resolution, and an ending. It is important to recognize that there are many different kinds of story structures (Resnick and Snow, 2008). Some cultures string together a series of seemingly unrelated events that ultimately work together to make a point. Others include many characters that are not necessary to the main theme but represent family values and community. Some families tell traditional stories that have been passed down for centuries while others tell stories from about their own family members. In some cultures, traditional stories have an element of fantasy that reveal a deeper truth about life. By recognizing and valuing the different ways children might have learned to tell stories, we can help expand children's understanding of what a story is and how stories work. Through the storytelling umbrellas, children learn to expand their understanding of story and further develop their language by

▶ listening to teachers tell their own stories,

▶ hearing classmates' stories,

▶ sharing their own stories and responding to questions about them,

Stories We Have Told

Baking Bread by Rocco

Losing a Tooth by Johan

Spider Bite by Ivy

Visiting Tía by Pedro

Figure 6-1: Keep a list of stories that children have told to remind them of ideas they can use when they make books.

- using picture cards to retell stories they have heard read aloud,

- recreating familiar stories with puppets, and

- acting out stories, taking on the parts of different characters.

The Literacy Continuum (Fountas and Pinnell 2017) contains a detailed list of the oral language behaviors important to develop in kindergarten children. Every section of this book contains minilessons to support the development of these behaviors. Children learn the routines and conventions of conversation through Management minilessons; they learn how to present their stories orally in the Telling Stories minilessons; and they learn how to share, expand, and discuss ideas for writing through minilessons in the Making Books, Drawing, Exploring Early Writing, and Writing Process sections. Language is the tool through which all learning is mediated.

Making Books

Weave minilessons for telling stories in between minilessons about making books because storytelling and bookmaking go hand in hand. That's why in the sequence we suggest teaching the minilessons in the first storytelling umbrella over the course of a few weeks. This allows children time in between minilessons to tell their stories, make books about their stories, and then tell more stories. The more stories they tell, the more ideas they have for books.

In the first umbrella in Section 4: Making Books (MBK.U1: Getting Started with Making Books), kindergartners are invited to make books. As children make books, refer them to the story charts you created with the class to record the stories they have told. Revisiting these charts helps children remember their stories and understand that they can write and draw about them. After this initial exposure, children are introduced in more depth throughout the year to the different kinds of books they can make, such as how-to books, all-about books, and memory books.

In all cases, they can go back to the stories they have told and not only write about those stories but use them as seeds to grow other books, as Rocco did. Rocco told his class a story about baking bread. Then he wrote a story about a time he baked with his cousin. Later in the year, he wrote a how-to book on how to bake bread. When all-about books were introduced, he wrote a book about all of the things he knows how to bake. When children learn to tell their own stories, they learn about themselves, what they love, and who they are. They are learning how to put themselves on the pages of a book.

Figure 6-2: Drew, age 5, used shapes to draw himself and the Gingerbread Man. Notice the rectangular bodies and arms. He wrote: *We made a gingerbread man.*

Figure 6-3: Drew included the details from his picture in his writing: *My birthday celebration was fun. I ate cupcakes. I turned six. My mom was there.*

Drawing

Drawing is important! Minilessons about drawing help writers tell stories in their books. Ray and Glover wrote that one of their core beliefs is that children do not need to "get ready" to be readers and writers, but rather they are already readers and writers (2008, xvii). Our job is to nurture them and encourage them to grow.

The umbrellas in Section 5: Drawing are designed to nurture children's ability to tell stories across the pages of a book. Even before children make representational drawings, they can tell us what their stories are about. You might even hear children acting out their stories with pencil in hand, playing in the same way they might play with action figures or stuffed animals. The scribbles and circles on a page often represent important people or things. When you teach children how to turn these early attempts at drawing into something representational, you give them the tools to express their ideas more clearly (Figure 6-2).

The first umbrella of Section 5: Drawing focuses on making self-portraits, which can then be used in a class book during interactive writing (IW.8: Making a Class Big Book) or framed and put on your wall to welcome people into your classroom. Through this umbrella, children learn that shapes are the building blocks for making a face. They look in a mirror to see the shapes that make up their faces and practice drawing them. In the next lesson, they learn about adding detail through color. As they think about the color of their skin, hair, and eyes, they notice that their classmates are unique and special in their own ways.

The second umbrella (DRW.U2: Learning to Draw) builds on the understanding that shapes help you draw people. The minilessons focus on how to draw a body, how to show facial expression, and how to create a simple background.

As you teach drawing, you are also nurturing children's development of writing. Once children are able to draw representationally, they begin to

add details that capture more of their stories. Later, when children are able to represent their ideas in print, they can add details from their pictures into their writing, as Drew did.

Drew learned how to draw the setting of his pictures. In Figure 6-3, he included the tables and chairs in his classroom, his classmates, his teacher, and his mom. He also learned to include smaller details in his pictures. Notice the cupcakes on the table. He continued to use shapes to draw people, but he used them to add clothing. Drew's attention to detail in his picture helped him expand his writing to include who is in the story (his mom) and what he did (ate cupcakes).

The more children learn about drawing, the more they learn about the process of revising their writing. They get excited to add new details to their pictures after talking about their stories. They begin to look at illustrations in books with a writer's/illustrator's eye. Through the last umbrella in Section 5: Drawing (U3: Making Pictures Interesting), they learn that they can borrow techniques used by writers and illustrators, such as collage, textured materials, flaps, and pop-ups (Figures 6-4-1 and 6-4-2) in their own books.

Children need time to tell their stories, experiment with making books, and learn ways to draw their ideas. It is our hope that the lessons in these three sections—Telling Stories, Making Books, and Drawing—will work together to help you nurture the writers in your classroom so they can share the important stories in their lives.

Figure 6-4-1: Kindergartner Tessa made a collage mouse for her story, imitating a technique used by author and illustrator Eric Carle.

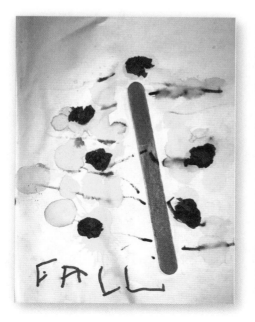

Figure 6-4-2: In the style of author and illustrator Lois Ehlert, Drew used different materials (a craft stick, tissue paper and cotton batting) to create different textures in his book about the seasons.

Chapter 7

Minilessons for Exploring Early Writing and the Writing Process

Play facilitates the development of intellectual skills and also allows for the application of academic skills. For example, a child playing with water might use intellectual skills to make a boat, but then apply academic skills to write the name of the boat on the side.

— Kristine Mraz

CHILDREN EAGERLY INCORPORATE WRITING INTO their play, where they constantly create and think of new ideas. Use the minilessons in Section 6: Exploring Early Writing and Section 7: Writing Process to help you build on that eagerness to teach children about early writing concepts such as understanding the directionality of print, how to hold a marker and paper, and the writing process.

Scribbles Mean Something

As children grow in their understanding of what it means to make a book, they begin to experiment more with writing. Marie Clay (1975) identified some important principles that describe what happens as young children learn to write.

Principles That Describe Writing Development

Clay's Principle	Description	Example
The Recurring Principle (Repeating What They Have Learned)	Children repeat what they know about writing and drawing over and over. In this example, Sam wrote the words she knows repeatedly.	
The Directional Principle (Exploring Direction)	As children begin to internalize the idea of writing from left to right and top to bottom, they often play around with it, starting their writing from different sides of the paper. Notice how Sam fit *Dad* and *Cally* onto her paper. Children also often reverse letters and words because they are just beginning to understand that direction makes a difference.	
The Inventory Principle (Using Everything)	You may see children include everything that they know about writing in their writing. Some children write all the letters and words they know. Lucas wrote the alphabet up one side of the page and also wrote all the names he knows.	
The Contrastive Principle (Putting Things Together)	Young children often like to compare things that are similar in some ways and different in others. You will often see them set up these comparisons in their writing. Tessa notices opposites. In the example, she drew an on/off switch and labeled her drawing.	

Figure 7-1: Clay's principles with descriptions and examples

Section 6: Exploring Early Writing was designed with Clay's principles in mind. The umbrellas and minilessons support children as they play with early approximations of writing and as they begin to make sense of the fact that the symbols they see (and make) in print carry meaning. Figure 7-1 shows examples of Clay's principles in children's writing.

Children Learn Early Concepts of Print and How to Write Words

Children need to learn that direction is important in print, words are made up of letters, and spaces between words create word boundaries. The first umbrella in Section 6: Exploring Early Writing (EWR.U1: Learning Early Concepts of Print) is designed to teach these important ideas. Through the shared writing and inquiry in these minilessons, children discover how print works and begin to apply these understandings to their own early writing attempts. The online resource shown in Figure 7-2 will help you track the progress of the class in these and other early writing behaviors.

Several lessons in this umbrella use children's names to teach minilesson principles. Through EWR.U1: Learning Early Concepts of Print and EWR.U3: Learning How to Write Words, children begin to recognize the letters in their names and make connections to their friends' names. They begin to talk about and identify the first and last letters of words, quickly learning that some words have the same beginnings and endings. They learn how to use classroom resources like the name chart and ABC chart to write new words. They also learn that they can develop their own personal word lists to support their writing.

Figure 7-2: Record when you notice consistent use of early writing behaviors on the Grade K Early Writing Behaviors Checklist.

Grade K Early Writing Behaviors Checklist

Observe children during independent writing and talk with them about their drawing and writing. Write the children's names in the first row. Record the date when you notice evidence of consistent use of an early writing behavior by a child.

Names	Santiago	Chris	Katie	Esperanza	Maggie	Luca	Talia	Farhan
Tells stories orally and attempts to transfer ideas to paper	9/9	9/22	9/17	11/2	9/8		10/2	9/30
Initiates writing quickly	10/27	9/22	10/1	2/16	10/1		10/15	
Draws to convey meaning	10/27	12/2	10/1	2/23	10/1		11/20	11/22
Scribbles or makes letter-like forms	11/16	10/4	9/16	4/3	10/1	10/5	11/20	11/22
Writes strings of random letters	12/1	12/9	1/14		12/1	11/15	12/15	12/12
Writes own name or some letters in name	12/1	11/7	12/5	5/1	11/5	10/20	11/20	1/13
Uses upper- and lowercase letters						1/20	12/5	2/16
Writes words from left to right						1/20	12/5	2/16
Returns to left when wrapping a line						1/20		2/16
Leaves spaces between words or letter strings meant to resemble words	1/13	1/16	12/5		12/15	1/20	2/4	2/16
Shows evidence of understanding letter-sound relationships	1/13	3/14	2/12		1/24		3/18	2/16
Writes words and phrases using approximated spelling	1/13	3/14	2/12		1/24		3/18	2/16
Uses resources such as name chart, ABC chart, and word wall	1/13	3/14	4/18		3/18		3/18	3/18
Writes approximately twenty-five high-frequency words with one, two, or three letters	3/18	4/12	4/18		3/18		5/5	5/5

The Writing Minilessons Book, Kindergarten

Children Learn to Form Letters Using Language

Minilessons on developing handwriting, including how to hold a writing tool, are found in EWR.U2: Introducing Handwriting. These lessons can be used over and over again to introduce how to write different letters in the alphabet. In this umbrella, as well as in most interactive writing lessons, we use specific language for how to form letters. The language comes from a resource called Verbal Path for Letter Formation (Figure 7-3), which is available in the online resources. When you consistently use the same direction words, you help children internalize the directions and support early attempts at letter formation.

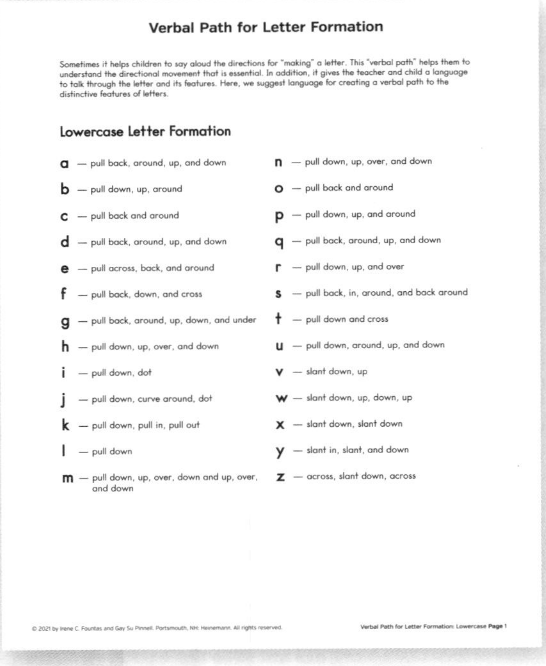

Verbal Path for Letter Formation

Sometimes it helps children to say aloud the directions for "making" a letter. This "verbal path" helps them to understand the directional movement that is essential. In addition, it gives the teacher and child a language to talk through the letter and its features. Here, we suggest language for creating a verbal path to the distinctive features of letters.

Lowercase Letter Formation

a — pull back, around, up, and down	n — pull down, up, over, and down
b — pull down, up, around	o — pull back and around
c — pull back and around	p — pull down, up, and around
d — pull back, around, up, and down	q — pull back, around, up, and down
e — pull across, back, and around	r — pull down, up, and over
f — pull back, down, and cross	s — pull back, in, around, and back around
g — pull back, around, up, down, and under	t — pull down and cross
h — pull down, up, over, and down	u — pull down, around, up, and down
i — pull down, dot	v — slant down, up
j — pull down, curve around, dot	w — slant down, up, down, up
k — pull down, pull in, pull out	x — slant down, slant down
l — pull down	y — slant in, slant, and down
m — pull down, up, over, down and up, over, and down	z — across, slant down, across

Verbal Path for Letter Formation: Lowercase **Page 1**

Figure 7-3: Use the language of the Verbal Path for Letter Formation consistently to support children in making letters.

Children Explore Writing Through Play

Another way to nurture early explorations of writing is to help children imagine the possibilities for writing in their play settings. Kindergartners look at writing and making books as another form of play, and you can teach them to see opportunities to write while they are playing in the play corner, block corner, science center, and so forth. EWR.U7: Learning to Draw and Write Through Play has minilessons with ideas for what children might write as they play. In the block center, children can label their towers. In the play corner, depending on how it is set up, they can write a menu for a restaurant, a letter for a post office, or a sign for a market. We recommended transforming your play corner several times across the year into spaces that will be meaningful to your children. We highlight particular settings because they connect with some of the themes and settings found in *Fountas & Pinnell Classroom™ Interactive Read-Aloud Collection* (2018) text sets.

Figure 7-4 lists the props and types of writing you might see in different play corner themes. The chart also includes some language you might use to promote writing. We also encourage you to review the suggestions in the Confer part of each minilesson.

Infusing Writing into the Play Corner

Play Corner Setting	Props and Materials	Types of Writing Children Might Try	Language to Promote Writing in the Play Corner
Market	• Credit cards (homemade), play money • Cash register or calculator • Name tags for workers • Telephone • Shelves for display • Pretend food • Shopping cards • Pads for list-making • Bags for bagging groceries • Empty food containers/cereal boxes	• Shopping list • Signs for food, sales, etc. • Receipts • Orders at the deli counter, bakery • Magazines for the checkout area • Recipes	• *What could you put on your shopping list?* • *How can you show something is on sale?* • *What can you make to help people find the food they want?* • *What can you make for a receipt once someone has paid?* • *What did you pretend to do today? You make a book about that.*
Airport	• Suitcases for baggage area • Index cards for baggage tags • Name tags for workers' badges • Pretend computer • Stamps to stamp IDs or passports • Security area–big box to walk through. • Paper for tickets to places • Posters of places to visit	• Signs for baggage, check in, security • Directions for security • Luggage tags • Maps • Posters of places to visit • Travel brochures • Boarding passes and tickets • Safety signs	• *I see you are pretending to use a ticket. Do you want to make one?* • *You could make some luggage tags for all of your bags.* • *What signs could you make for the airport?* • *How can you let people know where to pick up their bags?* • *You could make a book about what you played today.*
Restaurant	• Tables and chairs (1 or 2 settings) • Plates and cups • Plastic flatware • Aprons • Chef's hat • Big pieces of paper for menus • Order pads and pencils • Play money • Telephone • Play food • Chalkboard/whiteboard for specials	• Menus • Food orders • Specials board • Open/Closed signs • Hours • Recipes for chef • Check • Receipt	• *What food are you serving? You can make a menu.* • *What could you write on the check?* • *When you take a food order, what could you write on your notepad?* • *Can you write about the food you make at your restaurant?* • *You had so much fun playing restaurant. You could make a book about that.*

Figure 7-4: This chart shows how to infuse writing into the play corner.

Infusing Writing into the Play Corner (cont.)

Play Corner Setting	Props and Materials	Types of Writing Children Might Try	Language to Promote Writing in the Play Corner
Post office	• Envelopes • Stamps and stamp pad • Tape • Cardboard boxes to make individual mailboxes • Labels • Small boxes to make packages • Scale • Pens • Paper for letters • Map • Telephone book	• Letters • Make-your-own postcards • Signs (e.g., operating hours, out-of-town/in-town mail, etc.) • Labels for packages • Receipts	• *You are mailing a big box. You could make a label to tell where to send it.* • *Who are you sending it to?* • *You can write a letter. What could you say in your letter?* • *You could send an invitation to a party. What would you want to put on your invitation?* • *What can you do to let people know where to put their mail?* • *You could make a book about how post offices work.*
Animal hospital	• Toy medical tools—stethoscope, blood pressure cuff, syringe, bandages • White coats or blue "scrubs" • Plastic gloves • Clipboards for charts • Play computer • Box for X-ray machines • Telephone or cell phone • Stuffed animals • Food dishes/water bowls	• Medical chart • Instructions for owner • Bill • Appointment cards • Signs for the waiting room • Labels on pet food • Medicine/prescriptions • Books and magazines for the waiting room	• *What will you write on the chart when you check an animal?* • *How can you let people know where to wait for their appointment?* • *What do you give people to tell them how much to pay?* • *The vet might need to send home instructions for how to take care of a pet. You could make a list of directions to give the pet owner.*

Children Engage in the Writing Process

After children have experimented with making books, use the Writing Process umbrellas to show them that when authors make books they make important decisions and sometimes change those decisions to make their books better. These umbrellas introduce children to

▶ getting ideas for their writing,

▶ making their writing interesting,

▶ revising (adding, reorganizing, and deleting) and editing (proofreading for spacing, proper letter formation, and spelling of known words) their writing to make it better, and

◗ celebrating what they have written as well as new ideas they have tried and getting their books ready for others to read (publishing).

So many things contribute to young children's development in writing. When you surround children with literacy activities and print, infuse writing into their play, encourage their efforts with enthusiasm, and provide gentle guidance through writing minilessons, you create the right conditions for early writing behaviors to take root and grow. With a choice of interactive writing lessons and five types of writing minilessons, how do you decide which lesson to teach when? Most of your decisions will be based on your observations of the children. What do you see them doing on their own? What might they be able to do with your help? What are they ready to learn? Chapter 8 offers guidance and support for making those decisions.

Chapter 8

Putting Minilessons into Action: Assessing and Planning

With assessment, you learn what students know; the literacy continuum will help you think about what they need to know next.

—Irene Fountas and Gay Su Pinnell

THE INTERACTIVE WRITING LESSONS AND writing minilessons are examples of teaching that address the specific behaviors and understandings to notice, teach for, and support in *The Literacy Continuum* (Fountas and Pinnell 2017). Goals for each lesson are drawn from the sections on Writing; Writing About Reading; Phonics, Spelling, and Word Study; and Oral and Visual Communication. Taken together, the goals provide a comprehensive vision of what children need to become aware of, understand, and apply to their own literacy and learning about writing. Each lesson lists Continuum Connections, which are the exact behaviors from *The Literacy Continuum* that are addressed in the lesson.

Figure 8-1 provides an overview of the processes that take place when a proficient writer creates a text and represents what children will work toward across the years. Writers must decide the purpose of their text, their audience, and their message. They think about the kind of writing that will help them communicate the message (e.g., functional writing such

Figure 8-1: The writing wheel diagram, shown full size on the inside back cover, illustrates how the writing process encompasses all aspects of writing.

as a list or a letter). They make important craft decisions, such as how to organize the piece, what words to use, and how they want the writing to sound. While keeping the message in their heads, writers must also consider the conventions of writing, such as letter formation, capitalization, punctuation, and grammar. They work through a writing process from planning and rehearsing to publishing. All lessons in this book are directed to helping writers expand their processing systems as they write increasingly complex texts.

Genre — Informational, Persuasive, Poetic, Hybrid, Functional, Narrative

Planning and Rehearsing

Viewing Self as a Writer

Drawing

Conventions — Grammar and Usage, Capitalization, Punctuation, Spelling, Handwriting and Word-Processing

Drafting and Revising

Editing and Proofreading

Craft — Organization, Idea Development, Language Use, Word Choice, Voice

Publishing

Purpose · Audience · A PROCESSING SYSTEM FOR WRITING · Communicating Meaning

Text Layout

©2017 by Irene C. Fountas and Gay Su Pinnell. Portsmouth, NH: Heinemann.

Decide Which Interactive Writing Lessons and Writing Minilessons to Teach

You are welcome to follow the Suggested Sequence of Lessons (discussed later in this chapter and located in the appendix). However, first look at the children in front of you. Teach within what Vygotsky (1979) called the "zone of proximal development"— the zone between what the children can do independently and what they can do with the support of a more expert other (Figure 8-2). Teach on the cutting edge of children's competencies.

Select minilessons based on what you notice the majority of your class needs to learn to develop writing behaviors. Here are some suggestions and tools to help you think about the children in your classroom, the main resource being *The Literacy Continuum* (Fountas and Pinnell 2017):

▶ **Use the Writing continuum** to observe how children are thinking, talking, and writing/drawing. Think about what they can already do, almost do, and not yet do to select the emphasis for your teaching. Think about the ways you have noticed children experimenting with drawing and bookmaking. Observe children's contributions and participation during interactive writing lessons and writing minilessons. Use the Writing Process section to assess how children are developing their own independent writing process.

- Are they volunteering ideas when you talk about what to write?

- Do they demonstrate confidence in trying to write a letter on the chart when invited?

- How are children applying some of the things they are learning during writing minilessons to independent writing?

The Learning Zone

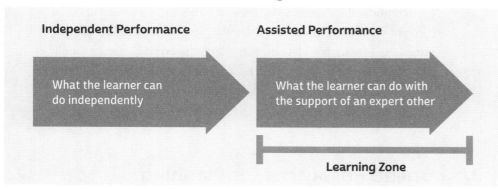

Figure 8-2: Learning zone from *Guided Reading: Responsive Teaching Across the Grades* (Fountas and Pinnell 2017)

▸ **Scan the Writing About Reading continuum** to analyze children's drawing and writing in response to the books you have read aloud. This analysis will help you determine next steps for having them respond to the books and poems you read together.

▸ **Review the Phonics, Spelling, and Word Study continuum** to assess what the children understand about early concepts of print (e.g., understanding the difference between pictures and print, directionality of print, word boundaries). This section will also help you evaluate children's phonological awareness, letter knowledge, and initial understanding of how to write words. These insights will help you make important choices about when to invite children to contribute during interactive writing lessons.

▸ **Consult the Oral and Visual Communication continuum** to help you think about some of the routines children might need for better communication between peers, especially as they begin to share their writing with one another. You will find essential listening and speaking competencies to observe and teach for.

▸ **Record informal notes** about the interactions you have while conferring or the interactions you see between children as they write and play during choice time. Look for patterns in these notes to notice trends in children's drawing and writing. Use *The Literacy Continuum* to help you analyze your notes and determine strengths and areas for growth across the classroom. Your observations will reveal what children know and what they need to learn next as they build knowledge about writing over time. Each goal becomes a possible topic for a minilesson. (See Conferring Record 1 and Conferring Record 2 in Figure 4-7.)

▸ **Consult district, state, and/or accreditation standards.** Analyze the suggested skills and areas of knowledge specified in your local and state standards. Align these standards with the minilessons suggested in this book to determine which might be applicable within your classroom.

▶ **Use the Assessment sections** within each lesson and at the end of each umbrella. Take time to assess the children's learning after the completion of each lesson and umbrella. The guiding questions on the last page of each umbrella will help you to determine strengths and next steps for your kindergartners. Your notes on the online resources shown in the next two sections will also help you make a plan for your teaching.

Use Online Resources for Planning and Teaching

The writing minilessons in this book are examples of how to engage kindergarten children in developing the behaviors and understandings of competent writers as described in *The Literacy Continuum*. To help you plan your teaching, use any of the various forms provided in the online resources (**resources.fountasandpinnell.com**).

The forms shown in Figure 8-3 will help you plan each part of a new interactive writing lesson or writing minilesson. You can design a lesson that uses a different set of example texts from the ones suggested in this book, or

Figure 8-3: Use these downloadable forms to plan your own interactive writing lessons and writing minilessons.

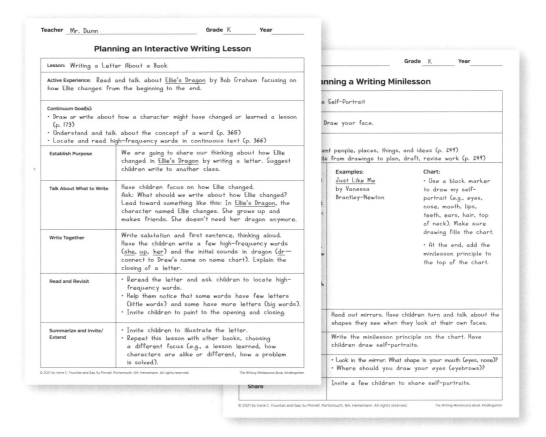

Teacher Ms. Schweiger   Grade K   Year

Curriculum Plan: Interactive Writing/Writing Minilessons

Month January	Interactive Writing/Writing Minilessons	Comments/Observations	✓ or Date
Week 1	IW.14: Writing About a Class Memory EWR.U3: Learning How to Write Words WML2: Listen for all the sounds in a word. WML3: Break apart words to help you write them. WML4: Write words that you know quickly.	1/10 Children were very engaged in IW.14—repeat with another class memory. 1/11 Skipped WML1; children ready to listen for all the sounds in a word.	
Week 2	WML5: Use what you know about words to write new words. MBK.U3: Making Memory Books WML1: Make a list of stories you remember. WML2: Tell a story you remember.	1/15 Teach STR.U2 to Juan, Olivia, and Alondra in guided writing group to help with their memory books.	
Week 3	WML3: Draw and write your story in the order it happened. WML5: Use pictures and words to show how you were feeling.	1/20 Skipped WML4. Children are already writing I and we. 1/22 Repeat WML5.	
Week 4	WPS.U2: Adding to Writing WML1: Add details to your drawings. WML2: Use a caret to add a word. WML3: Add a page to give more information.	1/27 Meet with Rohan, Will, and Sophie to help them find places to add (WML2).	

The Writing Minilessons Book, Kindergarten

Figure 8-4: Use this downloadable form to make notes about specific minilessons for future planning.

you can teach a concept in a way that fits the current needs of the children. The form shown in Figure 8-4 will help you plan which lessons to teach over a period of time to address the goals that are important for the children.

The minilessons are here for you to teach according to the instructional needs of your class. Do not be concerned if you do not use them all within the year. Record or check off the lessons you have taught so that you can reflect on the work of the semester and year. You can do this with the Interactive Writing and Writing Minilessons Record (Figure 8-5).

Teacher Mr. Pandey   Year

Interactive Writing and Writing Minilessons Record for Kindergarten

Interactive Writing Lesson Number	Lesson Title	Notes	✓ or Date
SECTION 1: INTERACTIVE WRITING			
IW.1	Making a Name Chart		9/4
IW.2	Writing About Our Classroom		9/9
IW.3	Creating a Job Chart	IW.4: Children love using the menu in play corner. Make a rules chart in IW for taking turns playing worker or shopper in the market.	9/12
IW.4	Making a Menu		9/18
IW.5	Making an ABC Book		10/1
IW.6	Making Labels for the Classroom		10/8
IW.7	Writing a Thank You Card	IW.7: Brinda, Mateo, Mia want to make thank you cards on their own.	10/14
IW.8	Making a Class Big Book	IW.9: Class loved using highlighter tape for high-frequency words. Repeat in small groups.	10/25
IW.9	Making a Color Chart		11/1
IW.10	Writing a Color Poem		11/13
IW.11	Writing from a Picture	IW.11: Children enjoyed this and want to bring photos from home to use in writing center.	12/2
IW.12	Making a Counting Book	IW.12: Moved to the writing center so children can add illustrations.	12/9
IW.13	Taking a Survey		12/16
IW.14	Writing About a Class Memory		1/13
IW.15	Writing About Our Creations	IW.15: Work in small group with Isaac, Piper, Asher.	2/3
IW.16	Making Signs		2/10

The Writing Minilessons Book, Kindergarten **Page 1**

The Writing Minilessons Book, Kindergarten **Page 2**

Figure 8-5: Interactive Writing and Writing Minilessons Record for Kindergarten

Meet Children's Needs and Build on Their Strengths

If you are new to interactive writing and writing minilessons, you may want to adhere closely to the suggested sequence, but remember to use the lessons flexibly to meet the needs of the children you teach and to build upon their strengths. Base your decisions about when or whether to use certain lessons on what you notice that children can already do, almost do, and not yet do.

- Omit lessons that you think are not necessary.
- Repeat lessons that you think need more time and instructional attention. Or, repeat lessons using different examples for a particularly rich experience.
- Move lessons around to be consistent with the curriculum that is adopted in your school or district.

Any of the following forms will help you determine where children are in their writing and provide information for making a plan for your teaching. Information from the Kindergarten Early Writing Behaviors Checklist (Figure 7-2) will help you identify where individual children are in acquiring specific writing behaviors. Use Analyzing Student Writing for Planning (Figure 8-6) along with the assessment questions on the last page of each umbrella to help you think about what individual children have learned through the minilessons. Use Guide to Observing and Noting Writing Behaviors (Figure 8-7) quarterly as an interim assessment. This observation form comes in two versions, one for individuals and one for the whole class.

Figure 8-6: Use this form to make a plan for teaching writing from information you have gathered.

Analyzing Student Writing for Planning

Use *The Literacy Continuum* and the Assessment section at the end of each umbrella you have taught to analyze a student's writing for evidence of writing behaviors and understandings.

Name: Sam **Grade:** K **Genre:** All-About Book **Date:** 1/24

Umbrellas Taught: MBK.U5: Making All-About Books, EWR.U6: Learning About Punctuation, EWR.U3: Learning How to Write Words

	Strengths	Next Steps	Plan (IW, WML, GW, IC)
Genre	• Writes about the same topic over several pages. • Labels drawings. • Groups information together (e.g., dog sleeps in room and hallway). • Pictures and words match.	• Help her tell more information by asking questions.	• GW: Meet with Sam, Jackson, Diego, and Milo to teach them to share their stories and ask each other questions about their writing.
Craft	• Understands the use of headings. • Demonstrates voice—talks directly to the reader. • Supports ideas with examples.	• Help her write about her pictures in detail. • Build on her use of examples to write more information. • Explore beginnings and endings (nonfiction).	• IC: Talk with her about her pictures. • IC: Read NF book introductions and suggest she try writing an introduction to her all-about book.
Conventions	• Can hear and write letters for most initial and ending sounds. • Uses some punctuation. • Uses some upper- and lowercase letters. • High-frequency words in control: my, the, on, a.	• Continue to work on hearing and writing predominant sounds. • Build on her understanding of punctuation; introduce exclamation points and question marks.	• IW: Invite her to share the pen for easily heard medial and ending sounds. • GW: Meet with Sam, Pedro, Jamal, and Magda to teach about other types of punctuation.
Writing Process	• Checks her letters to make sure they are clear.	• Teach her how to cross out instead of erasing. • Help her to add on to her writing.	• WML: Teach WPS.U3: Deleting and Reorganizing Writing, WML1 • WML: Teach WPS.U2: Adding to Writing

IW: Interactive Writing WML: Writing Minilesson GW: Guided Writing IC: Individual Conference

Guide to Observing and Noting Writing Behaviors—Individual Student
Kindergarten

Child's Name: Javier   Date: 1/24

IW: Interactive Writing • SW: Shared Writing • GW: Guided Writing •
WML: Writing Minilesson • IC: Individual Conference

Behaviors an...

| Genre |
| Draws and wr... |
| Makes picture... |
| Makes a book... |
| Makes all-abo... |
| Makes memo... |
| Writes a simp... |
| **Craft** |
| Writes the au... |
| Writes in first... |
| Writes and dr... the same sto... |
| Writes a story... an ending |
| Includes facts... |
| Provides desc... |
| Communicate... to understan... |
| Uses pictures... a topic |
| Adds speech... |
| Writes an eng... |

© 2021 by Irene C. Fou...

Guide to Observing and Noting Writing Behaviors—Whole Class
Kindergarten

Write students' names/initials and the date when each student consistently demonstrates this behavior.
Use this form quarterly if possible to assess your entire class.

Behaviors and Understandings	Marcos	Luca	Emmit	Valeria	Elle	Bryson	Myka	Sarena	Rafael	Mariana
Genre										
Draws and writes while playing	11/20	11/20	2/23	11/20	2/23	2/23		11/20		11/20
Makes picture books (with pictures and/or words)	2/23	2/23	11/20	2/23	2/23	11/20	11/20	11/20	2/23	11/20
Makes a book to teach something (how-to book)										
Makes all-about books										
Makes memory books	2/23	2/23	2/23	2/23	2/23	2/23	2/23	2/23	2/23	2/23
Writes a simple friendly letter										
Craft										
Writes the author's name and a title on the cover	11/20	11/20	11/20	2/23	2/23	2/23	2/23	2/23		2/23
Writes in first person when telling a story from own experience	2/23	2/23	11/20	2/23	2/23	11/20	11/20	11/20	2/23	2/23
Writes and draws across several pages with all pages related to the same story or topic	11/20	2/23	2/23	2/23	2/23	2/23	11/20	2/23	2/23	
Writes a story that has a beginning, a series of events, and an ending	2/23	2/23	2/23	2/23	2/23	2/23		2/23		
Includes facts and details in information writing	2/23			2/23		2/23	2/23			2/23
Provides descriptive details that make the writing interesting	2/23	2/23		2/23		2/23		2/23		
Communicates clearly the main points intended for readers to understand	2/23	2/23	2/23	2/23		2/23	2/23			2/23
Uses pictures and words to express thoughts and feelings about a topic	2/23	2/23	2/23	2/23	2/23	2/23	2/23	2/23	2/23	2/23
Adds speech and thought bubbles	2/23		2/23	2/23			11/20	2/23		2/23	2/23
Writes an engaging beginning or a satisfying ending to a story										
Uses drawings to represent people, places, things, and ideas										
Creates drawings that show attention to color or detail	2/23	2/23	11/20	2/23	2/23	11/20	11/20	11/20	2/23	11/20

The Writing Minilessons Book, Kindergarten **Page 1**

Figure 8-7: Use the observation forms about every quarter. One form helps you focus on an individual child. The other form offers a snapshot of the whole class.

Understand the Suggested Sequence of Lessons

The Suggested Sequence of Lessons (pp. 483–494 and in online resources) is intended to establish a strong classroom community early in the year, work toward more sophisticated concepts across the year, and bring together the instructional pieces of your classroom. The learning that takes place during interactive writing lessons and writing minilessons is applied in many situations in the classroom and so is reinforced daily across the curriculum and across the year.

Because many interactive writing lessons and writing minilessons use mentor texts as a starting point, the lessons are sequenced so that they occur after children have had sufficient opportunities to build some clear understandings of aspects of writing through interactive read-aloud, shared reading, interactive writing, and shared writing. From these experiences, you and the children will have a rich set of mentor texts to pull into writing minilessons.

The Suggested Sequence of Lessons follows the suggested sequence of text sets in *Fountas & Pinnell Classroom™ Interactive Read-Aloud Collection* (2018) and books in *Shared Reading Collection* (2018). If you are using either or both of these collections, you are invited to follow this sequence of texts. If you are not using them, the kinds of books children will need to have read are described on the first page of each umbrella (for the writing minilessons) and in Active Learning Experience (for the interactive writing lessons). Figure 3-12 shows how the text sets in *Fountas & Pinnell Classroom™ Interactive Read-Aloud Collection* connect to and support the interactive writing lessons.

The text sets in the *Interactive Read-Aloud Collection* are grouped together by theme, topic, author, or genre, not by skill or concept. That's why in many minilessons, we use mentor texts from several different text sets and why the same books are used in more than one umbrella.

We have selected the most concrete and clear examples from the recommended books. In most cases, the minilessons draw on mentor texts that have been introduced within the same month. However, in some cases, minilessons taught later in the year might draw on books you read much earlier in the year. Most of the time, children will have no problem remembering these early books because you have read and talked about them. Sometimes children have responded through art, dramatic play, or writing. Once in a while, you might need to quickly reread a book or a portion of it before teaching the umbrella so it is fresh in the children's minds, but this is not always necessary. Looking at pictures and talking about the book is enough.

In many cases, writing minilessons use pieces you have written with the children during interactive writing lessons. It is very supportive for children to experience an interactive writing lesson about a particular type of writing before they experience specific writing minilessons because they will have more context for understanding.

Use the Suggested Sequence to Connect the Pieces

To understand how the Suggested Sequence of Lessons can help you bring all of these instructional pieces together, let's look at a brief example from the suggested sequence. In month 9, we suggest reading the text set Exploring Nonfiction from the *Interactive Read-Aloud Collection*. One of the suggestions for extending learning after this text set is to do research on a topic of interest and then write about it. (You do not need any specific books in this text set; use any set of nonfiction books available.) In IW.24: Writing an All-About Book, the class uses what they have learned about plants to make an all-about book with a fact about plants on each page. Later, the class-made all-about book—along with books from the *Interactive Read-Aloud Collection* and *Shared Reading Collection*—becomes a mentor text in MBK.U5: Making All-About Books. These mentor texts help children learn specific understandings about making an all-about book, such as writing about the same topic on every page, adding labels to give facts, and using page numbers to help the reader (Figure 8-8).

Connecting All the Pieces

Read aloud and enjoy a nonfiction text set with the children.

Use interactive writing with the class to make a nonfiction all-about book.

Teach writing minilessons on specific aspects of all-about books.

Have children make their own all-about books.

Figure 8-8: The Suggested Sequence of Lessons helps you connect all the pieces of your classroom instruction and leads to children's own independent writing.

By the time this umbrella appears in the sequence, children will have already had lots of experience making books through some of the other umbrellas in Section 4: Making Books (e.g., MBK.U1: Getting Started with Making Books and MBK.U2: Expanding Bookmaking) and will be ready to experiment and play with this new kind of writing during independent writing and even during choice time.

Interactive read-aloud and shared/interactive writing experiences give children the background that helps them go deeper when they experience minilessons on specific topics. They are able to draw on their previous experiences with texts to fully understand the concepts in the minilessons. They can then apply this learning to their own independent writing and bookmaking. The Suggested Sequence of Lessons is one way to organize your teaching across the year to make these connections.

Add Interactive Writing Lessons and Writing Minilessons to the Day in Kindergarten

After deciding what to teach and in what order to teach it, the next decision is when. In *Fountas & Pinnell Classroom™ System Guide, Kindergarten* (2018), you will find frameworks for teaching and learning for a half day and a full day. Using those schedules and the information in this book as guides, think about when you might incorporate interactive writing lessons and writing minilessons as a regular part of your day in kindergarten. One suggestion is to provide a dedicated time each day for independent writing, which begins with a writing minilesson and ends with a share (Figure 1-6). Interactive writing can take place at any time of the day. Ideally, we recommend carving out a dedicated time each day for interactive writing, but if you are short on time, consider substituting interactive writing for a writing minilesson on certain days.

Kindergarten children thrive on structure, organization, and predictability. When you set routines and a consistent time for interactive writing and writing minilessons, you teach children what to expect. They find comfort in the reliability of the structure. Children write joyfully when they know they can count on time to experiment and play with their own drawing and writing. They delight in knowing that what they have to say is valued. Interactive writing lessons and writing minilessons are opportunities to build on the joy and enthusiasm children bring to all that they do in the classroom setting.

Section 1   Interactive Writing

INTERACTIVE WRITING ALLOWS children the opportunity to experience what it's like to be a writer before they become proficient writers themselves. With interactive writing, you are the guide. You guide the children as they think about what to write and help them express their ideas in language. Then you write together, sharing the pen with the children at selected points of learning value. The lessons in this section offer examples of the kinds of writing you and the children can do together. Each sample lesson is structured to take you and the children through the process of interactive writing.

1 Interactive Writing

You Will Need

- chart paper or a large piece of card stock
- red and black markers
- long, thin pointer
- To download the following online resource for this lesson, visit **resources.fountasandpinnell.com**:
  - Verbal Path for Letter Formation

Academic Language/ Important Vocabulary

- name
- letter
- word
- first

Continuum Connection

- Notice capital letters in names (p. 247)
- Understand and talk about the concept of a word (p. 365)
- Understand and talk about the concepts of first and last in written language (p. 365)
- Recognize and talk about the sequence of letters in a word (p. 365)
- Begin to make connections among words by recognizing the position of a letter: e.g., _was_, _we_; _good_, _said_; _just_, _put_ (p. 365)

ACTIVE LEARNING EXPERIENCE

- Prior to the lesson, make a card with the first letter in each child's name written large enough so that children can glue tissue paper onto it. Write the remaining letters in each child's name for them. Display the cards in alphabetical order.

GOAL

- Understand the concept of a letter and a word.
- Understand that a word is made up of distinct letters.
- Recognize one's name.
- Begin to connect visual features of letters to sounds in words.

RATIONALE

- Children's names are a powerful and engaging resource for literacy learning. Often, children's names are the first words children recognize. This learning can be used to make connections to other names and words.

ASSESS LEARNING

- Observe for evidence that children understand the concept of a word and that a word is made up of distinct letters.
- Look for evidence that children can connect visual features of letters to sounds in words.
- Notice if children can recognize their names.

INTERACTIVE WRITING LESSON

We recommend that you write the names on the name chart so that the letters are legible and provide a reference for children to recognize the letters in their names.

Establish Purpose

Refer to the children's name cards from the Active Learning Experience.

> Your name is a word, and a word is made up of letters. Today we are going to make a name chart so that you can see how your name looks and how your friends' names look.

Talk About What to Write

Talk about what you will write on the name chart.

- Point to the child whose name comes first in alphabetical order.

  > Who is this? Yes, this is _____.

  > The first letter in Alex's name is _A_. _A_ is the first letter in the alphabet, so _Alex_ will be the first name we will put on our name chart.

Write Together

Make a name chart.

▶ Write *Alex* on the chart using red for the first letter and black for the remaining letters. Invite Alex to trace the letter *A* with a finger while the other children write the letter in the air using the Verbal Path for Letter Formation.

Slant down, slant down, across.

Point under your name, Alex, and we will all read it together.

▶ Continue this process in alphabetical order. This may be extended to another day depending upon the number of children in the classroom.

Read and Revisit

Read the names with the children as you point under them. You might have children revisit the name chart for one or more of the following reasons.

▶ Invite children to observe that some of the names begin with the same letter. Draw a line around the names that begin with the same letter.

▶ Invite children to point to the first letter in their names.

▶ Invite children to count the letters in their names.

Summarize and Invite/Extend

Summarize the lesson. You might also decide to extend the learning.

You can look at the name chart to know how to write your name and the names of your friends.

▶ Display the name chart near the meeting area so that you and the children can use it whenever you do shared or interactive writing.

▶ Provide plenty of opportunities for children to work with the name chart (e.g., match a name card to the corresponding name on the chart, use a finger to trace the first letter in one's name, find names in other places in the room).

Alex	Jasmine
Andrew	Jaxson
Anna	
	Layla
Carlos	Mateo
Cecelia	Maya
	Michael
Drew	
Eva	William
Hanna	Zach

Section 1: Interactive Writing

You Will Need

- familiar books about school, such as the following from *Fountas & Pinnell Classroom™ Interactive Read-Aloud Collection* Text Set: Learning and Playing Together: School:
  - *The Bus for Us* by Suzanne Bloom
  - *Wemberly Worried* by Kevin Henkes
  - *Look Out Kindergarten, Here I Come!* by Nancy Carlson
  - *Miss Bindergarten Gets Ready for Kindergarten* by Joseph Slate
- chart paper and marker
- To download the following online resources for this lesson, visit **resources.fountasandpinnell.com**:
  - Alphabet Linking Chart
  - Verbal Path for Letter Formation
  - chart art (optional)

Academic Language/ Important Vocabulary

- agreement
- period
- word
- sentence
- letter

Continuum Connection

- Understand that a procedural text helps people know how to do something (p. 244)
- Say words slowly to hear a sound and write a letter that represents it (p. 248)
- Understand and talk about the concept of a letter (p. 365)
- Understand and talk about the concept of a word (p. 365)

ACTIVE LEARNING EXPERIENCE

- Prior to the lesson, read and discuss books about school (see You Will Need). Then, talk with the children about how they can help each other learn and play together well at school.

GOAL

- Understand the concept of a letter and the concept of a word.
- Write consonant letters for easily heard sounds at the beginning and end of words.

RATIONALE

- Putting children's ideas in writing provides a demonstration of a real purpose for writing. When children participate actively in this process (deciding what to say and sharing the pen), they think about the ideas and how to say them in their own words, and they learn that their ideas can be put into writing. Because they are active participants in creating the text and the sentences are reread while writing, they will be more likely to be able to read it with you.

ASSESS LEARNING

- Notice children's participation in creating the class agreement.
- Observe whether children can identify some letters in familiar words.
- Notice whether children can identify some familiar written words.
- Look for evidence that children can identify some consonant sounds at the beginning and end of words.

INTERACTIVE WRITING LESSON

This lesson is designed as an interactive writing lesson. Alternatively, you might choose to do all the writing yourself (shared writing). Keep the completed class agreement displayed so that children can refer to it often.

Establish Purpose

Display some of the books about school that you have read aloud.

> We've been reading and talking about good ways to learn and play together. What are some of the good things we can all do?

> Let's make a list of things that everyone in our class can agree to do. It is called a class agreement.

Talk About What to Write

Plan what to write for the class agreement.

> What is one thing we should write?

> We could say, "Be kind."

Write Together

Write a title for the class agreement. Then write the text with the children. Keep all children engaged while one child shares the pen by having them make the letter in the air or on the carpet in front of them.

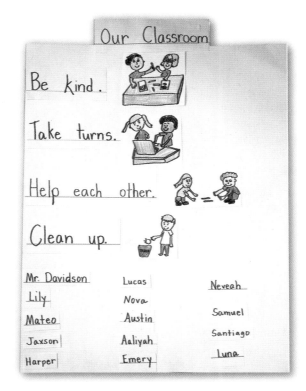

▶ Write *Be*. Point under the word as you read it with children to help them anticipate the next word.

> What is the next word in our sentence?

> The next word is *kind*. Say *kind* with me. Listen for the first sound. What sound do you hear at the beginning of *kind*?

> The first sound is /k/. The letter that goes with that sound is *k*.

▶ Point to the letter *k* on the ABC chart. Then use the verbal path to guide a volunteer to write the letter *k*.

> Pull down, pull in, pull out.

▶ Explain that a period at the end of a sentence shows that the sentence is finished.

▶ Reread the whole sentence together.

▶ Repeat the process of composing and writing several more sentences. Invite two or three more children to add letters for easy-to-hear sounds at the beginning or end of words, such as the *T* in *Take*, the *p* in *Help*, or the *C* in *Clean*.

Read and Revisit

Ask the children to read the class agreement with you as you point under each word. You might have children revisit the text for one or both of the following reasons.

▶ After reading the sentences, ask children whether they want to make any changes to the text—add another sentence, delete a sentence, or change a sentence.

▶ Invite children to point to a particular letter (e.g., *t*) or word (e.g., *Clean*).

Summarize and Invite/Extend

Summarize the lesson. You might also decide to extend the learning.

> Today we wrote a class agreement together. Later, we will put our names on the agreement to show that we agree to do all the things we wrote about.

▶ Use the chart to help children learn to recognize their names (e.g., match name cards, trace the first letter with a finger, find two names that have the same letter).

You Will Need

- a book that children are familiar with that shows classroom experiences, such as *Miss Bindergarten Gets Ready for Kindergarten* by Joseph Slate, from *Fountas & Pinnell Classroom™ Interactive Read-Aloud Collection* Text Set: Learning and Playing Together: School

- materials for creating a job chart, such as chart paper, sentence strips cut to size and glue stick, or a pocket chart and note cards

- markers

- name chart

- To download the following online resources for this lesson, visit **resources.fountasandpinnell.com**:
  - Alphabet Linking Chart
  - Verbal Path for Letter Formation
  - chart art (optional)

Academic Language/ Important Vocabulary

- job
- name
- chart

Continuum Connection

- Make lists in the appropriate form with one item under another (p. 244)

- Recognize and point to one's name (p. 365)

- Hear and say the beginning phoneme in a word; e.g., *sun*, /s/ (p. 365)

- Say a word slowly to hear the initial sound in the word (p. 366)

ACTIVE LEARNING EXPERIENCE

- Prior to the lesson, read aloud and enjoy several books about school, such as *Miss Bindergarten Gets Ready for Kindergarten* by Joseph Slate.

GOALS

- Recognize one's name.
- Listen for and say the beginning phoneme in a word.

RATIONALE

- When children learn to create a class job chart, they not only gain experience in recognizing their own names and the names of others, but they also gain independence as they take on responsibilities for maintaining an organized classroom community.

ASSESS LEARNING

- Notice whether children participate in creating a classroom job chart.
- Observe whether children recognize their names on the job chart.
- Notice whether children can hear and say the beginning sound in a word.

INTERACTIVE WRITING LESSON

This lesson is designed as an interactive writing lesson in which you and the children will compose the text together and share the pen. Alternatively, you might choose to do all the writing yourself (shared writing).

Establish Purpose

- Talk with children about the things Miss Bindergarten does to get the classroom organized in *Miss Bindergarten Gets Ready for Kindergarten*.

  What are some things Miss Bindergarten does to get the classroom ready?

- Reread the last two pages.

  What are some things the children might do to organize the classroom?

Talk About What to Write

Plan the jobs children can do to help keep the classroom organized and running smoothly.

  Let 's talk about some of the jobs you can have to help keep our classroom organized. What are some ideas?

- Engage children in a conversation about different classroom jobs they might do. You might walk around the classroom and point to different areas of the room or objects to help spark their ideas.

Write Together

Write the jobs that children have decided on. Keep all children engaged as one child shares the pen by having the others practice forming the letter in the air using the verbal path.

> *Calendar Assistant* **has two words.** *Calendar* **is the first word, and it begins with the letter** *C***. Can you find a** *C* **on the ABC chart?**

▶ Point to the letter *C* on the ABC chart. Use the verbal path to guide children in making the letter in the air as the volunteer uses the pen to write a *C* on a word card.

> **To make a** *C***, pull back and around.**

▶ Write the rest of the word *Calendar*. Have children read the word with you as you point under the word. Then write *Assistant*.

▶ Have children read the word with you as you point under each part of the word.

▶ Finish the rest of the jobs for the jobs chart in the same manner. Point out that in a list, each item goes under the one before it.

Read and Revisit

Ask the children to read the jobs with you as you point under each word. You might have children revisit the job chart for one or both of the following reasons.

▶ Have children whose names are on the job chart point to their names.

▶ Say a word on the job chart (e.g., *Song*). Then say two words, only one of which begins with /s/ (e.g., *sun, kite*). Have children identify which word begins with the same sound and say the sound.

Summarize and Invite/Extend

Summarize the lesson. You might also decide to extend the learning.

> **Today we made a job chart. You can look at the job chart each day and see what jobs different children in the classroom have.**

▶ Prepare a name card for each child. Add the names of children who will have jobs this week to the chart. Consider drawing children's names from a jar. Remove the cards once children have had a job. Replenish the jar when all have had a turn.

▶ Place art on or have children draw art for the job chart.

You Will Need

- a book about grocery stores or markets, such as *On Market Street* by Arnold Lobel, from *Fountas & Pinnell Classroom™ Interactive Read-Aloud Collection* Text Set: Letters at Work: The Alphabet
- chart paper and markers
- To download the following online resources for this lesson, visit **resources.fountasandpinnell.com**:
  - Alphabet Linking Chart
  - Verbal Path for Letter Formation

Academic Language/ Important Vocabulary

- menu
- market
- restaurant
- letter
- word

Continuum Connection

- Draw and write, extracting ideas from particular environments: e.g., restaurants, house, shops, doctor's office (p. 248)
- Form upper- and lowercase letters efficiently in manuscript print (p. 248)
- Use one's name to learn about words and to make connections to words and to other names (p. 365)
- Use the initial letter in a name to make connections to other words: e.g., *Max, Maria, make, home, from* (p. 366)

ACTIVE LEARNING EXPERIENCE

- Prior to the lesson, read aloud and enjoy books about food, grocery stores, or markets, such as *On Market Street* by Arnold Lobel. Then convert your classroom's play corner into a market or grocery store. Brainstorm with children what could be in the store.

GOAL

- Use background experience to generate ideas for writing.
- Use one's name to learn about words and to make connections to words and to other names.

RATIONALE

- When you help children make a menu, they learn that writing has a practical purpose and that writing is used in everyday life. Children can also make a clear connection between pictures and print. Use this opportunity to talk about foods to celebrate the similarities and differences in the children's home cuisines.

ASSESS LEARNING

- Notice whether children use past experiences and background knowledge as inspiration for writing and drawing.
- Look for evidence that children can make connections between the first letter of their name and other words that begin with the same letter.

INTERACTIVE WRITING LESSON

This lesson is designed as an interactive writing lesson in which you and the children will compose the text together and share the pen. Alternatively, you might choose to do all the writing yourself (shared writing).

Establish Purpose

Display *On Market Street*.

> We read this book about a boy who goes to Market Street and buys lots of different things. Some markets have a restaurant and you can buy meals to eat. A restaurant has a menu. A menu is a list that shows customers all the foods they can eat at the restaurant. Let's make a menu for our play-corner market.

- Write *Menu* at the top of the sheet of chart paper.

Talk About What to Write

Brainstorm a list of menu items for a restaurant.

> What could we put on our menu? Think about things that you like to eat.

- Encourage children to think about foods they have eaten at home or at restaurants.

Write Together

Write the text for the menu. To keep all children engaged while one child shares the pen, have them form the letter in the air or on the carpet in front of them.

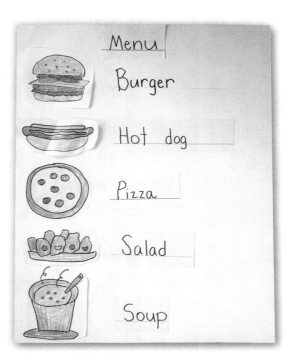

> The first thing we chose for our menu is a burger.

▶ Say *burger* slowly, emphasizing the /b/. Then have the children say *burger* with you to listen for the first sound.

> What sound do you hear first in the word *burger*?

> *Burger* begins with /b/. The letter that goes with that sound is *B*. Does anyone know another word or name that begins with the letter *B*?

▶ Point to *B* on the ABC chart, the name chart, or another place the letter *B* is visible in the classroom. Invite a volunteer to come to the chart to write the letter *B*.

> To make *B*, pull down, up, around and in, back and around.

▶ Write the rest of the word.

> Who can point to where we should start writing the next word?

▶ Use interactive writing to finish the rest of the menu. Invite different volunteers to share the pen, adding easily heard letters such as *t*, *P*, and *S*.

Read and Revisit

Ask the children to read the menu with you as you point under each word. You might have children revisit the text for one or both of the following reasons.

▶ Have children identify two words that start with or contain the same letter.

▶ Invite children to come up and point to a word that contains the first letter of their names.

Summarize and Invite/Extend

Summarize the lesson. You might also decide to extend the learning.

> Today, we made a menu for our market in the play corner. You can use the menu when you are playing with your friends!

▶ Display the menu in the play corner and invite children to take turns playing customers or workers at the market.

▶ Use interactive writing to make a shopping list for the play corner.

You Will Need

- several familiar alphabet books, such as those from *Fountas & Pinnell Classroom™ Interactive Read-Aloud Collection* Text Set: Letters at Work: The Alphabet
- chart paper or other paper for making a big book
- pictures of items that can be purchased at a store (optional)
- markers
- long, thin pointer
- To download the following online resources for this lesson, visit **resources.fountasandpinnell.com**:
  - Alphabet Linking Chart
  - Verbal Path for Letter Formation
  - chart art (optional)

Academic Language/ Important Vocabulary

- alphabet
- letters
- word
- sentence

Continuum Connection

- Understand and talk about the concept of a letter (p. 365)
- Understand and talk about the concept of a word (p. 365)
- Understand and talk about the concept of a book (p. 365)
- Say a word slowly to hear the initial sound in the word (p. 366)

ACTIVE LEARNING EXPERIENCE

- Prior to the lesson, read and enjoy alphabet books with the children. Help children notice the features of an alphabet book.

GOALS

- Understand the concept of a letter and a word.
- Use sound analysis to say and isolate the beginning and ending sounds in words.

RATIONALE

- Children are learning that there are twenty-six different letters in the alphabet, each with a name, a form, and a sound. They may also understand that letters come together to form words. When you make an ABC book about a topic (e.g., a market, animals), children might also develop some new vocabulary.

ASSESS LEARNING

- Look for evidence that children understand the concepts of a letter and of a word.
- Notice if children can say a word slowly to listen for and identify the beginning and ending sounds.

INTERACTIVE WRITING LESSON

This lesson is about making an alphabet book of items children would buy if they went to Market Street or to any store. The items might be real (*apples*) or silly (*alligators*). Children might want to make a book about a different topic or no topic at all.

Establish Purpose

Review several familiar ABC books with children.

> Why do you think the authors wrote these ABC books?

> We can make our own ABC book to teach the letters of the alphabet.

Talk About What to Write

Talk about what will be on the pages of the ABC book. Guide children toward the letter, a picture, and a sentence.

> What do you notice about the ABC books we have read?

- Prompt children to notice features such as the letters in order, pictures of items that begin with each letter, and uppercase and lowercase letters.

> What letter goes on the first page of our book?

> What else goes on the first page?

Write Together

Engage children in thinking about an item they would like to buy at a store that begins with the letter *a* (*apples*). To keep all children engaged while one child shares the pen, have them practice the letter in the air or on the carpet.

▶ Write *Aa* at the top of the page.

Where is a good place to start writing?

▶ Indicate the starting point on the left at the top or bottom, where children indicate.

Let's say the sentence together. *A is for apples*.

▶ Invite a child to write *A*. Guide the child using the verbal path.

To make an *A*, slant down, slant down, across.

▶ Ask children to check the letter that the child wrote against the ABC and name charts. Use correction tape as needed.

▶ If a child knows how to write the high-frequency word *is*, invite the child to write it. Complete the sentence, inviting one more child to write *a* in *apples*. Draw or add an illustration to the page.

▶ Make as many pages as time allows and continue the book in later interactive writing lessons. Each time, review the completed pages before starting the next page.

Read and Revisit

Ask the children to read the sentences with you as you point under each one. You might have children revisit the text for one or both of the following reasons.

▶ Have children point to the space between words. Talk about why the spaces are there.

▶ Use the ABC book to discuss the concept of a book (e.g., has pages, all the pages are about the same thing).

Summarize and Invite/Extend

Summarize the lesson. You might also decide to extend the learning.

Today we started an ABC book about things we can buy at the store. We will add more pages until we have pages for all twenty-six letters in the alphabet.

▶ Have children find pictures or make drawings for the ABC book. Use the finished book for shared and independent reading.

▶ Provide materials for children to make their own ABC books in the writing center.

You Will Need

- four word cards for labels
- markers
- To download the following online resources for this lesson, visit **resources.fountasandpinnell.com**:
  - Alphabet Linking Chart
  - Verbal Path for Letter Formation

Academic Language / Important Vocabulary

- label
- word
- letters

Continuum Connection

- Write a label for an object in the classroom (p. 244)
- Understand that a label provides information (p. 244)
- Realize that what you say (oral language) can be put into writing (p. 246)
- Say words slowly to hear a sound and write a letter that represents it (p. 248)
- Write some words with consonant letters appropriate for sounds in words (beginning and ending) (p. 248)

ACTIVE LEARNING EXPERIENCE

- Prior to the lesson, give children ample time to explore the classroom. Point out and name objects in the classroom (items such as a table or clock; materials such as markers or glue) that you will eventually label.

GOAL

- Understand that a label gives information.
- Say words slowly to hear the initial sound and identify the letter that goes with it.

RATIONALE

- When you engage children in writing labels for the classroom they begin to take ownership for creating a print-rich environment to help them manage their classroom. Labels expose children to writing and reading with purpose, promote letter and word recognition, and offer visual cues to the location of objects.

ASSESS LEARNING

- Look for evidence of what children know about labels.
- Listen to children say words slowly. Can they hear and identify the initial sound?

INTERACTIVE WRITING LESSON

This lesson is designed as an interactive writing lesson in which you and the children will compose the text together and share the pen. Alternatively, you might choose to do all the writing yourself (shared writing). It will be helpful to have an ABC chart, a name chart, and/or a word wall nearby so that children can refer to the letters to help them write words.

Establish Purpose

Review what children learned about the classroom.

> You had a chance to explore the classroom and to see where things are. We can write labels for some of those things. The labels will help you know where things belong and they will also help you when you write words.

Talk About What to Write

Plan what to write on the labels. Help children decide on about four objects to label.

> What are some things in our classroom that we could label?
>
> What should we write on the label for this?
>
> Let's write *Pencils* on the first label.

Write Together

Write the labels. Invite several children to share the pen. Engage the others by having them try the letter in the air or on the carpet in front of them.

▶ Say the word *Pencils* slowly with the children, accentuating the first sound, /p/.

> **What sound do you hear first in *Pencils*?**
>
> *Pencils* **begins with /p/, and the letter that goes with that sound is *P*.**

▶ Locate *P* on the ABC chart, name chart, or word wall. Invite a child to write the *P* on the label. Write the rest of the word yourself.

> **To make the letter *P*, pull down, up, and around.**

▶ Read the label together slowly while you point under the letters.

▶ Repeat this process for the remaining labels, inviting children to add letters for easy-to-hear consonant sounds such as *S* and *M*.

Read and Revisit

Ask the children to read the labels with you as you point under each one. You might have children revisit the labels for one or both of the following reasons.

▶ Have children point to a word that begins with a certain letter.

▶ Ask one or more of the children to point to a word on the ABC chart or name chart that begins with the same letter.

Summarize and Invite/Extend

Summarize the lesson. You might also decide to extend the learning.

> **Today we wrote labels for our classroom. What helped you write the letters on the labels?**
>
> **The ABC chart, name chart, and word wall can help you find the beginning letter in each word. When you do you own writing, remember to say the word slowly and write the letters for the sounds you hear.**

▶ Continue labeling items in the classroom across several days and as new items are added to the classroom.

You Will Need

- a book that children are familiar with that shows families helping each other, such as *Do Like Kyla* by Angela Johnson, from *Fountas & Pinnell Classroom™ Interactive Read-Aloud Collection* Text Set: Taking Care of Each Other: Family

- chart paper and markers

- name chart

- highlighter tape

- To download the following online resources for this lesson, visit **resources.fountasandpinnell.com**:
  - Alphabet Linking Chart
  - Verbal Path for Letter Formation

Academic Language/ Important Vocabulary

- thank you
- card
- space

Continuum Connection

- Understand that written communication can be used for different purposes: e.g., to give information, to invite, to give thanks (p. 244)

- Understand that the sender and the receiver must be clearly shown (p. 244)

- Use spaces between words to help readers understand the writing (p. 247)

- Recognize, point to, and say the same beginning consonant sound and the letter that represents the sound: e.g., *bag*, *bee* (p. 365)

- Recognize and use high-frequency words with one, two, or three letters: e.g., *a, I, in, is, of, to, and, the* (p. 366)

ACTIVE LEARNING EXPERIENCE

- Prior to the lesson, read aloud and enjoy several books about family members helping each other.

GOALS

- Use spaces between words.
- Recognize and use some high-frequency words, such as *is*, *and*, *the*, and *to*.
- Recognize the same beginning consonant sound and the letter that represents it.

RATIONALE

- When children write a thank you card, they learn that writing has a practical purpose and that it can be used to convey feelings and to show appreciation toward others.

ASSESS LEARNING

- Look for evidence that children understand the purpose of a thank you card.
- Observe children's writing for evidence that they understand words are separated by spaces.
- Look for evidence that children are making the connection between the same beginning consonant sound and the letter that represents that sound.
- Notice the high-frequency words that children are beginning to recognize.

INTERACTIVE WRITING LESSON

This lesson is designed as an interactive writing lesson in which you and the children will compose the text together and share the pen. Alternatively, you might choose to do all the writing yourself (shared writing).

Establish Purpose

Talk with children about ways family members help each other.

- Show a few pages that show Kyla helping her sister (pp. 12, 24).

    What are some ways that Kyla helps her little sister?

    What are some ways that people in your family help you?

Talk About What to Write

Talk about people at school who help the children and who might appreciate a thank you card.

    Just like the people in your family help you, there are also people at school who help you. You can write a thank you note to thank them for helping you.

- Engage children in a conversation about people at school to whom they might write a thank you card, such as the media specialist or art teacher.

Write Together

Write the text for the thank you card. As one child shares the pen and shows the space after the word, have the others use their hands to show the space and practice the letter in the air.

> A thank you card starts with the word *Dear* and then the name of the person you are writing to.

▶ Write the salutation.

> The next thing you write is what you are thanking her for. Watch how I start on the line below and how I make a space between each word.

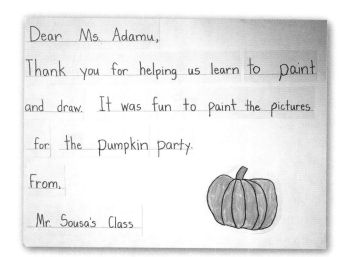

▶ Begin writing the first line, saying initial consonant sounds and using your hand to leave a space before you begin the next word. Stop before you get to *paint*.

> Say the word *paint* with me. What sound do you hear first in *paint*?
>
> The letter that goes with that sound is *p*.

▶ Ask a volunteer to use her hand to make a space and then write the letter *p*.

> To make a *p*, pull down, up, and around.

▶ Continue writing the card in this manner, having children contribute a letter that is repeated at the beginning of several words.

Read and Revisit

Ask the children to read the thank you card with you as you point under each word. You might have children revisit the thank you card for one or both of the following reasons.

▶ Have several children point to a letter on the chart that is repeated, name the letter, and say the sound.

▶ Identify high-frequency words (e.g., *to*, *and*, *the*) by placing highlighter tape over them and talking about them with children.

Summarize and Invite/Extend

Summarize the learning. You might also wish to extend the learning.

> Today you learned about thank you cards and we wrote one together.

▶ Have children illustrate the thank you card and deliver it to the recipient.

▶ Provide materials in the writing center for children to write their own thank you cards.

You Will Need

- books about friendship, such as the following from *Fountas & Pinnell Classroom™ Interactive Read-Aloud Collection* Text Set: The Importance of Friendship:
  - *A Visitor for Bear* by Bonny Becker
  - *Big Al and Shrimpy* by Andrew Clements
  - *I'm the Best* by Lucy Cousins
  - *Jessica* by Kevin Henkes
  - *Yo! Yes?* by Chris Raschka
- children's self-portraits (see Active Learning Experience)
- chart paper and markers
- To download the following online resources for this lesson, visit **resources.fountasandpinnell.com**:
  - Alphabet Linking Chart
  - Verbal Path for Letter Formation

Academic Language/ Important Vocabulary

- word
- letter
- space
- sentence
- period

Continuum Connection

- Use spaces between words to help readers understand the writing (p. 247)
- Say words slowly to hear a sound and write a letter that represents it (p. 248)
- Use initial letter in a name to make connections to other words: e.g. *Max, Maria, make, home, from* (p. 366)
- Recognize and find names (p. 366)

ACTIVE LEARNING EXPERIENCE

- Prior to the lesson, read and enjoy books about friendship, such as those in The Importance of Friendship text set. Then help children draw self-portraits to make a class big book (see DRW.U1: Making a Self-Portrait).

GOAL

- Say words slowly to hear a sound and write a letter that represents it.
- Learn that there is a space between words.
- Use the initial letters in names to make connections to other words.
- Recognize and find names.

RATIONALE

- When you share the pen with children, you show them how to put writing on the page–starting on the left, moving to the right, and leaving a space between each word. Having children say their name, listen for the first sound, and identify the letter reinforces the relationship between the sounds of language and the letters that represent them.

ASSESS LEARNING

- Observe for evidence that children are actively engaged in creating a class big book.
- Notice whether children say words slowly to hear a sound and identify the letter that represents it.
- Observe whether children can identify their own or their classmates' names.

INTERACTIVE WRITING LESSON

This lesson is designed as an interactive writing lesson in which you and the children will compose the text together and share the pen. However, you might choose to do all the writing yourself (shared writing).

Establish Purpose

Display familiar books about friendship and some of the children's self-portraits.

> We've been reading lots of books about friends. Let's put your self-portraits together to make a class big book about all the friends in our class. We can name the book *We Like Our Friends!*

Talk About What to Write

Talk about a simple sentence pattern with the children, such as _____ likes _____.

- Display one child's self-portrait.

> Alex drew this picture of himself. We can write words on this page to tell people about something Alex likes. Alex, what do you like?
>
> Alex says that he likes dogs. So what should we write?

Write Together

Write the text for the book. Keep all children engaged while one child shares the pen by having them practice the letter in the air or on the carpet in front of them.

> The first word in our sentence is *Alex*. *Alex* begins with the letter *A*, like *apple* and *acorn*.

❱ Point to *A* on the ABC chart or name chart. Then invite Alex to come to the chart to write the first letter in his name.

> To make an *A*, slant down, slant down, across.

❱ If Alex knows any of the other letters in his name, work together to finish writing the name. Write the word *likes*. Help the children notice that you need to leave a space after each word.

❱ Together, read what has been written so far to anticipate the next word.

> The next word in our sentence is *dogs*. Say *dogs*. What sound do you hear at the start of *dogs*?
>
> *Dogs* starts with /d/. The letter that goes with that sound is *d*.

❱ Point to *d* on the ABC chart or name chart. Then invite Alex or another child to write the letter *d*. Write the rest of the word.

❱ Reread the whole sentence together. Explain that you put a period at the end to show that the sentence is finished.

❱ Repeat the process for a few other children's self-portraits.

Read and Revisit

Call the children to the easel as you reread their pages. They point under the words with your support as the rest of the children read together. You might have children revisit the text for one or both of the following reasons.

❱ Have children find *Alex* and the other names on the name chart.

❱ Invite children to find a word that begins like a classmate's name.

Summarize and Invite/Extend

Summarize the learning and invite the rest of the class to add to the book.

> Today we started to make a big book about our friends. Later, we will add more pages to the book so everyone will have a page.

❱ Continue the lesson over a few more days to finish the book.

You Will Need

- a book that children are familiar with about colors, such as the following from *Fountas & Pinnell Classroom*™:
  - *Dog's Colorful Day* by Emma Dodd and *Red Is a Dragon* by Roseanne Thong, from *Interactive Read-Aloud Collection*™ Text Set: Noticing the Way the World Looks: Colors
  - *A Rainbow of Fruit* by Brooke Matthews, from *Shared Reading Collection*
- chart paper prepared with four rows
- markers
- highlighter tape
- To download the following online resources for this lesson, visit **resources.fountasandpinnell.com**:
  - Alphabet Linking Chart
  - Verbal Path for Letter Formation
  - High-Frequency Word List
  - chart art (optional)

Academic Language/ Important Vocabulary

- color
- chart
- column

Continuum Connection

- Recognize and use beginning consonant sounds and the letters that represent them: *b, c, d, f, g, h, j, k, l, m, n, p, qu, r, s, t, v, w, y, z* (p. 365)
- Recognize and use concept words: e.g., color names, number words, days of the week, months of the year, seasons (p. 366)

ACTIVE LEARNING EXPERIENCE

- Prior to the lesson, read aloud and enjoy several books about colors with children (see You Will Need). Have children draw pictures of things that are red, green, blue, etc.

GOALS

- Become familiar with color names and several high-frequency words.
- Say words slowly to hear a sound and write the letter that represents that sound.
- Use letters in names to make connections to other words.

RATIONALE

- Making a color chart is an opportunity for children to categorize items that are related and develop familiarity with concept (color) words and high-frequency words.

ASSESS LEARNING

- Notice whether children can say words slowly to hear a sound and recognize the letter that represents that sound.
- Look for evidence that children are beginning to recognize concept (color) words.
- Notice whether children are beginning to recognize high-frequency words.

INTERACTIVE WRITING LESSON

This lesson is designed as an interactive writing lesson in which you and the children will compose the text together and share the pen. Alternatively, you might choose to do all the writing yourself (shared writing).

Establish Purpose

- Briefly review the color books you and the children have read together.

  We have read books about colors. We could show what we know about colors by making a color chart.

Talk About What to Write

Make a plan for a color chart.

- Display the prepared chart paper.

  We can put things that are the same color in each row. What color should we put in the first row?

  We can also write a sentence: *We see red.*

Write Together

Make the chart. As one child shares the pen, keep the others engaged by having them find the letter on the ABC chart.

▶ Using a couple of children's ideas, briefly sketch or place art for red items.

What color do we see?

We see red. **Let's write that sentence.**

▶ Write the first two words, which are high-frequency words. Read what you have written so far to help children anticipate the next word.

What sounds do you hear in *red*?

▶ Guide children in identifying the initial /r/ sound and the ending /d/ sound.

▶ Have a volunteer come up to write the letter *r*. Write the *e*, and have the volunteer write the *d*. Use the verbal path to guide letter formation.

To make *r*, **pull down, up, and over. To make** *d*, **pull back, around, up, and down.**

▶ Choose another color for the next row and repeat the process. Have children write one of the high-frequency words (*we*, *see*) or continue writing letters for the beginning and ending sounds that are easily heard (e.g., *g* and *n* in *green*, *b* in *blue*).

Read and Revisit

Ask the children to read the color chart with you as you point under each word. You might have children revisit the color chart for one or both of the following reasons.

▶ Place highlighter tape over the high-frequency words (e.g., *we*, *see*). Have children read the words with you.

▶ Have children recognize and point to the color words.

Summarize and Invite/Extend

Summarize the learning. You might also decide to extend the learning.

Today we made a color chart. You can choose another color and write and draw about that color in the writing center.

▶ Have children add illustrations to the color chart.

▶ Set out baskets of objects that children can sort in different ways (e.g., by color, shape, or kind).

Section 1: Interactive Writing

You Will Need

- a familiar book about colors, such as *Cat's Colors* by Jane Cabrera, from *Fountas & Pinnell Classroom™ Interactive Read-Aloud Collection* Text Set: Noticing the Way the World Looks: Colors
- chart paper and markers
- To download the following online resources for this lesson, visit **resources.fountasandpinnell.com**:
  - Alphabet Linking Chart
  - Verbal Path for Letter Formation

Academic Language/ Important Vocabulary

- sound
- letter
- color
- poem

Continuum Connection

- Understand poetry as a way to communicate in sensory images about everyday life (p. 245)
- Understand that poems do not have to rhyme (p. 245)
- Place words on the page to look like a poem (p. 245)
- Closely observe the world (animals, objects, people) to get ideas for poems (p. 245)
- Understand that letters represent sounds (p. 248)

ACTIVE LEARNING EXPERIENCE

- Prior to the lesson, read aloud and enjoy several books about colors. One example of a color book that uses poetic language is *Cat's Colors.* Also provide opportunities for children to play with color through activities such as painting and using clay.

GOALS

- Begin to understand what a poem is and looks like.
- Understand that letters represent sounds.

RATIONALE

- When children write poems, they develop an understanding of the sounds of language, learning that they can make choices about the words they write and learning how to put words together.

ASSESS LEARNING

- Look for evidence that children are beginning to understand what a poem is and looks like.
- Look for evidence that children understand that letters represent sounds.

INTERACTIVE WRITING LESSON

This lesson is about writing a poem about the color blue, but write about any color that children choose. Use interactive writing or shared writing to construct the poem.

Establish Purpose

- Revisit pages 7–8 in *Cat's Colors.*

   What do you notice about the words on this page?

   These words about the color black sound like a poem when we read them.

Talk About What to Write

Plan to write a poem about the color blue.

- Revisit pages 17–18 in *Cat's Colors.*

   The words on this page describe something that is blue. What other words describe something that is blue?

- Guide children to think of something blue and some words that describe it. Then talk through what some of the language of the poem could be, including repeated words and descriptive language.

   You talked about a river being blue, so we can write a poem about a blue river.

Write Together

Write a color poem. While one child shares the pen, keep other children engaged by having them practice making the letter in the air.

- Make a sketch of the river to inspire children to think of language for the poem.

  The first word is *Blue*. **What word on the ABC chart starts with the same sound as** *blue*?

  What letter goes with that sound?

  Who can come up and write the first letter, *B*, **in the word** *Blue*?

- Have a volunteer write an uppercase *B*.

  To make the letter *B*, **pull down, up, around and in, back and around.**

- Finish writing the word *Blue*. Point under the word as the children say it with you.

- Continue writing the poem. When you come to a word that begins with a child's name in the class, pause to make the connection between the child's name and the word.

- Point out that the lines of a poem are usually shorter than in a story or nonfiction book. Emphasize that poems do not need to rhyme.

Read and Revisit

Ask the children to read the color poem with you as you point under each word. You might have children revisit the color poem for one or both of the following reasons.

- As you reread the poem, emphasize each word as a whole by pointing under each word and having children echo the words after you.

- Talk about features of the poem (e.g., shorter lines, repeated words, descriptive words).

Summarize and Apply/Extend

Summarize the learning. You might also decide to extend the learning.

  Today you learned that you can write a poem about anything, including a color, and that poems do not have to rhyme.

- Share poems with children and talk about how the language looks and sounds.

- Encourage children to write color poems in the writing center.

You Will Need

- several picture or wordless books, such as the following from *Fountas & Pinnell Classroom™ Interactive Read-Aloud Collection* Text Set: Exploring Pictures: Wordless Books:
  - *Float* by Daniel Miyares
  - *The Boy and the Airplane* by Mark Pett
- a photo or picture attached to chart paper
- sentence strips
- marker
- long, thin pointer
- To download the following online resources for this lesson, visit **resources.fountasandpinnell.com**:
  - Alphabet Linking Chart
  - Verbal Path for Letter Formation

Academic Language / Important Vocabulary

- picture
- letter
- word
- begins
- space

Continuum Connection

- Tell about experiences or topics in a way that others can understand (p. 246)
- Realize that what you say (oral language) can be put into writing (p. 246)
- Use spaces between words to help readers understand the writing (p. 247)
- Recognize and use high-frequency words with one, two, or three letters: e.g., *a, I, in, is, of, to, and, the* (p. 366)

ACTIVE LEARNING EXPERIENCE

- Prior to the lesson, read aloud and enjoy books with interesting illustrations, including wordless picture books (see You Will Need). Invite children to talk about what they see in the pictures. Also encourage children to draw pictures and talk about things they are doing, such as activities in the classroom, with their families, or on the playground.

GOAL

- Identify spaces between words.
- Understand that writers get ideas from pictures.
- Recognize and use high-frequency words *we, like,* and *to.*

RATIONALE

- A picture is something concrete that children can talk about and write about. The oral rehearsal helps children create meaning through talk and then translate that to print on the page.

ASSESS LEARNING

- Observe how actively children talk about what is happening in a picture.
- Notice if children use the name chart and the ABC chart to make connections to other words.
- Look for evidence that children can write predominant sounds in some words.

INTERACTIVE WRITING LESSON

Use any photograph or picture that you think children will be interested in writing about. You and the children will compose the text together and share the pen. Alternatively, you might choose to do all the writing yourself (shared writing).

Establish Purpose

Display several familiar picture books and wordless books.

> Today we are going to look at a picture together. We will talk about what the illustrator or the photographer shows you and then write words to go with the picture.

Talk About What to Write

Plan what to write about a picture. Share a photo that will prompt discussion.

> What do you notice in this picture? Let's talk about that.

> Quinn is having fun on the slide at school. How can we say that?

- Help the children to reframe their thoughts into two simple sentences. Have the children say the sentences with you while you point to where they will be written.

The Writing Minilessons Book, Kindergarten

Write Together

Write the sentences about the picture. Invite several children to share the pen by writing a letter or a word. Keep the others engaged by having them look for the letters on the ABC chart, name chart, or word wall.

> Say the first sentence with me. What is the first word?

▶ Write Quinn's name.

> A name always starts with an uppercase letter.

▶ Read what has been written so far to anticipate the next word, *plays*. Say *plays*, emphasizing the first sound. Then have children say the word with you to listen for the first sound. Invite a child to write it. Use the verbal path to guide her.

> To make the letter *p*, pull down, up, around.

▶ Say the word *play* again. Invite the children to say it with you.

> What do you hear next?

▶ Write the *l* and invite a child to write *a*. Write the final letters.

▶ Continue in this manner until you have written all sentences. Invite children to write high-frequency words they are learning (e.g., *like, to*) and letters for easy-to-hear initial or final sounds, such as *p* in *playground* and *s* and *d* in *slide*.

Read and Revisit

Read the sentences with children as you point, using a pointer, under each one. You might have children revisit the text for one or both of the following reasons.

▶ Point to some high-frequency words (*on, like, to*).

▶ Ask one or more children to identify the space between two words.

Summarize and Apply/Extend

Summarize the lesson. You might also decide to extend the learning.

> A picture can give you ideas for something to write about.

▶ Provide an assortment of pictures in the writing center. Encourage children to plan their writing by talking about it first.

▶ Remind children that they can write words for the drawings in their books.

You Will Need

- several familiar books about numbers and counting, such as the following from *Fountas & Pinnell Classroom™ Interactive Read-Aloud Collection* Text Set: Numbers at Work: Counting:
  - *1, 2, 3 to the Zoo* by Eric Carle
  - *One Duck Stuck* by Phyllis Root
  - *Fish Eyes* by Lois Ehlert
  - *One Moose, Twenty Mice* by Clare Beaton
- chart paper and markers
- To download the following online resources for this lesson, visit **resources.fountasandpinnell.com**:
  - Alphabet Linking Chart
  - Verbal Path for Letter Formation

Academic Language/ Important Vocabulary

- counting
- number
- word
- letter
- book
- page

Continuum Connection

- Write a book with all of the pages and ideas related to the same topic or set of facts (p. 245)
- Write some words with consonant letters appropriate for sounds in words (beginning and ending) (p. 248)
- Distinguish and talk about the differences between pictures and print (p. 365)

ACTIVE LEARNING EXPERIENCE

- Prior to the lesson, read aloud and enjoy books about numbers and counting, such as those listed in You Will Need. Also provide objects to count in the math center.

GOAL

- Understand that every page in a book is related to the same thing (numbers).
- Use letter-sound relationships to help spell an unknown word.
- Distinguish between pictures and print.

RATIONALE

- When you help children make a counting book, they begin to see how the pages of a book are related to one another. Making a counting book also helps children connect the numeral, the number word, and the concept.

ASSESS LEARNING

- Observe children's participation in creating a counting book, including identifying the letter that represents a sound.
- Look for evidence that children understand that all the pages in a counting book are about numbers.
- Notice whether children can distinguish between pictures and print.

INTERACTIVE WRITING LESSON

This lesson begins the process of making a counting book. Make as many pages as the children can manage now and finish the book over the next day or two.

Establish Purpose

Revisit some of the counting books you have read with children.

- Display a few counting books. Briefly talk about the characteristics of the books (e.g., they have numbers, the pictures show how many).

  We've been reading books about numbers and counting. Today, we're going to make our own counting book!

Talk About What to Write

Plan what to write in the counting book.

  What should we put on the first page of our counting book?

  We can write *Here is one* _____.

Write Together

Write the text for the counting book. As you invite children to share the pen, keep the others engaged by having them form the letter in the air or on the carpet.

- Make a simple sketch on chart paper of whatever children suggested, such as a bear. Then write the first sentence up until the last word. Read it with children to think about the next word.

    What comes next in the sentence?

    Let's say _bear_ slowly together. What sound do you hear first in _bear_?

    Bear starts with /b/. The letter that goes with that sound is _b_.

- Point to _b_ on the ABC chart or name chart. Invite a volunteer to write the letter _b_. Remind him to leave a space after _one_. Then guide him to write the letter _b_.

    To make a _b_, pull down, up, around.

- Continue in a similar manner for the _r_ in _bear_, inviting a different volunteer to write it. Read the page together.

    What number should go on the next page of our counting book? What comes after _one_?

- Repeat the process for the remaining numbers from one to ten, deciding whether to use bears throughout the book or something different on each page.

Read and Revisit

When the counting book is finished, invite the children to read it with you. You may want to revisit the text for one or both of the following reasons.

- Ask children to point to the picture or the words on a page. Point out that the words are what is read.
- Talk about how all the pages in the book are about one thing: numbers.

Summarize and Invite/Extend

Summarize the lesson. You might also decide to extend the learning.

    Today we made our very own counting book

- Invite children to add illustrations to the counting book. Make small copies of the counting book for children to keep.
- Encourage them to make their own counting books in the writing center.

You Will Need

- books about numbers and counting, such as those from *Fountas & Pinnell Classroom™ Interactive Read-Aloud Collection* Text Set: Numbers at Work: Counting or *Counting on the Farm* by Tess Fletcher, from *Shared Reading Collection*

- chart paper and markers

- a name card for every child in the class

- To download the following online resources for this lesson, visit **resources.fountasandpinnell.com**:
  - Alphabet Linking Chart
  - Verbal Path for Letter Formation

Academic Language/ Important Vocabulary

- survey
- number
- letter
- word
- sentence
- question

Continuum Connection

- Ask questions and gather information on a topic (p. 248)

- Recognize and point to one's name (p. 365)

- Say a word slowly to hear the initial sound in the word (p. 366)

- Say a word slowly to hear the final sound in the word (p. 366)

ACTIVE LEARNING EXPERIENCE

- Prior to the lesson, read aloud and enjoy books about numbers and counting. Engage children in talking about numbers and counting various things.

GOALS

- Recognize and point to your own name.
- Say words slowly to hear the initial and final sound.

RATIONALE

- When you help children make a survey, you demonstrate that they can use writing to record information that they want to remember. When children locate their own names, they have to think about and search for particular letters. They gain familiarity with the letters in it.

ASSESS LEARNING

- Observe children's participation in creating a survey question and chart.
- Notice whether children can recognize and point to their own names.
- Notice whether children say words slowly to identify the initial and final sounds.

INTERACTIVE WRITING LESSON

This lesson is about using interactive writing (sharing the pen) to take a survey. Keep the survey posted in the room so that children can learn to recognize their names.

Establish Purpose

Display some of the books about numbers and counting that you have read aloud.

> We have read a lot of counting books, and we have been learning about our names. It would be interesting to know how many letters are in your friends' names. Let's make a survey about the number of letters in our names. When you make a survey, you ask a question and you write down the answers.

Talk About What to Write

Plan a survey question.

> First, we need to decide what question to ask for our survey. What question can we ask to find out how many letters are in each other's names?
>
> We can ask, "How many letters are in your name?"

Write Together

Write the text for the survey question. Keep all children engaged while one child shares the pen by having them look for the letter somewhere in the room (e.g., classroom label, name chart).

> The first word in our question is *How.* Say the word *How* slowly and listen for the first sound. What sound do you hear first?
>
> *How* begins with /h/, like *hat.* The letter that goes with that sound is *H.*

▶ Point to *H* on the ABC chart or name chart. Invite a volunteer to come to the chart to write the letter *H.*

> To make an *H,* pull down, pull down, across.

▶ Write the rest of the word *How.* Ask the children what word comes next.

▶ Write the rest of the sentence in a similar manner, inviting children to write letters for easy-to-hear sounds (e.g., *m, s,* and *n*).

▶ Add a question mark to the end of the sentence. Explain that you put a question mark at the end of a sentence that asks a question. Then read the question together.

▶ Write the numbers *3* through *10* (adjust as needed) at the bottom of the chart.

▶ Give each child a name card. Invite children to count the letters in their names, helping them as needed, and attach the name cards to the chart.

How many letters are in your name?							
		Zahra					
	Lily	Samir	Sophia	Gabriel		Charlotte	
Ava	Musa	Ethan	Yousef	Sariyah	Victoria	Elizabeth	
Eli	Noah	Pablo	Jimena	Ephraim	Benjamin	Salvatore	Alessandra
3	4	5	6	7	8	9	10

Read and Revisit

Ask the children to read all the names on the chart with you as you point under each name. You might have children revisit the text for one or both of the following reasons.

▶ Invite children to point to their own names and identify the first and last letter.

▶ Ask the children which name has the most/least letters.

Summarize and Invite/Extend

Summarize the lesson. You might also decide to extend the learning.

> Today, we made a survey about your names. The chart shows how many letters are in all of our names.

▶ Using shared or interactive writing, help children write about the results of the survey.

▶ Have the children count the names in the columns with you to find out the most common name length.

You Will Need

- a familiar book in which the author writes about a memory, such as *Jonathan and His Mommy* by Irene Smalls, from *Fountas & Pinnell Classroom™ Interactive Read-Aloud Collection* Text Set: Taking Care of Each Other: Family

- children's paintings of a shared class memory (see Active Learning Experience)

- chart paper and markers

- long, thin pointer

- To download the following online resources for this lesson, visit **resources.fountasandpinnell.com**:
  - Alphabet Linking Chart
  - Verbal Path for Letter Formation
  - masking cards

Academic Language/ Important Vocabulary

- memory
- remember
- sound
- letter
- sentence

Continuum Connection

- Understand that writers may tell stories from their own lives (p. 244)

- Understand that the writer can look back or think about the memory or experience and share thoughts and feelings about it (p. 244)

- Listen to and respond to the statements of others (p. 331)

- Recognize and name letters in words in continuous text (p. 365)

ACTIVE LEARNING EXPERIENCE

- Have children paint pictures of a shared experience (e.g., trip to the park, school tour, fire drill, class party). This lesson is based on a class trip to the park. Also read aloud and enjoy several books in which authors share memories, such as *Jonathan and His Mommy*.

GOALS

- Understand that you can talk, draw, and write about something that happened to you.
- Listen to and respond to the statements of classmates.
- Find letters from one's name within continuous text.

RATIONALE

- When you teach children to write about a class memory, they learn that what they say can be written down. The resulting text becomes a common text for the class to read and enjoy.

ASSESS LEARNING

- Observe how actively children participate in writing a memory story.
- Notice whether children can listen and respond to the statements of others.

INTERACTIVE WRITING LESSON

In addition to focusing on concepts of writing, this lesson also incorporates specific talk around deciding what to write. A child's drawing of a shared experience will be used to inform the writing.

Establish Purpose

- Show *Jonathan and His Mommy*. Talk about how the book tells about Jonathan's memory of a time he went for a walk with his mommy.

  The book is about what Jonathan remembered about a walk with his mommy. We can write memory stories about things we remember, too. We can write about the park.

Talk About What to Write

Engage children in specific talk to decide what to write about the experience.

- Show a few of the children's paintings. Ask children to talk about what they remember about the trip and how they were feeling. Support children in building on what classmates say. Use the following prompts as needed:

  - *What is important to say in our memory story?*
  - *Who can add to what _____ said?*
  - *How would you say that in our story?*
  - *What else do you want to remember?*

Write Together

Write sentences about a memory. Invite one or two children to share the marker by writing a letter. Keep the other children engaged by having them form the letter in the air.

- ⏵ Write the first part of the sentence, saying each word and pointing under it.

    The next word is *park.* Say *park* slowly with me. What sound do you hear at the beginning? Look at the ABC chart and find the letter that goes with that sound.

    The first sound in *park* is /p/, like in *pig.*

- ⏵ Use the verbal path to guide a volunteer to write the *p.* Write the *ar.*

    What sound do you hear at the end?

    The last sound is /k/, like in *kite.* Look at the ABC chart and find the letter that goes with that sound.

- ⏵ Have the child write the *k.* Invite one or two children to help you finish the sentences by writing letters that stand for easy-to-hear sounds or by helping to hold a space between words.

Read and Revisit

Read the sentences with children as you point, using a pointer, under each word. You might have children revisit the text for one or both of the following reasons.

- ⏵ Ask children to find a letter from their names on the name chart. Use a masking card.
- ⏵ Reread the text to decide if there is anything that should be added to the story.

Summarize and Apply/Extend

Summarize the lesson. You might also decide to extend the learning.

    We wrote sentences about a class memory. Today, you can make your own memory story. You can choose to make your story a book.

- ⏵ Repeat this lesson several times during the year to write stories about class memories (e.g., field trips, walks, an event that happened on the playground). Use the stories as mentor texts when children write independently (MBK.U3: Making Memory Books).

You Will Need

- several books about homes, such as the following from *Fountas & Pinnell Classroom™ Interactive Read-Aloud Collection* Text Set: The Place You Call Home:
  - *Houses and Homes* by Ann Morris
  - *A House Is a House for Me* by Mary Ann Hoberman
- several of the children's creations (see Active Learning Experience)
- photos of the creations attached to chart paper
- markers
- To download the following online resources for this lesson, visit **resources.fountasandpinnell.com**:
  - Alphabet Linking Chart
  - Verbal Path for Letter Formation
  - masking cards

Academic Language/ Important Vocabulary

- creation
- letter
- word
- sentence

Continuum Connection

- Provide supportive description or details to explain the important ideas (p. 246)
- Reread writing to be sure the meaning is clear (p. 249)
- Understand and demonstrate that one spoken word matches one group of letters (p. 365)

ACTIVE LEARNING EXPERIENCE

- Prior to the lesson, read aloud and enjoy several books about homes (see You Will Need) with children. Have children build their own houses in the creation station using a variety of supplies (e.g., shoeboxes, cereal boxes, paper towel tubes). Encourage them to build any type of house, such as their own home or an imaginary building.

GOALS

- Learn that you can write about what you know.
- Provide details to explain important ideas.
- Reread writing to be sure the message is clear.
- Hear and recognize word boundaries.

RATIONALE

- When children learn to write about their creations, they learn that they can use writing to share information that is meaningful and important to them.

ASSESS LEARNING

- Infer what children know about writing by observing what they write or draw about their creations.
- Look for evidence that children understand that one spoken word matches one group of letters.
- Observe children's willingness to reread a text to be sure the meaning is clear.

INTERACTIVE WRITING LESSON

This is an example of an interactive writing lesson in which children have made houses (see Active Learning Experience); however, use any creations that children have made.

Establish Purpose

- Display children's creations.

  We have been reading books about homes. You made homes in the creation station. We can write about your creations to share information about them.

Talk About What to Write

Plan what to write about the children's creations.

- Draw children's attention to one child's home.

  Simone, tell us something special about your creation.

  Simone said that her home is special because it is tall and thin. How can we say that?

- Say the sentence with children while you point to where it will be written.

Write Together

Write the sentences about the children's creations. Invite several children to write their names and letters. Keep the others engaged by having them look for the names on the name chart or the letters on the ABC chart.

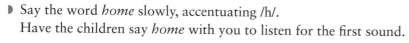

▶ Ask Simone to write any letters in her name that she can write quickly. Fill in the rest. Make sure the letters are written in order from left to right.

> **This is Simone's home, so I'm going to add 's to the end. What is the next word?**

▶ Say the word *home* slowly, accentuating /h/. Have the children say *home* with you to listen for the first sound.

> **Home begins with /h/, and the letter that goes with that sound is *h*, like in *hat*.**

▶ Point to the *h* on the ABC chart or name chart. Guide a volunteer with the verbal path.

> **To make an *h*, pull down, up, over, and down.**

▶ Write the *o*. Have children say *home* again, this time listening for the last sound. Use the verbal path to guide a volunteer to write the *m*. Write the rest of the sentence.

▶ Repeat the planning and writing process for one or two other creations. Have children write the letters for easy-to-hear sounds or high-frequency words.

Read and Revisit

Ask the children to read the sentences with you as you point under each word. You might have children revisit the sentences for one or both of the following reasons.

▶ Invite children to come up and point to individual words. You could have children use a masking card.

▶ Reread the sentences with children to be sure that the meaning is clear.

Summarize and Invite/Extend

▶ Summarize the lesson. You might also decide to extend the learning.

> **We wrote about our creations. What do you think of the sentences?**

▶ Provide drawing and writing materials in the creation station.

▶ Use the class-created sentences for shared reading.

You Will Need

- familiar books that contain signs, such as the following from *Fountas & Pinnell Classroom™ Interactive Read-Aloud Collection*:
  - *Float* by Daniel Miyares, from Text Set: Exploring Pictures: Wordless Books
  - *Flower Garden* by Eve Bunting and *Lost!* by David McPhail, from Text Set: The Importance of Kindness
  - *Alicia's Happy Day* by Meg Starr, from Text Set: Living and Working Together: Community
- chart paper prepared with the shapes of familiar signs
- markers
- To download the following online resources for this lesson, visit **resources.fountasandpinnell.com**:
  - Alphabet Linking Chart
  - Verbal Path for Letter Formation

Academic Language/ Important Vocabulary

- sign
- word
- letter

Continuum Connection

- Recognize and name letters in the environment (signs, labels, etc.) (p. 365)
- Recognize and point to the distinctive features of letter forms (p. 365)
- Understand and talk about the fact that some letters represent consonant sounds: e.g., the letter *b* stands for the first sound in *boy* (p. 365)

ACTIVE LEARNING EXPERIENCE

- Prior to the lesson, take children for a walk around the school or neighborhood. Help them notice and talk about signs (e.g., stop signs, street signs, exit signs). Encourage children to look for signs when they go out from home. You might also want to show and talk about pictures of signs in books (see You Will Need).

GOAL

- Recognize and point to letters that contain straight lines.
- Understand and talk about the fact that some letters represent consonant sounds.

RATIONALE

- Even before children can read, they recognize and attach meaning to signs that they see frequently, such as stop signs or the logo of a familiar store or restaurant. This lesson uses what children know about the meaning of the signs and connects it to new knowledge about words and letters.

ASSESS LEARNING

- Look for evidence that children understand that printed words have meaning.
- Notice whether children can point to letters that contain straight lines.
- Observe for evidence that children can identify the initial letter in some words.

INTERACTIVE WRITING LESSON

This lesson draws attention to print in the environment. Draw the sign shapes on chart paper as you discuss them, or prepare construction paper shapes.

Establish Purpose

Briefly discuss signs the children saw on their walk.

> We went for a walk around the neighborhood and you noticed lots of different signs. What signs did you see?
>
> How do signs help people?
>
> We can make our own signs, just like the ones you saw on our walk.

Talk About What to Write

Talk about a familiar sign.

- Point to the red octagon on the chart.

> We saw a sign that looked like this on our walk. What does this sign mean?
>
> This is a stop sign. It tells cars to stop. What word should be on the sign so everyone knows what it means?

Write Together

Write the text for the signs. To keep all children engaged while one child shares the pen, have them make the letters in the air or on the carpet.

▶ Say the word *stop* slowly, emphasizing /s/. Then have children say *stop* with you to listen for the first sound.

> What sound do you hear first in *stop*?
>
> *Stop* begins with /s/. The letter that we write for that sound is *s*. Do you know any other words or names that begin with *s*?
>
> Where can you find the letter *s* to see how it looks?

▶ Point to *S* on the ABC chart, a label in the classroom, or the name chart if there is a child whose name begins with *S*. Invite a volunteer to come to the chart to write the letter *S*. Guide him to write it.

> To make an *S*, pull back, in, around, down, and back around.

▶ Write the rest of the word yourself. Point to and name each letter. Then read the sign together.

▶ Repeat the interactive writing process for other familiar signs. Invite different children to write the letters for easy-to-hear consonant sounds, such as *M* in *Main*.

Read and Revisit

Ask the children to read the signs with you as you point under each word. You might have children revisit the text for one or both of the following reasons.

▶ Invite children to come up and point to a particular letter (e.g., *S*).

▶ Invite children to come up and point to letters with a particular feature (e.g., letters with straight lines).

Summarize and Invite/Extend

Summarize the lesson. You might also decide to extend the learning.

> Today, we made some signs that we know. You can make other signs you know in the writing center.

▶ Help children add some of these environmental print sign words to the word wall.

▶ Suggest that children make signs for the block center (e.g., if they make a block city with roads and cars).

You Will Need

- several familiar books about community, such as *Lola at the Library* by Anna McQuinn, from Text Set: Living and Working Together: Community from *Fountas & Pinnell Classroom™ Interactive Read-Aloud Collection*
- chart paper and markers
- note cards for labels
- tape or glue stick
- To download the following online resources for this lesson, visit **resources.fountasandpinnell.com**:
  - Alphabet Linking Chart
  - Verbal Path for Letter Formation

Academic Language / Important Vocabulary

- map
- label
- letter
- word
- first
- last

Continuum Connection

- Understand that a writer or illustrator can add a label to help readers understand a drawing or photograph (p. 244)
- Understand that a label provides important information (p. 244)
- Understand and talk about the concepts of first and last in written language (p. 365)
- Understand and talk about the fact that words are formed with letters (p. 365)
- Say a word slowly to hear the initial sound in the word (p. 366)
- Say a word slowly to hear the final sound in the word (p. 366)

ACTIVE LEARNING EXPERIENCE

- Read aloud and enjoy books about communities. Talk with children about their communities, including the school community. Take children on a walk through the school building. Then work together to make a map of the school. Labels will be added in this lesson.

GOALS

- Understand that writers use labels to provide information.
- Say words slowly to hear the initial and final sounds of a word.
- Write the letter that represents the sounds heard in a word.
- Understand and talk about the concepts of *letter* and *word*.

RATIONALE

- When children learn that labels give more information to a drawing, they recognize that they can add words to their own drawings to help explain what the drawings they represent. They learn that the pictures and writing together create one clear message.

ASSESS LEARNING

- Notice whether children understand that labels can be added to pictures to provide information.
- Listen to children say words slowly. Can they hear and identify the initial and final sounds?
- Look for evidence that children understand that when letters are put together they make one word.

INTERACTIVE WRITING LESSON

This lesson is designed as an interactive writing lesson in which you and the children will compose the text together and share the pen. Alternatively, you might choose to do all the writing yourself (shared writing).

Establish Purpose

- Show the map of the school.

  How can we make our map more useful?

  We can add labels to tell what each part is, like our room or the office.

Talk About What to Write

Plan what labels to add to the map.

- Revisit the different places on the map.

  Let's talk about the parts of our school map. What labels could we add?

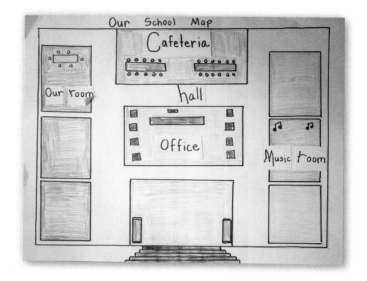

Write Together

Label the map. Invite several children to share the pen by adding a letter. Keep the others engaged by having them practice making the letter in the air or on the carpet in front of them.

> Watch as I write the word *Office* on a label.

▶ Write *Office* on a note card and attach it to the proper place on the map.

▶ Point to the music room on the map.

> *Music room* has two words. The first word is *Music*. Say *Music* slowly.

> The first sound in *Music* is /m/. What letter goes with that sound?

▶ Ask a child to write *M* on a note card.

> To make the letter *M*, pull down, slant down, slant up, pull down.

▶ Write the remaining letters, pausing before the *c*.

> *Music* ends with /k/. In the word *Music*, the last letter is the same as at the beginning of *cat*. Look at the ABC chart to find out what letter that is.

▶ As children identify *c*, ask a child to write the *c*.

▶ Have children listen for and identify the letters *r* and *m*. Have a child write *r* on a second note card. Write the *o*'s. Have a child write *m*. Attach the label to the map.

▶ Continue in this way, having children identify easy-to-hear first and last letters.

Read and Revisit

Ask the children to read the labels on the school map with you as you point under each word. You might have children revisit the text for one or both of the following reasons.

▶ Have children point to the first letter of a word and then point to the last letter of a word.

▶ Point to the letters in a word. Have children name each letter.

Summarize and Invite/Extend

Summarize the lesson. You might also decide to extend the learning.

> Today we added labels to the map of our school.

▶ Encourage children to make labels for their drawings and for different areas of and items in the classroom, including the centers and play area.

You Will Need

- chart paper and markers
- To download the following online resources for this lesson, visit **resources.fountasandpinnell.com**:
  - Alphabet Linking Chart
  - Verbal Path for Letter Formation

Academic Language / Important Vocabulary

- how-to
- steps
- space
- capital (uppercase) letters
- lowercase letters

Continuum Connection

- Understand that a procedural text can be written in various forms: e.g., list, directions with steps (how-to) (p. 244)
- Understand that a procedural text often shows one item under another item and may include a number or letter for each item (p. 244)
- Use spaces between words to help readers understand the writing (p. 247)
- Recognize and point to uppercase letters and lowercase letters: e.g., *B, b* (p. 365)
- Form upper- and lowercase letters proportionately in manuscript print (p. 248)

ACTIVE LEARNING EXPERIENCE

- Challenge pairs of children to build a tower using blocks from the block center. Take photos of the children with their towers, if possible, and have children make sketches of their towers. Support the process with prompts such as these: *What did you do first (next)? How did you decide which blocks to use? What did you do differently after the blocks fell? What did you do to make your tower strong?*

GOAL

- Understand that a how-to book teaches how to do something and often has numbered steps.
- Understand that words are separated from one another by spaces.
- Distinguish between capital and lowercase letters.

RATIONALE

- When you write a how-to book with children, they learn about a functional type of writing that can be used in everyday life to communicate a process.

ASSESS LEARNING

- Look for evidence of what children understand about procedural texts.
- Notice whether children understand the idea of good spacing between words.
- Notice whether children can distinguish between capital (uppercase) and lowercase letters.

INTERACTIVE WRITING LESSON

The how-to book can be used as a mentor text in MBK.U4: Making How-to Books. Write two steps per page as shown here or place one step per page. Do as much of the book as children can manage in one sitting. Continue writing the book across two or three days, as needed.

Establish Purpose

Talk about children's experiences making tall buildings out of blocks.

> We talked about building block towers and how you learned to keep them from falling over. We can make a how-to book to tell people how to make their own block towers.

Talk About What to Write

Talk about the steps children followed to construct their buildings.

> A how-to book has steps that people follow to do or make something. The steps must be in order. Let's think about how to build a tower. Your pictures can help us. What should we write as the first step?

Write Together

Write the text for the how-to book. Invite several children to share the pen. Keep the other children engaged by having them find the letter on the ABC chart, name chart, or word wall.

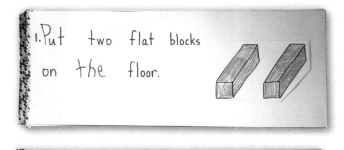

- On the first page, write the numeral *1*.

  The number *1* shows that this will be the first step. The first step is to put two blocks on the floor.

  Say *Put* slowly with me to listen for the first sound. What letter goes with that sound?

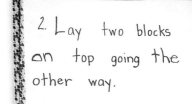

- Invite a child to write the letter *P*.

  The *P* is a capital letter. It is tall, so it starts up here. Pull down, up, and around.

- Write the rest of the word and sentence up to *the*.

  The is a word you are learning. Who can write *the*?

- Finish writing the sentence and point under it as you and the children read it aloud.

  The spaces show where one word ends and the next word begins. The period ends the sentence.

- Repeat the process to complete the remaining pages. Invite children to add letters for easy-to-hear sounds (e.g., *l*, *k*, and *m*) and familiar high-frequency words, such as *it*.

Read and Revisit

Read aloud the whole how-to book together, pointing under each word. You might have children revisit the text for one or more of the following reasons.

- Have children point to the space between two words.
- Ask children to identify a capital letter and a lowercase letter.

Summarize and Invite/Extend

Summarize the learning and invite children to make their own how-to books.

  Today we wrote a how-to book about how to build a tower out of blocks.

- To complete the book, work with children to add a cover and illustrations. An example of a complete how-to book is on page 158.
- Provide children with blank books (a few sheets of paper stapled together) to make their own how-to books. Invite them to read their books to you or to their classmates.

You Will Need

- a story with a simple plot, such as *The Three Billy Goats Gruff* by P. C. Asbjørnsen and J. E. Moe, from *Fountas & Pinnell Classroom™ Interactive Read-Aloud Collection* Text Set: Exploring Animal Tales
- a large sheet of butcher paper
- story characters
- sentence strips
- glue stick or tape
- marker
- To download the following online resources for this lesson, visit **resources.fountasandpinnell.com**:
  - Alphabet Linking Chart
  - Verbal Path for Letter Formation
  - chart art (optional)

Academic Language/ Important Vocabulary

- story map
- word
- letter
- sentence

Continuum Connection

- Represent a sequence of events from a text through drawing or writing (p. 172)
- Produce simple graphic representations of a story such as story maps or timelines (p. 173)
- Recognize and point to uppercase letters and lowercase letters: e.g., *B, b* (p. 365)
- Recognize and name letters in words (p. 365)

ACTIVE LEARNING EXPERIENCE

- Prior to the lesson, read aloud a story that has a clear order of events, such as *The Three Billy Goats Gruff*. Work with children to create a background of the story setting for a mural. Some children might draw pictures of the story characters to be used on a story map.

GOAL

- Understand that a story has a sequence.
- Recognize and point to uppercase and lowercase letters.
- Recognize and name letters in words.

RATIONALE

- By participating in making a story map, children begin to understand that the events in a story happen in sequential order. When you help them write about their illustrations, they learn to say words slowly to listen for the sounds.

ASSESS LEARNING

- Observe the accuracy of children's retellings of the story.
- Notice whether children can identify any vowel sounds in familiar words.

INTERACTIVE WRITING LESSON

This lesson is based on *The Three Billy Goats Gruff*, but any story with a clear, sequential plot could be used. Spread the writing across one or two days, depending on the attention span of the children in your class.

Establish Purpose

Use the prepared background plus drawings of the characters to create a story map.

- Remind children of *The Three Billy Goats Gruff*.

  We can make a story map to show what happened in *The Three Billy Goats Gruff*.

- Show the prepared sheet of butcher paper and read the title.

Talk About What to Write

Plan several sentences to write on the story map.

Think about what happened in the story. What is the first thing you remember?

How could we say that?

Write Together

Write sentences to tell about the story. Invite several children to share the pen by writing letters for easy-to-hear sounds or easy high-frequency words. Keep the others engaged by having them form the letters in the air or on the carpet.

> First, let's write the title of the story. Say it with me.

▸ Write *The*.

> What is the next word in the title?

> Say *Billy*. Billy starts with /b/, which we write with the letter *B*.

▸ Invite a volunteer to write the letter *B*. Use the verbal path to guide him.

> *Billy* is a name, so we need to make an uppercase *B*. To make a *B*, pull down, up, around and in, back and around.

▸ Write the rest of the word yourself. Complete the title together, inviting volunteers to write the *G* in *Goats* and *Gruff*. Read the title together.

▸ Repeat the process to write two or three sentences.

Read and Revisit

Read the sentences on the story map with the children. You might have the children revisit the story map for one or both of the following reasons.

▸ Invite the children who wrote letters to point to and name the letters or words they wrote.

▸ Ask children to point to uppercase and lowercase *Bb* and *Gg*.

Summarize and Invite/Extend

Summarize the lesson. You might also decide to extend the learning.

> Today we made a story map telling about *The Three Billy Goats Gruff*. You can use the story map to tell the story.

▸ Invite children to use the story map to retell the story. Consider attaching craft sticks to drawings of the characters for children to act out the story.

▸ Use interactive writing to make speech bubbles to show what the characters are saying on the story map.

Section 1: Interactive Writing

You Will Need

- a familiar folktale, such as the following from *Fountas & Pinnell Classroom™ Interactive Read-Aloud Collection* Text Set: Sharing Stories: Folktales:
  - *The Gingerbread Boy* by Paul Galdone
  - *The Magic Fish* by Freya Littledale
  - *Stone Soup* by Heather Forest
- chart paper and markers
- long, thin pointer
- To download the following online resources for this lesson, visit **resources.fountasandpinnell.com**:
  - Alphabet Linking Chart
  - chart art (optional)

Academic Language/ Important Vocabulary

- letter
- word
- story
- sentence
- ending

Continuum Connection

- Compose innovations on very familiar texts by changing the ending, the series of events, characters, or the setting (p. 173)
- Begin to make connections among words by recognizing the position of a letter: e.g., *was*, *we*; *good*, *said*; *just*, *put* (p. 365)
- Understand and talk about the fact that some letters represent vowel sounds (p. 365)
- Hear, say, clap, and identify syllables in one- or two-syllable words: e.g., *big, frog, gold, lit/tle, mon/key, sil/ver* (p. 366)

ACTIVE LEARNING EXPERIENCE

- Prior to the lesson, read aloud and enjoy several folktales with the children (see You Will Need).

GOAL

- Begin to make connections between words by recognizing the position of a letter.
- Write easily heard vowel sounds in words.
- Use known words to help spell unknown words.

RATIONALE

- Writing an alternative ending for a familiar story is a way of responding to reading. In this lesson, children not only have an opportunity to think about how familiar characters might act differently but also to see that their ideas can be written down and read by others.

ASSESS LEARNING

- Notice whether children use known words to help spell unknown words.
- Observe whether children can identify and write some vowels.
- Notice whether children can make connections between words by recognizing the position of a letter.

INTERACTIVE WRITING LESSON

This lesson is based on *The Gingerbread Boy*, but any familiar story could be used. Spread the writing across one or two days, depending on the attention span of the children in your class.

Establish Purpose

Display *The Gingerbread Boy* and briefly review the story.

> We read and enjoyed *The Gingerbread Boy*. What happened at the end of this story?

> The author made up that ending, but we can write a different ending.

Talk About What to Write

Plan an alternative ending to the story.

> What's another way that the story could end?

> The Gingerbread Boy could run away. Let's write about that. What should we write?

- Once the children have agreed upon an ending, say the sentences together while you illustrate the new ending on the chart paper.

Write Together

Write the text for the new ending. Invite several children to share the pen by writing a letter or a word. Engage the others by having them find the letter on the ABC chart or the word on the word wall.

> Say the first sentence with me.
>
> Who can write the word *The*?

- Before the child writes the high-frequency word *The*, establish where the writing will begin.

- Write *Gingerbread Boy* and then read aloud what has been written to help children anticipate the next word.

> Say the word *runs*. What sound do you hear first? What letter is that?

- Ask a child to write the letter *r*. Finish writing the sentence and read it aloud.

- Continue in a similar manner to write two or three more sentences. Invite children to write high-frequency words that they are learning (e.g., *he*, *is*) and easy-to-hear beginning and ending consonants (e.g., *f*, *t*, *d* and vowels (e.g., *e* in *free*).

Read and Revisit

Read the alternative ending together, using a pointer to point under the words. You might have children revisit the text for one or both of the following reasons.

- Have children listen for, say, and clap the syllables in words.

> Let's clap the parts we hear in *Boy*. Now let's clap the parts in *away*. Now let's clap the parts in *Gingerbread*.

- Explain that some letters are called vowels. Have children find *a, e, i, o,* or *u* in the alternative ending. Note that every word has at least one vowel.

Summarize and Invite/Extend

Summarize the learning. You might also decide to extend the learning.

> Today we wrote a new ending for a story that we knew.

- Invite children to make stick puppets for the characters in the story and use them to retell the story, including the new ending.

- Invite children to change the plot, the characters, or the setting in other familiar tales.

You Will Need

- familiar question-and-answer books, such as the following from *Fountas & Pinnell Classroom*™:

  - *Morning on the Farm* by Jane Simon and *On the Go* by Abbey Grace Moore, from *Shared Reading Collection*

  - *What Color Is Nature?* by Stephen R. Swinburne and *Cat's Colors* by Jane Cabrera, from *Interactive Read-Aloud Collection* Text Set: Noticing the Way the World Looks: Colors

- several familiar nonfiction books about animals, such as *Actual Size* by Steve Jenkins and *Elephants Swim* by Linda Capus Riley, from *Interactive Read-Aloud Collection* Text Set: Sharing the Earth: Animals

- chart paper and markers

Academic Language / Important Vocabulary

- question
- answer
- information
- capital letter
- period
- question mark

Continuum Connection

- Write books or short pieces that are enjoyable to read and at the same time give information to a reader about a topic (p. 245)

- Use periods, exclamation marks, and question marks as end marks (p. 247)

- Distinguish and talk about the differences between the uppercase and lowercase forms of a letter (p. 365)

ACTIVE LEARNING EXPERIENCE

- Read several nonfiction books about animals along with nonfiction books that have a question-and-answer format (see You Will Need). If possible, share question-and-answer books that have a variety of formats, including lift-the-flap books.

GOALS

- Understand that sentences begin with a capital letter.
- Talk about the differences between capital and lowercase letters.
- Understand when to use appropriate punctuation.

RATIONALE

- When children learn that some books ask questions and provide answers as a way to give the reader information, they know what to expect from question-and-answer books and can choose to write a book in this format.

ASSESS LEARNING

- Look for evidence of what children understand about question-and-answer books.
- Notice what children understand about using capital letters and punctuation marks.
- Observe whether children can hear and identify the first and last sounds in words.

INTERACTIVE WRITING LESSON

The question-and-answer book can be turned into a flap book in a later lesson about making books fun to read (DRW.U3.WML2). In this lesson, we use the term *capital letters*, but you may choose to use *uppercase letters*.

Establish Purpose

- Show several examples of animal books and question-and-answer books.

  We have been reading books about animals. We have also read some question-and-answer books. Together, we can make a question-and-answer book about animals.

Talk About What to Write

Use *Morning on the Farm* to help plan what to write in a question-and-answer book.

  Morning on the Farm asks questions about farm animal sounds and then gives the answers. What are some other questions you could ask about animals?

- Have children use the examples in *Morning on the Farm* to come up with some questions and answers for the book you will write together, perhaps about what animals eat.

Write Together

Begin writing the question-and-answer book. Invite several children to share the pen by writing a letter. Keep the others engaged by having them find the letter on the ABC chart or name chart.

> **What kind of letter goes at the beginning of a sentence?**

▶ Assist children in determining that a capital letter is needed.

> **Who can show where to write capital *W* on the page?**

▶ Ask a child to write the letter *W*. Finish the words up to *eat*.

> **Say the word *eat* slowly. What sound do you hear first?**

▶ Ask a volunteer to write *e*. Write *a*.

> **What sound do you hear last?**

▶ Have the volunteer add the letter *t*.

> **Listen to how I read the sentence. My voice goes up at the end because it is a question. What goes at the end of a question?**

▶ Ask a child to write the question mark. Then write and read the next sentence.

> **My voice stops at the end, but it does not go up. What goes at the end of this sentence?**

▶ Continue writing as many pages as children can manage in one sitting. Invite them to write letters that have easy-to-hear sounds (e.g., *h*, *s*) and known words (e.g., *do*).

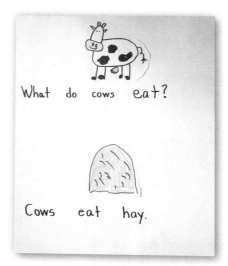

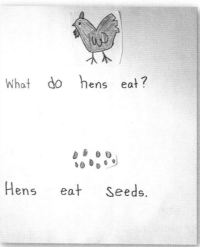

Read and Revisit

Ask the children to read the sentences with you as you point under each word. You might have children revisit the text for one or more of the following reasons.

- Practice reading the sentences with children to reflect the end punctuation.
- Talk about how capital letters and lowercase letters look different.

Summarize and Invite/Extend

Summarize the lesson. You might also decide to extend the learning.

> **Today we made a question-and-answer book.**

▶ Work with several children to add illustrations to the question-and-answer book.

▶ Invite children to play with animals at the water table or in the block center and write a question-and-answer book about those animals.

You Will Need

- results of a science experiment (see Active Learning Experience)

- a book about things that float or sink, such as *Float* by Daniel Miyares from *Fountas & Pinnell Classroom™ Interactive Read-Aloud Collection* Text Set: Exploring Pictures: Wordless Books

- chart paper and markers

- To download the following online resource for this lesson, visit **resources.fountasandpinnell.com**:
  - Verbal Path for Letter Formation

Academic Language/ Important Vocabulary

- sink
- float
- experiment
- observation

Continuum Connection

- Hear and divide onsets and rimes: e.g., *m-en, bl-ack* (p. 365)

- Use known words to help spell an unknown word (p. 366)

- Write a letter for easy-to-hear vowel sounds (p. 248)

- Understand and talk about the fact that some letters represent consonant sounds: e.g., the letter *b* stands for the first sound in *boy* (p. 365)

- Understand and talk about the fact that some letters represent vowel sounds (p. 365)

ACTIVE LEARNING EXPERIENCE

- Prior to the lesson, engage children in a science experiment. This lesson is based on observing which objects float and which sink. Use a water table or a tub of water and objects such as keys, blocks, marbles, rocks, foam shapes, corks, bathtub toys, and crayons. You might also read aloud books about boats or things that sink and float, such as *Float* by Daniel Miyares.

GOAL

- Hear and divide onset and rimes, for example, *bl-ock, r-ock*.
- Use known words to help spell an unknown word.
- Listen for and identify easy-to-hear consonant and vowel sounds.

RATIONALE

- When you record scientific observations with children, they learn to look closely and discuss, draw, and write about what they notice. This helps children understand that writers have many purposes for writing.

ASSESS LEARNING

- Look for evidence that children can hear and divide onset and rimes.
- Notice how well children can use words they know to help spell new words.
- Notice whether children can identify some consonant and vowel sounds in words.

INTERACTIVE WRITING LESSON

This lesson is designed to use interactive writing to record observations about objects that float and sink, but use any experiment that you have done with the class. Make sure children understand *sink* and *float* as used in this lesson.

Establish Purpose

Talk about the science experiment that the children conducted.

> In our experiment, we tested objects to see if they float or sink. We can write our scientific observations. Our observations are what we noticed when we did the experiment.

Talk About What to Write

Talk about which objects floated and which objects sank.

- Create two labeled columns (*Sink, Float*) on chart paper. Then display one of the objects that you used in the experiment (e.g., a block).

  > Did the block float or sink?

  > The block sank. We can write *Block* under the word *Sink*.

Write Together

Create a chart. When you invite a child to share the pen by writing a letter, engage the others by having them form the letter in the air or on the carpet.

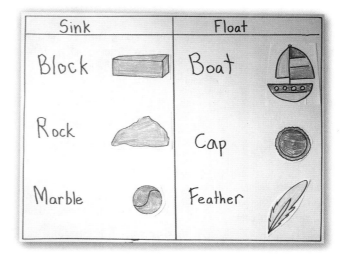

> The first word that we will write on our chart is *Block.* Say it with me slowly: *Block.* What's the first sound you hear in *Block*?

> What is the letter that goes with that sound? The letter is *B.* Do you know any other words or names that start with *B*?

▶ Use the verbal path to guide a volunteer to write the letter *B.*

▶ Write the rest of the word *Block.*

> Did the rock sink or float?

> *Block* and *Rock* have different sounds at the beginning, but they both end with the same sound: /ock/. We can break *Block* down into /bl/ /ock/ and *Rock* into /r/ /ock/. We already know how to write *Block,* so we can figure out how to write *Rock.* What sound does *Rock* start with?

> *Rock* starts with /r/. The letter that goes with that sound is *R.*

▶ Invite a volunteer to write at least the letter *R.*

▶ Continue by holding up each item and asking children in which column to write the word. Invite several children to write letters for easy-to-hear sounds such as *M* or *F.*

Read and Revisit

Invite the children to read the chart with you as you point under the words. You might have children revisit the text for one or both of the following reasons.

▶ Ask children to identify the words that end the same way (*Block/Rock, Float/Boat*).

▶ Ask children to identify consonants (e.g., *s, b, r*) and vowels (e.g., *i, a, o*).

Summarize and Invite/Extend

Summarize the lesson. You might also decide to extend the learning.

> Today we wrote like scientists. We wrote scientific observations.

▶ Work with children to add illustrations to the chart.

▶ Choose other objects to test. Ask children to predict which will sink and which will float and to explain their predictions.

Section 1: Interactive Writing

You Will Need

- a familiar book that has interesting characters who learn something, such as *Three Hens and a Peacock* by Lester L. Laminack, from *Fountas & Pinnell Classroom™ Interactive Read-Aloud Collection* Text Set: Learning How to Be Yourself

- chart paper and markers

- To download the following online resources for this lesson, visit **resources.fountasandpinnell.com**:
  - Alphabet Linking Chart
  - High-Frequency Word List

Academic Language/ Important Vocabulary

- letter
- character
- sound

Continuum Connection

- Draw or write about how a character might have changed or learned a lesson (p. 173)

- Understand and talk about the concept of a word (p. 365)

- Locate and read high-frequency words in continuous text (p. 366)

- Read and write approximately twenty-five high-frequency words (p. 366)

- Recognize and use more common phonograms with a VC pattern: *-ab, -ad, -ag, -am, -an, -ap, -at, -aw, -ay; -ed, -en, -et, -ew; -id, -ig, -im, -in, -ip, -it; -ob, -od, -og, -op, -ot, -ow* (as in *show* or as in *cow*); *-ub, -ug, -um, -un, -ut* (p. 366)

ACTIVE LEARNING EXPERIENCE

▶ Read and have rich conversations about books with interesting characters who learn something, such as *Three Hens and a Peacock*.

GOALS

▶ Understand that readers write letters to share their thinking about a character in a book.

▶ Locate and read high-frequency words in continuous text.

▶ Read and write several high-frequency words in continuous text.

RATIONALE

▶ When children write about books they have read, they develop a deeper understanding of the text while recognizing that they can use writing to share their thinking with others.

ASSESS LEARNING

▶ Look for evidence that children understand that writing can be used to share their thinking about a book.

▶ Take note of which high-frequency words children know how to read and write.

INTERACTIVE WRITING LESSON

For this lesson, use any story with rich characters that learn a lesson. If you have *The Reading Minilessons Book, Kindergarten* (Fountas and Pinnell 2019), you might teach any of the Literary Analysis umbrellas about characters (Umbrellas 14, 15, and 16) as a foundation for this lesson.

Establish Purpose

Decide how to share thinking about a book that has been shared.

> When we read *Three Hens and a Peacock*, you talked about your thinking. Another way to share your thinking is by writing a letter. Let's write a letter to another class to share your thinking about this book.

Talk About What to Write

Plan what to write in the letter.

▶ Have the children focus their thinking on how a character changed (e.g., the peacock learned to be helpful by switching to a job just right for him).

> What do you remember about the peacock in this book? How did he change?

> In the letter, what should we write about how the peacock changed?

Write Together

Write the letter by inviting several children to write easy high-frequency words they are learning. Engage the others by having them write the words in the air or on the carpet.

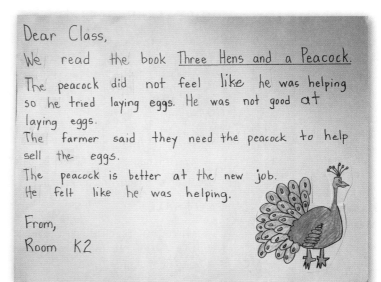

Dear Class,
We read the book <u>Three Hens and a Peacock.</u>
The peacock did not feel like he was helping so he tried laying eggs. He was not good at laying eggs.
The farmer said they need the peacock to help sell the eggs.
The peacock is better at the new job.
He felt like he was helping.

From,
Room K2

- Write the salutation and the first sentence, thinking aloud as you do.

    First, we write *Dear Class*, so we know to whom we are writing. Next, we can tell the readers what book we read.

- Have in mind several high-frequency words (e.g., *we, the, like, he, so, at*) that children are learning and could contribute as well as some easy-to-hear initial and final sounds in words. If you have a word wall with any of the words, point them out as they come up in the letter.

    The first word is *We*. That's a word you know. Who would like to write *We*?

- Continue writing the letter, pausing before several more high-frequency words that children could write.

- Explain that a letter ends with a closing that tells whom the letter is from.

Read and Revisit

Read the sentences with children, using a pointer to point under each word. You might have children revisit the letter for one or both of the following reasons.

- Help children use what they know about *not* and *at* to make other words (e.g., *dot*, *hot*; *cat*, *hat*).

- Help children notice that some words have few letters and some words have more letters by having them identify little words and big words.

Summarize and Apply/Extend

Summarize the lesson. You might also decide to extend the learning.

    We wrote a letter about a book we read.

- Have children illustrate the letter.

- Have children write their own letters about books they have read.

You Will Need

- several informational nonfiction books including at least one about plants, such as *A Fruit Is a Suitcase for Seeds* by Jean Richards, from *Fountas & Pinnell Classroom™ Interactive Read-Aloud Collection* Text Set: Exploring Nonfiction

- chart paper and markers

- To download the following online resources for this lesson, visit **resources.fountasandpinnell.com**:
  - Alphabet Linking Chart
  - Verbal Path for Letter Formation

Academic Language/ Important Vocabulary

- all-about book
- page
- letter
- word
- sentence

Continuum Connection

- Understand how to write a factual text from listening to mentor texts read aloud and discussing them (p. 245)

- Say words slowly to hear a sound and write a letter that represents it (p. 248)

- Use simple resources to help in spelling words or check on spelling (word walls, personal word lists) (p. 248)

- Hear, say, and clap syllables: e.g., *farm, be/fore, a/ni/mal* (p. 365)

ACTIVE LEARNING EXPERIENCE

- Prior to the lesson, read aloud and enjoy several informational nonfiction books. Then choose one topic to focus on in particular. This lesson uses plants as an example, but you can choose any topic that interests the children. Read books about plants aloud and engage children in a discussion about what they know about plants.

GOAL

- Listen for a sound in a word and write a letter to represent it.
- Use the name chart, ABC chart, and word wall as a resource for spelling.
- Hear, say, clap, and use syllables to write multisyllable words.

RATIONALE

- When you help children write an all-about book, you demonstrate that writing can be used to share information. Children also begin to understand the difference between fiction and nonfiction.

ASSESS LEARNING

- Notice whether children can identify and record some sounds in a word.
- Observe whether children use classroom resources to help them with spelling.
- Notice whether children can identify and clap syllables.

INTERACTIVE WRITING LESSON

This lesson results in a book all about plants, but make the book about whatever the children in your class have been reading and learning. Make as many pages of the book as children can manage in one sitting. Continue the book across the next day or two.

Establish Purpose

Display some of the nonfiction books that you have read aloud.

> The authors wrote about what they know a lot about. We can make a book about something we know a lot about. Let's write a book about plants. We can name our book *All About Plants*.

- Write the title on the cover of the book.

Talk About What to Write

Plan what to write on at least the first page of the book.

> What have you learned about plants?
>
> What could we write about plants on the first page of our book?

Write Together

Write the text for the all-about book. When you invite one child to share the pen by writing a letter, keep the others engaged by having them find the letter on the ABC chart.

> The first word in our sentence is *Plants.*
>
> Say *Plants* with me slowly. What sound do you hear at the beginning of *Plants*?
>
> *Plants* begins with /p/, which we write with the letter *P.* Who has the letter *p* in your name?

▶ Point to *P* on the ABC chart or name chart. Invite a volunteer to come to the chart to write the letter.

> To make a *P,* pull down, up, and around.

▶ Write the rest of the word. Continue in a similar manner with *n* and *d* in *need.*

▶ Ask a child to write *w* in *water.* As you write the rest of the word, have children clap the syllables.

▶ Invite a child to write the high-frequency word *and.* Finish writing the sentence, having children clap the syllables as you write *sunlight.*

▶ Continue using the interactive writing process to make several pages for the book. Together, read each page as it is finished.

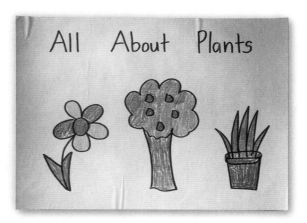

Read and Revisit

Invite the children to read the all-about book with you as you point under each word. You might have children revisit the text for one or both of the following reasons.

▶ Point to individual letters and have children identify them.

▶ Ask children to point to words that contain, for example, the letter *a.*

Summarize and Invite/Extend

Summarize the lesson and invite children to make their own all-about books.

> We made an all-about book to share what we know about plants. What would you like to make your own all-about book about?

▶ Invite children to illustrate the book. Make the finished book available to children.

▶ Provide blank books for children to make their own all-about books.

You Will Need

- a familiar book that uses rhythm, such as *Mary Wore Her Red Dress and Henry Wore His Green Sneakers* by Merle Peek, from *Fountas & Pinnell Classroom™ Interactive Read-Aloud Collection* Text Set: Rhythm and Rhyme: Joyful Language
- chart paper and markers
- name chart (see IW.1)
- color chart (see IW.9)
- To download the following online resource for this lesson, visit **resources.fountasandpinnell.com**:
  - High-Frequency Word List

Academic Language / Important Vocabulary

- letter
- sound
- name
- color

Continuum Connection

- Compose innovations on very familiar texts by changing the ending, the series of events, characters, or the setting (p. 173)
- Recognize, point to, and say the same beginning consonant sound and the letter that represents the sound: e.g., *bag*, *bee* (p. 365)
- Use known words to help spell an unknown word (p. 366)
- Read and write approximately twenty-five high-frequency words (p. 366)
- Hear, say, and clap syllables: e.g. *farm*, *be/fore*, *a/ni/mal* (p. 365)

ACTIVE LEARNING EXPERIENCE

- Read and enjoy books with rhythm and rhyme, such as those in the Rhythm and Rhyme: Joyful Language text set. Prior to the lesson, read *Mary Wore Her Red Dress and Henry Wore His Green Sneakers* enough times that children can recite it along with you.

GOALS

- Recognize, point to, and say the same beginning consonant sound and the letter that represents the sound.
- Hear, say, clap, and use syllables to write multisyllable words.

RATIONALE

- When children innovate on a text by inserting their own names into a familiar poem or song, they discover early concepts of print such as letter formation, saying words slowly to listen for consonant sounds, and recognizing high-frequency words. For this lesson, the text of the story will be changed slightly to use the pattern _____ *is wearing* _____ so that children can gain experience recognizing *is* (a high-frequency word).

ASSESS LEARNING

- Notice whether children participate in composing innovations on a familiar text.
- Observe whether children can recognize and write letters of beginning consonant sounds.
- Observe children's ability to hear and clap syllables.

INTERACTIVE WRITING LESSON

This lesson is designed as an interactive writing lesson in which you and the children will compose the text together and share the pen. Alternatively, you might choose to do all the writing yourself (shared writing).

Establish Purpose

- Show *Mary Wore Her Red Dress and Henry Wore His Green Sneakers*.

  Writers can use books as ideas for writing. We can write our own version of *Mary Wore Her Red Dress and Henry Wore His Green Sneakers*.

Talk About What to Write

Plan what to write in the new version of the text.

- Have the children talk about using their own names and the colors of the items they are wearing to write a new version.

  Robert is wearing a red shirt, so we could write *Robert is wearing a red shirt, red shirt, red shirt.* What else could we write?

Write Together

Begin writing the new text. As one child writes a word or letter, engage the others by having them find the names on the name chart and the colors on the color chart.

> *Robert* and *red* both begin with *r.*

▶ Have Robert write his name.

> You know the next word, *is*, so I will write it quickly.

▶ As you write *wearing*, have children clap the syllables.

> Who can write the word *red*?

▶ After a child writes *red*, finish writing the first sentence. Then read it aloud.

> *Red* looks the same here as it does on the color chart. What is our next sentence?

▶ Have Nora write her name. Write *is wearing* and then pause before *purple*.

> *Purple* is a long word. Let's clap it. It has two parts.

> What do you notice about how *purple* and *pants* begin?

▶ Ask a child to write the *p* in *purple* and *pants*. Finish the words yourself.

▶ Continue in this way, adding a few more sentences and asking one or two more volunteers to share the pen. You might have them write the color words.

Read and Revisit

Ask the children to read the sentences with you as you point under each word. You might have children revisit the text for one or both of the following reasons.

▶ Say and clap the syllables of other multisyllable words, such as *yellow.*

▶ Have several children point to the word *is*. Ask children where they can look to make sure *is* is spelled correctly (e.g., High-Frequency Word List, word wall).

Summarize and Invite/Extend

Summarize the lesson. You might also decide to extend the learning.

> Today we wrote our own version of a chant by using some of your names.

▶ Have children add an illustration for each sentence in the text.

▶ Innovate on the text of another familiar poem or song.

Section 1: Interactive Writing

Interactive writing is a way to provide modeling and support for children as you introduce them to the idea of making their own books. Below is a complete how-to book that shows what is possible when you show children what they can do. Once a class book is complete, it can be used for shared reading and as a mentor text when children make their own similar books.

1. Put two flat blocks on the floor.

2. Lay two blocks on top going the other way.

3. Keep doing step 2.

4. Make it tall!

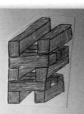

Section 2 | Management

MANAGEMENT MINILESSONS WILL help you set up routines for playing, learning, and working together in the classroom. They allow you to teach effectively and efficiently and are directed toward the creation of an orderly, busy classroom in which children know what is expected and how to behave responsibly and respectfully in a community of learners. A class that has a strong feeling of community is a safe place for all children to do their best work, and have fun. Most of the minilessons at the beginning of the school year will come from this section.

2 Management

Minilessons in This Umbrella

WML1 Get to know your classmates.

WML2 Use an appropriate voice level.

WML3 Move from one spot to another quickly and silently.

WML4 Turn and talk to share your thinking with others.

WML5 Listen carefully to each other.

WML6 Do your best work.

WML7 Find ways to solve problems when you need help.

WML8 Take good care of classroom materials.

Before Teaching Umbrella 1 Minilessons

This set of minilessons helps you establish a respectful and organized classroom community. If you use *The Reading Minilessons Book, Kindergarten* (Fountas and Pinnell 2019) and have already taught the first Management umbrella, you do not need to teach this umbrella.

After teaching each minilesson, provide a drawing and writing activity so that children have something to do for about ten minutes as they apply what they have learned about working together. MGT.U1.WML1 asks children to make an identity web. The web could be continued for another day or two. On subsequent days, children could be asked to draw and write about their families, their friends, what they like to do at home or school, or places they like to go.

We recommend that toward the middle or end of this umbrella, you teach IW.2: Making a Class Agreement. In addition to explicitly teaching routines through minilessons, encourage children to communicate their thinking through drawing and writing following interactive read-aloud. Read books from your own library or use books from *Fountas & Pinnell Classroom™ Interactive Read-Aloud Collection* text sets about what it means to be part of a caring community.

Interactive Read-Aloud Collection

Sharing Stories and Songs: Nursery Rhymes

I'm a Little Teapot as told by Iza Trapani

Baa Baa Black Sheep as told by Iza Trapani

Interactive Read-Aloud
Nursery Rhymes

Section 2: Management

Writing Minilesson Principle
Get to know your classmates.

Working Together in the Classroom

You Will Need

- chart paper prepared with a sketch or photo of yourself and a web of details to help children get to know you
- chart paper and markers
- To download the following online resource for this lesson, visit **resources.fountasandpinnell.com**:
  - chart art (optional)

Academic Language / Important Vocabulary

- community
- proud
- special
- unique

GOAL

Learn to value one another's unique identities as part of a community of learners.

RATIONALE

When children learn to value the unique identities of others and embrace diversity, you create a rich, interesting classroom community in which children feel comfortable expressing themselves in writing.

ASSESS LEARNING

- Observe whether children show an interest in getting to know classmates.
- Look for evidence that children are sharing details about themselves.
- Observe for evidence that children can use vocabulary such as *community*, *proud*, *special*, and *unique*.

MINILESSON

Engage children in a conversation about getting to know one another using a web with a sketch or photograph of yourself. Then provide a lesson to help children brainstorm ways to get to know each other. Here is an example.

- Show the prepared chart and read the words to children.

  What do you notice that I have done here?

  I made a web to show you information about me. I want you to get to know things about me. What kinds of things did I share about myself?

- As children respond, use a clean sheet of chart paper to make a web of general categories.

  What other things could we tell each other to get to know each other?

- Continue adding to the chart.

  How will getting to know each other make our classroom community a better place?

- Guide children to understand that sharing things that make them proud, special, and unique allows classmates to learn about each other. Help them understand that when they know each other, they feel more comfortable sharing and helping each other.

Have a Try

Invite children to turn and talk to get to know each other.

> Choose one of the things on the chart to talk about to your partner.

▶ After time for discussion, ask a few volunteers to share what they learned about their partners.

Summarize and Apply

Summarize the lesson. Invite children to make their own webs during writing time.

▶ Write the principle on the chart and read it aloud.

> Today you learned ways to get to know your classmates so you can enjoy and appreciate each other. During writing time, draw a picture of yourself and add drawings and words to show ways you are special and unique. Bring your web to share when we meet later.

▶ Alternatively, instead of having children draw themselves, you might take a photo of each child to use for the center of the web.

Confer

▶ During independent writing, move around the room to confer briefly with as many individual children as time allows. Sit side by side with them and invite them to talk about their webs. Use the following prompts as needed.

- *What is something you are proud of?*
- *What makes you special?*
- *What makes your family special?*
- *What is your favorite thing to do with your family?*

Share

Following independent writing, gather children in the meeting area to share something about themselves.

> What did you draw or write about yourself today? Share something to show how special you are.

Writing Minilesson Principle
Use an appropriate voice level.

Working Together in the Classroom

You Will Need

- sticky notes
- chart paper and markers
- To download the following online resource for this lesson, visit **resources.fountasandpinnell.com**:
  - chart art (optional)

Academic Language / Important Vocabulary

- voice level
- appropriate

Continuum Connection

- Speak at an appropriate volume (p. 331)

GOAL

Learn to monitor appropriate voice volume.

RATIONALE

Voice volume needs to be taught explicitly so that children are able to independently determine the acceptable noise level for various settings, routines, and activities both inside and outside of the classroom.

ASSESS LEARNING

- Observe whether children can identify appropriate activities for each voice level.
- Look for evidence that children are able to use the appropriate voice level during independent writing.
- Observe for evidence that children can use vocabulary such as *voice level* and *appropriate*.

MINILESSON

To help children think about the minilesson principle, engage them in a conversation about voice levels and constructing a reference chart. Here is an example.

- Talk about why you use a loud voice sometimes and a soft voice sometimes.

  One way to help each other do your best work in our classroom is to use a good voice for the activity you are doing. For example, when you are outside for recess, would you use a loud voice or a soft voice?

  When you are drawing and writing, how might your voice sound?

  We can talk about the kind of voice to use by using a number. A zero voice means you are silent; you are not saying anything.

- Write the word *silent* on the chart and a speech bubble with *SHHH*. Write the numeral *0* on a sticky note. Ask a child to place the sticky note next to the word on the chart.

- Repeat the procedure for each voice level on the chart. Show that a *1* means whispering, a *2* means using a soft voice, and a *3* means using a loud voice.

Have a Try

Invite children to turn and talk about voice level.

▶ Call out a voice level number and have the children practice by saying *hello* using the appropriate voice level.

Summarize and Apply

Summarize the learning. Have the children practice using the appropriate voice level in an actual learning situation.

> Look at the chart. What does it show you about which voice level to use?

▶ Add the principle to the top of the chart and read it aloud.

> During writing time, think about the appropriate voice level for the activity you are doing and practice using that voice level.

▶ Keep the voice level chart posted so children can refer to it.

Confer

▶ During independent writing time, move around the room to confer briefly with as many individual children as time allows. Sit side by side with them and invite them to talk about using an appropriate voice level. Use the following prompts as needed.

- *What are you working on?*
- *What voice level are you using?*
- *Why is it important to use a zero level voice when you are writing independently?*
- *What voice level will you use when you share your writing?*

Share

Following independent writing, gather children in the meeting area to share how they used appropriate voice levels.

> Talk about what voice levels you used today at different times.

Section 2: Management

Writing Minilesson Principle
Move from one spot to another quickly and silently.

Working Together in the Classroom

You Will Need

- three children prepared in advance to demonstrate the principle
- voice level chart from WML2
- chart paper and markers
- To download the following online resource for this lesson, visit **resources.fountasandpinnell.com**:
  - chart art (optional)

Academic Language / Important Vocabulary

- meeting area

GOAL

Learn routines for classroom transitions.

RATIONALE

Setting clear expectations for transitions in the classroom increases time spent on learning.

ASSESS LEARNING

- ▶ Observe whether children are able to describe how to move during transitions.
- ▶ Look for evidence that children can identify the appropriate voice level for moving around the classroom.
- ▶ Observe for evidence that children can use vocabulary such as *meeting area*.

MINILESSON

To help children think about the minilesson principle, engage them in a demonstration and discussion of transitions. Here is an example.

> You do your work in many different places in the classroom. Sometimes you sit at tables. Sometimes everyone comes to the meeting area. Why should you move (but not run) quickly and silently when you move from one place to another?
>
> Why is it helpful to sit in your own spot?

▶ Invite three volunteers to demonstrate.

> We are going to watch _____, _____, and _____ walk from the meeting area back to the writing area. Remember to walk quickly and silently, but do not run.

▶ After time for the demonstration, talk about what they did. As children discuss, record each step of the transition process on chart paper.

> How did they walk?

▶ Point to the voice chart.

> Look at the voice chart. What voice level did they use when they moved?

▶ Ask the volunteers to return to the meeting area.

> Where did they put their hands and feet when they sat down in their spots?

▶ Record responses.

The Writing Minilessons Book, Kindergarten

Have a Try

Invite children to apply the new thinking about moving from one spot to another.

> Now everyone will have a chance to practice moving about the classroom.

▶ Have children participate in various common transitions.

Summarize and Apply

Help children summarize the lesson. Remind them to practice what they learned when they move about the classroom.

> How should you move from one spot to another in the classroom? Did you do that when you practiced?

▶ Add the principle to the top of the chart and read it aloud.

> Today, think about how you will move around the classroom as you get your materials for writing time.

> Move from one spot to another quickly and silently.

> Walk quickly, but do not run.

> Use a 0 level voice.

> Keep your hands and feet in your own space.

Confer

▶ During independent writing, move around the room to confer briefly with as many individual children as time allows. Sit side by side with them and invite them to talk about how they move from one spot to another. Use the following prompts as needed.

· *What are you working on?*

· *How did you move to the writing center today?*

· *If you need drawing and writing materials, how will you move to get them?*

Share

Following independent writing, gather children in the meeting area to talk about how they moved about the classroom.

> Tell how you moved about the classroom today.

> Why is it important that you move quickly and silently in the classroom?

Writing Minilesson Principle
Turn and talk to share your thinking with others.

Working Together in the Classroom

You Will Need

- one or two familiar texts that children enjoy, such as *I'm a Little Teapot* and *Baa Baa Black Sheep* as told by Iza Trapani, from Text Set: Sharing Stories and Songs: Nursery Rhymes
- chart paper and markers
- To download the following online resource for this lesson, visit **resources.fountasandpinnell.com**:
  - chart art (optional)

Academic Language / Important Vocabulary

- turn and talk

Continuum Connection

- Engage actively in conversational routines: e.g., turn and talk in pairs, triads (p. 331)

GOAL

Develop guidelines for the routine of turn and talk.

RATIONALE

Turn and talk is a technique that provides all children an opportunity to articulate their thinking and engage in conversation with others. When you establish clear guidelines for the procedure, you allow every child the opportunity to practice thinking and speaking in a comfortable situation.

ASSESS LEARNING

- Observe whether children actively listen to one another when they turn and talk.
- Notice whether children take turns, make eye contact, and use body language to show they are listening.
- Observe for evidence that children can use vocabulary such as *turn and talk*.

MINILESSON

To help children think about the minilesson principle, choose familiar texts to use in a demonstration and discussion of turning and talking. As an alternative, you could use child-made drawings or writing samples to practice the turn and talk procedures. Here is an example.

- Show the front cover of *I'm a Little Teapot* or a child's drawing or writing sample.

  Sometimes when you read a book or draw or write something, you turn and talk to a partner about your thinking. When you share your thinking with a partner, everyone gets to talk.

- Ask for a volunteer to talk to you about something interesting about the book or writing sample.

  While we turn and talk, notice what we are doing with our bodies and voices.

- Briefly model the turn and talk procedure, making sure to face your partner, look at your partner, listen to your partner, wait for your partner to finish speaking before you speak, and so forth. However, take into consideration that some children may not be comfortable with establishing or able to establish eye contact because of cultural conventions or for other reasons,

  What did you notice about the way we turned and talked to each other?

- List children's responses on chart paper to create guidelines for turn and talk.

Have a Try

Invite children to apply the new thinking with a partner.

▶ Show the cover of *Baa Baa Black Sheep* or a child's drawing or writing sample.

> Turn and talk to your partner about what you notice or find interesting.

▶ After time for discussion, have children review the chart and give themselves a thumbs-up or thumbs-down for each action.

Summarize and Apply

Summarize the lesson. Remind children to think about what to do when they turn and talk.

> Today you learned a way to share your thinking with others. You learned to turn and talk.

▶ Write the principle on the chart and read it aloud.

> During writing time today, draw or write something you found interesting from a story. Later, you will turn and talk to share your drawing or writing with a partner.

> **Turn and talk to share your thinking with others.**
>
> Turn to your partner.
>
> Look at your partner.
>
> Wait for your partner to finish talking.
>
> Use a soft voice.
>
> Listen to your partner's thinking.
>
> Stop talking and turn back when the teacher signals.

Confer

▶ During independent writing, move around the room to confer briefly with as many individual children as time allows. Sit side by side with them and invite them to talk about sharing their thinking. Use the following prompts as needed.

- *What would you like to draw or write today? You will be sharing it with a partner.*
- *What voice level will you use when you share your drawing with a partner?*
- *Why is it important to look at your partner when you turn and talk?*

Share

Following independent writing, gather children in the meeting area. Have them bring the drawing or writing they worked on today so that they can share it with partners.

> What do you remember about how to turn and talk to a partner?

> Turn and talk to your partner to share your drawing or writing. Look at the chart to remember how to turn and talk.

Section 2: Management

Working Together in the Classroom

You Will Need

- voice level chart from WML2
- chart paper and markers
- To download the following online resource for this lesson, visit **resources.fountasandpinnell.com**:
  - chart art (optional)

Academic Language / Important Vocabulary

- listen
- meeting area
- small group
- whole group

Continuum Connection

- Look at the speaker when being spoken to (p. 331)
- Speak at an appropriate volume (p. 331)

GOAL

Learn expectations for listening during small- or whole-group meetings.

RATIONALE

When children listen to classmates during small- or whole-group instruction, they become effective communicators and collaborators.

ASSESS LEARNING

- Observe whether children understand why it is important to listen to each other and the teacher.
- Look for evidence that children follow the classroom expectations for listening carefully.
- Observe for evidence that children can use vocabulary such as *listen*, *meeting area*, *small group*, and *whole group*.

MINILESSON

To help children think about the minilesson principle, engage them in discussing effective listening behaviors. Here is an example.

> When one person in the classroom is talking, the rest of the people are listening. What does it look like to be a good listener in the classroom?

- Guide the conversation to help children talk about what a good listener looks and sounds like. Show the voice level chart from WML2 to help children make the connection between voice level and listening. Prompt the conversation as needed with questions such as the following.
  - *When a classmate is speaking, what are you doing?*
  - *What do you do when you have a question?*
  - *Which voice level should the person who is listening use?*
  - *What does listening in a small group (whole group) look and sound like?*

- As children provide ideas, create guidelines on chart paper for how to be a good listener. If children mention that it's important to look at the speaker, take into consideration that some children may not be comfortable with establishing or able to establish eye contact because of cultural conventions or other reasons.

- Post the chart to help children remember to listen carefully to each other.

Have a Try

Invite children to turn and talk about how to listen carefully.

> Turn and talk to your partner about something you will do the next time you listen to someone speak during a group meeting.

▶ Ask a few volunteers to share. Add new ideas to the chart.

Summarize and Apply

Summarize the lesson and write the principle on the chart. Remind children to listen carefully to each other.

> What are some ways to show that you are listening carefully? Look at the chart to remember. During writing time today, be a good listener when someone else is speaking.

Confer

▶ During independent writing, move around the room to confer briefly with as many individual children as time allows. Sit side by side with them and invite them to talk about how they are listening carefully. Use the following prompts as needed.

- *What are you working on today?*
- *When your friends share something, why is it important for you to be a good listener?*
- *How will you show you are listening carefully?*

Share

Following independent writing, gather children in the meeting area to talk about when they listened carefully to a classmate.

> Tell about a time you listened carefully today.

WML6

Writing Minilesson Principle
Do your best work.

Working Together in the Classroom

You Will Need

- four children prepared in advance to demonstrate the principle
- paper, pencils, and crayons
- chart paper and markers
- To download the following online resource for this lesson, visit **resources.fountasandpinnell.com**:
  - chart art (optional)

Academic Language / Important Vocabulary

- best
- classmates
- goals
- focus

GOAL

Learn ways to work well in the class.

RATIONALE

When you explicitly teach children to begin working promptly, work quietly, stay focused, and follow directions, you promote independence. Setting the foundation early for independent work frees you to work effectively with children individually and in small groups.

ASSESS LEARNING

- Observe whether children can articulate a goal for doing their best work.
- Look for evidence that children are able to follow directions and work quietly.
- Observe for evidence that children can use vocabulary such as *best*, *classmates*, *goals*, and *focus*.

MINILESSON

To help children think about the minilesson principle, engage them in a demonstration and discussion of how to do their best work. Here is an example.

> The work you do by yourself is important. Watch as your classmates do their best work.

- Give directions to the four children you have prepared in advance to go to the writing area and start writing or drawing. Have the rest of the class observe just long enough to see the four children follow directions, begin promptly, work quietly, and stay focused. Call the four children back to the meeting area, allowing others to observe how they put materials away and then move silently and quickly as they return.

> What did you notice about how your classmates did their work?

- Guide children to notice the behaviors, such as getting to work quickly, working quietly, following directions, and staying focused.
- Record responses on chart paper.

Have a Try

Invite children to turn and talk about how they can do their best learning.

> Think about what you need to practice the most. Turn and talk to your partner about your goal for doing your best work. A goal is something you try to do. You can start by saying "I am going to try to _____."

▷ After time for discussion, ask a few volunteers to share.

Summarize and Apply

Write the principle on the chart. Remind children to do their best work by reviewing the chart.

> During writing time today, you can practice all the ways to do your best work. You can look at the chart to remember.

Confer

▷ During independent writing, move around the room to confer briefly with as many individual children as time allows. Sit side by side with them and invite them to talk about how they are doing their best work. Use the following prompts as needed.

- *How can you do your best work today?*
- *What are you doing right now to do your best work?*
- *How can you show that you are following directions during writing time?*

Share

Following independent writing, gather children in the meeting area. Invite a few children to talk about how they did their best work. To support children's oral language, provide a sentence frame as needed: *Today I tried _____ to do my best work*.

> Who did your best work today? Tell about what you did to meet your goals.

> Do your best work.

 Begin right away.

 Work quietly.

 Stay focused.

 Follow directions.

Best Work

Writing Minilesson Principle

Find ways to solve problems when you need help.

Working Together in the Classroom

You Will Need

- chart paper and markers
- To download the following online resource for this lesson, visit **resources.fountasandpinnell.com**:
  - chart art (optional)

Academic Language / Important Vocabulary

- directions
- word wall
- classmate

GOAL

Learn how to problem solve independently.

RATIONALE

When children learn how to problem solve independently, they gain confidence. It also allows you to work with small groups of individuals without interruption.

ASSESS LEARNING

- Observe whether children are independently trying one or two ideas for problem solving.
- Look for evidence that children are choosing appropriate solutions to problems.
- Observe for evidence that children can use vocabulary such as *directions*, *word wall*, and *classmate*.

MINILESSON

To help children think about the minilesson principle, engage them in a discussion of how to problem solve independently. Here is an example.

> Sometimes when you are working, you may need help. When I am talking to another child or working with a group, I may not be available to help you right away.

> What are some things you can do to get help on your own?

- Record ideas on chart paper. If children have trouble generating ideas, help them think through different scenarios. For example, if they do not know how to spell a word, where could they look to find out? Guide them to think of resources in the room (e.g., word wall) they can use and to understand that they can ask a classmate or, as a last resort, you.

> If you have done some of your work and are stuck, what could you do while you are waiting for help?

Have a Try

Invite children to turn and talk to a partner about problem solving.

> Imagine that you finish with your work and do not know what to next. How can you solve the problem? Turn and talk about that.

▶ After time for discussion, ask a few volunteers to share ideas.

Summarize and Apply

Help children summarize the lesson. Remind children to try to solve problems on their own.

> What does the chart help you know how to do?

▶ Write the principle on the chart and read it aloud.

> When you are working on your writing today, try to solve any problem you have by yourself, ask a classmate, or do your best until I can help you.

Find ways to solve problems when you need help.

Reread the directions.

Use the word wall.

Ask a classmate in a soft voice.

Ask the teacher when he is not busy.

Confer

▶ During independent writing, move around the room to confer briefly with as many individual children as time allows. Sit side by side with them and invite them to talk about finding ways to solve problems on their own. Use the following prompts as needed.

- *What are you working on today?*
- *What can you do if you forget how to write your name on your paper?*
- *What can you do if you don't know how to write a word?*
- *If you need to cut some paper, but cannot find the scissors, what can you do?*

Share

Following independent writing, gather children in the meeting area. Ask a few children to share their experiences solving problems.

> Did you solve a problem today? Tell about what you did.

Writing Minilesson Principle
Take good care of classroom materials.

Working Together in the Classroom

You Will Need

- two children prepared in advance to demonstrate the principle
- materials for activity in meeting area
- chart paper and markers
- To download the following online resource for this lesson, visit **resources.fountasandpinnell.com**:
  - chart art (optional)

Academic Language / Important Vocabulary

- take good care
- materials

GOAL

Learn to take care of and return materials and supplies independently.

RATIONALE

When you teach children how to take care of materials and return them to the same place, they learn responsibility and independence so that others can use materials when they need them.

ASSESS LEARNING

- Observe whether children take good care of classroom materials.
- Look for evidence that children are able to get supplies and return them to the appropriate place.
- Observe for evidence that children can use vocabulary such as *take good care* and *materials*.

MINILESSON

To help children think about the minilesson principle, engage them in a demonstration and discussion of the different materials they use, where to find them, and how to care for them. Here is an example.

> What are some of the materials you use to draw and write in the classroom?

> Watch _____ and _____ get the materials they need to do their work. Pay attention to what they do with the materials when they finish working.

- Provide a few minutes for the children to demonstrate getting, using, and returning the supplies. Point out that the materials are labeled at the place they belong. Guide the children to understand how to take good care of the materials.

> What did you notice?

> How did your classmates take good care of the materials when they used them?

- Add responses to chart paper. If you have shelves and materials boxes labeled, show children how to match a materials box to its label on the shelf.

> How should the classroom sound when you are cleaning up? At the end of writing time, return materials quickly and quietly.

Have a Try

Invite children to practice taking care of classroom materials.

▶ Ask a few more children to model taking out different drawing and writing supplies and returning them. Have them explain how they can take care of the materials when they use them.

Summarize and Apply

Summarize the lesson. Remind children to take good care of classroom materials during writing time.

> Today you learned to get, care for, and return materials to the place where they belong so others can use them.

▶ Write the principle on the chart and read it aloud.

> During writing time, remember to take good care of the materials.

Take good care of classroom materials.

* Get your materials.

* Use them carefully.

* Put materials back in the same place quickly and quietly.

Confer

▶ During independent writing, move around the room to confer briefly with as many individual children as time allows. Sit side by side with them and invite them to talk about taking good care of classroom materials. Use the following prompts as needed.

- *What do you need to color your drawing? Where will you find it?*
- *What writing materials will you use today? How will you use them?*
- *How can you show that you are taking care of these materials?*
- *What will you do with the markers when you finish using them?*

Share

Following independent writing, gather children in the meeting area. Ask a few children to share what they did to take care of materials.

> Tell what you did to take good care of classroom materials today.

Assessment

After you have taught the minilessons in this umbrella, observe children in a variety of classroom activities. Use *The Literacy Continuum* (Fountas and Pinnell 2017) to notice, teach for, and support children's learning as you observe their attempts at building a classroom community.

▶ What evidence do you have of new understandings children have developed related to working together in the classroom community?

- Are children showing an interest in getting to know each other?
- Are they easily finding their spots in the meeting area?
- Do they actively listen when the teacher and classmates are speaking?
- Do they move quickly and quietly from one place to another?
- Do they follow the procedures for turn and talk?
- Do they start new work right away and stay focused?
- In what ways are they able to solve problems without your help?
- Are they returning materials and supplies and keeping the classroom clean and organized?
- Are they using vocabulary such as *community*, *unique*, *voice level*, *appropriate*, *meeting area*, *listen*, *small group*, *whole group*, *turn and talk*, *best*, *classmates*, *goals*, *focus*, *directions*, *word wall*, *take good care*, and *materials*?

▶ In what ways, beyond the scope of this umbrella, are children showing an understanding of building a positive classroom community?

- Do they treat each other with respect when in the play and work centers?
- Are they able to work on their writing independently?

Use your observations to determine the next umbrella you will teach. You may also consult Suggested Sequence of Lessons (pp. 483–494) for guidance.

EXTENSIONS FOR WORKING TOGETHER IN THE CLASSROOM

▶ From time to time, have children role-play different classroom activities to show how responsible classroom community members act. This is especially important as new children join the classroom community.

▶ Repeat minilessons throughout the year as needed to promote positive community behaviors.

Minilessons in This Umbrella

WML1   Get started on your writing quickly and quietly.

WML2   Draw and write until the end of writing time.

WML3   Put your writing in your writing folder.

WML4   Reread your writing to think what to do next.

WML5   Talk with your teacher about your writing.

WML6   Share your writing with an audience to get ideas.

WML7   Return your writing materials to where they belong.

Before Teaching Umbrella 2 Minilessons

Learning the routines for independent writing time will help children build self-confidence by achieving a sense of agency and responsibility for their own work while also allowing you time to work with individual children or small guided writing groups. We suggest that children have the opportunity for independent writing time each day. Opportunities and invitations for writing are discussed on pages 12–15. Minilesssons in Section 6: Exploring Early Writing are specific lessons about how to teach independent writing skills.

Before teaching the minilessons in this umbrella, design the classroom writing center to facilitate easy access to materials. Materials may include but not be limited to paper, pens, pencils, crayons, markers, and staplers. As children become familiar with these materials, introduce other materials and tools, such as different kinds of paper (including the paper templates in the online resources), a hole punch, tape, glue sticks, and scissors. Some of the Section 2: Management minilessons, such as using the writing center and learning about appropriate voice levels, will provide helpful background for the lessons in this umbrella.

Writing Minilesson Principle
Get started on your writing quickly and quietly.

Establishing Independent Writing

You Will Need

- a child prepared to demonstrate getting started writing quickly and quietly
- chart paper and markers
- To download the following online resource for this lesson, visit **resources.fountasandpinnell.com**:
  - chart art (optional)

Academic Language/ Important Vocabulary

- quickly
- quietly

Continuum Connection

- Keep working independently rather than waiting for a teacher to help (p. 249)
- Listen with attention and understanding to directions (p. 331)

GOAL

Learn a routine for beginning independent writing time quickly and quietly.

RATIONALE

Teaching children to begin their independent writing time quickly and quietly promotes independence and a sense of responsibility, allows the class to function efficiently, and gives you time to confer with individual children or small guided writing groups.

ASSESS LEARNING

- Notice whether children can function independently to get ready for their writing time.
- Observe for evidence that children can use vocabulary such as *quickly* and *quietly*.

MINILESSON

Consider assigning children to one of four folder colors and keeping each color in a separate corner of the classroom in a crate to alleviate traffic jams when children retrieve their folders. To help children learn an independent writing routine, engage them in a short demonstration. Here is an example.

- Gather children in the meeting area.

  Each day we have time for writing. What are some of the things you do during writing time?

- Help children frame their answers to emphasize that writing time is used to learn about writing, spend time drawing and writing on their own, and come together to share what they wrote.

- Invite the child prepared to demonstrate the writing time routine to come forward.

  Watch _____ as he gets started during writing time.

  What did you notice _____ did?

  What could you hear when he went to get his writing materials?

  What did you notice about how quickly he got started?

Have a Try

Invite a few more children to demonstrate getting started on their writing quickly and quietly.

▶ As children observe the demonstrations, ask them what they notice.

> What do you notice about how your friends are getting ready for writing time?

▶ Record children's responses on chart paper.

Summarize and Apply

Write the principle at the top of the chart. Help children summarize the learning.

> How do you get started during writing time?

> Today during writing time, remember to get started quickly and quietly. You can look at the chart to help you remember. When we come back together we will talk about how getting started quickly and quietly helped you.

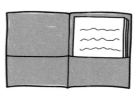

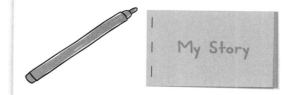

Confer

▶ If you notice children who need support starting their writing quickly and quietly, remind them to refer to the chart and to think about the lesson. During independent writing, move around the room to confer briefly with as many individual children as time allows. Sit side by side with them and invite them to talk about their writing. Use the following prompts as needed.

- *What are you writing about?*
- *Where did you get the idea for your writing?*
- *What will you write about on this page?*
- *What will you write on the next page?*

Share

Following independent writing, gather children in the meeting area. Ask a few children to share their experiences getting started drawing and writing quickly and quietly.

> How did you get started during writing time today?

> How does getting started quickly and quietly help you?

WML2
MGT.U2.WML2

Writing Minilesson Principle
Draw and write until the end of writing time.

Establishing Independent Writing

You Will Need

- chart paper and markers
- To download the following online resource for this lesson, visit **resources.fountasandpinnell.com**:
  - chart art (optional)

Academic Language/ Important Vocabulary

- add
- reread

Continuum Connection

- Keep working independently rather than waiting for a teacher to help (p. 249)
- Think of what to work on next as a writer (p. 249)
- Produce a quantity of writing within the time available: e.g., one or two pages per day (p. 249)

GOAL

Learn how to work independently and build stamina during independent writing.

RATIONALE

Teaching children to write independently and to utilize all of the time at their disposal allows them to develop as writers and build their stamina for and interest in writing.

ASSESS LEARNING

- Look for evidence that children can work independently during writing time.
- Notice whether children are able to write for the whole writing time. Do they always know what they will write next?
- Observe for evidence that children can use vocabulary such as *add* and *reread*.

MINILESSON

To help children learn to work independently and build stamina during independent writing, engage them in discussion about using the entire amount of time allowed for drawing and writing. Here is an example.

- Gather children in the meeting area.

  We have talked about how to do your best work during writing time. What are some things you can do if you think you have finished your writing?

- To keep the focus on writing and drawing, prompt children to think about actions such as checking the pictures to make sure they are clear and not in need of further details, rereading their writing to make sure the meaning is clear, and starting a new book.

- Add responses to chart paper.

Have a Try

Invite children to talk to a partner about what they do to keep writing until the end of their writing time.

> Look at the chart. Choose one idea to talk about. Have you done something like that to keep writing during writing time? Turn and talk to your partner about that.

Summarize and Apply

Summarize the learning and remind children to continue working until the end of writing time. Write the principle on the chart. Read it to the children.

> Writers are always thinking about what they are going to work on next.

> So today and every day, when you think you have finished writing, remember what you can do to keep drawing and writing until the end of writing time.

Draw and write until the end of writing time.

Check your pictures.

Reread your writing.

ELEPHANTS

Start a new book.

Confer

▶ During independent writing, move around the room to confer briefly with as many individual children as time allows. Sit side by side with them and invite them to talk about writing until the end of writing time. Use the following prompts as needed.

- *Talk about the picture on this page.*
- *Did you reread your writing? Is there anything you need to add?*
- *What are you thinking about working on next?*
- *You kept drawing and writing all the way until the end of writing time!*

Share

Following independent writing, gather children in the meeting area. Invite children to talk with a partner about how they kept their writing going. Then ask a few to share with the group. Add new ideas to the chart.

> If you finished a book today, what did you do?

> Continuing to write or draw when you have finished a book helps you to grow as a writer.

Writing Minilesson Principle

Put your writing in your writing folder.

Establishing Independent Writing

You Will Need

- a child prepared to demonstrate putting writing in a writing folder
- a writing folder for each child
- chart paper and markers
- To download the following online resource for this lesson, visit **resources.fountasandpinnell.com**:
  - chart art (optional)

Academic Language/ Important Vocabulary

- organized
- folder

Continuum Connection

- Listen with attention and understanding to directions (p. 331)

GOAL

Learn to keep writing organized inside a writing folder.

RATIONALE

Teaching children to put their writing in a writing folder helps them to keep their writing organized and builds a routine for independent writing time that makes it easier to write more, confer with other writers, and share writing.

ASSESS LEARNING

- Notice whether children keep writing organized inside a writing folder.
- Observe for evidence that they can use vocabulary such as *organized* and *folder*.

MINILESSON

Before teaching this minilesson, make sure children are familiar with keeping their writing in progress in a writing folder. Make sure children know where to place finished work. To help children learn to use a writing folder, engage them in a short demonstration. Here is an example.

Gather children in the meeting area.

> When you finish your writing for the day, you can keep your writing organized in a special way. Why is that a good idea?

> You have a writing folder to keep your writing organized. The writing folder is in a place where you can always find it.

- Invite the prepared child to demonstrate how to put writing that is finished or in progress in a writing folder.

> Watch _____ put her writing away. What do you notice _____ did?

> What do you notice about the way she put the writing into the folder?

Have a Try

Invite a few more children to demonstrate putting their writing in their writing folders.

▶ As children observe the demonstrations, ask them what they notice.

> Where do they put their writing in the folder?

Summarize and Apply

Write the principle on the chart. Read it to the children.

> What did you learn today about putting your writing in your writing folder?

▶ Record responses on chart paper.

> At the end of writing time, remember to put your writing in your writing folder. Today I will ask you to bring your folder to the rug to share.

Confer

▶ During independent writing, move around the room to confer briefly with as many individual children as time allows. Sit side by side with them and invite them to talk about using a writing folder. Use the following prompts as needed.

- *What are you working on today?*
- *What will you draw [write] on the next page?*
- *Where can you look to see what that letter looks like?*
- *You put your writing back into your folder neatly.*

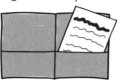

Put your writing in your writing folder.

Put your writing in the pocket.

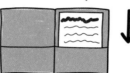

Put the paper all the way down.

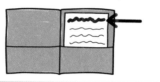

Make sure you can see the front.

Share

Following independent writing, gather children in the meeting area with their writing folders. Invite children to talk to a partner about how they put their writing away neatly. Partners, or you, can use this time to further demonstrate for children who are having difficulty placing the writing in the pocket.

> Now when writing time is over, you know how to put your writing away neatly in your writing folder.

WML4

MGT.U2.WML4

Writing Minilesson Principle
Reread your writing to think what to do next.

Establishing Independent Writing

You Will Need

- a simple piece of your own writing in a booklet to read aloud
- each child's writing folder
- chart paper and markers
- To download the following online resource for this lesson, visit **resources.fountasandpinnell.com**:
  - chart art (optional)

Academic Language/ Important Vocabulary

- reread
- information

Continuum Connection

- Reread writing each day (and during writing on the same day) before continuing to write (p. 249)
- Think of what to work on next as a writer (p. 249)

GOAL

Understand that rereading writing helps one remember what to work on next.

RATIONALE

Teaching children to reread their writing helps them remember what they were working on—whether on the same day or on subsequent days—so that they can write more and that what they write next makes sense with what has been already written. This is the foundation for the process of revision.

ASSESS LEARNING

- Look for evidence that children reread their writing in order to write more.
- Observe for evidence that children can use vocabulary such as *reread* and *information*.

MINILESSON

To help children learn to reread their writing, engage them in a short demonstration. You will need a brief piece of your own writing to read from a writing booklet. Here is an example.

> We have talked about what to do each day during writing time. Today I am going to reread a piece of my own writing so I can think about what to do next.

- Demonstrate rereading a short piece of your own writing. Think aloud about what you might do next as a writer.

> Rereading helped me remember what I wrote about already so that I can think about what I want to do next.

> Is there anything I can do to make sure readers understand my writing?

> If my book is finished, what should I do?

- As children share ideas, add them to chart paper.

Have a Try

Distribute the writing folders. Invite children to reread their own writing to a partner and talk about what they want to do next.

> Turn and talk to a partner. Take out your writing. Read it to your partner. What do you want to do next with your writing?

Summarize and Apply

Summarize the lesson and remind children to reread their writing. Write the principle on the chart and read it to the children.

> Writers reread their writing to remember their ideas and to be sure their readers will understand it. When you reread your writing each day, you can remember what you have written and think about what you want to draw or write next. As you are writing today, ask yourself, *Will my readers understand? What do I want to do next?*

Confer

▶ During independent writing, move around the room to confer briefly with as many individual children as time allows. Sit side by side with them and invite them to talk about rereading their writing. Use the following prompts as needed.

- *Reread your writing while I listen.*
- *What will you add to your words?*
- *What will you add to your pictures?*
- *Is it time to start a new book?*

Share

Following independent writing, gather children in the meeting area. Invite children to talk with a partner about rereading their writing.

> Did you reread your writing? What did you do next?

WML5

MGT.U2.WML5

Talk with your teacher about your writing.

Establishing Independent Writing

You Will Need

- a child prepared to demonstrate a writing conference
- chart paper and markers
- To download the following online resource for this lesson, visit **resources.fountasandpinnell.com**:
  - chart art (optional)

Academic Language/ Important Vocabulary

- reread
- understand
- ideas

Continuum Connection

- Understand that it is helpful to talk about your writing with another person (teacher) (p. 248)
- Generate and expand ideas through talk with peers and teacher (p. 248)

GOAL

Understand that it is helpful to talk about one's writing with another person.

RATIONALE

When children reread their writing they can listen for what they are communicating to others. Helping children understand why and how to talk to the teacher about their writing can give them an audience and help them generate and expand their ideas to write or draw more.

ASSESS LEARNING

- Notice how and why children discuss their writing with you.
- Observe for evidence that children can use vocabulary such as *reread*, *understand*, and *ideas*.

MINILESSON

To help children understand why and how to talk to you about their writing, engage them in a short demonstration. Select a child in advance who is willing and able to talk with you about her writing in front of the class. Here is an example.

- Sit on a low chair with the child in front of the group.

  Please read your writing, _____.

  I understand that _____ and _____.

  Telling what I understand lets you know what your writing says to me. We can talk about information that I didn't understand. Talking with another person about your writing can help you make your writing better.

- Model some of the prompting language you might use to support the writers in your classroom, such as the following.

  - *What will you work on next?*
  - *What information will you add?*
  - *What information will you add to your pictures?*
  - *Is it time to start a new book?*

The Writing Minilessons Book, Kindergarten

Have a Try

Invite children to talk to a partner about what they noticed from the teacher-writer conversation.

> What are some things you and I could talk about when we meet about your writing? Turn and talk to a partner.

❯ Write their noticings on chart paper.

Summarize and Apply

Summarize the learning and remind children that talking about their writing helps them grow as writers. Write the principle on the chart. Read it to the children.

> How does talking about your drawing and writing help you be a better writer?

> Today when you write, I will sit with some of you just like I sat with _____. You will read your writing to me and then we will talk together so you can decide what you want to work on next.

Talk with your teacher about your writing.

- Read your writing out loud.

  I went to the fair.

- Tell what you will write about next.

- Tell what you want to draw next.

- Answer the teacher's questions.

Confer

❯ During independent writing, move around the room to confer briefly with as many individual children as time allows. Sit side by side with them and invite them to talk about their writing. Use the following prompts as needed.

- *Reread your writing while I listen.*
- *What are you working on today?*
- *What will you write on the next page?*
- *Talk more about the pictures you drew.*
- *How might you let your readers know who the people are in your pictures (labeling)?*

Share

Following independent writing, gather children in the meeting area. Invite children that had a writing conference with you to talk about what that was like. Add new ideas to the chart.

> What did you do as a writer after talking to me?

Writing Minilesson Principle
Share your writing with an audience to get ideas.

Establishing Independent Writing

You Will Need

- a simple piece of your own writing (with pictures) in a booklet or on chart paper to read aloud
- chart paper and markers
- To download the following online resource for this lesson, visit **resources.fountasandpinnell.com**:
  - chart art (optional)

Academic Language/ Important Vocabulary

- audience
- share

Continuum Connection

- Understand that writers get help from other writers (p. 248)
- Speak with confidence (p. 331)
- Look at the audience (or other person) while speaking (p. 331)
- Listen actively to others read or talk about their writing and give feedback (p. 331)
- Look at the speaker when being spoken to (p. 331)
- Form clear questions to get information (p. 331)

GOAL

Learn that speaking to an audience about one's writing is a way to get ideas.

RATIONALE

Helping children understand why and how to share their writing with one another helps them generate and expand their ideas, build off of each other's comments, and reinforce their listening skills.

ASSESS LEARNING

- Look for evidence that children understand how and why to share their writing with one another.
- Notice whether children share their writing as a means to generate new ideas for writing.
- Observe for evidence that children can use vocabulary such as *audience* and *share*.

MINILESSON

Before teaching this minilesson, make sure children are familiar with the concepts of MGT.U1: Working Together in the Classroom, particularly WML2, WML4, and WML5. To help children understand why and how to share their writing, engage them in a short demonstration. You will need a brief piece of your own writing to read from a writing booklet or displayed on chart paper. Here is an example.

> Writers share their writing with an audience. An audience is a group of people that watch and listen to what is being shared. Today I am going to share my writing with you. You will be my audience. As I read, think about what I do as the writer and what you do as the audience.

- Demonstrate reading a short piece of your own writing. Use a strong voice, be sure to look at the audience, and share any pictures.

> What did you notice I did when I shared my writing?

> What did you notice about what the audience did?

- Use the words or picture icons to indicate children's responses (eyes or dotted lines for what they saw, an ear for what they heard, a question mark for questions, speech or thought bubbles) as you record responses on chart paper.

- If children engage in a discussion about looking at the audience, take into consideration that some children are not comfortable with establishing or cannot establish eye contact for cultural or for other reasons.

Have a Try

Invite children to ask you questions and have a conversation about your writing. Add their actions and observations to the chart.

> I am going to give you—the audience—a chance to share your ideas and ask me questions about my writing. Think about starting your sentences with *Your picture shows that _____; I wonder why _____; or You told us about _____.*

▶ Demonstrate asking the children questions and model responses such as these: *What did my writing make you think about? What did you understand about my writing? Do you have any questions about my writing? I can go back and add that idea to my book. I can add that to this illustration.*

Share your writing with an audience to get ideas.

Show your writing.

Look at the audience.

Listen.

Answer questions.

Summarize and Apply

Help children summarize the learning and remind them that sharing their writing can help them get new ideas. Write the principle on the chart. Read it to the children.

> How does sharing your writing help you become a better writer?

> When you share, remember to use a strong voice, show your pictures, and ask your audience what they think. You can look at the chart to remind you.

Confer

▶ During independent writing, move around the room to confer briefly with as many individual children as time allows. Sit side by side with them and invite them to read their writing. Then tell the writer what you understood and what you wonder. Use the following prompts as needed.

- *What are you hoping the audience will understand about your story?*
- *I understand that _____.*
- *I wonder if _____.*
- *Where might you add that to your pictures? To your words?*

Share

Following independent writing, gather children in the meeting area. Invite a few children to share their writing with the group.

> Who would like to share your writing today?

Section 2: Management

Writing Minilesson Principle
Return your writing materials to where they belong.

Establishing Independent Writing

You Will Need

- two or three children prepared to demonstrate putting their writing materials away where they belong
- chart paper and markers
- To download the following online resource for this lesson, visit **resources.fountasandpinnell.com**:
  - chart art (optional)

Academic Language/ Important Vocabulary

- materials

Continuum Connection

- Listen with attention and understanding to directions (p. 331)

GOAL

Learn the routine of putting materials away at the end of writing time.

RATIONALE

Teaching children what is expected of them about putting away their writing materials at the end of independent writing time builds good habits of caring for materials and creates an organized learning environment. This builds independence and allows children to quickly find their materials. It also helps you find children's writing to review.

ASSESS LEARNING

- Notice how carefully children put their materials away at the end of writing time.
- Observe for evidence that children can use vocabulary such as *materials*.

MINILESSON

Before teaching this minilesson, make sure children are familiar with the materials in the writing center and how they are organized. If the writing center materials are not yet labeled, teach IW.6: Making Labels for the Classroom. To help children learn a routine for putting their writing materials away, engage them in a short demonstration. Right before teaching the lesson, ask two or three children to place their writing materials at their writing spots. Here is an example.

> We looked at the materials in the writing center together. What materials did you notice?
>
> Writers keep their materials organized so they can find them and get started writing quickly and quietly. How do you know where each of the materials goes?

- Invite the children prepared to demonstrate to pick up the writing materials that have been placed at their writing spots, and put the materials away.

> Watch as they put away their writing materials.
>
> What do you notice they did?

- Record children's responses on chart paper.

The Writing Minilessons Book, Kindergarten

Have a Try

Invite children to talk not just about returning their writing materials to where they belong but also about the accompanying behaviors.

> It's important to do all the things we wrote on the chart, but what else should you remember when it's time to put everything away?

▶ Use prompts such as the following to help children think about the behaviors that accompany the end of independent writing time: *How should it sound when you put materials away? What should you do if someone else is putting a folder away when you want to? Where should you go after you clean up? How should you walk there?*

Summarize and Apply

Summarize the learning and remind children to put their writing materials where they belong after writing time. Write the principle on the chart. Read it to the children.

> Why is it important to return materials to where they belong when writing time is over?

> Today when it is time to put your writing materials away, take a look at the chart and do all of the important things we talked about.

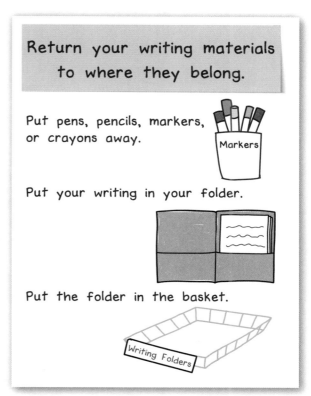

Return your writing materials to where they belong.

Put pens, pencils, markers, or crayons away.

Markers

Put your writing in your folder.

Put the folder in the basket.

Writing Folders

Confer

▶ During independent writing, move around the room to confer briefly with as many individual children as time allows. Sit side by side with them and invite them to talk about putting away their materials. Take the opportunity to review what to do when writing time ends. Use the following prompts as needed.

- *Talk about what you have in your writing folder. What will you work on next?*
- *Look for the label to know where to put that.*
- *You are quietly putting your materials away.*
- *You are waiting your turn to put your folder in the basket.*

Share

Following independent writing, gather children in the meeting area. Invite children to talk to a partner about how they put away their writing materials.

> Now every time you finish writing time, you know how to put your materials away.

Assessment

After you have taught the minilessons in this umbrella, observe children as they prepare for, progress through, and conclude independent writing time each day. Use *The Literacy Continuum* (Fountas and Pinnell 2017) to notice, teach for, and support children's learning as you observe their attempts at reading and writing.

▶ What evidence do you have of new understandings children have developed related to the routines for independent writing time?

- Do children get started on their writing quickly and quietly?
- Do they draw and write until the end of independent writing time?
- Do they keep their writing in a writing folder in an orderly way?
- Do they reread their writing to remember their ideas?
- How are they talking with you about their writing?
- How are they sharing their writing with an audience to get ideas?
- Do they return their writing materials to where they belong?
- Do they understand and use vocabulary such as *reread*, *organized*, *ideas*, *audience*, and *materials*?

▶ In what other ways, beyond the scope of this umbrella, are children getting started with independent writing?

- Are children choosing drawing and writing as a choice time activity?
- Are they using drawing and writing tools appropriately?
- Are they writing about their imaginative play?

Use your observations to determine the next umbrella you will teach. You may also consult Suggested Sequence of Lessons (pp. 483–494) for guidance.

EXTENSIONS FOR ESTABLISHING INDEPENDENT WRITING

▶ Teach children to use resources in their writing folders, such as a list of finished writing, a list of ideas for writing, an ABC chart, a personal word list, and a proofreading checklist (see EWR.U4 and WPS.U5).

▶ Support children in understanding how to be a specific and supportive audience when writers share their writing. Help children progress from statements like "I like your picture," to "Your picture shows you and your mom went to the park together."

▶ Teach children the kinds of questions that are helpful to a writer, using *who*, *what*, *where*, *when*, *how*, and *why*.

Minilessons in This Umbrella

WML1   Write and draw in the writing center.

WML2   Play with blocks in the block center.

WML3   Play, write, and draw in the play corner.

WML4   Play at the sand/water table.

WML5   Make a choice at choice time.

WML6   Make art in the art center.

WML7   Play with letters and words in the word work center.

WML8   Create things in the creation station.

WML9   Explore in the science center.

Before Teaching Umbrella 3 Minilessons

We suggest that children have choice time each day in addition to a time dedicated solely to independent writing. The writing center activities are in addition to what children are working on during independent writing time. Opportunities and invitations for writing are infused into all of these choices, as discussed on pp. 12–15. See EWR.U7: Learning to Draw and Write Through Play for specific lessons about how to use writing in each of the classroom centers. You may choose to schedule some of the activities/centers listed here during a dedicated literacy work time (see p. 77).

Before teaching the minilessons in this umbrella, design classroom space to facilitate easy transitions and smooth movement between activity areas. Introduce choice time by having every child work on one activity, for example, writing and drawing in the writing center (WML1). When you introduce a second activity, assign half of the class to do the new activity and the other half to work on the familiar activity or to look at books. Switch the children halfway through or at another time during the day so that everyone has an opportunity to try the new routine on the first day. When children are familiar with about four routines, teach WML5 so that children can learn to make their own choices. Continue to add routines through the year as you freshen the activity centers. (If you use *The Reading Minilessons Book, Kindergarten* [Fountas and Pinnell 2019], you may have already taught minilessons on using the writing center and word work center.)

Section 2: Management

Writing Minilesson Principle
Write and draw in the writing center.

Learning About Choice Time

You Will Need

- writing center materials
- chart paper and markers
- To download the following online resources for this lesson, visit **resources.fountasandpinnell.com**:
  - writing center icon
  - chart art (optional)

Academic Language/ Important Vocabulary

- choice time
- writing center
- directions
- materials

 ### Continuum Connection

- Remember and follow simple directions with two to three steps (p. 331)

GOAL

Learn how to follow routines in the writing center.

RATIONALE

Whether children work in a writing center or at their tables, they need to be taught explicitly how to choose materials, write, put materials away, and place their finished writing where it belongs. The writing center holds the supplies children will use during independent writing. It is also a choice time activity that allows children to extend their work from independent writing and to play with writing in different ways.

ASSESS LEARNING

- Observe children's use of the writing center and the materials in it.
- Look for evidence that children can use vocabulary such as *choice time* and *writing center*.

MINILESSON

If items in the writing center are not already labeled, teach IW.6: Making Labels for the Classroom. (If you use *The Reading Minilessons Book, Kindergarten* (Fountas and Pinnell 2019) and have taught MGT.U3.RML4, you may not need to teach this lesson.) To help children think about the minilesson principle, engage them in a short demonstration of a writing center activity. Here is an example.

- Show the writing center icon.

  This picture is for the writing center. When you put your name beside it, it means you will do writing and drawing in the writing center.

- Hold up some of the materials (for example, pencils, markers, staplers, paper, covers, correction tape, glue sticks, blank books) and point to the labels.

  What do you notice about the materials in the writing center?

  The materials are organized and labeled to help you find them.

- Have a child model how to get a marker, glue stick, and paper and return them to their labeled spots.

  What did you notice about how _____ borrowed and returned the materials?

- If you plan to provide a list of the kinds of writing children can choose from a weekly writing prompt, show them where you will post the directions.

  In the writing center, you can write letters or make signs for the play corner. Sometimes you will write about a book we have read together.

  What do you do when you are finished with your writing center work?

- Show children where to put their finished work.

Have a Try

Invite children to talk to a partner about what they will do in the writing center.

> Turn and talk to your partner about what you will do today in the writing center.

Summarize and Apply

Summarize the learning and remind children how to work in the writing center.

▶ Create a chart as the children summarize their learning.

> What are some things you learned today about using the writing center?

> Now everyone will have a chance to write and draw. You can continue working on a piece of writing that you've already started, or you can start something new.

▶ Provide some writing materials on the children's tables.

> Some materials are on your tables, but if you need more, get what you need from the writing center. Remember to use the materials carefully and return them to where they belong when you are finished.

Writing Center

- Get the materials you need.

- Draw and write.

- Return materials.

- Put your work in the basket or your writing folder.

Confer

▶ During choice time, move around the room to confer briefly with as many individual children as time allows. Sit side by side with them and talk about what they are working on in the writing center. Use the following prompts as needed.

- *What will you work on in the writing center today?*
- *Where does the marker go when you are finished with it?*
- *Where should you put your finished work?*

Share

Following choice time, gather children in the meeting area. Ask several children who worked in the writing center to share what they did.

> Is there anything we need to add to the chart to help you remember what to do when you write and draw in the writing center?

Writing Minilesson Principle
Play with blocks in the block center.

Learning About Choice Time

You Will Need

- a well-organized block center, prepared with blocks of various shapes and sizes, as well as paper, labels, and markers

- two children prepared to demonstrate using the block center

- chart paper and markers

- To download the following online resources for this lesson, visit **resources.fountasandpinnell.com**:

  - block center icon

  - chart art (optional)

Academic Language/ Important Vocabulary

- blocks

- block center

- organized

- respect

- choice time

Continuum Connection

- Remember and follow simple directions with two to three steps (p. 331)

GOAL

Learn the routine for using the block center.

RATIONALE

A block center with various types and sizes of blocks encourages children's imaginations and the building and exploration of different shapes and materials. When children are explicitly taught how to use the block center—and especially how to share the block center with others—they are more likely to engage in constructive and cooperative play.

ASSESS LEARNING

- Observe whether children share the block area and respect other children's buildings.

- Listen to how children talk about their block creations.

- Look for evidence that children can use vocabulary such as *blocks*, *block center*, *organized*, *respect*, and *choice time*.

MINILESSON

To help children think about the minilesson principle, engage them in a demonstration and discussion about how to use the block center. If this is one of the first centers children are learning about, assign some children to try the routine while others look at books. Then switch the groups.

- Show the block center icon.

  This picture is for the block center. You can build buildings, roads, bridges, and lots of other structures in the block center. What do you notice about how the materials are put in the block center?

  The materials in the block center are neatly organized.

- Invite two children who have been prepared beforehand to model playing with blocks in the block center side by side, but separately.

  What did you notice about how _____ and played _____ with blocks?

  What did they do with the blocks?

  How did they share blocks and respect each other's buildings?

- Tell the two children that it's time to clean up.

  What did you notice your classmates did when it was time to clean up?

  They put all their blocks back neatly where they belong. How did they take apart their creations?

  When you take apart your creations, start taking blocks off the top and go down.

Have a Try

Invite children to talk to a partner about what they might make in the block center.

> Turn and talk to your partner about what you might make in the block center.

▌ Tell children that in addition to building with the blocks, they can make labels for their block buildings.

Summarize and Apply

Summarize the learning and remind children how to play in the block center during choice time.

> What did you learn today about using the block center?

▌ Create a chart to summarize the learning.

> During choice time today, some of you will play in the block center. The rest of you will have a chance to play in the block center later.

Block Center

- Share the blocks.

- Make a label.

Yasmin's Tower

- Put the blocks away.

BLOCKS

Confer

▌ During choice time, move around the room to confer briefly with as many individual children as time allows. Sit side by side with them and invite them to talk about using the block center. Use the following prompts as needed.

- *What do you think you might build with these blocks?*

- *What kind of blocks could you use to build a bridge?*

- *You put that block on your building very gently.*

- *Show how you put away the blocks when you're finished playing.*

- *Do you want to tape a name on your construction?*

Share

Following choice time, gather children in the meeting area to talk about using the block center.

> Who played in the block center today?

> What did you build with the blocks? Tell about it.

> Did anyone make a label for your construction? What does it say?

Writing Minilesson Principle

Play, write, and draw in the play corner.

You Will Need

- a play corner that has been set up according to a particular theme (e.g., as a market; see EWR.U7)
- chart paper and markers
- To download the following online resources for this lesson, visit **resources.fountasandpinnell.com**:
  - play corner icon
  - chart art (optional)

Academic Language/ Important Vocabulary

- choice time
- play corner
- play
- write
- draw

Continuum Connection

- Remember and follow simple directions with two to three steps (p. 331)

GOAL

Learn that you can play, write, and draw in the play corner.

RATIONALE

Play is essential for young children. Through self-directed play, children exercise their imaginations, develop language, and learn self-regulation and interpersonal skills. When children are explicitly taught how to use the play corner, they are more likely to play cooperatively with other children and get the most out of their playtime.

ASSESS LEARNING

- Observe whether children choose the play corner as one of their choice activities.
- Notice whether they play cooperatively in the play corner and then clean up.
- Look for evidence that children can use vocabulary related to the play corner.

MINILESSON

To help children think about the minilesson principle, guide them through how to play in the play corner. This lesson assumes the play corner is set up as a market, but any environment (e.g., restaurant, fire station) will work. Here is an example.

- Show the play corner icon.

  This is the picture for the play corner. When you put your name next to this picture, you will play in the play corner during choice time. Look around the play corner. Talk about how it looks. Does it look like a place you know?

  Today our play corner looks like a market, but it will change to other places on other days. How could you play in a market? What could you pretend?

  What do you see in the market?

- Help children notice the different materials in the play corner, including the writing and drawing materials.

  What can you write or draw if you are pretending to work in the market?

- Talk with children about playing with others in the play corner.

  How should you play with others when you are playing in the play corner?

  What kind of voice should you use, an indoor voice or an outdoor voice?

  What should you do when you have finished playing in the play corner?

  Before you start to play in the play corner, think about *how* you are going to play. For example, if you are playing with a friend, decide who is going to work in the market and who is going to shop.

Have a Try

Invite children to talk to a partner about what they will do in the play corner.

> Turn and talk to your partner about what you will do in the play corner. How will you play well together with your friends?

Summarize and Apply

Summarize the learning and remind children how to play in the play corner during choice time.

> What are some things you learned today about what to do when you are in the play corner?

▶ Create a chart as the children summarize their learning.

> Some of you will play in the play corner during choice time today. The rest of you will have a chance to play there later.

Play Corner

• Plan your play.

• Use an indoor voice.

• Share. Take turns.

• Draw and write.

SHOPPING LIST

• Clean up!

Confer

▶ During choice time, move around the room to confer briefly with as many individual children as time allows. Sit side by side with them and invite them to talk about using the play corner. Use the following prompts as needed.

- *What would you like to play in the play corner today?*
- *You could make a shopping list.*
- *What could you do with _____?*
- *What kind of voice should you use in the play corner?*
- *What should you do now that you have finished playing?*

Share

Following choice time, gather children in the meeting area to talk about what they did in the play corner.

> Who played in the play corner today? What did you do there?

> Did anyone write or draw in the play corner? What did you write or draw?

Writing Minilesson Principle
Play at the sand/water table.

You Will Need

- a sand/water table filled with sand, water, pasta, beans, or rice; various containers; small plastic toys
- two children prepared to demonstrate playing at the sand/water table
- chart paper and markers
- To download the following online resources for this lesson, visit **resources.fountasandpinnell.com**:
  - sand/water table icon
  - chart art (optional)

Academic Language/ Important Vocabulary

- sand/water table
- choice time

Continuum Connection

- Remember and follow simple directions with two to three steps (p. 331)

GOAL

Learn to use the sand/water table.

RATIONALE

Sand or water tables (either one works for this lesson) offer sensory opportunities for discovering concepts about volume and capacity as well as how the material behaves when poured. When children are explicitly taught the rules for playing at the sand/water table, they are more likely to play constructively and cooperatively.

ASSESS LEARNING

- Observe whether children choose the sand/water table as one of their choice activities.
- Notice whether they take care of the materials in the sand/water table and play cooperatively.
- Look for evidence that children can use vocabulary related to the sand/water table.

MINILESSON

To help children think about the minilesson principle, guide them through how to use the sand/water table. This lesson involves the use of a water table, but use whatever kind of sensory apparatus is available in your classroom.

- Show the sand/water table icon.

  This is the picture for the water table. What do you notice about the water table? What materials do you see in it?

  There are lots of different things in the water table for you to play with. Watch how _____ and _____ play at the water table.

- Invite two children who have been prepared beforehand to demonstrate different ways to play at the water table (e.g., filling and pouring water from different containers, seeing whether different objects float or sink).

  How did your classmates play at the water table? What did they do with the water?

  What else did you notice about how they played?

  When you play at the water table, keep all the water in the table. Remember that the water is for playing and exploring, not for splashing. Share the water table with your classmates.

Have a Try

Invite children to talk to a partner about how they will play at the water table.

> Turn and talk to your partner about how you will play at the water table.

▶ Tell children that they can write about what they do at the water table. For example, they could make a list of what sinks and what floats.

Summarize and Apply

Summarize the learning and remind children how to play at the water table during choice time.

> What did you learn today about using the water table?

▶ Create a chart as the children summarize their learning.

> During choice time today, some of you will play at the water table. The rest of you will have a chance to play there later.

Confer

▶ During choice time, move around the room to confer briefly with as many individual children as time allows. Sit side by side with them and invite them to talk about their exploration and play at the water table. Use the following prompts as needed.

- *Do you think that this cup or that cup can hold more water? Let's find out.*
- *Do you think a rubber band would float? What about a paper clip? Try it and see what happens.*
- *You can make a list of what sinks and what floats.*
- *Remember that the water stays in the water table.*

Share

Following choice time, gather children in the meeting area to talk about what they did at the water table.

> Who played at the water table today? What did you do with the water?

Writing Minilesson Principle
Make a choice at choice time.

Learning About Choice Time

You Will Need

- a choice time board (see pp. 15, 80)
- a name card ready to affix to the board for each child
- a child prepared to demonstrate how to use the board
- chart paper and markers
- To download the following online resource for this lesson, visit **resources.fountasandpinnell.com**:
  - chart art (optional)

Academic Language/ Important Vocabulary

- choice time board
- choose

Continuum Connection

- Remember and follow simple directions with two to three steps (p. 331)

GOAL

Learn how to make choices for choice time.

RATIONALE

When children make choices about which activities to participate in, they develop self-regulation, independence, and confidence. They learn to plan their own time and to commit to a single activity for a sustained period. Consider teaching this lesson again after you have introduced a few more centers.

ASSESS LEARNING

- Observe whether children use the choice time board to indicate their choices.
- Notice whether they follow through with their choices and stick with them for a sufficient period of time.
- Notice whether they work productively in the creation station, take care of the materials, and put them back where they belong.

MINILESSON

To teach children how to indicate what they will do during choice time, demonstrate with the method that you use in your classroom. Here is an example based on a choice time board (or work board) to which children attach their name cards.

- Display the choice time board.

  You've been learning about and trying out the many different activities you can do during choice time! Today, you will learn how to choose the activity you want to do. Look at our choice time board. What do you notice about it?

  The choice time board shows all the activities that are available today. What does the picture of the blocks mean?

- Review each icon on the board.

  Some days there will be different choices on the board.

  Juan is going to demonstrate how to use the choice time board. Watch him.

- Give the child his name card and instruct him to put it on the board next to his choice.

  What did you choose?

  Juan has chosen to play in the block center today. How can you tell?

- If time allows, ask another child to make a choice.

- Explain that each choice on the board has a limited number of spaces available. Tell children that if the choice they want is full they will have to make a different choice.

Have a Try

Invite children to talk to a partner about how they will use the choice time board.

> Turn and talk to your partner about which activity you would like to choose for choice time.

Summarize and Apply

Help children summarize their learning and remind them how to use the choice time board to choose an activity for choice time.

> What did you learn today about how to make a choice during choice time?

▶ Remind children of the centers that are open today. Invite them to come up to the board one at a time to make their choices. Encourage them to try a variety of activities over time.

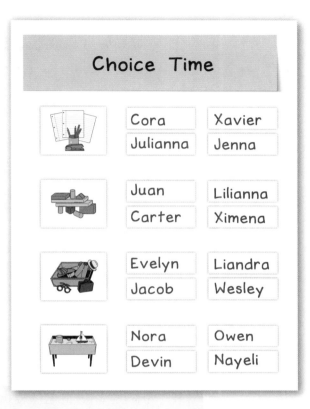

Confer

▶ During choice time, move around the room to confer briefly with as many individual children as time allows. Sit side by side with them and invite them to talk about their choices. Use the following prompts as needed.

- *Which activities are open today?*
- *Which activity would you like to do today?*
- *Is there room for you to do that activity? If not, what other activity would you like to try?*
- *Which picture is for writing and drawing in the writing center?*

Share

Following choice time, gather children in the meeting area to share what they did during choice time. Support children's oral language as needed by providing a sentence frame, such as *During choice time, I _____.*

> What did you do during choice time today? Tell about it.

> What do you think you will choose tomorrow?

Writing Minilesson Principle
Make art in the art center.

Learning About Choice Time

You Will Need

- an art center stocked with various art supplies, such as paints, markers, paper, and glue, in labeled bins or baskets

- chart paper and markers

- To download the following online resources for this lesson, visit **resources.fountasandpinnell.com**:

    - art center icon

    - chart art (optional)

Academic Language/ Important Vocabulary

- art

- art center

- materials

- choice time

Continuum Connection

- Remember and follow simple directions with two to three steps (p. 331)

GOAL

Learn about how to handle supplies and understand the routines of the art center.

RATIONALE

A well-stocked art center offers children the opportunity to develop their creativity while working on teacher-led projects or on independent projects (e.g., creations for the play corner, artwork for their own books). You'll find a suggested list on page 78. Children need to be taught explicitly how to handle art supplies carefully and put them back where they belong (see Management Umbrella 4: Using Drawing and Writing Tools).

ASSESS LEARNING

- Observe children's interactions when they work in the art center.

- Notice children's level of independence when they work in the art center.

- Notice whether children take care of the art supplies and put them back where they belong.

- Look for evidence that children can use vocabulary related to the art center.

MINILESSON

To help children think about the minilesson principle, guide them through how to use the art center. Here is an example.

- Display the art center icon.

    This is the picture for the art center. When you put your name next to this picture, you can make art in the art center during choice time. Sometimes you will all do the same art project. Other times, you can make whatever you want!

    What do you notice about how the materials in the art center are stored?

- Show children where individual art supplies are located. Point out and read the labels.

    What should you do when other children are working in the art center at the same time as you?

    What if someone else wants to use the same materials as you want to use?

    What do you think you should do when you are finished making art in the art center?

- Demonstrate putting away the materials and putting finished artwork in the basket.

Have a Try

Invite children to talk to a partner about what they will do in the art center.

> Turn and talk to your partner about what you might make in the art center.

Summarize and Apply

Summarize the learning and remind children that they can choose to work in the art center during choice time.

> What is something important to remember when you work in the art center?

▶ Create a chart as the children summarize their learning.

> The art center will be one of the activities available today during choice time. If you go to the art center today, remember to take good care of the materials and put them back where they belong when you are finished with them.

Art Center

Get the materials you need.

Share.

Clean up.

Put your art in the basket.

Confer

▶ During choice time, move around the room to confer briefly with as many individual children as time allows. Sit side by side with them and invite them to talk about using the art center. Use the following prompts as needed.

- *What would you like to make today? Would you like to make a _____?*
- *What materials do you need to make that?*
- *_____ is using the red marker now. Wait until she is finished.*
- *What words could you add to your drawing?*
- *Did you remember to write your name on your drawing?*

Share

Following choice time, gather children in the meeting area to talk about working in the art center.

> Who worked in the art center today? What did you make?

> How did you take good care of the art supplies?

WML7
MGT.U3.WML7

Writing Minilesson Principle
Play with letters and words in the word work center.

Learning About Choice Time

You Will Need

- word work materials chart
- directions for an activity related to a recent phonics lesson
- chart paper and markers
- magnetic letters
- To download the following online resources for this lesson, visit **resources.fountasandpinnell.com**:
  - word work center icon
  - chart art (optional)

Academic Language/ Important Vocabulary

- choice time
- word work
- directions
- materials

Continuum Connection

- Remember and follow simple directions with two to three steps (p. 331)

GOAL

Learn how to work in the word work center.

RATIONALE

This minilesson establishes the basic routines for children to work independently in the word work center or at their seats so that only a brief introduction to the specific task will be required. Word work activities should reinforce the concepts learned during the whole-class phonics lesson.

ASSESS LEARNING

- Look for evidence that children can use the word work center independently.
- Notice how they handle materials and whether materials are put away properly.
- Look for evidence that children can use vocabulary related to the word work center.

MINILESSON

To help children think about the minilesson principle, engage them in a short demonstration of the routines of the word work center. Here is an example.

- Show children the word work icon.

  This is the picture for the word work center. When you put your name next to this picture, you will go to the word work center during choice time.

  What do you think you might do in the word work center?

- Show children the word work center with the materials placed there or where word work materials are kept in the classroom if they will need to get them.

  What do you notice about the materials in the word work center?

  The materials are organized and labeled so you can find and return them easily.

- Show children where the charts will be displayed.

  There will always be two charts posted in the word work center: one chart is a list of the materials you need, and the other tells you how to do the activity.

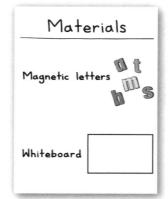

Have a Try

Invite children to talk to a partner about what they will do in the word work center.

> Turn and talk to your partner about what you will do first in the word work center.

Summarize and Apply

Summarize the learning and remind children how to work and play with words in the word work center.

▶ Summarize the steps with children and record them on chart paper.

> Let's make a chart to help remember what to do in the word work center.

> Today some of you will do the activity I showed you. The rest of you will have a chance to try the word work center later.

Confer

▶ During choice time, move around the room to confer briefly with as many individual children as time allows. Sit side by side with them and invite them to talk about using the word work center. Use the following prompts as needed.

- *What do you need to do first? Let's look at the materials chart together.*
- *What is the first letter in* bat*? Can you find a* b*?*
- *You made the word* mat*! Let's read it together.*
- *What should you do now that you're finished with the activity?*

Share

Following choice time, gather children in the meeting area to talk about what they did in the word work center.

> Who went to the word work center today?

> Give a thumbs-up if you did the activity, handled the materials carefully, and put them back where you found them.

> What are some things you will remember to do when you go to the word work center?

Word Work Center

- Read the list.

- Take out the materials.

- Read the directions.

- Do the activity.

- Return the materials.

Materials
Magnetic letters

Directions
- Make the word at

bat

Section 2: Management

Writing Minilesson Principle
Create things in the creation station.

Learning About Choice Time

You Will Need

- a creation station stocked with various materials for 3D building (e.g., cardboard, shoeboxes, paper towel rolls, yarn, wheels)

- a creation that you have started to make in the creation station (e.g., a building)

- a place to display/store creations

- chart paper and markers

- To download the following online resources for this lesson, visit **resources.fountasandpinnell.com**:

  - creation station icon

  - chart art (optional)

Academic Language/ Important Vocabulary

- creation station

- build

- materials

- creation

- choice time

Continuum Connection

- Remember and follow simple directions with two to three steps (p. 331)

GOAL

Learn that you can build things in the creation station.

RATIONALE

A creation station—or maker space or whatever term you use—offers children the opportunity to develop their creativity, exercise their imagination, and learn about different materials while building 3D creations. Teaching children how to use the creation station helps ensure that they will use the materials carefully and safely.

ASSESS LEARNING

- Observe whether children choose the creation station as one of their choice activities.

- Notice whether they work productively in the creation station, take care of the materials, and put them back where they belong.

- Look for evidence that children can use vocabulary related to the creation station.

MINILESSON

To help children think about the minilesson principle, guide them through how to use the creation station. Here is an example.

- Show the creation station icon.

  > This is the picture for the creation station. When you put your name next to it, you will build something in the creation station during choice time. When you go to the creation station, think about what you want to make and what materials you will need. Where will you find the materials you need?

  > The materials are neatly organized to help you find what you need.

- Show children the creation that you started to make and demonstrate adding a new feature to it (e.g., adding a roof to a building). Then demonstrate putting the materials back.

  > What did you notice about how I used the materials?

  > What did I do with the materials when I was finished with them?

  > When you build in the creation station, remember to take good care of the materials so your classmates can use them, too.

  > If other children are working in the creation station at the same time you are, how can you make sure that everyone has the materials and space to work?

  > Try to find your own space to work on your creation, and let other children have their own space, too.

- Show children where to store their finished creations. Point out that there are paper and pencils that children can use for planning their creations or writing about them afterward (see EWR.U7.WML2).

Have a Try

Invite children to talk to a partner about what they might build in the creation station.

> Turn and talk to your partner about one thing you might like to build in the creation station.

Summarize and Apply

Summarize the learning and remind children that they can choose to create things in the creation station.

> What do you need to remember to do when you are working in the creation station?

▶ Create a chart as the children summarize their learning.

> The creation station will be one of the activities available today during choice time. If you build something in the creation station today, remember to find your own space, take good care of the materials, and put them back where they belong.

Creation Station

• Get your materials.

• Share.

• Plan your creation.

• Take good care of materials.

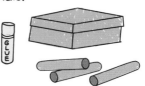

CREATIONS

• Clean up!

Confer

▶ During choice time, move around the room to confer briefly with as many individual children as time allows. Sit side by side with them and invite them to talk about using the creation station. Use the following prompts as needed.

- *What would you like to make today?*
- *What materials will you need to make that?*
- *Will you have enough space to work there?*
- *What could you write about your creation?*
- *Where should you put your finished creation?*

Share

Following choice time, gather children in the meeting area. Support children's oral language as needed by providing a sentence frame, such as *I made a* _____.

> Who built something in the creation station today? What did you build?

> How did you take good care of the materials?

Writing Minilesson Principle
Explore in the science center.

Learning About Choice Time

You Will Need

- a science center set up with materials such as magnifying glasses, magnets, various natural materials (e.g., leaves, rocks), science books, and writing and drawing supplies
- a basket of leaves of various sizes, shapes, and colors or other materials to observe closely
- a notebook and writing utensil to record observations
- chart paper and markers
- To download the following online resources for this lesson, visit **resources.fountasandpinnell.com**:
  - science center icon
  - chart art (optional)

Academic Language/ Important Vocabulary

- science
- science center
- leaf/leaves
- observation
- magnifying glass
- choice time

Continuum Connection

- Remember and follow simple directions with two to three steps (p. 331)

GOAL

Learn that the science center is a place to explore and record your observations.

RATIONALE

A science center (or wonder center) offers children the opportunity for focused inquiry using concrete materials. Children need to be explicitly taught how to use and take care of the materials in the science center.

ASSESS LEARNING

- Observe whether children choose the science center as one of their choice activities.
- Notice whether they use the materials in the science center properly and put them back where they belong.
- Look for evidence that children can use vocabulary related to the science center.

MINILESSON

To help children think about the minilesson principle, demonstrate how to use the science center. This lesson focuses on observing, but teach a similar lesson each time a new activity is introduced in the science center.

- Show the science center icon.

  This picture is for the science center. When you put your name beside it, you will go to the science center during choice time. In this center, you will do different science activities and experiments. You can also make observations of things. Making an observation means that you look closely at something. You can write and draw about what you notice.

- Demonstrate how to look closely at objects, ideally with a magnifying glass. Think aloud as you do your observation.

  What did you notice about what I did?

  I used a magnifying glass to look closely at the leaves. This leaf is interesting to me because it has lots of different colors. I'm going to draw a picture of it so I will remember what I noticed.

- Model drawing and labeling the leaf.

- If time allows, demonstrate sorting the leaves into two or more categories (e.g., oval leaves and hand-shaped leaves).

  What should you do when you have finished working in the science center?

Have a Try

Invite children to talk to a partner about what they will do in the science center.

> Turn and talk to your partner about what you will do in the science center.

Summarize and Apply

Summarize the learning and remind children that they can choose to work in the science center during choice time.

> What did you learn today about exploring in the science center?

▶ Create a chart as the children summarize their learning.

> The science center will be open today during choice time. You can make observations of leaves, just like I did. I will be there to help you.

Confer

▶ During choice time, move around the room to confer briefly with as many individual children as time allows. Sit side by side with them and invite them to talk about using the science center. Use the following prompts as needed.

- *What do you notice about _____? What do you find interesting about it?*
- *How are these two things different?*
- *What can you draw and write to show what you observed?*
- *What should you do before you leave the science center?*

Share

Following choice time, gather children in the meeting area to talk about what they did in the science center.

> Who went to the science center today? What did you do there?

Assessment

After you have taught the minilessons in this umbrella, observe children as they work in various areas of the room during choice time. Use *The Literacy Continuum* (Fountas and Pinnell 2017) to notice, teach for, and support children's learning as you observe their reading and writing attempts.

▶ What evidence do you have of new understandings children have developed related to the routines for choice time?

- Do children understand and follow the routines for each center?
- How well do children manage their own choices during choice time?
- How are they sharing their choice time experiences during share time?
- Are they integrating drawing and writing into their choice time activities?
- Do they understand and use vocabulary related to choice time, such as *choice time*, *block center*, *play corner*, and *choose*?

▶ In what other ways, beyond the scope of this umbrella, are children using classroom materials and centers?

- Are children using drawing and writing tools appropriately?
- Are they playing and working together well?

Use your observations to determine the next umbrella you will teach. You may also consult Suggested Sequence of Lessons (pp. 483–494) for guidance.

EXTENSIONS FOR LEARNING ABOUT CHOICE TIME

▶ Provide instructions and materials in the centers for a variety of kinds of writing, for example, poster, response to interactive read-aloud, book recommendation, poem, or recipe. Consider integrating social studies or science content into the writing center activities.

▶ Fill the water table with different materials throughout the year (e.g., sand, dried beans, rice). Develop children's vocabulary by prompting conversations with them as they play. Ask questions about what they are doing (e.g., pouring, measuring), how something feels (e.g., rough, wet, cold), or what they like about playing with the material.

▶ Expand opportunities for the creation station by collecting donations of more materials (e.g., broken toys, small paper cups, craft sticks, yarn or string, clean egg cartons, and other clean food packaging).

▶ Use children's recorded observations in the science center as the basis for a class all-about book (e.g., *All About Butterflies, All About Plants*). See IW.24: Writing an All-About Book.

▶ Introduce math activities into the science center or create a math center where children can play and work with manipulatives.

Minilessons in This Umbrella

WML1 Learn how to use glue.

WML2 Take good care of the markers.

WML3 Use the scissors safely.

WML4 Choose your paper.

Before Teaching Umbrella 4 Minilessons

Learning to use writing and drawing tools and working in the writing center support children in developing their literacy skills. At the beginning of the school year, decide how to organize the writing center. Choose containers for materials and label them with pictures and words. Also label the areas where the containers will be stored. Labeling helps with organization and also helps children recognize words and understand that print carries meaning. Provide space for glue, markers (sorted in sets or by color), scissors, pencils, pens, colored pencils, staple remover, blank paper of different sizes, and blank paper stapled into booklets. Several kinds of paper templates for writing and making books are available in the online resources. Start with just a few materials initially to help children find the materials and learn to return materials to the proper location after use. As you do these minilessons with children and provide time for them to gain experience with the materials, you can increase the mix of items, such as adding different kinds of paper.

Use books to show familiar school situations, such as those from the following *Fountas & Pinnell Classroom™ Interactive Read-Aloud Collection* text set or from the classroom library.

Learning and Playing Together: School

Miss Bindergarten Gets Ready for Kindergarten by Joseph Slate

I Love You All Day Long by Francesca Rusackas

Read and enjoy these texts together to help children notice and talk about the different drawing and writing materials authors and illustrations use to make their books.

Writing Minilesson Principle
Learn how to use glue.

Using Drawing and Writing Tools

You Will Need

- a familiar picture book that shows materials being used in the classroom, such as *Miss Bindergarten Gets Ready for Kindergarten* by Joseph Slate, from Text Set: Learning and Playing Together: School

- glue stick

- a picture and a piece of paper upon which to glue the picture

- designated, labeled container(s) for storing glue sticks

- chart paper and markers

- To download the following online resource for this lesson, visit **resources.fountasandpinnell.com**:

    - chart art (optional)

Academic Language/ Important Vocabulary

- draw
- write
- tools
- glue stick·

Continuum Connection

- Listen with attention and understanding to directions (p. 331)

- Remember and follow simple directions with two to three steps (p. 331)

GOAL

Learn the routines for using glue.

RATIONALE

In order to use materials (such as glue sticks) in the writing center safely, appropriately, and independently, children need to be taught explicit steps for using the materials.

ASSESS LEARNING

- Notice whether children know where to get the glue sticks and return them when finished.

- Notice whether they can use a glue stick properly.

- Observe for evidence that children can use vocabulary such as *draw*, *write*, *tools*, and *glue stick*.

MINILESSON

Before teaching this minilesson, make sure children are somewhat familiar with using glue sticks and know where glue sticks are stored in the classroom. To help children learn how to use a glue stick properly, engage them in a short demonstration and inquiry-based lesson. Here is an example.

- Show pages 7, 11–12, and 15–16 from *Miss Bindergarten Gets Ready for Kindergarten*.

    Remember how Miss Bindergarten spent time getting the room ready for the kindergartners to arrive? I did the same thing. What are some things you notice that I did to get the writing center ready?

    Sometimes when you make a picture, you might want to stick something onto the paper. Talk about how you do that.

- As children suggest using a glue stick, ask a volunteer to model getting a glue stick from the writing center. Continue to guide children through the steps of gluing a picture to a piece of paper, modeling as children describe each step (e.g., take off the cap, turn the glue stick up a little, put the cap on, return the glue stick).

- Consider using one or more of these prompts to talk about using glue sticks.

    - *What do you know about using a glue stick?*

    - *Why is it important to turn up (down) the glue stick just a little?*

    - *Why do you put the cap back on after using a glue stick?*

    - *What do you do when you have finished using a glue stick?*

Have a Try

Invite children to talk to a partner about using glue in the classroom.

> Turn and talk to your partner about how much glue you should use.

▶ Ask a few volunteers to share the importance of using the right amount of glue, but not too much.

Summarize and Apply

Write the principle on the chart. Read it to the children and summarize the learning.

> What are the important things to remember about using a glue stick?

▶ On chart paper, briefly sketch each step as children share ideas, guiding the conversation as needed.

> Today if you make a book or a picture during writing time, you might want to use a glue stick. You can look at the chart to help you remember the important things about using a glue stick.

Confer

▶ During independent writing, move around the room to confer briefly with as many individual children as time allows. Sit by side with them and invite them to talk about how they are using glue. Use the following prompts as needed.

- *Show how to move the glue stick up and down.*
- *How do you know the cap is on tight?*
- *Where will you put the glue stick when you are finished?*

Share

Following independent writing, gather children in the meeting area. Ask a few children to share their experiences using glue sticks.

> If you used a glue stick today, tell about that.

> What did you use the glue stick for?

> Tell one step you did when you used a glue stick.

Using Drawing and Writing Tools

You Will Need

- a familiar picture book that shows a child drawing a colorful picture, such as *I Love You All Day Long* by Francesca Rusackas from Text Set: Learning and Playing Together: School
- markers (multiple sets in multiple colors, organized in the writing center)
- labeled container(s) for storing markers
- chart paper and markers
- To download the following online resource for this lesson, visit **resources.fountasandpinnell.com**:
  - chart art (optional)

Academic Language/ Important Vocabulary

- draw
- write
- tools
- markers

Continuum Connection

- Listen with attention and understanding to directions (p. 331)
- Remember and follow simple directions with two to three steps (p. 331)

GOAL

Learn routines for taking good care of markers.

RATIONALE

When children know how to use markers appropriately, they take good care of them so that everyone will have tools for writing and drawing. Having the proper tools for writing and drawing allows children to create drawings with careful attention to color.

ASSESS LEARNING

- Notice whether children know where to both get the markers and return them when finished.
- Notice whether they use markers appropriately.
- Observe for evidence that children can use vocabulary such as *draw*, *write*, *tools*, and *markers*.

MINILESSON

Before teaching this minilesson, make sure children have had experiences using markers and know where markers are stored in the classroom. To help children learn how to use markers properly, engage them in a short demonstration and inquiry-based lesson. Here is an example.

▶ Show page 9 from *I Love You All Day Long*.

> Look at the picture Owen made. What do you notice about the colors he chose to make his apple tree?

> When you draw your pictures, be sure the colors you choose match what you are drawing. You also need to be careful about how you use your markers.

> What is the first thing you do if you want to use markers to draw a picture?

▶ Select several markers to use to draw a picture. Guide children through the steps of properly using the markers. As they describe each step, model it with markers (e.g., choose a color, take off the cap, put the cap back on with a click, return the markers to the proper location).

▶ Consider using one or more of these prompts to encourage talk about using markers:

> - *Where can you put the cap so you do not lose it while you are drawing?*
> - *How do you know the cap is on tight?*
> - *Why do you always return the markers to the correct spot in the writing center when you are finished?*

Have a Try

Invite children to talk to a partner about using markers in the classroom.

> Turn and talk to your partner about some ways you take care of markers in the classroom.

Summarize and Apply

Write the principle on the chart. Read it to the children and summarize the learning.

> What are the steps to help you remember how to use markers in the classroom?

▶ On chart paper, briefly sketch each step as children share ideas, guiding the conversation as needed.

> Today if you make a book or a picture during writing time, you might want to use markers to draw your pictures. Look at the chart to help you remember each step.

Take good care of the markers.

Click!

BLUE MARKERS

Confer

▶ During independent writing time, move around the room to confer briefly with as many individual children as time allows. Sit side by side with them and invite them to talk about how they are using markers. Use the following prompts as needed.

- *Why is it important not to push too hard on the paper with a marker?*
- *Show how to make the cap click.*
- *Where will you put the marker when you have finished drawing?*

Share

Following independent writing, gather children in the meeting area. Ask a few children to share their experiences using markers.

> If you used a marker today, tell how you took good care of it.

> What did you do with the marker?

Section 2: Management

Writing Minilesson Principle
Use the scissors safely.

Using Drawing and Writing Tools

You Will Need

- a pair of scissors and paper to use for modeling
- scissors (one per child)
- designated, labeled container(s) for storing scissors
- chart paper and markers
- To download the online resource for this lesson, visit **resources.fountasandpinnell.com**:
  - chart art (optional)

Academic Language/ Important Vocabulary

- draw
- write
- tools
- scissors

Continuum Connection

- Listen with attention and understanding to directions (p. 331)
- Remember and follow simple directions with two to three steps (p. 331)

GOAL

Learn to use scissors safely.

RATIONALE

When you teach children to use scissors safely and carefully, they not only keep themselves and others from getting hurt, but they also develop independence with writing and drawing projects and fine motor skills.

ASSESS LEARNING

- Notice whether children understand the importance of using scissors in a safe way.
- Notice whether they can use scissors appropriately.
- Observe for evidence that children can use vocabulary such as *draw*, *write*, *tools*, and *scissors*.

MINILESSON

Before teaching this minilesson, make sure children have had experiences using scissors and know where scissors are stored in the classroom. To help children learn how to use scissors properly, engage them in a short demonstration. Here is an example.

- Hold up a pair of scissors.

  Turn and talk to your partner about what you know about using scissors safely.

- After time for a brief discussion, ask a few volunteers to share ideas.

  Notice the way I use these scissors to cut a piece of paper.

- Model the correct way to hold the scissors and use them to cut a piece of paper.

  What did you notice about what I did?

- Encourage children to talk about what they noticed. Include a conversation about safety rules, such as sitting with scissors instead of walking around and always cutting away from your body.

- Pass out a pair of scissors to each child, or as an alternative, have children use finger movements. Have them practice *open*, *shut them* with the scissors or finger movements. Ask volunteers to model proper scissor behavior.

- Collect the scissors.

Have a Try

Invite children to talk to a partner about using scissors in the classroom.

> Turn and talk to your partner about how you walk with scissors in a safe way. Then talk about how you hand scissors to someone.

▶ Ask a few volunteers to share. Highlight the importance of holding the bottom of the scissors with the blades closed, pointing blades down while walking, and facing the handle away from you when handing someone scissors.

Summarize and Apply

Write the principle on the chart. Read it to the children and summarize the learning.

> What are some things to remember when using scissors?

▶ On chart paper, briefly sketch each step as children share ideas, guiding the conversation as needed.

> Today if you make a book or a picture during writing time, you might want to use scissors. You can look at the chart to help you remember the important things about using the scissors safely.

Use the scissors safely.

Sit.

Cut away from you.

Turn the handle out to pass the scissors.

Hold the scissors in a safe way when you walk.

Confer

▶ During independent writing time, move around the room to confer briefly with as many individual children as time allows. Sit side by side with them and invite them to talk about how they are using scissors. Use the following prompts as needed.

- *Show how you give scissors to a partner.*
- *Show how you hold scissors when you walk.*
- *Why is it important that you follow safety rules when using scissors?*

Share

Following independent writing, gather children in the meeting area. Ask a few children to share their experiences using scissors.

> If you used scissors, tell about that.

> What did you make with the scissors?

Writing Minilesson Principle

Choose your paper.

Using Drawing and Writing Tools

You Will Need

- children's writing samples that use different kinds of paper (e.g., a book, a sign, a card)
- various kinds of paper choices
- tape
- chart paper and markers

Academic Language/ Important Vocabulary

- draw
- write
- tools
- paper

Continuum Connection

- Choose paper to match desired organization and the genre (p. 248)
- Listen with attention and understanding to directions (p. 331)

GOAL

Learn that writers choose different paper depending on what they are planning to write.

RATIONALE

Children begin to feel like writers even before they can use all the conventions of writing. When children learn to think about what kind of paper they might use, they understand that writers choose different paper for different writing activities (e.g., a card, a book, or a menu).

ASSESS LEARNING

- Notice whether children understand that writers select different kinds of paper depending on what they are writing.
- Notice whether they can select paper that is appropriate for what they are writing.
- Observe for evidence that children can use vocabulary such as *draw*, *write*, *tools*, and *paper*.

MINILESSON

Before teaching this minilesson, make sure children have had experiences using paper and know where paper is stored in the classroom. To help children learn to select different kinds of paper (e.g., size, color, thickness) depending on what they are writing, engage them in a short demonstration and inquiry-based lesson. Here is an example.

- Show examples of the children's writing samples using different kinds of paper.

  Look at all of the different kinds of paper you have used for writing. What do you notice?

- Have a conversation about the different kinds of paper and why the writers chose the particular kind of paper for what they wrote. Also discuss other things the kinds of paper might be used for. Use one or more of these prompts as needed:

  - *What could these big pieces of paper be used for?*
  - *What kinds of writing could you do with a small piece of paper?*
  - *This has pages that are stapled together. What could you use this for?*
  - *How could you use this piece of folded paper?*

Have a Try

Invite children to talk to a partner about using different paper for different purposes.

> Look around the room. Turn and tell your partner one kind of paper that you see. What would you do with it?

▶ Ask a few volunteers to share.

Summarize and Apply

Write the principle on the chart. Read it to the children and summarize the learning.

▶ Show a variety of paper choices available in the writing center.

> What are some different ways you could use this paper?

▶ On chart paper, tape the several kinds of paper and record children's ideas for what they might do with that paper, guiding the conversation as needed.

> Today if you make a book or a picture during writing time, choose the kind of paper that is best for your writing.

Choose your paper.

	Stapled book
	Colors book cover animal poster
	Big supermarket sign street sign
	Folded birthday card get well card

Confer

▶ During independent writing, move around the room to confer briefly with as many individual children as time allows. Sit side by side with them and invite them to talk about choosing paper. Use the following prompts as needed.

- *What kind of paper will you choose to write that?*
- *What kind of paper might work well for a list?*
- *What kind of paper might work well for a recipe?*

Share

Following independent writing, gather children in the meeting area. Ask a few children to share their experiences using different kinds of paper.

> If you made a paper choice today, tell about that.

> What kind of paper will you use for your next writing? Why?

Assessment

After you have taught the minilessons in this umbrella, observe children as they learn to use drawing and writing tools. Use *The Literacy Continuum* (Fountas and Pinnell 2017) to notice, teach for, and support children's learning as you observe their attempts at reading and writing.

▶ What evidence do you have that children understand how to use drawing and writing tools?

- Do children know how to appropriately use glue sticks?
- Do they understand how to take care of markers?
- Are they able to hold scissors carefully when using them?
- Are they selecting paper that is appropriate for what they are writing?
- Do they understand the terms *draw*, *write*, *tools*, *glue*, *markers*, *scissors*, and *paper*?

▶ In what ways, beyond the scope of this umbrella, are the children using drawing and writing tools?

- Are children making books?
- Are they paying careful attention to how they make their illustrations?

Use your observations to determine the next umbrella you will teach. You may also consult Suggested Sequence of Lessons (pp. 483–494) for guidance.

EXTENSIONS FOR USING DRAWING AND WRITING TOOLS

▶ Repeat the lesson on how to use glue using different kinds of glue and applicators (e.g., liquid glue, glue bottle and brush, cotton swabs, paintbrushes).

▶ Teach minilessons like these for other items children use in the writing center or art center.

▶ As you change the theme of the imaginative play area, include different kinds of paper that can be used for that theme (e.g., mailing envelopes and box labels for the post office, a medical notepad for the animal hospital, shopping list paper for the supermarket).

▶ When children are ready, add other kinds of paper for them to use (e.g., postcards, greeting cards, envelopes, invitations, gift tags, colored copy paper).

Section 3 | Telling Stories

THE LESSONS IN this section build children's oral language and storytelling abilities by reminding them that they can tell stories from their lives. They can tell stories to the class or to one other. They can even use puppets! Once children can *tell* stories, they can learn to draw and write their stories on paper.

3 Telling Stories

Minilessons in This Umbrella

WML1 Tell stories about what you know and care about.

WML2 Tell stories about things you did.

WML3 Tell stories about places you don't want to forget.

WML4 Tell stories about things from your Me Box.

Before Teaching Umbrella 1 Minilessons

Prior to teaching these minilessons, provide opportunities for children to hear and talk about a diversity of stories from many different authors. Hearing stories will enable children to understand that people share what they are thinking through language. Include stories from your own life as well. Telling stories will help children rehearse and organize their ideas before putting them on paper.

The focus of these lessons is to help children realize that they can get story ideas from their own lives. It is not recommended that you teach the minilessons within this umbrella one right after another because you will want children to have opportunities to tell their own stories between each of the lessons. Save the charts from these minilessons because they are referenced in WPS.U1: Getting Ideas for Writing. For mentor texts, use the books listed below from *Fountas & Pinnell Classroom™ Interactive Read-Aloud Collection*, or choose books from the classroom library that tell stories that are personal to the authors.

Letters at Work: The Alphabet

B Is for Bulldozer: A Construction ABC by June Sobel

Taking Care of Each Other: Family

Do Like Kyla by Angela Johnson

Jonathan and His Mommy by Irene Smalls

Elizabeti's Doll by Stephanie Stuve-Bodeen

As you read and enjoy these texts together, help children

- talk about what events from their own lives the stories make them think about, and

- imagine what events from an author's life she may have used to decide what to write about.

The Alphabet

Family

Writing Minilesson Principle
Tell stories about what you know and care about.

Storytelling

You Will Need

- several familiar books about topics that are personal to the author, such as the following:

  - *B Is for Bulldozer: A Construction ABC* by June Sobel, from Text Set: Letters at Work: The Alphabet

  - *Do Like Kyla* by Angela Johnson, from Text Set: Taking Care of Each Other: Family

- chart paper and markers

Academic Language / Important Vocabulary

- stories
- know
- care

Continuum Connection

- Understand that writers may tell stories from their own lives (p. 244)

- Generate and expand ideas through talk with peers and teacher (p. 248)

- Look for ideas and topics in personal experiences, shared through talk (p. 248)

- Use storytelling to generate and rehearse language that may be written later (p. 248)

GOAL

Understand that you can tell stories about what you know about and care about.

RATIONALE

Telling stories fosters the ability to progress from telling to writing. When children tell stories about things that they know and care about, they learn that writers get ideas from personal experiences and that those ideas can be written down.

ASSESS LEARNING

- Listen for evidence that children are using ideas from their own lives to tell stories.

- Look for evidence that children can use vocabulary such as *stories*, *know*, and *care*.

MINILESSON

Use familiar stories to engage children in thinking and talking about storytelling. Here is an example.

- Show *B Is for Bulldozer: A Construction ABC*. Review a few pages.

  What is this book about?

  How do you think the author, June Sobel, knew what to write about the building of an amusement park?

- Show *Do Like Kyla*. Review a few pages.

  What is this book about?

  How do you think the author, Angela Johnson, thought of things that two sisters might do together?

- As children discuss their thoughts, guide them to realize that the authors chose something they knew about from their own lives (e.g., construction sites, amusement parks, experiences with siblings).

  I know a lot about hiking because I go hiking a lot with my family. I could tell about that.

- Tell a simple story about any topic that you know and care about (e.g., hiking). The goal is to choose an authentic subject and tell about it.

  Why do you think people tell stories about things they know and care about?

Have a Try

Invite children to tell a story about something they know and care about.

> Think about something you know and care about. Turn and tell your partner your story.

▶ After time for discussion, ask several children to share their story topics. Record the ideas on chart paper with a simple sentence and sketch.

Summarize and Apply

Write the principle at the top of the chart. Summarize the learning and invite children to tell a story and write about it during independent writing.

> During writing time, you can tell me a story about something you know about or care about. Then you can draw and write about your story. Look at the chart to help you think of ideas.

Tell stories about what you know and care about.

Oliver collects rocks.

Kinsley plays the piano.

Giana bathes her dog.

Obi likes to draw.

Confer

▶ During independent writing, move around the room to confer with as many individual children as time allows. Sit side by side with them and invite them to tell stories from their own lives. Use the prompts below as needed.

- *Tell more about what happened.*
- *What happened next? after that?*
- *Who was with you?*
- *You wrote what you know about _____ . What do you like about _____ ?*

Share

Following independent writing, gather children in the meeting area. Ask several children to share their stories.

> Tell a story you were thinking about today.

▶ Add more story ideas to the chart.

Writing Minilesson Principle
Tell stories about things you did.

Storytelling

You Will Need

- a book that children know that includes familiar experiences, such as *Jonathan and His Mommy* by Irene Smalls, from Text Set: Taking Care of Each Other: Family
- chart paper and markers

Academic Language / Important Vocabulary

- stories
- ideas

Continuum Connection

- Understand that writers may tell stories from their own lives (p. 244)
- Tell stories from personal experience (p. 331)
- Tell personal experiences in a logical sequence (p. 331)

GOAL

Understand that you can tell stories about things you have done.

RATIONALE

When children tell stories from their own lives, they practice expressing thoughts and ideas through language. Telling stories supports their ability to move from oral to written language.

ASSESS LEARNING

- Observe whether children are telling stories about their own experiences.
- Look for evidence that children can use vocabulary such as *stories* and *ideas*.

MINILESSON

To help children think about the minilesson principle, use a familiar book and a simple oral story of your own to demonstrate that people tell stories about things they have done. Here is an example.

- Show *Jonathan and His Mommy*.

  In this book, *Jonathan and His Mommy*, what did Jonathan tell about?

- Go through a few pages with children and engage them in a conversation about the things Jonathan and his mother do together. Help them realize that the author may have used ideas from her own life in the book.

  This story makes me think about things I have done that I can tell a story about.

- Tell a story about something you have done with a family member (e.g., bike riding) or something the class has done together (e.g., field trip). Engage children by telling it like a storyteller using details and basic story structure (beginning, middle, and end). Consider modeling telling the story across your fingers—tell about the first event on the thumb, the next event on the next finger, and so forth.

  You can tell stories about things you have done, too.

Have a Try

Invite children to talk to a partner about an experience from their own lives.

> Think of something you did with your family or a friend. Turn and tell your partner about that.

▶ After time for discussion, invite a few children to quickly share their stories. After each story, make a sketch on chart paper to help children think of ideas for storytelling. Write each child's name next to the sketch. Post the chart and continue to add ideas as children tell stories about their experiences.

Summarize and Apply

Write the principle at the top of the chart. Summarize the learning and invite children to tell stories about their own lives during independent writing.

> During writing time, you can tell me your story. You can also tell the story to a partner or act it out when you play in the play corner.

Tell stories about things you did.

Hailey

Jack

Taavi

Hikari

Confer

▶ During independent writing, move around the room to confer briefly with as many individual children as time allows. Sit side by side with them and invite them to tell you stories about themselves. Use the prompts below as needed to encourage children to tell more. Repeat the story you heard back to the child.

- *What did you do last night? (over the weekend? last week?)*
- *Tell the story across your fingers. Point to your thumb. What happened first?*
- *How will your story end?*
- *Tell more about that.*

Share

Following independent writing, gather children in the meeting area. Ask several children to share their stories.

> Tell a story you told about today.

Writing Minilesson Principle
Tell stories about places you don't want to forget.

Storytelling

You Will Need

- a familiar book that includes a setting, such as *Elizabeti's Doll* by Stephanie Stuve-Bodeen, from Text Set: Taking Care of Each Other: Family

- chart paper and markers

Academic Language / Important Vocabulary

- stories

- places

Continuum Connection

- Generate and expand ideas through talk with peers and teacher (p. 248)

- Look for ideas and topics in personal experiences, shared through talk (p. 248)

- Use storytelling to generate and rehearse language that may be written later (p. 248)

GOAL

Understand you can tell stories about places you have been.

RATIONALE

Teaching children to express their ideas by telling stories about places that are familiar to them helps them understand that the things they know about the world have value. As children tell their stories, help them clarify information and add details by asking questions and restating what you heard.

ASSESS LEARNING

- Notice whether children tell stories about places they have been.

- Look for evidence that children can use vocabulary such as *stories* and *places*.

MINILESSON

To help children think about the minilesson principle, use a familiar book that has a setting and tell a simple story about a place you have been. Here is an example.

- Show *Elizabeti's Doll*. Review a few pages and read the note about the author on the inside cover.

  The author, Stephanie Stuve-Bodeen, tells a story about a place in Africa called Tanzania. This place is special to her, and she shared a story about that place by writing a book.

- Tell a simple story about a place that is special to you. Here is an example, but tell your own personal story.

  A place that is special to me is the lake near where I grew up. The water was so clear that I could see all the way to the bottom. I would open my eyes underwater and look at the brown rocks, tan sand, and green plants. The water was cold, but I did not mind. Sometimes, we would find crawdads, which look like small lobsters, under rocks. We would have to be careful because they had claws that could pinch your toes!

- After telling your story, engage children in a conversation about using a special place to tell a story.

  What did you learn about a place that is special to me?

  What words helped you know what the lake looked like?

  When you tell a story about a place that is special to you, tell about what you did there and what the place looked like.

Have a Try

Invite children to talk to a partner about places they want to remember.

> Turn and tell your partner about a place that you want to remember.

▶ After time for discussion, invite a few children to share ideas. On chart paper, draw a quick sketch of the place and add the child's name.

Summarize and Apply

Write the principle on the chart. Summarize the learning and invite children to tell and write stories during independent writing.

> You can tell stories about places you want to remember. During writing time today, you can tell me a story about a place that is special to you. Then you can make a book about it.

Tell stories about places you don't want to forget.

Nari

Ajani

Charles

Grace

Confer

▶ During independent writing, move around the room to confer briefly with as many individual children as time allows. Sit side by side with them and invite them to tell stories from their own lives. Use the prompts below as needed.

- *Can you add to that idea?*
- *Tell more about that.*
- *How did you feel when you were in that place? Did you feel excited, happy, surprised?*
- *What did you see (hear, smell, feel) there?*

Share

Following independent writing, gather children in the meeting area. Choose several children to share their stories about places they want to remember.

> Tell about a place that is special to you.

▶ Add the story ideas to the chart.

Writing Minilesson Principle

Tell stories about things from your Me Box.

Storytelling

You Will Need

- Me Boxes for you and each child or objects to use for storytelling
- chart paper and markers

Academic Language / Important Vocabulary

- stories
- Me Box
- item

Continuum Connection

- Understand that writers may tell stories from their own lives (p. 244)
- Generate and expand ideas through talk with peers and teacher (p. 248)
- Look for ideas and topics in personal experiences, shared through talk (p. 248)
- Use storytelling to generate and rehearse language that may be written later (p. 248)

GOAL

Understand you can tell stories about items that represent important memories.

RATIONALE

When children choose topics from their own lives for telling stories, they learn to value their lives and understand that they have unique stories to tell. Telling stories orally helps children develop their use of language before they write their ideas.

ASSESS LEARNING

- Notice whether children tell stories about items in their Me Boxes.
- Look for evidence that children can use vocabulary such as *stories*, *Me Box*, and *item*.

MINILESSON

To help children understand that they can use special items for story ideas, engage them in thinking and talking about items from their Me Boxes. Here is an example.

- Before teaching, have each child prepare a Me Box filled with meaningful objects. Make a Me Box for yourself as well.

- Choose an item to show from your Me Box. Tell a story about the object you have chosen. Here is an example, but tell your own personal story.

  In my Me Box is a toy frog. When I was younger, I went to a carnival with my dad. There was a game at the carnival that we loved to play. To win a prize, you had to throw a ball into a bowl filled with water. It was hard because the balls were hard to aim and the bowls seemed so far away! My dad missed all his throws. When it was my turn, I actually got a ball into a bowl. In that bowl was a toy frog, and here it is! I have saved it to remind me how much fun my dad and I had at the carnival.

- Engage children in a conversation about the story you told and have them think about what items from their Me Boxes they might tell a story about.

  What did you learn about this item from my Me Box?

  Look at the items in your Me Box. What is an item you could tell a story about?

- Ask a few children to share ideas. Create a chart with a sketch of the item they have chosen, along with the child's name and a simple sentence. Post the chart to help children remember ideas they can tell stories about.

Have a Try

Invite children to tell a partner about something from their Me Boxes.

> Choose one item from your Me Box. Tell your partner about that item.

▶ After time for discussion, invite a few children to share. Add new ideas to the chart.

Summarize and Apply

Write the principle at the top of the chart. Summarize the learning and invite children to tell and write stories during independent writing.

> Today we talked about telling stories about things in your Me Boxes. During writing time today, you can tell me a story about an item in your Me Box. Then you can write a story about your item.

> **Tell stories about things from your Me Box.**
>
> Carlos won an award.
>
> Yon found a penny.
>
> Spencer saw an elephant at the zoo.
>
> Rosa found a feather on a hike.

Confer

▶ During independent writing, move around the room to confer briefly with as many individual children as time allows. Sit side by side with them and invite them to tell stories about themselves. Use the following prompts below as needed.

- *Tell about this item in your Me Box.*
- *Why did you choose to include this item in your Me Box?*
- *Tell more about that.*
- *Can you add to that?*

Share

Following independent writing, gather children in the meeting area. Have several children share their stories.

▶ Ask a few children to share their stories.

> Tell about something in your Me Box.

▶ Then add the story ideas to the chart.

Assessment

After you have taught the minilessons in this umbrella, observe children as they tell stories. Use *The Literacy Continuum* (Fountas and Pinnell 2017) to notice, teach for, and support children's learning as you observe their attempts at storytelling.

▶ What evidence do you have of new understandings children have developed related to storytelling?

- Do children use ideas from their own lives to tell stories?

- Can they develop stories about items from their Me Boxes?

- Do they understand and use vocabulary such as *stories*, *know*, *care*, *ideas*, *places*, and *Me Box*?

▶ In what ways, beyond the scope of this umbrella, are children showing readiness for storytelling?

- Do they show an interest in acting out their stories?

- Are they using ideas from their own lives when making books?

Use your observations to determine the next umbrella you will teach. You may also consult Suggested Sequence of Lessons (pp. 483–494) for guidance.

EXTENSIONS FOR STORYTELLING

▶ Post the charts from each minilesson in the writing center so children can use the story ideas for making books. Refer to the charts when you teach WPS.U1: Getting Ideas for Writing

▶ Have children tell their stories to partners, rotating the children so they have opportunities to hear stories from different classmates.

▶ Encourage children to use photographs or drawings for story ideas.

▶ Invite families to make a Family Box and fill it with items that represent shared family experiences. Children can use those items to tell stories.

Minilessons in This Umbrella

WML1 Tell the story from the pictures.

WML2 Pretend you are the characters in a story.

WML3 Use puppets to act out a story.

Before Teaching Umbrella 2 Minilessons

If you have *The Reading Minilessons Book, Kindergarten* (Fountas and Pinnell 2019), we recommend teaching LA.U17: Using Pictures in a Book to Tell the Story.

Read and discuss stories that are easy to retell and/or act out, such as those with few characters, simple plots, and plenty of repetition. Use the following books from *Fountas & Pinnell Classroom*™ *Interactive Read-Aloud Collection* text sets, or choose books from the classroom library that have similar characteristics. We recommend that these lessons be taught after you and the children have read books together that lend themselves to being acted out. Notice that the list below includes books from text sets that you may not have read yet with the class if you are following the *Interactive Read-Aloud Collection* sequence. If that is the case, read and enjoy the books with children now and revisit them in detail later.

Learning and Playing Together: School
The Bus for Us by Suzanne Bloom

Exploring Animal Tales
The Little Red Hen by Paul Galdone

Sharing Stories: Folktales
The Gingerbread Boy by Paul Galdone

As you read and enjoy these texts together, help children

- think about what is happening in the story,
- talk about the words, actions, and personality of each character, and
- notice how the illustrations help tell the story.

School

Animal Tales

Folktales

Section 3: Telling Stories

Writing Minilesson Principle
Tell the story from the pictures.

Acting Out Stories

You Will Need

- a familiar book that can be easily retold from the illustrations, such as *The Bus for Us* by Suzanne Bloom, from Text Set: Learning and Playing Together: School

- chart paper and markers

- a basket of wordless picture books

- To download the following online resource for this lesson, visit **resources.fountasandpinnell.com**:

  - Sequence Cards (*The Bus for Us*)

Academic Language/ Important Vocabulary

- picture
- story
- order

Continuum Connection

- Retell familiar stories or stories from texts (p. 331)

- Share knowledge of story structure by telling what happened, mostly in order (p. 331)

GOAL

Use the pictures in a book to retell the story.

RATIONALE

To tell a story using the illustrations, children have to look closely at the illustrations and construct their thinking about what is happening in the story. By putting those ideas into words, children become familiar with the parts of a story–the plot, the setting, and the characters. They also develop a sense of the story's structure.

ASSESS LEARNING

- Notice whether children can use the illustrations to tell the story.

- Listen to children tell a story they have heard or read. Do they tell the events in the correct sequence?

- Look for evidence that children can use vocabulary such as *picture*, *story*, and *order*.

MINILESSON

Use a familiar book and related sequence cards to demonstrate retelling a story from the illustrations.

- Show the cover of *The Bus for Us* and read the title. Show some of the pages as a quick review.

  > We read this story about two children who are waiting for the bus. We can tell what happens in the story just by looking at the pictures. Watch what I do.

- Retell the beginning of the story. As you retell each part, attach the corresponding sequence card to chart paper.

  > Tess and Gus are waiting for the bus. Tess asks, "Is this the bus for us, Gus?" But it's not the bus. It's a taxi. Then another vehicle arrives. Tess asks again, "Is this the bus for us, Gus?" This time, it is a tow truck.

- After you finish retelling the beginning of the story, ask children what they noticed.

  > How did I know what happens in the story?

  > I looked at the pictures. What picture did I tell about first?

  > What picture did I tell about next?

  > When you tell a story from the pictures, remember to tell what happens in the right order. Start by saying what happens in the first picture. Then, keep going in order until you get to the last picture and the end of the story.

Have a Try

Invite children to retell *The Bus for Us* to a partner.

▶ Add the remaining sequence card to the chart.

> Now it's your turn. Look at the pictures and tell the story to your partner.

Summarize and Apply

Write the principle at the top of the chart. Read it to children. Help children summarize the learning and remind them to tell the story in the right order when they tell a story from the pictures.

> What did you learn today about how to tell a story from the pictures?

> This basket has books without words. Today during writing time, you will practice telling one of these stories either to me or to a partner.

Tell the story from the pictures.

First

Next

Then

Last

Confer

▶ During independent writing, move around the room to confer briefly with as many individual children as time allows. Invite them to look at a wordless picture book and then tell the story to you. Use prompts such as the following if needed.

- *Look at the first picture. What happens first in the story?*
- *What happens next?*
- *What are these characters doing?*
- *Remember to tell the story in the same order that the pictures are in.*

Share

Following independent writing, gather children in the meeting area. Ask one or two children to tell a story (or part of a story) from the pictures.

> Who would like to tell a story from the pictures in a book?

Section 3: Telling Stories

WML 2
STR.U2.WML2

Writing Minilesson Principle
Pretend you are the characters in a story.

Acting Out Stories

You Will Need

- a familiar story that can be easily acted out, such as *The Little Red Hen* by Paul Galdone, from Text Set: Exploring Animal Tales
- three children prepared to act out *The Little Red Hen* with you
- props and/or costumes for acting out *The Little Red Hen,* such as cat ears, a broom, and a cake pan
- chart paper and markers
- To download the following online resource for this lesson, visit **resources.fountasandpinnell.com**:
  - chart art (optional)

Academic Language/ Important Vocabulary

- pretend
- character
- story
- act

Continuum Connection

- Act out stories with or without props (p. 331)

GOAL

Retell a familiar story by acting it out.

RATIONALE

Acting out a familiar story helps children notice that the characters are an integral part of a story. They will reflect this knowledge in the stories they tell and write.

ASSESS LEARNING

- Observe children as they act out familiar stories. Do their dramatizations reflect the story (the characters, the events, the sequence) accurately?
- Look for evidence that children can use vocabulary such as *pretend, character, story,* and *act.*

MINILESSON

With help from a small group of children, model how to act out a story. Then engage the other children in a discussion about what they noticed.

- Show the cover of *The Little Red Hen* and read the title. Briefly review the story.

    Some of your classmates and I are going to act out this story by pretending to be the characters. Watch what we do.

- With your three helpers, act out the story of *The Little Red Hen* (or a portion of it). Use props and/or costumes (e.g., cat ears, a broom, a cake pan), if possible.

- Ask the other children what they noticed about how you acted out the story.

    What character did I pretend to be?

    What character did _____ pretend to be? How could you tell?

    How did we know what to say?

    What did we do with our bodies? How did we know what to do?

    How did we make the story seem real?

Have a Try

Invite children to talk to a partner about how to act out a story.

> Turn and talk to your partner about what to do when you act out a story.

▶ Record children's responses on chart paper.

Summarize and Apply

Write the principle at the top of the chart. Read it to children. Summarize the learning and remind children to pretend to be a character when they act out a story.

> Today you will work with a group of three other children to act out *The Little Red Hen*.

Confer

▶ During independent writing time or choice time, guide a small group of children to act out *The Little Red Hen*. Use prompts such as the following if needed.

- *Who wants to be the hen?*
- *How can you make your voice sound like the hen?*
- *What does the hen do?*
- *What happens first in the story? What happens next? What happens at the end?*

Pretend you are the characters in a story.

- Pretend to be a character.

- Say what the character says.

Not I!

- Do what the character does.

- Wear a costume.

- Use objects from the story.

Share

After children have had a chance to act out a story, gather them together to talk about what they did and how they make themselves seem like the characters.

> How did you make yourself seem like the characters in *The Little Red Hen*?

Writing Minilesson Principle
Use puppets to act out a story.

Acting Out Stories

You Will Need

- a familiar story that can be acted out with puppets, such as *The Gingerbread Boy* by Paul Galdone, from Text Set: Sharing Stories: Folktales

- several children prepared to act out the story with you

- stick puppets for each character

- chart paper and markers

- To download the following online resources for this lesson, visit **resources.fountasandpinnell.com**:

  - Character Puppets (*The Gingerbread Boy*)

  - chart art (optional)

Academic Language/ Important Vocabulary

- puppet

- act

- character

- order

Continuum Connection

- Act out stories with or without props (p. 331)

GOAL

Use puppets to retell a familiar story.

RATIONALE

Retelling familiar stories helps children internalize story structure and language, knowledge that they will use when they write their own stories. Using a visual aid such as a puppet helps them engage more deeply and concretely with a story.

ASSESS LEARNING

- Notice whether children can accurately retell some of the events in a story's plot when they act out a story using puppets.

- Observe whether children retell the events in the correct order.

- Look for evidence that children can use vocabulary such as *puppet*, *act*, *character*, and *order*.

MINILESSON

Before the lesson, glue the character puppets from online resources onto craft sticks. With help from a small group of children, use the stick puppets to demonstrate using puppets to act out a story.

- Show the cover of *The Gingerbread Boy* and read the title. Briefly review the pages.

  We read this story about a gingerbread boy. Watch us act out the story with our puppets.

- With the children who have been prepared beforehand, act out the story (or a portion of the story) using the stick puppets.

- Ask the other children what they noticed about how you acted out the story. Record children's responses on chart paper.

  What did we do with the puppets?

  What did we say? How did we know what to say?

  What part of the story did we tell first? How did we know what order to tell the story in?

  When you tell a story with puppets, first tell the beginning of the story, then the middle, and then the end. Tell the story in the same order that it happens in the book.

Have a Try

Invite children to talk to a partner about how to use puppets to act out a story.

> Turn and talk to your partner about how you can use puppets to act out a story.

Summarize and Apply

Write the principle at the top of the chart. Read it to children. Summarize the learning and remind children to tell the story in the right order when they use puppets to act out a story.

> Today you will work in small groups to act out *The Gingerbread Boy* using puppets. Remember to tell the story in the order that it happens in the book.

Confer

▶ During independent writing or choice time, help a small group of children act out *The Gingerbread Boy* using stick puppets. Use prompts such as the following if needed.

- *What happens first in the story? How can you show that with your puppets?*
- *Use your puppet to show what the gingerbread boy does next.*
- *What happens at the end of the story?*

Share

After children have had a chance to act out a story with puppets, gather them in the meeting area to talk about what they did.

> How did you use puppets to act out a story?

Use puppets to act out a story.

- **Say** what the characters say.
- **Do** what the characters do.
- **Tell** the story in the order it happens.

Assessment

After you have taught the minilessons in this umbrella, observe children as they tell their own stories and retell familiar stories. Use *The Literacy Continuum* (Fountas and Pinnell 2017) to notice, teach for, and support children's learning as you observe their oral communication.

▶ What evidence do you have of new understandings children have developed related to acting out stories?

- Can children retell the major events in a story from the illustrations?
- Do they act out or retell the events in a story in the correct sequence?
- Can they pretend to be the characters in a story?
- Can they use puppets to act out a story?
- Do they understand and use vocabulary such as *character*, *puppet*, *act*, and *story*?

▶ In what other ways, beyond the scope of this umbrella, are children ready to develop their storytelling?

- Do they speak loudly and clearly enough?
- Do they look at the audience?

Use your observations to determine the next umbrella you will teach. You may also consult Suggested Sequence of Lessons (pp. 483–494) for guidance.

EXTENSIONS FOR ACTING OUT STORIES

▶ Regularly share wordless picture books and ask children to help you tell the story from the illustrations. Alternatively, have them retell a familiar story (that does have words) from the illustrations.

▶ Help children make stick or sock puppets for a familiar story in the art center and then use the puppets to act out the story.

▶ Give children plenty of opportunities to act out stories in the dramatic play corner, stocked with various props and costumes.

▶ Help children make props, costumes, or sets for their drama productions in your classroom's art center or creation station.

▶ Plan and rehearse an end-of-year class play and invite an audience to come and watch it.

Minilessons in This Umbrella

WML1 Speak with a strong voice.

WML2 Look at your audience.

WML3 Tell your story in the order it happened.

Before Teaching Umbrella 3 Minilessons

Before teaching the minilessons in this umbrella, teach Umbrella 1: Storytelling. In addition, give children plenty of opportunities to listen to stories read aloud and told by you and to share stories of their own. Tell various kinds of stories (e.g., about your own experiences and shared class experiences, retellings of familiar stories) and model effective storytelling techniques, such as speaking at an appropriate volume and rate, making eye contact with the audience, and telling the events in the story in the correct sequence.

As you share stories together, help children

- think about what is happening at the beginning, the middle, and the end of the story, and

- notice how you use your voice and hold your body while you read or tell a story.

Writing Minilesson Principle
Speak with a strong voice.

Learning How to Tell Stories

You Will Need

- an idea for a story (e.g., a personal experience or a retelling of a familiar book)
- chart paper and markers
- To download the following online resource for this lesson, visit **resources.fountasandpinnell.com**:
  - chart art (optional)

Academic Language/ Important Vocabulary

- story
- strong
- voice

Continuum Connection

- Talk about a topic with enthusiasm (p. 331)
- Speak with confidence (p. 331)
- Tell stories in an interesting way (p. 331)
- Speak at appropriate volume to be heard, but not too loud (p. 331)
- Speak at an appropriate rate to be understood (p. 331)

GOAL

Speak with confidence and enthusiasm and in a way that can be heard and understood.

RATIONALE

When children understand that the way they speak (volume, rate, etc.) matters, they are better able to communicate their ideas effectively. Telling stories orally will help them put their ideas into writing later on.

ASSESS LEARNING

- Observe children as they tell stories to note the volume and rate of their speaking.
- Look for evidence that children can use vocabulary such as *story*, *strong*, and *voice*.

MINILESSON

To help children think about the minilesson principle, engage them in an inquiry around how you use your voice when telling a story.

- Tell a brief story about a personal or shared class experience (e.g., a recent school trip) or a brief retelling of a familiar story (e.g., "Little Red Riding Hood"). First, tell the story too quietly.

  What did you notice about my voice when I told the story?

  How should I change my voice the next time I tell the story?

- Tell the story again, this time at an appropriate volume but too quickly.

  What did you notice about my voice this time? Could you understand what I was saying?

  What should I do next time so that you can understand the story better?

- Tell the story one last time with an appropriate volume and rate. Ask children to share what they noticed about how you used your voice.

  This time, I used a strong voice to tell my story. I didn't speak too loudly or too quietly. I didn't speak too fast or too slow. You could hear me and understand what I was saying. Did I sound excited to tell my story?

- Write on chart paper what children noticed about your storytelling.

Have a Try

Invite children to tell a partner a story about a personal experience.

> Think of something fun you did recently. Turn and tell a story about it to your partner. Remember to use a strong voice so your partner can hear you and understand your story.

Summarize and Apply

Write the principle at the top of the chart and read it to the children. Summarize the learning and remind children to speak with a strong voice when they tell stories.

> Today during writing time, you will tell a story to me or to a classmate. Remember to speak with a strong voice so that the listener can hear and understand your story. If you have time, write your story in a book.

Speak with a strong voice.

• Not too quiet.

• Not too loud.

• Not too fast.

• Not too slow.

Confer

▸ During independent writing, move around the room to confer briefly with as many individual children as time allows. Sit side by side with them and invite them to tell you a story. Use prompts such as the following if needed.

- *Try speaking a little louder. I don't want to miss anything!*
- *Try saying that a little more slowly.*
- *You used a good strong voice to tell your story!*

Share

Following independent writing, gather children in the meeting area to practice telling stories.

> Who would like to tell a story? Remember to use a strong voice so everyone can hear and understand what you're saying.

WML2

Writing Minilesson Principle
Look at your audience.

Learning How to Tell Stories

You Will Need

- an idea for a story (e.g., a personal experience or a retelling of a familiar book)
- chart paper and markers
- To download the following online resource for this lesson, visit **resources.fountasandpinnell.com**:
  - chart art (optional)

Academic Language/ Important Vocabulary

- story
- audience

Continuum Connection

- Look at the audience (or other person) while speaking (p. 331)

GOAL

Look at the audience (or other person) while speaking.

RATIONALE

When children understand the importance of maintaining eye contact, they are better able to communicate with their audience. This in turn will make them more confident and more motivated to continue telling stories.

ASSESS LEARNING

- Observe whether children make eye contact with their audience when they tell stories.
- Look for evidence that children can use vocabulary such as *story* and *audience*.

MINILESSON

To help children think about the minilesson principle, model how to effectively make eye contact with the audience while telling a story. However, take into consideration that some children are not comfortable with establishing or cannot establish eye contact because of cultural conventions or for other reasons. Here is an example.

- Tell a very short story about a personal or a shared class experience or a retelling of a familiar story. For this first telling, do not look directly at the children.

  What did you notice about how I told my story? Where was I looking?

  Where do you think I should look when I tell a story?

- Tell the story again, this time making eye contact with the children.

  What did you notice about how I told my story this time? Where was I looking?

  Do you think I told my story better when I looked at you or when I looked at the floor and around the room? Why?

  Remember to look at your audience when you tell a story. Your audience is the person or the people who are listening.

- Make a chart to help children remember to look at the audience when they tell a story.

Have a Try

Invite children to tell their partner a story.

> Turn and tell your partner a story about something you did yesterday. Remember to look at your partner!

Summarize and Apply

Write the principle at the top of the chart and read it to the children. Summarize the learning and remind children to look at their audience when they tell a story.

> Today during writing time, you will practice telling stories. You can tell a story to me or to your classmates. Remember to look at your audience when you're telling your story! Then, if you have time, write your story in a book.

Confer

▶ During independent writing, move around the room to confer briefly with as many individual children as time allows. Sit side by side with them and invite them to tell you a story. Use prompts such as the following if needed.

- *Where should you look when you're telling a story?*
- *Say that part again, but this time remember to look at me.*
- *I like how you looked at me while you told your story.*

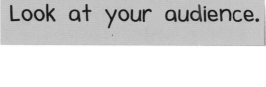

Share

Following independent writing, gather children in the meeting area to share their stories. Remind the storytellers to look at the audience.

> Who would like to share your story?

> Would anyone like to tell us about someone else's story?

Writing Minilesson Principle

Tell your story in the order it happened.

Learning How to Tell Stories

You Will Need

- an idea for a story (e.g., a personal experience or a retelling of a familiar book)
- chart paper and markers
- To download the following online resource for this lesson, visit **resources.fountasandpinnell.com**:
  - chart art (optional)

Academic Language/ Important Vocabulary

- story
- order

Continuum Connection

- Tell personal experiences in a logical sequence (p. 331)
- Present information or ideas in a logical sequence (p. 331)
- Demonstrate knowledge of story structure (p. 331)

GOAL

Tell stories in a logical sequence.

RATIONALE

When children understand how to tell stories in a logical sequence, they are better able to tell stories that their audience will understand and enjoy.

ASSESS LEARNING

- Observe whether children tell stories in a logical sequence.
- Look for evidence that children can use vocabulary such as *story* and *order*.

MINILESSON

To help children think about the minilesson principle, model telling a story in a logical sequence and engage children in a discussion about what they noticed. Here is an example.

- Tell a very brief story about a personal or a shared class experience or a retelling of a familiar story. Hold a finger up as you tell each part and explain that each part will be a page.

  What happened first in my story?

  What happened next?

  What happened after that?

  What happened last in my story?

  How did I know what to say first, next, after that, and last in my story?

  I told my story in the order that it happened. First I told what happened first, then I told what happened next, then I told what happened after that, and finally I told what happened last. Why do you think it's important to tell a story in the order that it happened?

  When you tell your story in the order it happened, your audience will understand and enjoy the story.

Have a Try

Invite children to tell a story to their partner.

> Turn and tell your partner a story about what you did this morning. Remember to tell your story in the order it happened. Hold up a finger as you tell about what will go on each page.

▶ Choose a volunteer to tell a story. Make a chart to show the order of the story.

Summarize and Apply

Write the principle at the top of the chart and read it to the children. Summarize the learning and remind children to tell a story in the order it happened.

> Today during writing time, tell a story to me or to a classmate. Make sure to tell your story in the order it happened. If you have time, write your story in a book.

Tell your story in the order it happened.

First
↓
Next
↓
Then
↓
Last

Confer

▶ During independent writing, move around the room to confer briefly with as many individual children as time allows. Sit side by side with them and invite them to tell you a story. Use prompts such as the following if needed.

- *What happened first in your story?*
- *What happened next?*
- *Then what happened?*
- *What happened last?*
- *Did _____ happen before or after _____ ?*

Share

Following independent writing, gather children in the meeting area to share their stories. Have children pay attention to the order of events.

> Who would like to share your story?

Section 3: Telling Stories

Assessment

After you have taught the minilessons in this umbrella, observe children as they tell stories. Use *The Literacy Continuum* (Fountas and Pinnell 2017) to notice, teach for, and support children's learning as you observe their oral communication skills.

- ▶ What evidence do you have of new understandings children have developed related to storytelling?
  - When children tell a story, do they use a strong voice?
  - Do they make eye contact with their audience?
  - Do they tell the events in their story in the order that they occurred?
  - Do they understand and use vocabulary such as *story*, *strong*, *voice*, *audience*, and *order*?
- ▶ In what other ways, beyond the scope of this umbrella, are children extending their knowledge of telling stories?
  - Are children using interesting words when they tell their stories?
  - Do they tell stories as part of their play?

Use your observations to determine the next umbrella you will teach. You may consult Suggested Sequence of Lessons (pp. 483–494) for guidance.

EXTENSIONS FOR STORYTELLING

- ▶ Give children daily opportunities to share stories with their classmates, such as in morning meeting or in the dramatic play corner. Also provide various ways for telling a story, such as with puppets, from a picture, or to a stuffed animal.

- ▶ When children tell stories, prompt them to give more details with questions such as *What did you do after that? How did you feel when that happened? What did it smell/taste/look/sound like? What did you like about that?*

- ▶ When children listen to stories told by others, ask questions such as *What happened first in the story? What happened next? What happened at the end of the story? What did you notice about how _____ told his story?*

- ▶ Use interactive or shared writing to write stories with children. Use the stories for shared reading.

- ▶ Provide models of good storytelling by inviting a local author or professional storyteller to the class or playing professional recordings of stories.

Section 4 | Making Books

CHILDREN KNOW ABOUT telling stories and they have had books read to them. Making their own picture books is a logical step for them. As children make books, they learn about making books and they learn more about telling stories. When they tell more stories, they have more ideas for making books. The lessons in this section introduce the basics of making books and suggest several kinds of books that children might make.

4 Making Books

Minilessons in This Umbrella

WML1 Make a book.

WML2 Write your name on your book.

WML3 Make a book with pictures and writing.

WML4 Plan what to put on each page.

WML5 Decide when your book is finished.

Before Teaching Umbrella 1 Minilessons

Children will benefit from having experienced at least some of the minilessons in Section 3: Telling Stories and from having enjoyed a variety of books, such as fiction stories, pattern books, wordless books, and nonfiction books. Use the books listed below from *Fountas & Pinnell Classroom™ Interactive Read-Aloud Collection* text sets and *Shared Reading Collection* as well as the complete text sets Sharing Stories and Songs: Nursery Rhymes and Letters at Work: The Alphabet. Also consider using the class-made book from IW.8: Making a Class Big Book. Alternatively, or in addition, use a variety of books from the classroom library that children have enjoyed.

Interactive Read-Aloud Collection
Taking Care of Each Other: Family

Do Like Kyla by Angela Johnson

Elizabeti's Doll by Stephanie Stuve-Bodeen

Jonathan and His Mommy by Irene Smalls

Learning and Playing Together: School

The Bus for Us by Suzanne Bloom

Shared Reading Collection

School Days by Carlos Perez

Interactive Writing Lessons

IW.8: Making a Class Big Book

As you read and enjoy these texts together, help children notice that

- writers and illustrators make books,
- there are words and/or pictures on every page,
- writers tell about different things in their books,
- writers tell stories in their books, and
- writers give information in their books.

Interactive Read-Aloud
Family

School

Shared Reading

Interactive Writing

Writing Minilesson Principle
Make a book.

Getting Started with Making Books

You Will Need

- a variety of familiar picture, wordless, alphabet, and informational books
- a prepared book of your own
- a stapled blank book (about four pages) with colorful cover
- crayons and washable markers
- charts from STR.U1: Storytelling (optional)
- chart paper and markers
- To download the following online resource for this lesson, visit **resources.fountasandpinnell.com**:
  - chart art (optional)
  - paper templates (optional)

Academic Language/ Important Vocabulary

- author
- front cover
- words
- pictures

Continuum Connection

- Create a picture book as one form of writing (p. 246)
- Have ideas to tell, write, draw about (p. 249)
- Demonstrate confidence in attempts at drawing and writing (p. 249)

GOAL

Make books using drawing and approximated writing.

RATIONALE

When you introduce children to making books, you help them view themselves as writers and illustrators. They learn the power of their own ideas and that drawing and writing can communicate ideas to others.

ASSESS LEARNING

- Observe for evidence of what children know about making books.
- Notice children's use of representational drawings or writing in their books.
- Look for evidence that children can use vocabulary such as *author*, *front cover*, *words*, and *pictures*.

MINILESSON

To help children explore bookmaking, show examples of the different ways authors/ illustrators put pictures and words on paper to tell their stories or give information. Include an example of a picture book you have made yourself (e.g., *My Garden*). Here is an example.

- Display different types of books, including picture books, wordless books, alphabet books, and informational books.

    Who made these books?

    A person who makes books is called an author. What are these books about?

    Authors tell many different things. Some tell stories, and some tell information. Some tell about the alphabet.

    You could make a book about school or about something that happened to you. You could make an ABC book.

- Read each page of the book that you made and show the pictures.

    My book has a front cover, and there are words and pictures on the pages that tell about my garden.

- Show a blank book. Then show children where the blank books are kept.

    You can make a book like I made and like the authors made.

    When you are ready to write your own book, you can get one from here.

- Save your book for WML2, where you will add your name to the cover.

Have a Try

Invite children to talk to a partner about what they could make a book about. As needed, refer to the charts created in STR.U1: Storytelling.

> Think of something that you could make a book about. Turn and tell your partner.

▶ Invite a few children to share what their books will be about.

Summarize and Apply

Write the principle on the chart paper and attach the book you made or display it on the easel. Read the principle.

> Today during writing time, each of you will make your own book. I will come around to talk to some of you about the book you are making. Bring your book to share when we meet later.

▶ Allow children to choose blank booklets or any of the paper templates available in the online resources to make their books.

Confer

▶ During independent writing, move around the room to confer briefly with as many individual children as time allows. Sit side by side with them and invite them to talk about the books they are making. Use the following prompts as needed.

- *What are you making a book about?*
- *You know a lot about _____. You could make a book about that.*
- *Tell a story about something you have done. Let's plan what you will make on each page.*
- *Tell the story that goes with this part of the book.*
- *Look at the chart. Which idea interests you?*

Share

Following independent writing, gather pairs of children in the meeting area with their books. Ask partners to share their books with one another.

> Tell your partner about the book you made.

Umbrella 1: Getting Started with Making Books

Getting Started with Making Books

You Will Need

- several familiar books, such as the following:
  - *School Days* by Carlos Perez, from *Shared Reading Collection*
  - *Elizabeti's Doll* by Stephanie Stuve-Bodeen, from Text Set: Taking Care of Each Other: Family
- book you made for WML1
- books children made in WML1
- markers

Academic Language/ Important Vocabulary

- author
- illustrator
- front cover

Continuum Connection

- Write a title and author's name on the cover of a story or book (p. 246)
- Write name and date on writing (p. 248)
- Use letters from one's name to represent it or to write a message (p. 365)

GOAL

Understand that the person who writes a book is the author and the author's name is on the cover.

RATIONALE

When you teach children that the person who wrote a book is the author and that the author's name is on the cover of the book, they understand they can write their own names on the books they write.

ASSESS LEARNING

- Look for evidence that children know that the author is the person who wrote the book.
- Notice whether children can point to the author's name on the cover of a book.
- Observe children's ability to write their names on the books they write.
- Look for evidence that children can use vocabulary such as *author*, *illustrator*, and *front cover*.

MINILESSON

Share a number of books with children to help them notice the author's name on the cover. Consider using enlarged texts so the author's name is large enough for the children to see. Refer to the book you began in WML1. Here is an example.

- Display familiar books, such as *School Days* and *Elizabeti's Doll*. Read the name of the author while pointing to it on each book.

  What do you notice the writer did to show he/she wrote the book?

  Each book has the author's name on the front cover.

- Attach your book to the chart or display it on the easel. Write your name on the cover of the book. Demonstrate beginning at the left and adding each letter to the right.

  My book has a front cover. Since I am the author of this book, I will write my name on the cover. Watch how I write my name.

  You will write your name on the cover of the books you make. If you need help writing your name, you can look at our name chart.

- Save your book for WML3. Be sure there is a page that has both words and a picture.

Have a Try

Invite children to think about where they will write their names on the books they made.

▶ Give each child the book they made in WML1.

Point to where you wrote your name, or talk to your partner about where you will write your name.

▶ Allow time for children to write their names on the WML1 books before starting new books.

Summarize and Apply

Summarize the learning and remind children to write their names on the books they make.

▶ Write the principle at the top of the chart.

You are writers and illustrators. You can make books about lots of different things.

To show everyone you wrote the book, put your name on it. I will talk to several writers today about the books they are making. I can't wait to see your names on your books!

Confer

▶ During independent writing, move around the room to confer briefly with as many individual children as time allows. Sit side by side with them and invite them to talk about the books they are making. Use prompts such as the following as needed to support children's writing. For children ready to start a new book, use prompts from WML1.

- *Start here [indicating where to begin name]. Write the next letter here.*
- *Listen to how I say words to help me. Say the words to help you write the letters.*
- *Use the name chart (or ABC chart) to help you.*

Share

Following independent writing, gather children in pairs in the meeting area with their books. Ask partners to share their books with one another, pointing to the name on the cover.

Point to where you wrote your name on the cover of your book.

You are the author of your books. Whenever you begin a new book, be sure to write your name on it like you did today.

WML 3
MBK.U1.WML3

Writing Minilesson Principle
Make a book with pictures and writing.

Getting Started with Making Books

You Will Need

- several familiar picture books, such as *Jonathan and His Mommy* by Irene Smalls and *Elizabeti's Doll* by Stephanie Stuve-Bodeen, from Text Set: Taking Care of Each Other: Family

- class-made book from IW.8: Making a Class Big Book

- your book from WML2

- markers

- charts from STR.U1: Storytelling (optional)

- To download the following online resource for this lesson, visit **resources.fountasandpinnell.com**:
  - chart art (optional)

Academic Language/ Important Vocabulary

- pictures
- words

Continuum Connection

- Create a picture book as one form of writing (p. 246)

- Draw or write a continuous message on a simple topic (p. 249)

- Use words and drawings to compose and revise writing (p. 249)

- Understand how writing and drawing are related (p. 249)

- Demonstrate confidence in attempts at drawing and writing (p. 249)

GOAL

Understand that a picture book has pictures and words about the same idea.

RATIONALE

Making a book with pictures and words helps children view themselves as writers and builds their stamina and enthusiasm for writing.

ASSESS LEARNING

- Look for evidence that children can distinguish between the pictures and the words in a book and understand that the pictures and words are related.

- Look for evidence that children can use vocabulary such as *pictures* and *words*.

MINILESSON

To help children think about the minilesson principle, use familiar books that have both pictures and print, the class book created in IW.8: Making a Class Big Book, and the book you added your name to in WML2. Here is an example.

- Show several pages from a book, such as the class writing from IW.8. Read the words. Point under the words as you read and then point to the picture.

  What do you notice is on these pages?

  Each page has a picture and some words. The pictures and the words tell about our friends and what they like.

- Show several pages from another book, such as *Jonathan and His Mommy*.

  What do you notice is on these pages?

  They have pictures and words about the walk that Jonathan took with his mommy.

- Attach the book used for WML2 to chart paper. Point to the pictures and words.

  Here is the book I wrote. On this page, I drew a picture and wrote the words that go with the picture.

- Save the book for WML5.

Have a Try

Invite children to talk to their partners about a story they might draw and write. As needed, refer to the charts from STR.U1: Storytelling.

> Talk to your partner about a story you could tell. What pictures will you draw to go with that story? What words will you write?

▶ Listen to partners as they talk. After a few moments, share with the class several ideas as examples.

Summarize and Apply

Help children summarize what they have learned about making books. Then invite them to work on their books.

> What will you do to make your book?

▶ Write the principle at the top of the chart. Read it aloud.

> During writing time, I will be sitting with different writers to help you plan the pictures and words.

Confer

▶ During independent writing, move around the room to confer briefly with as many individual children as time allows. Sit side by side with them and invite them to talk about the books they are making. Use the following prompts as needed.

- *What is your book about?*
- *Talk more about your story.*
- *What happened first . . . next . . . ?*
- *What will you draw for that part of the story?*
- *Start here. Write the next word here.*

Share

Following independent writing, gather children in the meeting area. Ask a few children to point out the words and pictures in their books. Choose books on a variety of topics to show the breadth of possibilities. As needed, support children's oral language by providing a sentence frame, such as *This is a story about _____. Here is the picture and here are the words.*

Section 4: Making Books

WML4

MBK.U1.WML4

Writing Minilesson Principle
Plan what to put on each page.

Getting Started with Making Books

You Will Need

- several familiar picture books, such as the following:
  - *The Bus for Us* by Suzanne Bloom, from Text Set: Learning and Playing Together: School
  - *Do Like Kyla* by Angela Johnson, from Text Set: Taking Care of Each Other: Family
- chart paper and markers
- To download the following online resource for this lesson, visit **resources.fountasandpinnell.com**:
  - chart art (optional)

Academic Language/ Important Vocabulary

- plan
- across

Continuum Connection

- Tell one part, idea, or group of ideas on each page of a book (p. 246)
- Write and/or draw about one idea on a page (p. 246)

GOAL

Learn to think about and plan what to put on each page of a book.

RATIONALE

Part of making a book is learning to think about and plan what goes on each page. By helping children learn to tell a story across their fingers, they realize that a story has many parts and they must make the decision about which part to draw and write about on each page.

ASSESS LEARNING

- Look for evidence that children know to plan what goes on each page of their books.
- Notice whether they write about one idea or group of ideas on a page.
- Look for evidence that children can use vocabulary such as *plan* and *across*.

MINILESSON

To help children think about the principle, use familiar picture books to show how the authors tell about one part of the story on each page. Here is an example.

- Briefly review what happens in the story *The Bus for Us*, pointing to a finger for each part of the story (tell the story across your fingers).

  There are many parts to this story. How did the author, Suzanne Bloom, show the parts of the story in the book?

  The author put one part of the story on each page. First she wrote about the taxi, then the tow truck—all the way until the bus came.

- Use *Do Like Kyla* to talk about how another author told her story across all the pages.

  When you make books, think about what part of the story you will tell on each page. You can tell your story across your fingers. Tell one part of the story for each finger. Then you can put the part for each finger on its own page.

Have a Try

Invite children to tell a story across their fingers to their partners, perhaps about an activity they did at school that day.

> Tell your partner a story you could write. Tell it across your fingers. Maybe you want to tell a story about what happened when you got to school this morning.

▶ After time for children to tell their stories, ask one or two volunteers what they might write on the first page of a book. It should correspond to the part of the story they told on the first finger.

Summarize and Apply

Make a chart to summarize the learning. Then invite children to work on their books.

> Let's make a chart to help you remember how to plan your book.

▶ Write the principle on the top of the chart. Read it aloud.

> During writing time, I will sit with some writers. I can help you plan the pages of your book.

Plan what to put on each page.

Think of a story.

Tell it across your fingers.

Put one part on each page.

Confer

▶ During independent writing, move around the room to confer briefly with as many individual children as time allows. Sit side by side with them and invite them to talk about how they are deciding what to put on each page. Use prompts such as the following as needed.

- *Tell your story across your fingers.*
- *What will you put on the first page? on the next page?*
- *What will you draw for that part of the story?*
- *What words go with that picture?*

Share

Following independent writing, invite children to share their books in pairs or trios, or show one book to the whole class.

> How did you decide what to put on each page?

Writing Minilesson Principle
Decide when your book is finished.

Getting Started with Making Books

You Will Need

- your book from WML3
- a child's book and the child prepared to talk about the book
- chart paper and markers

Academic Language/ Important Vocabulary

- decide
- finished

Continuum Connection

- Think of what to work on next as a writer (p. 249)
- Keep working independently rather than waiting for a teacher to help (p. 249)

GOAL

Decide when a book is finished and when to start another one.

RATIONALE

When you teach children how to decide when a book is finished and what to do next, it builds a foundation for revising and editing their writing (perhaps over several days) and supports them as independent writers.

ASSESS LEARNING

- Observe whether children can evaluate when they have finished making a book.
- Look for evidence that children can use vocabulary such as *decide* and *finished*.

MINILESSON

To help children think about the minilesson principle, use the book you created to demonstrate thinking about whether a book is finished. Here is an example.

- Show and read your book from WML3.

  Does this book seem finished to you?

  What's missing?

  I haven't told very much about my garden, so I could add some more pages. I could tell what else I do to take care of my garden.

- Show the child's book.

  Here is Sam's book. It might be finished, but how can he decide?

  He can reread the book.

- Record the response on the chart paper.

  When you reread your own book, think about whether you told everything that the reader needs to know. If you didn't, you can add some words to your book.

  Besides the words, what else can Sam check?

  He can check the pictures to be sure that all the right details are there.

- Record responses on chart paper.

Have a Try

Invite children to talk to a partner about what to do when they finish a book.

> If you have already reread your book and checked the words and pictures, what should you do next? Turn and talk to your partner.

▶ Talk about what they should do to start the next book—where to get a new booklet, how to think of an idea, and so forth.

Summarize and Apply

Summarize the learning and invite children to start a new book when they finish one.

▶ Write the principle at the top of the chart.

> Today we talked about how to decide when you have finished making a book. During writing time each day, before you start a new book, look at the chart and think about whether your book is finished. When you are sure, put your finished book where it belongs, get another booklet, and start making a new book.

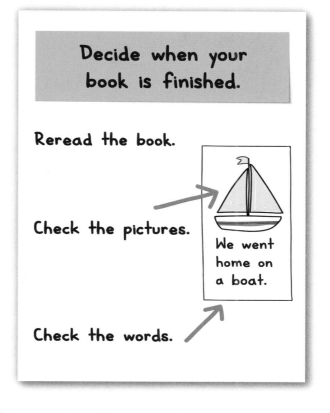

Confer

▶ Observe children for a few minutes at the beginning of independent writing. If there are children who get a new booklet immediately, sit side by side with them individually or in a small group and talk more about the principle. Use prompts such as the following as needed.

- *I noticed you are starting a new book. Let's look together at your last book and think about what to do to make sure it is finished.*
- *What can you add to the illustrations to help your reader understand more?*
- *What can you add to your words to help the reader understand _____ ?*
- *You reread your book and checked the pictures. Now what will you do?*

Share

Following independent writing, invite a few children to share how they added to the words and/or illustrations in their books before deciding they were ready to begin a new book.

> How did you know you were finished with your book?

Assessment

After you have taught the minilessons in this umbrella, observe children as they draw and write. Use the behaviors and understandings in *The Literacy Continuum* (Fountas and Pinnell 2017) to notice, teach for, and support children's learning as you observe their drawing and writing attempts.

▶ What evidence do you have of new understandings children have developed related to making books?

- Do children understand that they can make their own books?
- Do they demonstrate confidence in their attempts at drawing and writing?
- What part of their name can they write on the front cover of the book?
- Do they put pictures and/or words on each page of the book?
- Are children able to plan what goes on each page?
- Are they beginning to understand the routine of what to do when they think their book may be finished?
- Do they understand and use vocabulary related to bookmaking, such as *author*, *front cover*, *pictures*, *words*, *plan*, *illustrator*, and *finished*?

▶ In what other ways, beyond the scope of this umbrella, are children ready to expand their bookmaking experience?

- Are they adding details to their illustrations to help the reader understand their message?
- Are they ready to learn more about how to write words?
- Would they benefit from more experience with storytelling?

Use your observations to determine what you will teach next. You may also consult Suggested Sequence of Lessons (pp. 483–494) for guidance.

EXTENSIONS FOR GETTING STARTED WITH MAKING BOOKS

▶ Gather several books by the same author to show that one person can write more than one book.

▶ Gather several books by someone who both wrote and illustrated the books. Talk about what it might have been like for this person to make the book: *Where did the ideas come from? How long do you think it took to make the book? What did the person do to make the pictures?*

▶ Gather together a guided writing group of several children who need support in a specific area of writing.

▶ Create a chart that lists the titles of the books children have made.

Minilessons in This Umbrella

WML1 Write labels on your pictures.

WML2 Write a title on your cover.

WML3 Add sentences to match your pictures.

WML4 Add speech and thought bubbles.

WML5 Write an author page.

Before Teaching Umbrella 2 Minilessons

The minilessons in this umbrella add to the learning gained in MBK.U1: Getting Started with Making Books and are best taught once children are comfortable with the bookmaking routine and you observe them using letterlike forms or approximated writing. Thus, you do not need to teach the minilessons one right after another.

Give children plenty of opportunities to write and draw freely and without constraints. Read and discuss simple books from a variety of genres. Use the following books from *Fountas & Pinnell Classroom™ Interactive Read-Aloud Collection* text sets and from *Shared Reading Collection*, class writing from interactive writing lessons, the text you made for MBK.U1, or books from the classroom library.

Interactive Read-Aloud Collection

Letters at Work: The Alphabet

On Market Street by Arnold Lobel

The Importance of Friendship

I'm the Best by Lucy Cousins

Learning and Playing Together: School

The Bus for Us by Suzanne Bloom

Shared Reading Collection

A Rainbow of Fruit by Brooke Matthews

City ABCs by Finnoula Louise

School Days by Carlos Perez

Spots by Judy Kentor Schmauss

Ten in the Bed by Inna Chernyak

City Kid, Country Kid by David Andrews

Interactive Writing Lessons

IW.8: Making a Class Big Book

As you read and enjoy these texts together, help children notice that authors

- label pictures,
- write a title on the cover and sentences that match the pictures,
- use speech and thought bubbles, and
- sometimes include an author page.

Interactive Read-Aloud
The Alphabet

Friendship

School

Shared Reading

Interactive Writing

WML1

Writing Minilesson Principle
Write labels on your pictures.

Expanding Bookmaking

You Will Need

- several familiar picture books with labels, such as the following:
  - *On Market Street* by Arnold Lobel, from Text Set: Letters at Work: The Alphabet
  - *City ABCs* by Finnoula Louise and *A Rainbow of Fruit* by Brooke Matthews, from *Shared Reading Collection*
- teacher-made text from MBK.U1
- chart paper and markers
- books that the children are working on
- To download the following online resource for this lesson, visit **resources.fountasandpinnell.com**:
  - chart art (optional)

Academic Language/ Important Vocabulary

- label
- picture
- illustration
- drawing

Continuum Connection

- Understand that a writer or illustrator can add a label to help readers understand a drawing or photograph (p. 244)
- Understand that a label provides important information (p. 244)
- Create a label for an illustration that accompanies a written piece (p. 244)
- Write some words with consonant letters appropriate for sounds in words (beginning and ending) (p. 248)

GOAL

Label pictures to help the reader understand more.

RATIONALE

Having children write labels for their drawings helps them take a first step toward writing the text of a book. A label is just enough to challenge children, conveying meaning without being overwhelming.

ASSESS LEARNING

- Observe for evidence of what children know about labels.
- Notice if children begin to label drawings in their own books.
- Look for evidence that children can use vocabulary such as *label*, *picture*, *illustration*, and *drawing*.

MINILESSON

To help children think about the minilesson principle, use several texts with clear examples of labels, including the text you made for MBK.U1. Here is an example.

- Display *On Market Street* and show several pages. Point to the labels as you speak.

   In this book the author wrote a word to go with a picture for each letter of the alphabet.

   This word is called a label. The label is a word or a few words that tell you about the picture.

- Display *City ABCs*, choosing a page such as page 17 (*Nn/nest*).

   What do you notice near each photo?

   The label tells you this is a nest. The label gives information about the photograph.

- Repeat this process with *A Rainbow of Fruit*.

- Attach the book you made for MBK.U1 to chart paper.

   What could I write that would tell readers about this picture?

- Write the label.

   You can write labels in your book.

Have a Try

Invite the children to talk to a partner about a label they could write in their books.

▶ Give children a book that they are working on.

> Look to see if there is a page in your book where you could write a label. What label could you write? Tell your partner about that.

Summarize and Invite

Write the principle at the top of the chart. Read the principle and invite children to label their drawings.

> Labels give information about the pictures. Today, when you are making a book during writing time, think about where you could add a label. I will talk to some writers today to help you think about the labels you can add to your writing.

Confer

▶ During independent writing, move around the room to confer briefly with as many individual children as time allows. Sit side by side with them and invite them to talk about writing labels. Use prompts such as those below to help them think about labeling their drawings.

- *What could you write to tell the reader about the picture?*
- *What information does your reader need to understand this drawing? Write that here.*
- *Say the word slowly and listen for sounds you hear in the first (last) part.*
- *Write that letter here.*

Share

Following independent writing, gather children in the meeting area to share their labels.

> Who would like to share a book you worked on?

> This book has a label. The drawing is here, and the label is here.

Section 4: Making Books

Expanding Bookmaking

You Will Need

- several familiar picture books, such as *School Days* by Carlos Perez, from *Shared Reading Collection*
- teacher-made text from MBK.U1
- chart paper prepared with a book cover (no title)
- markers
- cut-out paper arrow
- glue stick or tape
- To download the following online resource for this lesson, visit **resources.fountasandpinnell.com**
  - chart art (optional)

Academic Language/ Important Vocabulary

- cover
- title
- author

Continuum Connection

- Select an appropriate title for a poem, story, or informational book (p. 246)
- Place titles and headings in the appropriate place on a page (p. 247)

GOAL

Write a title using approximated writing on the front cover of a book.

RATIONALE

When you teach children that books have titles on the cover and authors choose the titles for their books, they will learn to add titles to their own books.

ASSESS LEARNING

- Observe whether children can point to the titles on a book.
- Look for evidence that children understand that a title tells what a book is about.
- Notice if children add titles to their own books.
- Look for evidence that children can use vocabulary such as *cover*, *title*, and *author*.

MINILESSON

To help children think about the minilesson principle, use several familiar texts, including the text you made for MBK.U1, to start a discussion about book titles. Here is an example.

- Display the covers of several books. Point to and read each title.

  The front of a book is called the cover. What do you notice about the covers?

  The covers have words on them, and some of these words are called the title. The title is the name of the book.

- Display *School Days*.

  What is this book about?

  Because the book is about a day in school, the author chose the title *School Days*.

- Repeat this process as needed with the book you made for MBK.U1.

  You can write a title on your books, too. The title helps the reader know what the book is about.

Have a Try

Have children help you write a title for the prepared cover.

> **Here's a book cover that needs a title. What do you think would be a good title for this book? Turn and talk to your partner about that.**

▶ Accept ideas from children and choose one that all agree on. Then discuss where on the cover you should write the title. Write the title.

▶ Attach (or have a child attach) the arrow so that it points to the title.

Summarize and Invite

Help children summarize what they learned about titles. Then have them add titles to their books.

> **What did you learn today about book titles?**

▶ Write the principle on the chart and read it aloud.

> **Today during writing time, write a title on the cover of your book. Be sure the title matches your story. Bring your book to share when we meet.**

Write a title on your cover.

In the Ocean

Confer

▶ During independent writing, move around the room to confer briefly with as many individual children as time allows. Sit side by side with them and invite them to talk about their book titles. Use the following prompts as needed.

- *What is your book all about?*
- *What could be the title of your book?*
- *You can say the word slowly, listening for the sound at the beginning (end).*
- *Leave some space before you start the next word.*

Share

Following independent writing, gather children in the meeting area to share their books with partners. As needed, support children's oral language by providing a sentence frame, such as *The title of my book is _____.*

> **Turn and talk to your partner about the title of your book. Point to it. Does it tell what your book is about?**

Writing Minilesson Principle

Add sentences to match your pictures.

Expanding Bookmaking

You Will Need

- several familiar books such as the following:
  - *Spots* by Judy Kentor Schmauss, from *Shared Reading Collection*
  - *I'm the Best* by Lucy Cousins, from Text Set: The Importance of Friendship
- class-made book from IW.8: Making a Class Big Book
- markers
- To download the following online resource for this lesson, visit **resources.fountasandpinnell.com**:
  - chart art (optional)

Academic Language/ Important Vocabulary

- sentence
- words
- pictures
- drawings
- photographs

Continuum Connection

- Realize that what you say (oral language) can be put into writing (p. 246)
- Use known oral language in writing even if unsure how to spell some words (p. 246)
- Place words in lines, starting left to right, top to bottom (p. 247)
- Understand that when both writing and drawing are on a page, they are mutually supportive, with each extending the other (p. 249)

GOAL

Add sentences to match pictures and to explain more to the reader.

RATIONALE

It is important to teach children that the combination of drawing and writing supports a reader's understanding of a story. When children are ready to move beyond labeling their pictures, help them learn to write sentences. This inspires children to begin using approximated writing to translate what they say (oral language) into writing that matches their illustrations.

ASSESS LEARNING

- Look for evidence of children's understanding that writing and illustrations work together to give meaning to the reader.
- Observe children's ability to write approximated sentences that match their pictures.
- Notice if children use drawings and approximated writing to convey meaning.
- Look for evidence that children can use vocabulary such as *sentence*, *words*, *pictures*, *drawings*, and *photographs*.

MINILESSON

To help children think about the minilesson principle, use several familiar books to engage children in a discussion about how sentences and pictures work together to give meaning to the reader. Here is an example.

- Show and read several two-page spreads from *Spots*.

  What do you notice on the pages?

  One page has a sentence about the photograph on the other page.

- Repeat this process for *I'm the Best* and the class book from IW.8, guiding children to the understanding that the words and pictures are about the same thing. You might also note that sometimes sentences give more information than the pictures and vice versa.

  The author of each book wrote sentences that tell about the pictures. You can write sentences to tell about the drawings in your books.

Have a Try

Have children help you add a sentence to a picture.

▶ Draw a picture or place the drawing from online resources on chart paper.

> What is happening in the picture?

> What could we write about the picture?

▶ Guide children to think about who the character is (give him a name) and what the character is like so that the sentence tells about the picture and also gives more information.

▶ Write the final sentence on the chart.

Summarize and Apply

Help children summarize what they learned about sentences and pictures. Then remind them that they can add sentences to the pictures in their books.

> What did we talk about today?

▶ Write the principle at the top of the chart.

> Today, when you are working on your book, look to see if there are any pictures that need a sentence. If you already have pictures and sentences in your book, make sure they are about the same thing.

Add sentences to match your pictures.

Noah missed the bus again!

Confer

▶ During independent writing, move around the room to confer briefly with as many individual children as time allows. Sit side by side with them and invite them to talk about their sentences and pictures. Use prompts like the following as needed.

- *What is happening in this picture? What could you write to let your reader know that?*

- *You said _____ . You can write that sentence to match your picture.*

- *Start writing your sentence here.*

Share

Following independent writing, gather children in the meeting area. Invite partners to share their books with one another. If time allows, share a few books with the whole class.

> Does the writing match the picture?

Writing Minilesson Principle

Add speech and thought bubbles.

You Will Need

- several familiar picture books with speech or thought bubbles, such as the following from *Shared Reading Collection*:
  - *Ten in the Bed* by Inna Chernyak
  - *City Kid, Country Kid* by David Andrews
- chart paper prepared with examples of speech and thought bubbles
- markers
- To download the following online resource for this lesson, visit **resources.fountasandpinnell.com**:
  - chart art (optional)

Academic Language/ Important Vocabulary

- speech bubbles
- thought bubbles
- illustrations
- author
- writer
- character

Continuum Connection

- Explain one's thoughts and feelings about an experience or event (p. 244)
- Use dialogue as appropriate to add to the meaning of the story (p. 245)
- Notice craft decisions that the author or illustrator has made and try out some of these decisions in one's own writing with teacher support (p. 245)
- Tell a story or give information in an interesting way (p. 247)

GOAL

Add speech and thought bubbles to make your writing interesting.

RATIONALE

Discussing how authors use speech and thought bubbles helps children learn to include dialogue and inner dialogue in their own writing to make a story more interesting.

ASSESS LEARNING

- Look for evidence that children understand what speech and thought bubbles are.
- Notice if children begin to add speech and thought bubbles to their writing.
- Look for evidence that children can use vocabulary such as *speech bubbles*, *thought bubbles*, *illustrations*, *author*, *writer*, and *character*.

MINILESSON

To help children think about the minilesson principle, use several familiar texts to engage children in a discussion about including speech and thought bubbles in their writing. Here is an example.

- Read and show a few pages of *Ten in the Bed*, pointing to the speech bubbles.

  What are these?

  A shape like this pointing to a person's mouth is called a speech bubble. A speech bubble tells you what a person is saying.

- Repeat this process with the thought bubble on page 4 of *City Kid, Country Kid*. Read the page and point to the thought bubble.

  What do you notice about this bubble? How is it different from the speech bubble?

  A bubble shape with smaller bubbles below it is called a thought bubble. A thought bubble tells you what a person is thinking. In the book, he is not saying the words out loud. He is saying them inside his own head.

  Why do you think some authors use speech bubbles and thought bubbles in their books?

Have a Try

Have children help you decide what to write in a speech bubble and a thought bubble.

▶ Draw two children speaking or place the art from online resources on chart paper.

Here are two children speaking. What might they be saying to one another?

▶ Repeat the process for the thought bubble.

Summarize and Apply

Help children summarize the learning. Then remind them that they can add speech bubbles or thought bubbles to their books.

▶ Review the chart with children. Write the principle at the top and read it aloud.

As you are making a book today, think about what the people in your story might say and try adding a speech bubble to your writing. Or, think about what they are thinking and try adding a thought bubble. Write the words first and then draw the bubble around the words so that they will fit. Be ready to share your writing when we come back together.

Confer

▶ During independent writing, move around the room to confer briefly with as many individual children as time allows. Sit side by side with them and invite them to talk about using speech and thought bubbles. Use prompts like the following as needed.

• *Let's go back into this story and think about what the characters said or thought.*

• *Is there part of the story where a character is thinking something? Write that here. Then put a bubble around it with smaller bubbles pointing to the head.*

• *Think about how to write the words.*

Share

Following independent writing, gather children in the meeting area. Identify one or two clear examples of speech or thought bubbles. Have those children share their books.

What does the speech/thought bubble show you about this part of the story?

Expanding Bookmaking

You Will Need

- several familiar picture books with an author page, such as the following:
  - *The Bus for Us* by Suzanne Bloom, from Text Set: Learning and Playing Together: School
  - *City Kid, Country Kid* by David Andrews, from *Shared Reading Collection*
- chart paper and markers
- To download the following online resource for this lesson, visit **resources.fountasandpinnell.com**:
  - paper templates (optional)

Academic Language/ Important Vocabulary

- author
- author page
- writer

Continuum Connection

- Write an author page at the beginning or end of a book that gives information about the author (picture, writing) (p. 246)
- Talk about oneself as a writer (p. 249)

GOAL

Write an author page to share information about yourself.

RATIONALE

Studying author pages and supporting children in writing their own author pages helps children view themselves as writers. It encourages children to take pride in and celebrate their writing and share important information about themselves with their readers.

ASSESS LEARNING

- Look for evidence that children understand the purpose of an author page.
- Notice if children begin to write an author page in their books.
- Look for evidence that children can use vocabulary such as *author*, *author page*, and *writer*.

MINILESSON

To help children think about the minilesson principle, show them author pages from several familiar texts. Engage children in a discussion about the information that authors share about themselves. Below is an example. When children make their author pages, they can use plain paper or the author page from the paper templates in online resources.

- Read parts of the author page at the end of *The Bus for Us*.

  This page isn't part of the main part of the book. What is it?

  It's called an author page. What do you notice about the author page?

  This author page includes the author's name (Suzanne Bloom), where she got the idea for the book, the names of other books she has written, and where she is from.

- Repeat this process with *City Kid, Country Kid*.

  What does the author, David Andrews, include in his author's note?

  Why might an author write an author page?

  Knowing a little bit about the author or where the idea for the book came from can help you enjoy or understand the book more.

Have a Try

Have children help write an author page about one of the writers in your class.

> Let's help Bryn write an author page for her book. Bryn, tell us a little bit about yourself.

▶ Work with the children to decide what information to share on an author page.

Summarize and Apply

Write the principle at the top of the chart and read it aloud. Remind children that they can write an author page for their books.

> You can write an author page for the book you are working on or one that you have already made. Decide what information you want to share with the readers. Use the chart as an example.

Confer

▶ During independent writing, move around the room to confer briefly with as many individual children as time allows. Sit side by side with them and invite them to talk about adding an author page to their books. Use prompts such as the following as needed.

- *What do you want your readers to know about you?*
- *Where did you get the idea for writing this book?*
- *What are the names of other books you have written?*

Share

Following independent writing, gather children in the meeting area. Have partners share their author pages with one another, or have several children share with the whole class.

> Did anyone add an author page to your book?

> What does it tell about you?

Write an author page.

Author Page

Bryn is six years old.

She has one brother and one sister.

Her favorite color is blue.

Bryn wants to be a writer.

Assessment

After you have taught the minilessons in this umbrella, observe children as they draw, write, and talk about their writing. Use the behaviors and understandings in *The Literacy Continuum* (Fountas and Pinnell 2017) to notice, teach for, and support children's learning as you observe their attempts at drawing and writing.

▶ What evidence do you have of new understandings children have developed related to making books?

- Do children write labels near their drawings?
- Are they adding a title to the cover?
- How well do their sentences match their drawings?
- Do they experiment with speech and thought bubbles?
- Can they write an author page about themselves?
- Are they understanding and using vocabulary related to making books, such as *drawing, illustration, pictures, label, author, title, cover, photographs, words, sentence, character, writer, thought bubbles, speech bubbles*, and *author page*?

▶ In what other ways, beyond the scope of this umbrella, are children ready to expand their experience with making books?

- Are they moving beyond scribbles to more representational drawing?
- Are they ready to add more pages or page numbers to their books?
- Would they benefit from more experience with storytelling?

Use your observations to determine the next umbrella you will teach. You may also consult Suggested Sequence of Lessons (pp. 483–494) for guidance.

EXTENSIONS FOR EXPANDING BOOKMAKING

▶ Review and encourage writing labels by photocopying children's writing that shows examples of labels. Display the examples in the writing center.

▶ Review and encourage writing sentences by photocopying children's writing that shows examples of how one might write sentences to go with the pictures. Place examples in the writing center.

▶ Gather together a guided writing group of several children who need support in a specific area of writing.

▶ Study dedications of several familiar books. Encourage children to write a dedication for their own books.

Minilessons in This Umbrella

WML1 Make a list of stories you remember.

WML2 Tell a story you remember.

WML3 Draw and write your story in the order it happened.

WML4 Say *I* and *we* when you tell a story about yourself.

WML5 Use pictures and words to show how you were feeling.

Before Teaching Umbrella 3 Minilessons

For young writers, understanding that they can make a book about anything they have personally experienced is an important realization.

Prior to teaching these minilessons, make sure children have an understanding of story structure. If you have *The Reading Minilessons Book, Kindergarten* (Fountas and Pinnell 2019), consider teaching LA.U13: Understanding How Stories Work. Additionally, you can teach IW.14: Writing About a Class Memory so that the text you and the children create can be used as a mentor text for these lessons. For other mentor texts, use first-person texts from the classroom library or that you have created with the class. Also consider the following books from *Fountas & Pinnell Classroom™ Interactive Read-Aloud Collection* and *Shared Reading Collection*. If you are following the *Interactive Read-Aloud Collection* sequence, note that some of these books come later in the year, but you can read the stories aloud now to use as examples of a memory story and then again later where they fall in the sequence.

Interactive Read-Aloud Collection
Grace Lin: Exploring Family and Culture

The Ugly Vegetables

Kite Flying

Taking Care of Each Other: Family

Do Like Kyla by Angela Johnson

Jonathan and His Mommy by Irene Smalls

Living and Working Together: Community

My Steps by Sally Derby

The Importance of Kindness

Flower Garden by Eve Bunting

Shared Reading Collection

The Sleepover by Judith E. Nayer

Interactive Writing Lessons

IW.14: Writing About a Class Memory

As you read and enjoy these texts together, help children

- connect texts to memories in their lives,

- notice the sequence of story events and the use of *I* and *we*, and

- talk about what the pictures and words show about how characters are feeling.

Interactive Read-Aloud
Grace Lin

Family

Community

Kindness

Shared Reading

Interactive Writing

Section 4: Making Books

Writing Minilesson Principle
Make a list of stories you remember.

You Will Need

- several familiar books that tell about memories, such as the following:
  - *The Ugly Vegetables* by Grace Lin, from Text Set: Grace Lin: Exploring Family and Culture
  - *The Sleepover* by Judith E. Nayer, from *Shared Reading Collection*
- class writing from IW.14: Writing About a Class Memory (optional)
- markers
- To download the following online resource for this lesson, visit **resources.fountasandpinnell.com**:
  - Ideas for Memory Stories

Academic Language / Important Vocabulary

- list
- stories
- memory
- remember

Continuum Connection

- Understand that writers may tell stories from their own lives (p. 244)
- Think about topics, events, or experiences from your own life that are interesting to write about (p. 244)
- Generate and expand ideas through talk with peers and teachers (p. 248)
- Look for ideas and topics in personal experiences, shared through talk (p. 248)

GOAL

Understand that writers generate ideas for stories from memories that are important to them.

RATIONALE

When children learn that they can make books about personal memories, they realize that their own memories have value and that each child has a unique story to tell.

ASSESS LEARNING

- Observe for evidence that children understand that their personal experiences can be the topics for books they write.
- Listen to children talk about their memories. How well can they shape a story from a memory?
- Look for evidence that children can use vocabulary such as *list*, *stories*, *memory*, and *remember*.

MINILESSON

Prior to teaching this lesson, it would be useful to teach IW.14: Writing About a Class Memory. Use familiar stories to demonstrate that authors write stories about their own memories. Here is an example.

- Display books that are about something the author remembers, such as the *The Ugly Vegetables* and *The Sleepover*.

  The writers of these books all wrote about special memories. What are some of the memories we read about?

- Have children briefly recall the memory each book tells about.

  If I want to write a memory book, first I think about some things I remember.

- Display the blank online resource Ideas for Memory Stories. Talk about a couple of personal memories and sketch something to represent each memory. The ideas here are merely examples.

  Here is a chart that you can use to write down your ideas. I'm going to make a big version on chart paper. The first memory I am thinking about is the time I went fishing. I was so excited because I caught a fish! I will draw a fish and a fishing pole to help me remember.

- Quickly sketch a fish and a fishing pole in the first box on the chart.

  Another memory I have is when I fell off my bike last year. I can draw something in the next box to help me remember this idea.

- Quickly sketch an adhesive bandage in the next box on the chart.

Have a Try

Invite children to turn and talk about a memory.

> Think of a memory you have. Turn and tell your partner about your memory.

- Ask a few children to share ideas (e.g, baked bread with dad, went to the zoo with family). Add children's ideas to the blank boxes on the chart.

- Keep the completed chart to use in the next minilesson.

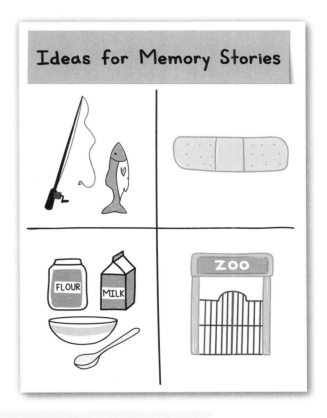

Summarize and Apply

Summarize the learning and have children make a list of story ideas.

> During writing time, make a list of story ideas using a chart like the one we used today. In each box, draw a picture or write words about something you remember doing. You can tell about a different memory in each box.

Confer

- During independent writing, move around the room to confer briefly with as many individual children as time allows. Sit side by side with them and invite them to talk about their ideas for memory stories. Use the following prompts as needed to help children expand their thinking.

  - *Tell more about this memory.*

  - *Which idea will make the best story? Why?*

  - *What other ideas do you have?*

Share

Following independent writing, gather children in pairs in the meeting area to share their ideas for memory stories. As needed, support children's oral language by providing a sentence frame, such as *My memory is about* _____.

> Share the memories you wrote down. Talk about which memory you are the most excited to make a book about.

WML 2

MBK.U3.WML2

Writing Minilesson Principle
Tell a story you remember.

Making Memory Books

You Will Need

- several familiar books that tell about memories, such as the following:
  - *Kite Flying* by Grace Lin, from Text Set: Grace Lin: Exploring Family and Culture
  - *Do Like Kyla* by Angela Johnson, from Text Set: Taking Care of Each Other: Family
  - *My Steps* by Sally Derby, from Text Set: Living and Working Together: Community
- class writing from IW.14: Writing About a Class Memory (optional)
- chart from WML1

Academic Language / Important Vocabulary

- tell
- story
- memory
- remember

Continuum Connection

- Tell a story across several pages in order to develop the story or idea (p. 245)
- Tell about experiences or topics in a way that others can understand (p. 246)
- Use storytelling to generate and rehearse language that may be written later (p. 248)
- Tell stories from personal experience (p. 331)

GOAL

Tell the important events in a story orally to an audience.

RATIONALE

Telling a story orally is a rehearsal for writing a story. As children move their ideas into words, they can work out how best to tell the story before committing the words to paper.

ASSESS LEARNING

- Notice whether children are telling stories about a memory.
- Look for evidence that children can use vocabulary such as *tell*, *story*, *memory*, and *remember*.

MINILESSON

Prior to teaching this lesson, it would be useful to teach IW.14: Writing About a Class Memory. Use familiar stories to demonstrate that authors write stories about their own memories. Use your own story to model how to tell a story. Here is an example.

- Briefly revisit several books that tell about the authors' memories.

  These authors all wrote books about special memories. Turn and talk about what memory each author wrote about.

- After a brief time, ask one or two children to share.
- Display the chart completed in the previous minilesson.

  Here is our chart of memory story ideas. I am going to choose one of my memories from this chart and tell a story about it. Watch how I do that.

- Choose one of the story ideas and tell a story, modeling how you can tell it across your fingers. You might find the following prompts helpful.
  - *The first thing that happened is _____ (point to thumb).*
  - *Then, _____ (point to index finger).*
  - *After that, _____ (point to middle finger).*
  - *At the end, _____ (point to pinky finger).*

Have a Try

Invite children to turn and talk about what they understood from your memory story.

> Turn and talk to your partner about the important things you heard in the memory story I told. Share with your partner if there is anything you wondered about.

 ◗ After a brief discussion, ask a few volunteers to share ideas.

Summarize and Apply

Summarize the learning and have children tell a memory story.

> During writing time, you can choose a memory story of your own to tell to a partner across your fingers. You can look at the chart to help you think of ideas. When you are ready, start writing your memory book. Bring your book to share when we meet later.

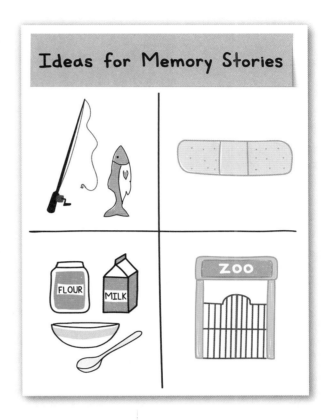

Confer

 ◗ During independent writing, move around the room to confer briefly with as many individual children as time allows. Sit side by side with them and invite them to tell memory stories across their fingers. Use the following prompts as needed.

- *What happened first?*
- *Then what happened?*
- *Now point to your ring finger and tell what happened.*
- *Tell the story across your fingers. Write what you told on your first finger on the first page.*

Share

Following independent writing, gather children in the meeting area to share their stories.

> Who would like to share your memory story? Tell it across your fingers the way I showed you.

Draw and write your story in the order it happened.

Making Memory Books

You Will Need

- familiar books that tell about memories in chronological order, such as the following:
  - *The Sleepover* by Judith E. Nayer, from *Shared Reading Collection*
  - *Flower Garden* by Eve Bunting, from Text Set: The Importance of Kindness
- several pages of a memory story you have written, attached to chart paper
- markers
- To download the following online resource for this lesson, visit **resources.fountasandpinnell.com**:
  - chart art (optional)

Academic Language / Important Vocabulary

- order
- beginning
- middle
- end

Continuum Connection

- Tell events in order that they occurred in a personal narrative (p. 245)
- Tell a story across several pages in order to develop the story or idea (p. 245)
- Present ideas in a logical sequence (p. 246)

GOAL

Understand that the pictures and writing in a story appear in chronological order.

RATIONALE

Teaching children that authors tell stories in chronological order helps them become aware that the order of events in a story matters.

ASSESS LEARNING

- Look for evidence that children understand that stories are told in chronological order.
- Observe whether children draw and write memory stories in the order in which events happened.
- Look for evidence that children can use vocabulary such as *order*, *beginning*, *middle*, and *end*.

MINILESSON

Use familiar stories plus an original story to engage children in thinking and talking about sequential order in memory stories. Here is an example.

- Ahead of time, write a simple story in sequential order based on the oral memory story you told in the previous lesson. The story used in this minilesson is merely an example.

- Show page 2 of *The Sleepover,* helping children notice that the thought bubble shows that Jake is thinking about a memory. Then show page 3, a few different pages from the middle, and the last page.

- Guide a conversation about the sequence of events in the book using a few prompts about the beginning, middle, and end of the story such as the following.

  - *Why do you think the author started this story with Jake sharing how he felt about going on his first sleepover?*

  - *What happened in the middle of the story?*

  - *Why do you think the author ended this story with Josh coming to Jake's house the next week for a sleepover?*

  - *How can you tell that the author wrote about the story events in order?*

- Repeat if needed with another memory story that is written in chronological order, such as *Flower Garden*.

  Authors write their stories in the order that they happened.

Have a Try

Invite children to turn and talk to a partner about whether a memory is written in the order it happened.

▶ Show the prepared chart with the memory story.

> As I read my memory story, think about whether it is written in the right order. When I finish, turn and talk to your partner about whether it is written the way the story happened.

▶ After a brief discussion, ask children to share. As they do, add (or have volunteers add) numbers to the chart to show the story sequence.

▶ This memory story will be used in WML5.

Summarize and Apply

Summarize the learning. Remind children to draw and write their stories in the order they happened.

> In what order should you draw and write your story?

▶ Write the principle at the top of the chart.

> When you make a memory book, make sure you draw the pictures and write the words in the order the story happened.

Draw and write your story in the order it happened.

1. I went fishing.

2. I put my pole in the water.

3. I caught a fish!

4. I was surprised!

Confer

▶ During independent writing, move around the room to confer briefly with as many individual children as time allows. Sit side by side with them and invite them to talk about their memory stories. Use the following prompts as needed.

  • *What happened first? next? last?*

  • *Tell the story across your fingers to help you know what goes on each page.*

  • *Read your story. Is everything in the right order?*

Share

Following independent writing, gather children in the meeting area to share their stories.

▶ Choose several volunteers whose memory books you know are written in order.

> Let's listen to _____'s memory book. Notice how the drawings and words are in the order that the story happened.

WML 4
MBK.U3.WML4

Writing Minilesson Principle
Say *I* and *we* when you tell a story about yourself.

Making Memory Books

You Will Need

▸ several familiar books that are told in first-person point of view, such as the following:

- *The Sleepover* by Judith E. Nayer, from *Shared Reading Collection*
- *Jonathan and His Mommy* by Irene Smalls, from Text Set: Taking Care of Each Other: Family

▸ class writing from IW.14: Writing About a Class Memory (optional)

▸ chart paper prepared with simple drawings: one person, two people

▸ projector (optional)

▸ highlighter tape

▸ marker

▸ To download the following online resource for this lesson, visit **resources.fountasandpinnell.com**:

- chart art (optional)

Academic Language / Important Vocabulary

▸ story

▸ memory

▸ yourself

▸ I

▸ we

Continuum Connection

▸ Understand that a story from your life is usually written in first person (using *I* and *we*) (p. 244)

GOAL

Learn to use the words *I* and *we* when telling a story about yourself.

RATIONALE

Teaching children to use the words *I* and *we* when writing a story about themselves helps them recognize that authors choose particular words in order to give information. They also learn that a memory story is one that is written about an author's own life.

ASSESS LEARNING

▸ Look for evidence that children can identify the words *I* and *we* in a story.

▸ Notice whether children use the words *I* and *we* when they write memory stories.

▸ Look for evidence that children can use vocabulary such as *story*, *memory*, *yourself*, *I*, and *we*.

MINILESSON

Use familiar stories told in the first person to engage children in thinking and talking about writing memory books. If possible, use a projector so that children can see the words. Here is an example.

▸ Show page 14 from *The Sleepover*.

> As I read this page from *The Sleepover*, listen for the words the author uses to help you know who is telling the story.

▸ Slowly read page 14, pointing under each word as you do.

> I notice the author uses the word *I* to show who is telling the story. Listen as I read it again and put your thumb up when you hear the word *I*.

▸ Reread the page. As children identify *I*, add highlighter tape to the word. If children comment on the word *my*, include the word in your discussion.

▸ Show page 5 from *Jonathan and His Mommy*.

> While I read this page from *Jonathan and His Mommy*, listen for any words that help you know who is telling the story.

▸ Guide the conversation so children notice both *I* and *we*, adding highlighter tape as before. Have them discuss how *I* and *we* help the reader know who is telling the story. If children identify the word *us*, include the word in your discussion.

▸ Repeat with the class memory story (IW.14) if it includes the words *I* and/or *we*.

Have a Try

Invite children to turn and talk about the words *I* and *we*.

▶ Display the prepared chart with the sketches. Point to the drawing of the single figure.

Why is it important to use the word *I* when you write a story about yourself?

▶ Point to the drawing of the two figures.

When do you use the word *we* when you are writing a story?

Summarize and Apply

Summarize the learning and remind children to use *I* and *we* when they write books about themselves.

What words do you use when you write a story about yourself?

▶ Write the principle at the top of the chart.

When you work on your memory book today, remember to use the words *I* and *we* when you write a story about yourself. Bring your book to share when we meet later.

Confer

▶ During independent writing, move around the room to confer briefly with as many individual children as time allows. Sit side by side with them and invite them to talk about their memory stories. Use the following prompts as needed.

- Who is your story about?
- How will the reader know who your story is about?
- Where can you look to know how to write the word *we*?
- Where did you use the words *I and we*?

Share

Following independent writing, gather children in the meeting area to share their memory books.

Who used the word *I* or *we* in your memory book? Share a page that uses *I* or *we.*

WML 5

Writing Minilesson Principle
Use pictures and words to show how you were feeling.

Making Memory Books

You Will Need

- familiar books with pictures that show feelings, such as the following:
  - *Flower Garden* by Eve Bunting, from Text Set: The Importance of Kindness
  - *Jonathan and His Mommy* by Irene Smalls, from Text Set: Taking Care of Each Other: Family
- chart paper prepared with a page from the memory story in WML3
- markers
- several cut-out arrows to attach to the chart
- glue stick or tape
- To download the following online resource for this lesson, visit **resources.fountasandpinnell.com**:
  - chart art (optional)

Academic Language / Important Vocabulary

- tell
- story
- feeling

Continuum Connection

- Understand that the writer can look back or think about the memory or experience and share thoughts and feelings about it (p. 244)
- Explain one's thoughts and feelings about an experience or event (p. 244)

GOAL

Understand that the pictures and words in the story can tell how you feel.

RATIONALE

Teaching children to add pictures and words to show feelings when making a book helps them learn that authors reveal information in a variety of ways.

ASSESS LEARNING

- Notice whether children recognize that authors show feelings through words and pictures.
- Observe whether children add pictures and words to show feelings in their own writing.
- Look for evidence that children can use vocabulary such as *tell*, *story*, and *feeling*.

MINILESSON

Use familiar stories that have illustrations and words that show feelings to engage children in thinking and talking about making memory books. Here is an example.

- Show the illustrations on pages 27–29 from *Flower Garden*.

  Take a look at the family on these pages. How do you think they are feeling?

  How do you know?

- Guide the conversation to help children discuss the joyful, loving facial expressions and body language, both of which show that the family is happy.

- Read the text on pages 1 and 4.

  What do the words tell you about how the girl is feeling?

- Guide the conversation to help children identify language to show how happy and excited the girl feels about the flowers, such as *Doesn't it look great?* and *I can hardly wait.*

- Show *Jonathan and His Mommy*.

  As I read a few pages of *Jonathan and His Mommy*, think about what the words and pictures show you about how the characters are feeling.

- Have children talk about what feelings are revealed as you read and show pages 9–10 (feeling joyful and funny) and pages 19–20 (feeling loving and proud).

Have a Try

Invite children to turn and talk about how to show feelings in pictures and words.

▶ Show the chart paper that has been prepared with a page from the memory story in WML3.

> Here is the end of the memory story. How do you think I felt? How do you know? Turn and talk to your partner about that.

▶ After time for a brief discussion, ask volunteers to share.

▶ Choose volunteers to attach arrows to the chart.

Summarize and Apply

Summarize the learning and remind children to show emotion through pictures and words when they make books.

> What can you do to show feelings in your book?

▶ Write the principle at the top of the chart.

> When you work on your memory book, add pictures and words that show how you are feeling. Bring your book to share when we meet later.

Use pictures and words to show how you were feeling.

I was surprised!

Confer

▶ During independent writing, move around the room to confer briefly with as many individual children as time allows. Sit side by side with them and invite them to talk about their memory stories. Use the following prompts as needed.

- *How can you show how you were feeling?*
- *What words can you add to tell how you were feeling?*
- *Can you add something to your drawing to show how you were feeling?*

Share

Following independent writing, gather children in the meeting area to share their stories.

> Who would like to share the memory book you are working on?

> Share a page that shows feelings and tell about that.

Assessment

After you have taught the minilessons in this umbrella, observe children as they draw, write, and talk about their writing. Use *The Literacy Continuum* (Fountas and Pinnell 2017) to notice, teach for, and support children's learning as you observe their attempts at writing, drawing, and reading.

▶ What evidence do you have of new understandings children have developed related to making a memory book?

- Are children able to make a list of memories they might use for making a book?
- Can they tell stories about memories from their own lives?
- Do they draw and write story events in chronological order?
- Are they using *I* and *we* when telling a story about themselves?
- Are they using pictures and words to show feelings when they make books?
- Do they understand and use vocabulary related to making a memory book, such as *list, story, memory, remember, order, beginning, middle, end,* and *yourself*?

▶ In what ways, beyond the scope of this umbrella, are children making books?

- Do they show an interest in making a variety of kinds of books?
- Are they making connections to books they read and then talking about ideas for writing books about their own lives?

Use your observations to determine the next umbrella you will teach. You may also consult Suggested Sequence of Lessons (pp. 483–494) for guidance.

EXTENSIONS FOR MAKING MEMORY BOOKS

▶ Gather together a guided writing group of several children who need support in a specific area of writing.

▶ Teach children other words that are used in first-person stories: *me, my, us,* and *our*.

▶ Encourage children to talk about memories with their families to help them remember story ideas, details, and feelings associated with those memories.

▶ Refer to the storytelling charts you created with children in U1: Storytelling, in the Telling Stories section, to help them think about stories from their own lives.

Minilessons in This Umbrella

WML1   Make a book to teach something.

WML2   Write words and draw pictures to show what to do.

WML3   Write a number for each step.

WML4   Make a list of what you need.

Before Teaching Umbrella 4 Minilessons

Prior to teaching these minilessons, make sure children have had experiences reading how-to books. They should also have engaged in making and doing things that they could teach to others (e.g., blowing bubbles or making a sandwich) and have talked about those activities. Teach IW.18: Writing a How-to Book to prepare children for making how-to books independently. You will use the class-made book from that lesson as a mentor text for the minilessons in this umbrella. You may also choose the following books from *Fountas & Pinnell Classroom™ Interactive Read-Aloud Collection* and *Shared Reading Collection*, or you might use other how-to texts from the classroom. Recipes from cookbooks, on the back of boxes, or on websites are other good sources of examples for these lessons.

Interactive Read-Aloud Collection
Exploring Nonfiction

Building a House by Byron Barton

Shared Reading Collection

Animal Masks by Jennifer Blizin Gillis

Playing Basketball by Louis Petrone

Fly Away by Alina Kirk

A Rainbow of Fruit by Brooke Matthews

Interactive Writing Lessons

IW.18: Writing a How-to Book

As you read and enjoy these texts together, help children

- notice what the reader can learn from the text,
- talk about how the pictures help the reader learn how to do something,
- notice whether the steps are numbered, and
- talk about what items are needed.

Interactive Read-Aloud
Exploring Nonfiction

Shared Reading

Interactive Writing

Section 4: Making Books

Making How-to Books

You Will Need

- several books that show how to do something, such as the following:
  - *Animal Masks* by Jennifer Blizen Gillis and *Playing Basketball* by Louis Petrone, from *Shared Reading Collection*
  - *Building a House* by Byron Barton, from Text Set: Exploring Nonfiction
- chart paper and markers
- class how-to book from IW.18: Writing a How-to Book

Academic Language / Important Vocabulary

- how-to book
- writing
- drawing
- teach
- idea

Continuum Connection

- Understand that a procedural text helps people know how to do something (p. 244)
- Generate and expand ideas through talk with peers and teacher (p. 248)
- Look for ideas and topics in personal experiences, shared through talk (p. 248)
- Rehearse language for informational writing by retelling experiences, using chronological order, describing what they know, or repeating procedural steps in order (p. 248)

GOAL

Think of ideas for making a how-to book.

RATIONALE

When children learn to choose an idea and decide what pictures and words to include in a how-to book, they understand that both pictures and words convey meaning and that they are valued writers who have information to share.

ASSESS LEARNING

- ▶ Look for evidence that children understand that a how-to book teaches the reader how to do something.
- ▶ Observe whether children can choose an idea for writing a how-to book.
- ▶ Look for evidence that children can use vocabulary such as *how-to book*, *writing*, *drawing*, *teach*, and *idea*.

MINILESSON

Prior to teaching this lesson, teach IW.18: Writing a How-to Book and share various how-to books with children. To prepare them for making their own how-to books, revisit familiar books that teach how to do or make something. Here is an example.

- ▶ Show the cover and a few pages of *Animal Masks*.

  What are the children in this book doing?

- ▶ Show the back cover.

  What do you notice on the back cover?

- ▶ Engage children in a conversation, guiding them to understand that this book, including the back cover, shows the reader how to make an animal mask.

- ▶ Repeat with *Playing Basketball* and *Building a House*.

  How-to books teach the reader how to do something. What could you make a how-to book about?

- ▶ Ask a few volunteers to respond. As they do, record their names, their ideas, and sketches of their responses.

Have a Try

Invite children to turn and talk in threes about making how-to books.

> Turn and talk to two friends about an idea you have for making a how-to book.

▶ Ask a few volunteers to share ideas. Add new ideas to the chart. Keep the chart posted to help children generate ideas for making how-to books.

Summarize and Apply

Help children summarize what they learned about how-to books. Have children choose an idea and begin making a how-to book during independent writing.

> What does the chart show?
>
> These are some ideas for how-to books.

▶ Write the principle at the top of the chart and read it aloud.

> During writing time, begin making a how-to book to teach others how to do something.
> Look at the chart if you need help thinking of an idea.

Make a book to teach something.

Fatima   build a sandcastle

Eduardo   draw a car

Chati   shoot a basketball

Violet   fly a kite

Confer

▶ During independent writing, move around the room to confer briefly with as many individual children as time allows. Sit side by side with them and invite them to talk about their ideas for a how-to book. Use the following prompts as needed.

- *What is something you could teach a classmate how to do?*
- *What ideas do you have for making your own how-to book?*
- *What will you write and draw on the first page? the next page?*

Share

Following independent writing, gather children in the meeting area to talk about making how-to books.

> What is your how-to book about?
>
> What information will you give in your how-to book?

WML2

MBK.U4.WML2

Writing Minilesson Principle
Write words and draw pictures to show what to do.

Making How-to Books

You Will Need

- several procedural (how-to) books, such as *A Rainbow of Fruit* by Brooke Matthews from *Shared Reading Collection*

- class how-to book from IW.18: Writing a How-to Book

- three or four blank pages to model making a how-to book

- markers

- To download the following online resource for this lesson, visit **resources.fountasandpinnell.com**:

  - chart art (optional)

  - paper templates (optional)

Academic Language / Important Vocabulary

- how-to book
- pictures
- words
- recipe
- gather
- materials

Continuum Connection

- Understand that pictures can accompany the writing to help the readers understand the information (p. 244)

- Understand that a caption can be written under a picture to give people more information (p. 244)

- Use drawings in the process of drafting, revising, or publishing procedural writing (p. 244)

- Present ideas in logical sequence (p. 246)

GOAL

Learn that words and pictures help readers understand how to do something.

RATIONALE

When children learn that writers make choices about what words and illustrations to include in a text, they understand that both pictures and words convey meaning. This will encourage them to be thoughtful about what they place on each page as they make books.

ASSESS LEARNING

- Notice whether children understand that writers choose the words and illustrations to include.

- Observe whether the drawings and words that children include on a page are related.

- Look for evidence that children can use vocabulary such as *how-to book*, *pictures*, *words*, *recipe*, *gather*, and *materials*.

MINILESSON

To help children understand the role of words and pictures in a how-to book, model the making of a how-to book. Use familiar texts, including the class-made book from IW.18: Writing a How-to Book. Here is an example.

- Show the class-made how-to book from IW.18.

  What do you notice on the pages in this how-to book?

- Guide the conversation so children understand that there are pictures on each page to show what to do and that there is only one step per page.

- Show a few pages from *A Rainbow of Fruit* and then turn to the author's note that shows the directions for a rainbow fruit kabob.

  Here is a recipe for making a rainbow fruit kabob. Let's think about how to use this recipe to make a how-to book.

- Attach the book pages to the chart paper, or draw each page.

  Before you can make anything, you have to get the materials. What should I draw and write on the first page for this first step?

- As children provide suggestions, draw or place pictures and write a sentence under the pictures. Show children how you can look back at the pictures in the book to help know how to draw the different kinds of fruit.

- Continue for the next steps. (Note: Do not number the steps at this stage, as you will be numbering steps in the next minilesson).

Have a Try

Invite children to revisit the how-to book to check for completeness.

> Take a look at the pages in our how-to book. Are the steps clear? Are all the steps there? Turn and talk to your partner about whether anything should be changed.

▶ After a brief discussion, ask a few volunteers to share ideas. Make the suggested changes.

▶ Keep the how-to book to use in the next two minilessons.

Summarize and Apply

Help children summarize the learning. Then have children work on making a how-to book during writing time.

> What did you learn today about making how-to books?

▶ Write the principle at the top of the chart paper.

> Today you learned that the pictures and words together tell the reader what to do in a how-to book. During writing time, you will start a how-to book or continue working on one you have already started.

Confer

▶ During independent writing, move around the room to confer briefly with as many individual children as time allows. Sit side by side with them and invite them to talk about their how-to books. Use the following prompts as needed.

- *What words and pictures will go on this page?*
- *What drawing could you add to go with the words?*
- *What words could you add to go with the drawing?*
- *How will you show the reader how to do the next step?*

Share

Following independent writing, gather children in the meeting area to share their how-to books.

> Tell about the pictures and words on one page in your how-to book.

Writing Minilesson Principle

Write a number for each step.

Making How-to Books

You Will Need

- a familiar how-to book, such as the following from *Shared Reading Collection*:
  - *Animal Masks* by Jennifer Blizin Gillis
  - *Fly Away* by Alina Kirk
- class how-to book from IW.18: Writing a How-to Book
- the how-to book from WML2

Academic Language / Important Vocabulary

- how-to book
- number
- steps
- in order

Continuum Connection

- Understand that a procedural text can be written in various forms: e.g., list, directions with steps (how-to) (p. 244)
- Understand that a procedural text often shows one item under another item and may include a number or letter for each item (p. 244)
- Present ideas in logical sequence (p. 246)

GOAL

Put the steps in a set of directions in the right order and write the number for each step.

RATIONALE

When children learn to number the steps in a how-to book, they recognize that directions and books are read in a certain order. This will help them organize the pages of their own books sequentially.

ASSESS LEARNING

- Notice evidence that children understand the importance of sequential order in a how-to book.
- Look to see whether children number the steps in their how-to books.
- Look for evidence that children can use vocabulary such as *how-to book*, *number*, *steps*, and *in order* (meaning "sequence").

MINILESSON

To help children think about the minilesson principle, use familiar how-to books or sets of numbered directions to engage them in an inquiry about numbering the steps. Here is an example.

- Briefly revisit the pages of *Animal Masks* and *Fly Away* and ask children to recall what the books show the reader how to do.
- Show the back cover of *Animal Masks* and the last page of *Fly Away*.

  What do you notice about these pages?

- Guide the children to notice that there are steps that show the reader how to do something (e.g., make animal masks, make a paper airplane).

  Sometimes, writers use numbers. How have the writers used numbers on these pages?

- As children identify that the steps are numbered, have a conversation about why numbered steps are helpful to follow the directions in order.

- Show the first page from the how-to book you made in the previous lesson (making rainbow fruit kabobs).

  If I want to write a number for the first step, what number will I write?

  Why is it important to write number *1* for the first step?

- Continue asking children to identify which number to add to each step. As they do, add the correct number to each step.

- Keep the how-to book to use in the next minilesson.

Have a Try

Invite children to turn and talk to a partner about numbering the steps in a how-to book.

> Turn and talk to your partner about how writers can help the reader by using numbers in a how-to book.

Summarize and Apply

Help children summarize the learning. Then have children add numbers to the steps in their how-to books during writing time.

> What do some authors do to help you know the order of the steps in a how-to book?

▶ Add the principle to the top of the chart. (If you are using the chart from WML2, write the principle on a strip of paper and place it over the previous principle.) Read it aloud.

> When you work on your how-to books during writing time, write a number for each step. Bring your how-to book to share when we meet later.

Confer

▶ During independent writing, move around the room to confer briefly with as many individual children as time allows. Sit side by side with them and invite them to talk about their how-to books. Use the following prompts as needed.

- *What number goes with the first step?*
- *What number will you add to this step?*
- *Which number can I help you write?*

Share

Following independent writing, gather children in the meeting area to share their how-to books.

> Tell about the how-to book you worked on today.

> How did you decide which number to add to each step?

Writing Minilesson Principle
Make a list of what you need.

Making How-to Books

You Will Need

- an example of a how-to book that does *not* have a list of materials, such as *Animal Masks* by Jennifer Blizin Gillis from *Shared Reading Collection*
- the how-to book from WML2
- a recipe that has ingredients listed (e.g., from the back of a cake mix box)
- chart paper and markers
- To download the following online resource for this lesson, visit **resources.fountasandpinnell.com**:
  - chart art (optional)
  - paper templates (optional)

Academic Language / Important Vocabulary

- how-to book
- list
- need
- materials

Continuum Connection

- Understand that lists are a helpful way to organize information (p. 244)
- Use lists to plan activities or support memory (p. 244)
- Place items in the list that are appropriate for its purpose or category (p. 244)
- Understand that a procedural text can be written in various forms: e.g., list, directions with steps (how-to) (p. 244)

GOAL

Understand that sometimes writers include a list of materials needed to complete the instructions in a how-to book.

RATIONALE

Helping children learn that a list of materials is useful in a how-to book encourages them to think about their own writing from a reader's perspective. This enables them to think about and include necessary and important information in their own how-to books.

ASSESS LEARNING

- Look for evidence that children understand the purpose of a list of materials in a how-to book.
- Observe whether children include a list of materials in their own how-to books.
- Look for evidence that children can use vocabulary such as *how-to book*, *list*, *need*, and *materials*.

MINILESSON

To help children understand that a list of materials is helpful to include in a how-to book, provide a minilesson using familiar how-to books and a sample recipe. Here is an example.

- Show a recipe and point to the list of ingredients.

  At the beginning of this recipe, there is a list of materials, or ingredients. How will this list help you make the cake?

- Show page 1 from the how-to book you made in WML2.

  What are the materials needed to make a fruit kabob? Turn and tell your partner.

- After time for a brief discussion, ask a few children to share.

- Show the back cover of *Animal Masks*.

  Here are the numbered steps for making an animal mask, but there is no list of materials. Why would a list of materials be helpful to someone who wants to make this animal mask?

- Have a conversation about the usefulness of a list of materials.

Have a Try

Invite children to turn and talk to a partner about a list of materials in a how-to book.

▶ Continue showing the back cover from *Animal Masks*.

> Turn and talk about what to put on a list of materials for making an animal mask.

▶ After time for discussion, ask children to share. Using their suggestions, make a list on chart paper. Draw or place a sketch for each item. If needed, explain that some how-to books do not need a list of materials, but if the book is about making something, it probably will have one.

Summarize and Apply

Help children summarize the learning. Then have children make a list of materials in their how-to books.

> What did you learn today about making how-to books?

▶ Write the principle at the top of the chart paper. Read it aloud.

> As you work on a how-to book today, add a list of materials. Bring your how-to book to share when we meet later.

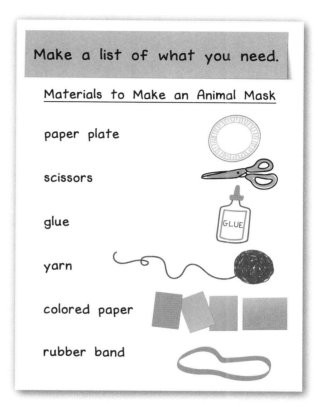

Make a list of what you need.

Materials to Make an Animal Mask

paper plate

scissors

glue

yarn

colored paper

rubber band

Confer

▶ During independent writing, move around the room to confer briefly with as many individual children as time allows. Sit side by side with them and invite them to talk about making their how-to books. Use the following prompts as needed.

- *What materials do you need?*
- *Does your list have everything on it that you need?*
- *How does your list help the reader?*

Share

Following independent writing, gather children in the meeting area to share their how-to books.

> Who added a list of materials in your how-to book today? Share what you put on the list.

Assessment

After you have taught the minilessons in this umbrella, observe children as they explore making books. Use *The Literacy Continuum* (Fountas and Pinnell 2017) to notice, teach for, and support children's learning as you observe their attempts at reading and writing.

- ▸ What evidence do you have of new understandings children have developed related to making how-to books?
  - Can children articulate the purpose of a how-to book?
  - Do they show an interest in making how-to books independently?
  - Do their how-to books contain pictures, numbers, and a list of materials?
  - Do they understand and use vocabulary related to making a how-to book, such as *how-to book*, *writing*, *drawing*, *teach*, *idea*, *pictures*, *words*, *number*, *steps*, *list*, *need*, and *materials*?
- ▸ In what ways, beyond the scope of this umbrella, are children making books?
  - Do they show an interest in celebrating their books?
  - Are they thinking about adding to, deleting from, or reorganizing the pages in their books?

Use your observations to determine the next umbrella you will teach. You may also consult Suggested Sequence of Lessons (pp. 483–494) for guidance.

EXTENSIONS FOR MAKING HOW-TO BOOKS

- ▸ Have children follow a recipe for a simple snack that has just a few steps and then talk about the steps with a partner. Following this, they can draw and write about the recipe to share with their families.

- ▸ Talk to children about their activities in the play corner and encourage them to make a how-to book to teach someone something they know how to do (e.g., give a dog a bath, make a pretend cake).

- ▸ If you and the class read how-to books, directions, or recipes that do not have numbered steps, use sticky notes to add the numbers.

- ▸ As children engage in science activities, use shared or interactive writing to make a list of materials.

- ▸ Gather together a guided writing group of several children who need support in a specific area of writing.

- ▸ Allow children to choose the kind of paper they want to use for their books. There is a selection of paper templates available in the online resources.

Minilessons in This Umbrella

WML1 Make an all-about book.

WML2 Write about the same topic on every page.

WML3 Write labels on your pictures to tell facts.

WML4 Use page numbers to help the reader.

Before Teaching Umbrella 5 Minilessons

Teach this umbrella late in the year so that children have learned about a wide variety of subjects and topics. This will enable them to generate many ideas for making all-about books. Before this umbrella, teach IW.24: Writing an All-About Book. The book you make with children in that lesson will be used as a mentor text throughout this umbrella. Prepare blank booklets (four to eight stapled pages with a cover) for children to use. You might also want to provide any of the paper templates from the online resources that are appropriate. Store the booklets and paper templates in the writing center.

Prior to teaching these minilessons, gather a variety of nonfiction books (some with labels and page numbers), both published mentor texts and children's writing. You may also choose the following books from *Fountas & Pinnell Classroom™ Interactive Read-Aloud Collection* and *Shared Reading Collection*. If you are using *The Reading Minilessons Book, Kindergarten* (Fountas and Pinnell 2019), LA.U9: Learning About Nonfiction Books would pair well with the minilessons in this umbrella.

Interactive Read-Aloud Collection

Exploring Nonfiction

A Fruit Is a Suitcase for Seeds by Jean Richards

Shoes Shoes Shoes by Ann Morris

Exploring Fiction and Nonfiction

Hats Hats Hats by Ann Morris

Shared Reading Collection

Fuzzy and Buzzy by Aaron Mack

Spin, Spin, Spin by Alina Kirk

Sticky by Cordelia S. Finn

Alligator Hide-and-Seek by Reese Brooks

Look Out! by Sue Bright-Moore

Interactive Writing Lessons

IW.24: Writing an All-About Book

As you read and enjoy these texts together, help children

- notice that the books have information,
- recognize that all of the pages in a book are about the same topic, and
- notice the use of labels and page numbers.

Interactive Read-Aloud
Exploring Nonfiction

Fiction and Nonfiction

Shared Reading

Interactive Writing

You Will Need

- several nonfiction books that give information about one topic, such as the following:

  - *Shoes Shoes Shoes* by Ann Morris and *A Fruit Is a Suitcase for Seeds* by Jean Richards, from Text Set: Exploring Nonfiction

  - *Fuzzy and Buzzy* by Aaron Mack and *Spin, Spin, Spin* by Alina Kirk, from *Shared Reading Collection*

- the class-made book from IW.24: Writing an All-About Book

- chart paper and markers

- blank, prepared all-about books for each child (stored in the writing center)

Academic Language / Important Vocabulary

- all-about book

Continuum Connection

- Understand how to write a factual text from listening to mentor texts read aloud and discussing them (p. 245)

- Include facts and details in information writing (p. 246)

- Begin to understand the difference between telling a story and telling facts about something (p. 246)

- Generate and expand ideas through talk with peers and teacher (p. 248)

GOAL

Understand that you can make a book to give readers information about something.

RATIONALE

When children write books with an authentic purpose, they learn that they can share their knowledge with others. Engaging in bookmaking enables children to use high-level thinking about the process of writing.

ASSESS LEARNING

- Notice evidence of what children understand about all-about books.
- Listen to children talk about a topic. Can they articulate their thinking?
- Look for evidence that children can use vocabulary such as *all-about book*.

MINILESSON

Prior to teaching this lesson, make sure children have been exposed to a variety of nonfiction books and have experienced making a class all-about book (see IW.24: Writing an All-About Book). To help children learn to write all-about books independently, engage them in a discussion about nonfiction books. Repeat *all about* throughout the lesson to reinforce the vocabulary. Here is an example.

- Show the cover and a few pages of *Shoes Shoes Shoes*.

  > Here is the book *Shoes Shoes Shoes*. What does Ann Morris tell all about in this book?

- As children identify that the book is all about shoes, create a chart with the book title on one side and what the book is about on the other side. Display the books on the easel.

- Show the cover of *A Fruit Is a Suitcase for Seeds* and revisit a few pages.

  > What does Jean Richards tell all about in this book, *A Fruit Is a Suitcase for Seeds*?

- Help children understand that the book is all about seeds. Add to the chart.

- Repeat with *Fuzzy and Buzzy*; *Spin, Spin, Spin*; and the class-made book from IW.24. Add to the chart.

Have a Try

Invite children to talk to a partner about all-about books.

> **What are some things you know a lot about? Tell your partner some ideas.**

▶ Ask a few children to share ideas, assisting the conversation as needed. Guide the conversation to help them understand that something they know a lot about can be the idea for a book.

Summarize and Apply

Summarize the learning. Then have children make all-about books.

▶ Write the principle at the top of the chart.

> **Today you learned that an all-about book tells information about something, like shoes or seeds or plants. During writing time, choose one of the ideas you talked to your partner about, or choose another idea to make an all-about book.**

▶ Make sure each child knows where the prepared blank books are stored in the writing center.

Make an all-about book.	
	shoes
	seeds
	animal descriptions
	things that spin
	plants

Confer

▶ During independent writing, move around the room to confer briefly with as many individual children as time allows. Sit side by side with them and invite them to talk about their plans for making their all-about books. Use the following prompts as needed.

- *What are some things you know a lot about and want to tell others?*
- *What could you write in a book about that?*
- *What will each page in this book be about?*
- *What will you put on the next page?*

Share

Following independent writing, gather children in the meeting area and choose several to share the all-about books they are working on. Support children's oral language by providing a sentence frame, such as *My all-about book is about _____.*

> **Who would like to share the all-about book you are working on?**

> **What is your book about?**

WML2

MBK.U5.WML2

Writing Minilesson Principle
Write about the same topic on every page.

Making All-About Books

You Will Need

- several familiar nonfiction books about a single subject, such as the following:
  - *Shoes Shoes Shoes* by Ann Morris, from Text Set: Exploring Nonfiction
  - *Hats Hats Hats* by Ann Morris, from Text Set: Exploring Fiction and Nonfiction
  - *Sticky* by Cordelia S. Finn, from *Shared Reading Collection*
- the class-made book from IW.24: Writing an All-About Book
- chart paper and markers

Academic Language / Important Vocabulary

- all-about book
- topic
- page

Continuum Connection

- Write a book with all pages and ideas related to the same topic or set of facts (p. 245)
- Make a drawing or series of drawings of objects or processes and talk or write about them (p. 245)
- Write and/or draw about one idea on a page (p. 246)
- Put together the related details on a topic in a text (p. 246)
- Tell one part, idea, or group of ideas on each page of a book (p. 246)

GOAL

Understand that every page in a book is related to the same topic.

RATIONALE

When children understand that all of the pages in an all-about book relate to the same topic, they learn the importance of staying on topic when making their own books.

ASSESS LEARNING

- Listen to children talk about all-about books. Do they recognize that all of the pages are about the same topic?
- Observe whether children write about the same idea on each page in the all-about books they make independently.
- Look for evidence that children can use vocabulary such as *all-about book*, *topic*, and *page*.

MINILESSON

To help children think about the principle, use familiar all-about books to engage them in noticing that all of the pages are about the same topic. Here is an example.

- Before teaching, gather several nonfiction books you have read with children. Include the book you created with them during IW.24: Writing an All-About Book.

- Show the covers and a few pages each of *Shoes Shoes Shoes* and *Hats Hats Hats*.

  Ann Morris wrote both of these all-about books. Turn and talk about what you notice about the pages of *Shoes Shoes Shoes* and what you notice about the pages of *Hats Hats Hats*.

- After a brief discussion, ask volunteers to share. Guide them to understand that each page of *Shoes Shoes Shoes* is all about shoes and each page of *Hats Hats Hats* is all about hats.

- Repeat with the class-made all-about book from IW.24.

  Each book is about a single topic. The topic of *Shoes Shoes Shoes* is shoes. The topic of *Hats Hats Hats* is hats.

Have a Try

Display the big book *Sticky* on the easel. Invite children to talk to a partner about what each page is about.

▶ Show the pages of *Sticky*, pausing long enough for children to notice each page.

> Turn and tell your partner what each page of this book is all about.

▶ Ask one set of partners what they think the book is about. Write the topic on chart paper. Continue asking each set of partners. Each time the children have the same answer, make a star.

Summarize and Apply

Help children summarize what they learned about the pages in an all-about book. Then remind children to make sure the pages in their all-about books are about the same topic.

> What should you write about on every page of your all-about book?

▶ Write the principle at the top of the chart and read it aloud.

> As you make an all-about book, make sure each page is about the same topic. Today you can work on the book you have already started or make a new book.

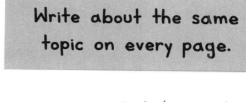

Confer

▶ During independent writing, move around the room to confer briefly with as many individual children as time allows. Sit side by side with them and invite them to talk about their all-about books. Use the following prompts as needed.

- *Your book is all about _____ . What will each page be about?*
- *What will you put on the next page?*
- *What else can you write about your idea?*

Share

Following independent writing, gather children in the meeting area to share their all-about books. Support children's oral language by providing a sentence frame, such as *All the pages are about _____* or *The topic of my book is _____.*

> Who would like to share the all-about book you are working on?

> What are all of the pages about?

WML3

MBK.U5.WML3

Writing Minilesson Principle
Write labels on your pictures to tell facts.

Making All-About Books

You Will Need

- familiar nonfiction books that have pictures with labels, such as the following from *Shared Reading Collection*:
  - *Alligator Hide-and-Seek* by Reese Brooks
  - *Sticky* by Cordelia S. Finn
  - *Spin, Spin, Spin* by Alina Kirk
- the class-made book from IW.24: Writing an All-About Book
- blank word cards
- tape or glue stick
- chart paper and markers
- To download the following online resource for this lesson, visit **resources.fountasandpinnell.com**:
  - chart art (optional)

Academic Language / Important Vocabulary

- all-about book
- facts
- labels
- information

Continuum Connection

- Understand that a writer or illustrator can add a label to help readers understand a drawing or photograph (p. 244)
- Understand that a label provides important information (p. 244)
- Create a label for an illustration that accompanies a written piece (p. 244)
- Use features (e.g., page numbers, title, labeled pictures, table of contents, or others) to guide the reader (p. 245)

GOAL

Understand that a label tells information about a picture.

RATIONALE

When children learn that labels add information to pictures in an all-about book, they understand that authors can provide information in different ways. They learn that they can add labels to pictures in the all-about books they make.

ASSESS LEARNING

- Notice whether children can explain that labels provide information about book illustrations.
- Observe whether children add labels to pictures in the all-about books they are making.
- Look for evidence that children can use vocabulary such as *all-about book*, *labels*, *facts*, and *information*.

MINILESSON

To help children think about the minilesson principle, use familiar nonfiction books to engage them in a discussion about labels. Here is an example.

- Show page 8 in *Alligator Hide-and-Seek* by Reese Brooks.

  What do you notice on this page?

- As needed, guide children to notice the label that points to *long, fat tail* and the line that connects the label to the picture.

- Repeat for *Sticky* by Cordelia S. Finn (p. 7), which shows labels for *tape* and *paper*, and *Spin, Spin, Spin* by Alina Kirk (p. 9), which shows labels for *plate* and *stick*.

  Why do you think these writers added labels to their pictures?

  You can add labels to tell facts about the pictures in our all-about book.

- Create a new page that could be added to the all-about book from IW.24.

  What label would tell the reader information, or facts, about the picture?

- Write the label on a blank word card.

  Who can show where the label should go on this page?

- Ask a volunteer to come up to attach the label to the page in the all-about book.

  You can also draw a line from your label to the part the label tells about.

- Draw a line from the label to the picture.

- Save the picture for WML4.

Have a Try

Invite children to turn and talk to a partner about adding another label in the all-about book.

▶ Show a different page from one of the nonfiction books or the class all-about book. (If the illustrations already have labels, cover them with sticky notes or choose a nonfiction book that does not have labels and add them with sticky notes).

Turn and talk about what label could be added to this page.

▶ After a brief discussion, ask a volunteer to share. Attach a new label or reveal the label.

Summarize and Apply

Help children summarize what they learned. Then remind children to add labels to the pictures in their all-about books.

What did you learn today about labels?

▶ Write the principle at the top of the chart paper.

Today during writing time, you can write labels to add facts to the pictures in your all-about book. You can continue working on a book you have already started or you can make a new book.

Write labels on your pictures to tell facts.

green leaves

Plants have green leaves.

Confer

▶ During independent writing, move around the room to confer briefly with as many individual children as time allows. Sit side by side with them and invite them to talk about their all-about books. Use the following prompts as needed.

• *Show me where you can add a label.*
• *Can you add a fact about this picture in a label?*
• *Say the word slowly. What sound do you hear first [next, last]?*
• *Write the letters for the sounds you hear.*

Share

Following independent writing, gather children in the meeting area to share their all-about books.

Who added a label to a picture in an all-about book? Tell about the label.

WML4

MBK.U5.WML4

Writing Minilesson Principle
Use page numbers to help the reader.

Making All-About Books

You Will Need

- several familiar all-about books that have page numbers, such as the following:
  - *Hats Hats Hats* by Ann Morris, from Text Set: Exploring Fiction and Nonfiction
  - *Fuzzy and Buzzy* by Aaron Mack and *Look Out!* by Sue Bright-Moore, from *Shared Reading Collection*
- the chart from WML3
- the class-made book from IW.24: Writing an All-About Book
- marker

Academic Language / Important Vocabulary

- all-about book
- page numbers

Continuum Connection

- Use features (e.g., page numbers, title, labeled pictures, table of contents, or others) to guide the reader (p. 245)
- Present ideas in logical sequence (p. 246)

GOAL

Understand that page numbers help to guide the reader.

RATIONALE

When children learn that page numbers are helpful guides for readers, they understand that they can add page numbers to the pages of their own books.

ASSESS LEARNING

- Notice evidence of what children understand about numbering the pages in a book.
- Observe whether children add page numbers in the all-about books they are making.
- Look for evidence that children can use vocabulary such as *all-about book* and *page numbers*.

MINILESSON

To help children think about the minilesson principle, provide an interactive lesson using familiar nonfiction books. Here is an example.

- Hold the book *Hats Hats Hats* close to the children so they can see the page numbers.

  What do you notice in the bottom corner of these pages?

  Those numbers are the page numbers.

- Show the pages of one or two other books.

  Where do you see page numbers in these books?

  Many books have page numbers on the bottom of each page. Why do you think books have page numbers?

- Guide children to realize that page numbers go in order and they can help you know how to find something in the book.

  You can add page numbers to the books you make.

Have a Try

Invite children to turn and talk to a partner about adding page numbers to the class all-about book.

▶ Display the all-about book created in IW.24 on the easel. (If you have not previously added page numbers to the book, add them now.)

> If we add the new page to our all-about book, what page would it be? Turn and talk about that.

▶ After a brief discussion, ask a few volunteers to share ideas. Then add the page number.

Summarize and Apply

Help children summarize what they learned about page numbers. Then remind them to add page numbers to their all-about books.

> Why are page numbers important?

▶ Write the principle on chart paper.

> Today during writing time, you can add page numbers to your all-about book. You can continue working on a book you already started or you can make a new book.

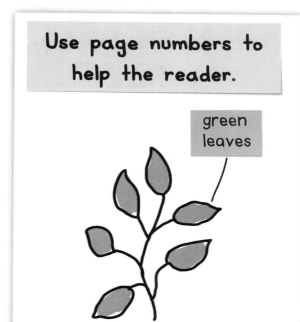

Confer

▶ During independent writing, move around the room to confer briefly with as many individual children as time allows. Sit side by side with them and invite them to talk about their all-about books. Use the following prompts as needed.

- *What page number comes next?*
- *This is page 2. What number comes after 2?*
- *Where will you put the page number on this page?*

Share

Following independent writing, gather children in the meeting area to share their all-about books.

> Who added page numbers in your all-about book?

> Show where you put the page numbers.

Assessment

After you have taught the minilessons in this umbrella, observe children as they explore making books. Use *The Literacy Continuum* (Fountas and Pinnell 2017) to notice, teach for, and support children's learning as you observe their attempts at writing and drawing.

▶ What evidence do you have of new understandings children have developed related to making all-about books?

- Are children able explain what an all-about book is?
- Are they making all-about books on their own?
- Do they write about the same idea on each page?
- Are they adding labels to their drawings to provide facts?
- Do they include page numbers in their all-about books?
- Do they understand and use vocabulary related to making a memory book, such as *all-about book*, *topic*, *pictures*, *labels*, *facts*, *information*, and *page numbers*?

▶ In what ways, beyond the scope of this umbrella, are children making books?

- Do they show an interest in making a variety of types of books?
- Are they starting to add to, delete from, or reorganize their writing?

Use your observations to determine the next umbrella you will teach. You may also consult Suggested Sequence of Lessons (pp. 483–494) for guidance.

EXTENSIONS FOR MAKING ALL-ABOUT BOOKS

▶ Provide assistance as children use a computer or other tech tools to make all-about books.

▶ Some children might be ready to add other features of nonfiction texts, such as a table of contents or sidebars. If you are using *The Reading Minilessons Book, Kindergarten* (Fountas and Pinnell 2019), see LA.U11: Using Text Features to Gain Information.

▶ Organize book-sharing opportunities with another class.

▶ When children show an interest in a topic, help them learn more by providing resources and encouraging them to make an all-about book with their newly acquired knowledge.

▶ Gather together a guided writing group of several children who need support in a specific area of writing.

Section 5 | Drawing

CHILDREN'S ABILITY TO draw recognizable people and objects develops throughout kindergarten. When you help children make their drawings more realistic looking and teach them how to add details, they gain the tools to express their ideas to others. The more details children include in their drawings, the more they will have to write about.

Minilessons in This Umbrella

WML1 Draw your face.

WML2 Color your face so it looks like you.

Before Teaching Umbrella 1 Minilessons

This umbrella is designed to teach children how to draw and paint a self-portrait that reflects realistic skin tones and hair and eye colors. To do this, children can use hand-held mirrors, which help them study their faces up close and also help them realize that the face drawing should fill the space. We recommend that children use a pencil in the first lesson. Once they have completed sketches of their faces, we suggest you outline the faces with a thin, black marker before children move on to the second lesson so they can see the lines to paint. The self-portraits made in this lesson can be used in IW.8: Making a Class Big Book.

In order to evaluate faces and how they are represented as drawings, children will benefit from looking carefully at the illustrations of characters in a variety of picture books. Choose a variety of genres from the classroom library that children have enjoyed and that offer close-ups of a variety of people so that children can study the facial features and color.

As you read and enjoy texts together, help children

- notice the illustrations, particularly where the author placed them on the pages,

- study how the illustrator drew faces,

- notice the illustrator's use of color, and

- notice how each face is unique, just like each child's face is unique.

WML1

Writing Minilesson Principle
Draw your face.

Making a Self-Portrait

You Will Need

- hand-held mirrors (preferably one per child or pair)
- chart paper and black marker
- drawing paper

Academic Language/ Important Vocabulary

- draw
- face
- shape
- self-portrait
- skin

Continuum Connection

- Use drawings to represent people, places, things, and ideas (p. 249)
- Add to or remove details from drawings to plan, draft, revise work (p. 249)

GOAL

Draw a self-portrait with details (e.g., eyes, nose, mouth, ears, hair).

RATIONALE

When children learn to draw self-portraits, they learn to observe details and identify shapes to make their drawings more representational. They also learn to embrace the diversity in human features.

ASSESS LEARNING

- Observe children's drawings. Do they include the main facial features (e.g., eyes, nose)? Are there any details (e.g., eyebrows, teeth)? How are the facial features placed?
- Look for evidence that children can use vocabulary such as *draw*, *face*, *shape*, *self-portrait*, and *skin*, as well as words describing face shape, facial features, and hair.

MINILESSON

Prior to teaching this lesson, provide children with experiences to help them notice and talk about facial illustrations in a variety of picture books. To help children learn how to draw a self-portrait, have them study their own faces by looking in the mirror. Model the experience.

- The initial self-portrait should be drawn with black marker by you and pencil by the children. Color will be added in the next lesson.

   Today you are going to learn how to draw your face. Your drawing of your face is called a self-portrait.

   I am going to make a self-portrait. The first thing I will do is look carefully in a mirror and think about the shape of my face.

- As you look in the mirror, use your finger to outline the outside of your face.

   What shape is my face?

- As children use a finger to draw your face shape in the air, guide the conversation to discuss shape (e.g., round, oval). Draw your face shape large enough to take up almost all of the space on the chart paper.

   What do you notice about how big I drew my face shape?

   Now look at my eyes. How would you describe them?

- Prompt children to notice details (e.g., shape, size, the circle and dot inside). Have a volunteer point to where the eyes should be drawn. Draw your eyes.

- Repeat the process for the remaining facial features, such as the nose (circle, oval), mouth (line or circle), lips, teeth, ears (half-circles), hair (curly, straight, side part), eyelashes, eyebrows, freckles, beauty marks, and pierced ears.

Have a Try

Invite children to use a mirror and talk to a partner about the shapes they see.

> Turn and talk to your partner about the shapes you see when you look at your face in the mirror.

▶ Invite a few children to share what they observed. Provide assistance with shape words as needed. Ask children to make the shapes they see in the air with their fingers.

Summarize and Apply

Write the principle on the chart. Read it to the children. Then invite children to draw self-portraits.

▶ You might have a few children work on their self-portraits in the art center, or you might want the whole class to work on them at the same time.

> Today you can draw a self-portrait using a pencil. I will be in the art center if you need help.

▶ Over the next few days, repeat the lesson as needed to provide time for children to add more detail.

▶ Save the chart for WML2, where children will add color to their self-portraits.

Draw your face.

Confer

▶ During choice time, sit side by side with individual children and invite them to talk about their drawings. Use the following prompts as needed.

- *Look in the mirror. What shape is your mouth (eyes, nose)?*
- *Where should you draw your eyes?*
- *Where will you draw your eyebrows?*

Share

Following choice time, gather children in the meeting area. Ask a few children to share their self-portraits.

> Tell about how you drew your face.

Writing Minilesson Principle
Color your face so it looks like you.

Making a Self-Portrait

You Will Need

- hand-held mirrors (preferably one per child or pair)
- self-portraits created in WML1
- paints or crayons in a wide variety of colors (include many skin tone choices)
- drawing paper

Academic Language/ Important Vocabulary

- self-portrait
- skin

Continuum Connection

- Create drawings that employ careful attention to color or detail (p. 249)

GOAL

Use color (e.g., paint, markers, colored pencils, or crayons) to color a self-portrait realistically.

RATIONALE

When children include color in creating their self-portraits, they learn to observe details and identify colors so that their drawings will become more representational.

ASSESS LEARNING

- Observe whether children notice facial feature details.
- Notice the colors children choose for their skin, eyes, and hair.
- Look for evidence that children can use vocabulary such as *self-portrait* and *skin* as well as words that describe facial features and hair.

MINILESSON

For their self-portraits, children should use the color they see in the mirror, which may or may not be exactly the same as how they describe themselves. To help children learn how to color a self-portrait, have them study their faces by looking in the mirror. Model the experience for them. Here is an example.

- Display the self-portrait you created in WML1, along with sufficient paints or crayons that children see a wide variety of colors.

    When you drew your self-portraits, you used shapes to make yourselves look like you do in real life. You can also use colors when you draw your self-portraits so that you look real.>

- Use the mirror to look at your face.

    What color is my skin? Which color matches my face?

- Have a volunteer choose a paint or crayon color. Paint or color the face on the self-portrait you created in WML1, including ears, nose, and neck.

- Look in the mirror again, touching or emphasizing your hair.

    What color should I choose for my hair color?

- Have a volunteer choose a color. Paint or color the hair on the self-portrait.

- Continue coloring the remaining features, having children provide color suggestions. If using paint, you may choose to wait a day until the face and hair are dry before repeating this process for the other facial features. It may be easiest to use markers or colored pencils for eyelashes, freckles, and beauty marks as the last step.

The Writing Minilessons Book, Kindergarten

Have a Try

Invite children to talk to a partner about the colors they see when they look at themselves in a mirror.

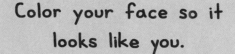

- Provide a hand-held mirror to each pair of children. Have them talk about the colors they see.

  Turn and talk to your partner about the colors you see when you look in the mirror.

- Invite a few children to share what they observed. Provide assistance with color words as needed.

Summarize and Apply

Write the principle on the chart. Summarize the learning and then invite children to add appropriate colors to their self-portraits.

- You might have a few children work on their self-portraits in the art center, or you might want the whole class to work on them at the same time.

  Today, you can paint or color your self-portrait. I will be in the art center to help you.

- Over the next few days, repeat the lesson as needed to provide time for children to add more detail and color. After the self-portraits are complete, children may want to outline features such as eyes, nose, mouth, and eyelashes with black marker or they may want to paint the background.

Confer

- During choice time, sit side by side with individual children and invite them to talk about their self-portraits. Use the following prompts as needed.
  - *Look in the mirror. What color is your skin (eyes, nose, mouth, hair)?*
  - *Make sure that you color in the shapes that you drew.*
  - *What other colors do you see when you look at your face?*

Share

Following choice time, gather children in the meeting area. Ask a few children to share their self-portraits.

Tell about the colors you used to draw your self-portrait.

How did you decide which colors to use?

Assessment

After you have taught the minilessons in this umbrella, observe children as they draw. Use *The Literacy Continuum* (Fountas and Pinnell 2017) to notice, teach for, and support children's learning as you observe their attempts at drawing and writing.

▶ What evidence do you have that children understand how to make a self-portrait?

- Are children able to name and draw the shapes of their faces?

- Can they select colors that accurately depict the colors of their faces?

- Do they understand and use vocabulary such as *draw*, *shape*, *face*, *self-portrait*, and *color*?

▶ In what ways, beyond the scope of this umbrella, are children showing readiness for drawing?

- Do children show an interest in drawing everyday objects, animals, and people?

- Are they noticing illustrations in books you read together and talking about the details in the illustrations?

Use your observations to determine the next umbrella you will teach. You may also consult Suggested Sequence of Lessons (pp. 483–494) for guidance.

EXTENSIONS FOR MAKING A SELF-PORTRAIT

▶ The self-portraits can be used to make a class big book (see IW.8: Making a Class Big Book). As an alternative, you could frame the portraits and hang them on the walls of the classroom.

▶ Continue discussions about shape and color as children draw other people and objects. Help them focus their attention on objects in the world around them, and help them notice shapes and colors.

▶ As you read books that have illustrations with facial details, have children talk about what decisions the illustrators made when drawing people.

Minilessons in This Umbrella

WML1 Use shapes to draw people.

WML2 Draw people in different positions.

WML3 Draw the background of your story.

WML4 Add color to your picture.

WML5 Make people look the same on every page.

WML6 Draw motion or sound lines to show something moving or making noise.

Before Teaching Umbrella 2 Minilessons

Before teaching the minilessons in this umbrella, read and discuss a variety of picture books with different styles of illustration and make sure children have had plenty of opportunities to draw and color without constraints. It will be helpful for you to have taught the first umbrella in this section (U1: Making a Self-Portrait).

Use the following texts from *Fountas & Pinnell Classroom™ Interactive Read-Aloud Collection* text sets, or choose books from the classroom library that show a variety of illustration styles and techniques.

Learning and Playing Together: School

Look Out Kindergarten, Here I Come! by Nancy Carlson

I Love You All Day Long by Francesca Rusackas

Taking Care of Each Other: Family

Elizabeti's Doll by Stephanie Stuve-Bodeen

Jonathan and His Mommy by Irene Smalls

The Importance of Friendship

I'm the Best by Lucy Cousins

As you read and enjoy these texts together, help children

- notice and talk about the illustrations,
- share what they notice about the characters,
- notice details in the background,
- notice the illusion of sound and motion, and
- talk about the colors in the illustrations.

School

Family

Friendship

Section 5: Drawing

Writing Minilesson Principle
Use shapes to draw people.

You Will Need

▶ a familiar book with illustrations of people that can be easily broken down into shapes, such as *Elizabeti's Doll* by Stephanie Stuve-Bodeen, from Text Set: Taking Care of Each Other: Family

▶ pencil

▶ chart paper and markers

Academic Language/ Important Vocabulary

▶ draw

▶ shape

▶ oval

▶ rectangle

▶ triangle

Continuum Connection

▶ Use drawings to represent people, places, things, and ideas [p. 249]

GOAL

Understand that shapes can be used to draw people.

RATIONALE

By teaching children that the human figure is made up of simple shapes, you provide guidance especially for children who are hesitant to draw because they "don't know how." Learning to recognize basic shapes forms a foundation for not just drawing but also life skills.

ASSESS LEARNING

▶ Notice how children use shapes to draw people.

▶ Look for evidence that children can use vocabulary such as *draw* and *shape*, as well as the names of specific shapes.

MINILESSON

Use a mentor text to engage children in an inquiry around drawings of people and then demonstrate how to use shapes to draw people. Select examples that show the person facing front. Here is an example.

▶ Show the cover of *Elizabeti's Doll*. Turn to page 5 and show the illustration.

> Look at the illustration of baby Obedi's head. What shape is it?

> What shapes do you see in his arms?

▶ Using your finger to trace over the body parts, show how the baby's body can be broken down into round shapes for the head, torso, upper arms, lower arms, and legs. Use terms that children know or can learn (e.g., *circle*, *oval*).

▶ Show the illustration on page 4.

> What shapes do you see in Elizabeti's dress?

▶ Help children use and understand shape names, such as *rectangle* and *triangle*, to describe the shapes of the dress.

> Help me draw a picture of a person. What shape should I use to draw the head?

▶ Continue drawing the person from the top down, soliciting participation from children. (This is shown on the first chart.)

> What clothes should our person wear?

> What shapes should I use to draw the pants?

▶ Draw the clothing using the children's suggestions. Show how you can draw clothing over the initial ovals and then erase the pencil lines under the clothing. (The finished drawing is shown on the second chart.)

Have a Try

Invite children to talk to a partner about how to draw the person's facial expression.

> How can I show that the person is happy? Turn and talk to your partner about what I should draw.

▷ After children turn and talk, ask a few children to share their ideas. Draw the person's face.

Summarize and Apply

Summarize the learning and remind children to use shapes when they draw people.

> What did you learn today about how to draw people?

▷ Write the principle at the top of the chart. Read it aloud.

> Today during writing time, you will draw a person. Remember to use shapes, like rectangles and triangles, in your drawings.

Confer

▷ During independent writing, move around the room to confer briefly with as many individual children as time allows. Sit side by side with them and invite them to talk about drawing people. If possible, provide children with a selection of photographs of people to use for reference. Use prompts such as the following to support children as they draw.

- *Look closely at the photo. What shapes do you see?*
- *What shapes do you see in the clothing?*
- *How can you use those shapes in your drawing?*

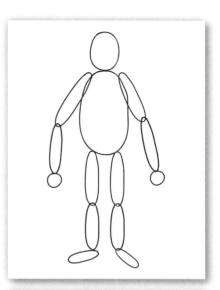

Use shapes to draw people.

Share

Following independent writing, gather children in the meeting area to share their drawings.

> Who would like to share the picture you drew?

> What shapes did you use to draw the person?

Writing Minilesson Principle
Draw people in different positions.

Learning to Draw

You Will Need

- a familiar book with illustrations of people in various positions, such as *Jonathan and His Mommy* by Irene Smalls, from Text Set: Taking Care of Each Other: Family
- chart paper and markers

Academic Language/ Important Vocabulary

- draw
- shape
- position
- oval

Continuum Connection

- Use drawings to represent people, places, things, and ideas (p. 249)

GOAL

Understand that shapes can be drawn in different arrangements to show people in different positions.

RATIONALE

Once children understand how to draw people using shapes, they can be taught to place the shapes to depict people in different positions. When children understand this principle, they can draw their stories' characters engaged in any activity or scenario. The possibilities are limitless.

ASSESS LEARNING

- Look for evidence that children understand the idea of drawing people in different positions.
- Notice how children draw people in different positions.
- Look for evidence that children can use vocabulary such as *draw*, *shape*, *position*, and *oval*.

MINILESSON

Use a mentor text to engage children in an inquiry around drawing people in different positions. Then demonstrate how to use shapes to draw people in these positions. Here is an example.

- Show the cover of *Jonathan and His Mommy*. Turn to page 6 and show the illustration.

  > What do you notice about how Jonathan and his mommy are standing?

  > How do you think the illustrator drew the people standing like this?

  > You learned how to draw people using shapes, like ovals. You can put the shapes in different places to draw people in different positions.

- Begin drawing one of the characters starting at with the head and using ovals for body parts. Explain the positioning of each oval you draw. Stop before drawing the final leg.

  > I need to draw Jonathan's left leg now. First, I will draw an oval for the top part of his leg. Which way should the oval point?

  > Next, I'll draw an oval for the bottom half of his leg. Which way should this oval point?

- Finish drawing the character using the children's suggestions.

Have a Try

Invite children to talk to a partner about how to draw a person in another position.

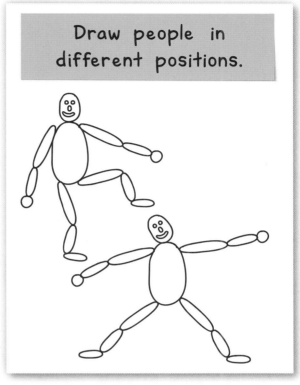

> ❱ Display a second illustration from the book.
>
>> Look at how Jonathan is standing in this picture. How can I draw him standing like this? Turn and talk to your partner about how I can draw him.
>
> ❱ Invite a few children to share their ideas. Draw the character in that position using the children's suggestions.

Summarize and Apply

Write the principle at the top of the chart. Read it to children. Summarize the learning and remind children to draw people in different positions.

> We used ovals to draw Jonathan standing in two different positions. Do our drawings look like Jonathan?
>
> Our drawings don't look like Jonathan yet. After you draw him in a certain position, draw his face, hair, and clothes.
>
> Today during writing time, try drawing the same person in two different positions.

Confer

> ❱ During independent writing, move around the room to confer briefly with as many individual children as time allows. Sit side by side with them and invite them to talk about drawing people. If possible, provide children with a selection of books or photographs that show people in different positions. Use prompts such as the following to support children as they draw.
>
> - *What do you notice about how the person in the photo is standing? What is she doing with her legs?*
> - *Where should you put the ovals for the person's legs?*
> - *Which way should this oval point? Try to make the leg point in the same direction as the leg in the picture.*

Share

Following independent writing, gather children in the meeting area to share their drawings.

> Who would like to show a picture of a person that you drew today?
>
> How is the person sitting/standing? Tell about how you drew the picture.

Section 5: Drawing

Writing Minilesson Principle
Draw the background of your story.

Learning to Draw

You Will Need

- a familiar book with detailed backgrounds, such as *Look Out Kindergarten, Here I Come!* by Nancy Carlson, from Text Set: Learning and Playing Together: School

- a black-marker line drawing of a child

- To download the following resource for this lesson, visit **resources.fountasandpinnell.com**:
  - chart art (optional)

Academic Language/ Important Vocabulary

- draw
- picture
- take place
- behind
- background
- detail

Continuum Connection

- Use drawings to represent people, places, things, and ideas (p. 249)

- Create drawings that are related to the written text and increase readers' understanding and enjoyment (p. 249)

GOAL

Understand that the background gives information about a story.

RATIONALE

When you draw children's attention to the information that they can learn from the background of an illustration, you help them understand that they, too, can give such information in their own drawings.

ASSESS LEARNING

- Look at children's drawings to see whether the backgrounds give information about the story.

- Look for evidence that children can use vocabulary such as *draw*, *picture*, *take place*, *behind*, *background*, and *detail*.

MINILESSON

Use a familiar mentor text to engage children in a discussion about what they can learn from an illustration's background. Here is an example.

- Show the cover of *Look Out Kindergarten, Here I Come!* and read the title. Turn to pages 1–2.

  Look at the picture. Where does this part of the story take place?

  How do you know this is Henry's bedroom?

  What do you notice about his bedroom?

  What do you see in the doorway? Whose head is peaking out?

  The illustrator included lots of little details in the background of the picture to help us understand more about Henry, his house, and his family. The background is the part of the illustration that's behind the main characters.

- Turn to page 11.

  Where is Henry in this illustration?

  What do you see in the background?

  What season is it? How can you tell?

  The illustrator drew colorful leaves falling from the trees to show that it is fall. Noticing details like this can help you learn a lot about the story.

Have a Try

Invite children to talk to a partner about what to put in a background.

▶ Display the prepared chart paper.

> I drew this illustration of a character. I want to show that the character is outside on a sunny day. What should I draw in the background to show this? Turn and talk to your partner about this.

▶ After children turn and talk, invite several children to share their ideas. Add the details that they suggest, using only a black marker.

▶ Save the chart for WML4.

Summarize and Apply

Write the principle at the top of the chart. Read it to children. Summarize the learning and remind children to think about the background when they draw.

> Today during writing time, you will work on making books. As you draw the pictures for your book, remember to draw the background so that the readers know where your story takes place.

Confer

▶ During independent writing, move around the room to confer briefly with as many individual children as time allows. Sit side by side with them and invite them to talk about drawing backgrounds. Use prompts such as the following to support children in drawing backgrounds.

- *Close your eyes and imagine the place where the story takes place. What do you see?*
- *What can you draw in the background to show where it's happening?*
- *What details can you add to give more information about the place?*

Share

Following independent writing, gather children in the meeting area to share their drawings. As needed, support children's oral language by providing a sentence frame, such as *My picture is about _____* or *The background of my picture shows _____.*

> Who would like to share a picture you drew today?

> Tell about the background of your picture.

Writing Minilesson Principle
Add color to your picture.

Learning to Draw

You Will Need

- a familiar book with illustrations with interesting use of color, such as *I'm the Best* by Lucy Cousins, from Text Set: The Importance of Friendship
- a sketch made using a black marker, such as the chart from WML3
- markers of different colors

Academic Language/ Important Vocabulary

- color
- illustration
- illustrator

Continuum Connection

- Create drawings that employ careful attention to color or detail (p. 249)

GOAL

Understand that illustrators choose colors with intention.

RATIONALE

As children study the illustrations in the books you share with them, they begin to notice how illustrators use color intentionally. When you talk with them about how illustrators use color, children learn that they can use color in similar ways in their own drawings.

ASSESS LEARNING

- Observe how children use color in their drawings.
- Look for evidence that children can use vocabulary such as *color, illustration, and illustrator*, as well as the names of specific colors.

MINILESSON

Use a mentor text to engage children in an inquiry around color. Then demonstrate adding color to a drawing. Here is an example.

- Show the cover of *I'm the Best* and read the title. Turn to pages 13–14.

   What colors do you see in this illustration?

   Why do you think the illustrator used so many different colors on these pages?

   All the different colors make it fun to look at the illustration.

- Turn to pages 15–16.

   What colors do you see on these pages?

   What color is the grass?

   Why did the illustrator make the grass green?

- Display the drawing that was created in WML3 or another drawing.

   My illustration needs some color because. I want it to look real. What color should I make the trees?

- With children's input, add color to the illustration, except for the person.

   Do the colors we used make the picture look real?

Have a Try

Invite children to talk to a partner about what colors to use for the person in the drawing.

> What colors do you think we should use for the person? Turn and talk to your partner about your ideas.

> ▶ After children turn and talk, invite a few children to share their ideas. Color the person as suggested.

Summarize and Apply

Write the principle at the top of the chart. Read it to children. Summarize the learning and remind children to think about color when they draw.

> Today during writing time, you will have a chance to work on your book. As you draw pictures for your book, remember to think carefully about the colors you choose. Bring your books to share when we meet later.

Add color to your picture.

Confer

> ▶ During independent writing, move around the room to confer briefly with as many individual children as time allows. Sit side by side with them and invite them to talk about how they are using color in their illustrations. Use prompts such as the following as needed.
>
> - *Why did you choose that color?*
> - *What color(s) would make that look real?*
> - *You used colors that make this page fun to look at.*

Share

Following independent writing, gather children in the meeting area to talk about the color in their drawings.

> Who would like to share a picture you made today?

> Tell about the colors in your picture. Why did you choose those colors?

Writing Minilesson Principle
Make people look the same on every page.

Learning to Draw

You Will Need

▸ a familiar book with illustrations of human characters, such as *Jonathan and His Mommy* by Irene Smalls, from Text Set: Taking Care of Each Other: Family

▸ the completed illustration made during WML4, or another illustration of a person

▸ chart paper

▸ markers of different colors

▸ To download the following online resource for this lesson, visit **resources.fountasandpinnell.com**:

  ▪ chart art [optional]

Academic Language/ Important Vocabulary

▸ people

▸ character

▸ page

▸ illustration

▸ illustrator

Continuum Connection

▸ Use drawings to represent people, places, things, and ideas [p. 249]

▸ Create drawings that employ careful attention to color or detail [p. 249]

GOAL

Understand that it is important to draw people consistently on every page.

RATIONALE

When characters are drawn consistently throughout a book, readers recognize the characters and are better able to follow the story. When children notice that illustrators draw people consistently, they learn to do the same thing in their own books.

ASSESS LEARNING

▸ Notice whether children draw characters consistently throughout their books.

▸ Look for evidence that children can use vocabulary such as *people*, *character*, *page*, *illustration*, and *illustrator*.

MINILESSON

Use a mentor text to engage children in a discussion about drawing people consistently. Then demonstrate doing so. Here is an example.

▸ Show the cover of *Jonathan and His Mommy* and read the title. Turn to pages 1–2. Point to Jonathan and his mother in the illustration.

> Who are these people?

> Take a good look at Jonathan and his mommy.

▸ Turn to pages 3–4 and point to Jonathan and his mother.

> Who are these characters?

> How do you know that this is Jonathan and his mommy?

> The illustrator drew the people so that you can recognize them on all the pages of the book. What if the illustrator made them look different on every page?

> If they looked different, you wouldn't know they are the same people.

▸ Display an illustration that includes a person, such as the one you made in WML4.

> I want to draw the same person walking down the street.

▸ Start drawing the person.

> I want to make her look the same on every page. What color should I make her hair?

> What should her hair look like?

▸ Continue drawing the character, soliciting children's participation when appropriate. Stop before coloring in the person's clothes.

The Writing Minilessons Book, Kindergarten

Have a Try

Invite children to talk to a partner about what color the person's clothes should be.

> What color should I use for the person's clothes? Remember, she should look the same on every page. Turn and talk to your partner about this.

▶ After they turn and talk, invite a few children to share. Color in the person's clothes as they are colored in the previous illustration.

Summarize and Apply

Write the principle at the top of the chart. Read it aloud. Summarize the learning and remind children to make people look the same on every page.

> Why is it important to make people look the same on every page?

> When you work on your book today, remember to make the people look the same on every page. Bring your book to share when we meet later.

Make people look the same on every page.

Confer

▶ During independent writing, move around the room to confer briefly with as many individual children as time allows. Sit side by side with them and invite them to talk about drawing people. Use prompts such as the following as needed.

- *Who are you drawing on this page? Have you drawn this person before?*
- *Let's take a look at your last drawing of this person. Try to make her look the same on this page.*
- *This person must be _____ . I can tell because she looks just like she did on the first page.*

Share

Following independent writing, gather children in the meeting area to share their drawings.

> Put your thumb up if you made a person look the same on every page in your book. Talk about how you made sure the person looked the same.

WML 6

Writing Minilesson Principle
Draw motion or sound lines to show something moving or making noise.

Learning to Draw

You Will Need

- a familiar book with illustrations that have motion and sound lines, such as *I Love You All Day Long* by Francesca Rusackas, from Text Set: Learning and Playing Together: School

- chart paper prepared with two drawings: a bell ringing (no sound lines) and a horse galloping (no motion lines)

- marker

- To download the following resource for this lesson, visit **resources.fountasandpinnell.com**:
  - chart art (optional)

Academic Language/ Important Vocabulary

- draw
- motion
- sound
- line
- noise

Continuum Connection

- Create drawings that employ careful attention to color or detail (p. 249)

- Create drawings that are related to the written text and increase readers' understanding and enjoyment (p. 249)

GOAL

Understand that adding lines in certain ways can make something look like it is moving or making noise.

RATIONALE

When children notice the ways illustrators create the impression of sound and motion in their illustrations, they can use the same techniques in their own books.

ASSESS LEARNING

- Look for evidence that children understand how to use motion and/or sound lines in their drawings.

- Look for evidence that children can use vocabulary such as *draw*, *motion*, *sound*, *line*, and *noise*.

MINILESSON

Use a mentor text to engage children in a discussion around motion and sound lines. Then demonstrate adding motion and sound lines to a drawing. Here is an example.

- Show the cover of *I Love You All Day Long* and read the title. Turn to page 11 and display the illustration.

  How can you tell that Owen's hands are moving?

  Sometimes illustrators draw little lines, called motion lines, to make something look like it is moving.

- Turn to page 12.

  Owen is playing musical instruments called cymbals. Why are there lots of lines around the cymbals? What do they show?

  The lines show that the cymbals are making a loud noise.

- Show the prepared chart paper.

  Here's a bell. I want to show that it is ringing. Where should I draw the lines?

- Add sound lines to the drawing using children's suggestions.

Have a Try

Invite children to talk to a partner about how to add motion lines to a drawing.

▶ Point to the drawing of a horse galloping.

Here's a picture of a horse running, or galloping. How can I show that the horse is moving? Turn and talk to your partner about this.

▶ After children turn and talk, invite a few children to share their ideas. Add motion lines to the drawing, following children's suggestions.

Summarize and Apply

Summarize the learning and remind children to think about adding sound or motion lines to their drawings.

How can you show that things are moving or making noise?

▶ Write the principle at the top of the chart.

When you work on your book today, look for a place to try using motion or sound lines to show something is moving or making noise. Bring your book to share when we meet later.

Draw motion or sound lines to show something moving or making noise.

Confer

▶ During independent writing, move around the room to confer briefly with as many individual children as time allows. Sit side by side with them and invite them to talk about adding motion or sound lines to their drawings. Use prompts such as the following as needed.

- *What can you add to your drawing to show that he is moving?*
- *How can you show that it's making a loud noise?*
- *Where should you put the motion/sound lines?*

Share

Following independent writing, gather children in the meeting area to share their drawings.

Who drew motion or sound lines today?

How do your motion/sound lines help readers understand the story?

Section 5: Drawing

Assessment

After you have taught the minilessons in this umbrella, observe children as they draw, write, and talk about their drawing and writing. Use the behaviors and understandings in *The Literacy Continuum* (Fountas and Pinnell 2017) to notice, teach for, and support children's learning as you observe their attempts at drawing and writing.

▶ What evidence do you have of new understandings children have developed related to drawing?

- Do children use shapes to draw people?
- Do they attempt to draw people in different positions?
- How well do the backgrounds show where the action is taking place?
- Do children choose colors with intention?
- Are the characters recognizable throughout children's books?
- Have they attempted to use sound and/or motion lines?
- Do they understand and use vocabulary related to drawing, such as *draw*, *shape*, *color*, *face*, and *background*?

▶ In what ways, beyond the scope of this umbrella, are children drawing?

- Do they know how to find and use drawing and writing tools?
- Are they attempting to make their drawings interesting?

Use your observations to determine the next umbrella you will teach. You may also consult Suggested Sequence of Lessons (pp. 483–494) for guidance.

EXTENSIONS FOR LEARNING TO DRAW

▶ Invite children to revisit books that they have made to apply what they learned about drawing backgrounds and using color.

▶ During interactive read-aloud, engage children in noticing how the illustrator used color in the illustrations. Talk about why the illustrator might have chosen to use certain colors (e.g., to make the illustration realistic or to convey a certain mood).

▶ Teach children how to mix paint colors (e.g., mixing yellow and blue to make green).

▶ Return to these lssons when you engage children in an illustrator study by looking closely at several books by the same illustrator. If you have *The Reading Minilessons Book, Kindergarten* (Fountas and Pinnell 2019), teach the minilessons in LA.U3: Studying Authors and illustrators, which focus on the work of Lois Ehlert and Eric Carle.

Minilessons in This Umbrella

WML1 Use collage to make your pictures interesting.

WML2 Make your book fun to read.

WML3 Use found objects to create art for books.

Before Teaching Umbrella 3 Minilessons

The lessons in this umbrella should be taught when they are relevant to the needs of the class rather than sequentially. Provide plenty of time for children to experiment with each technique before introducing another; the extra time will also help manage the volume of art supplies needed. In addition to the supplies suggested for each lesson, consider having the following available in your art or writing center: googly eyes, felt, fabric scraps, yarn, ribbon, textured paper (e.g., sandpaper), greeting cards, tissue paper, magazines, grocery circulars, and cardboard scraps.

Read and discuss picture books that illustrate a variety of art techniques (e.g., lift-the-flap, cut-outs, pop-ups, collage, mixed media). Use the following books from *Fountas & Pinnell Classroom™ Interactive Read-Aloud Collection* text sets, or choose books from your classroom library that have interesting features. We also suggest that you teach IW.21: Writing a Question-and-Answer Book before teaching WML2 so that the class writing can be turned into a lift-the-flap book.

Interactive Read-Aloud Collection
Eric Carle: Exploring the Natural World

Have You Seen My Cat?

Sharing Stories and Songs: Nursery Rhymes

This Is the House That Jack Built by Pam Adams

Lois Ehlert: Bringing Color and Texture to Life

Snowballs

Shared Reading Collection

Look Out! by Sue Bright-Moore

Alligator Hide-and-Seek by Reese Brooks

Interactive Writing Lessons

IW.21: Writing a Question-and-Answer Book

As you read and enjoy these texts together, help children

- discuss what makes the books fun to look at, and

- talk about how these techniques make the pictures interesting.

Interactive Read-Aloud
Eric Carle

Nursery Rhymes

Lois Ehlert

Shared Reading

Interactive Writing

Section 5: Drawing

Writing Minilesson Principle
Use collage to make your pictures interesting.

Making Pictures Interesting

You Will Need

- a familiar book with examples of collage, such as *Have You Seen My Cat?* by Eric Carle, from Text Set: Eric Carle: Exploring the Natural World

- green paper torn into pieces to make leaves

- brown paper cut to be a tree trunk

- yellow paper cut into the shape of a sun and rays of a sun

- glue stick

- chart paper and markers

Academic Language/ Important Vocabulary

- collage

- illustration

- illustrator

- color

- shape

Continuum Connection

- Try out techniques other writers and illustrators used (p. 249)

- Create drawings that are related to the written text and increase readers' understanding and enjoyment (p. 249)

- Create illustrations and writing as an integral part of the composing process (p. 249)

GOAL

Understand that writers and illustrators can use collage to make pictures interesting.

RATIONALE

When you help children notice ways that illustrators make their illustrations interesting, they can experiment with the same techniques in their own work.

ASSESS LEARNING

- Observe children's willingness to try different art techniques for their drawings.

- Notice whether children understand how to use collage.

- Look for evidence that children can use vocabulary such as *collage*, *illustration*, *illustrator*, *color*, and *shape*.

MINILESSON

Use a mentor text to engage children in an inquiry around collage as a way to make pictures interesting. Then demonstrate how to make a collage. Here is an example.

- Show the cover of *Have You Seen My Cat?* and read the title. Show a few of the illustrations.

  What do you notice about the illustrations in this book?

  The illustrator, Eric Carle, made the illustrations using collage. You do collage by tearing or cutting pieces of paper and gluing them on a sheet of paper to make a picture.

- Demonstrate how to use the prepared green and brown paper to use collage to make a picture of a tree.

  I want to make a picture of a tree using collage. First, I cut a tree trunk from brown paper. Now I will glue it on the paper in the place where I want the tree to be.

  What color are leaves in the summer?

  Leaves are green! I have torn some paper to make leaves. Who can show me where I should glue them in my picture?

- Attach the tree leaves.

  How would my tree look different if I drew it on the paper instead of using collage?

Have a Try

Invite children to talk about how to use collage to make a sun.

> I think our tree needs some sunlight, don't you? Turn and talk to your partner about how to use collage to make a sun. What color and shapes of paper do we need?

 Attach the prepared yellow paper to the chart.

Summarize and Apply

Write the principle at the top of the chart. Read it to children. Help children summarize what they have learned. Then remind them to think about using collage to make their pictures interesting.

> What did we talk about today?
>
> Why might an illustrator choose to use collage to make pictures?
>
> You can use collage in your own pictures, too! Today during writing time, try using collage.

 During independent writing, provide children with materials for collage making, such as paper of different colors, old magazines or catalogs, glue sticks, and scissors.

Use collage to make your pictures interesting.

Confer

 During independent writing, move around the room to confer briefly with as many individual children as time allows. Sit side by side with them and invite them to talk about making their pictures interesting. Use prompts such as the following if needed.

- *What is going to be in your picture?*
- *How could you make that using collage?*
- *What color paper do you need?*
- *What shapes do you need?*

Share

Following independent writing, gather children in the meeting area to share how they made their pictures interesting.

> Who would like to share a picture you made today using collage?
>
> Who did something else to make your pictures interesting?

Section 5: Drawing

Writing Minilesson Principle
Make your book fun to read.

Making Pictures Interesting

You Will Need

- books with features such as lift-the-flap, cut-out, pop-up, etc., such as the following:
  - *This Is the House That Jack Built* by Pam Adams, from Text Set: Sharing Stories and Songs: Nursery Rhymes
  - *Look Out!* by Sue Bright-Moore and *Alligator Hide-and-Seek* by Reese Brooks, from *Shared Reading Collection*
- class writing from IW.21: Writing a Question-and-Answer Book
- chart paper prepared to show lift-the-flap, cut-out, and pop-up
- glue stick and markers

Academic Language/ Important Vocabulary

- lift-the-flap
- cut-out
- pop-up

Continuum Connection

- Try out techniques other writers and illustrators used (p. 249)
- Understand that writers try to make their writing and drawings interesting and informative (p. 249)
- Create drawings that are related to the written text and increase readers' understanding and enjoyment (p. 249)

GOAL

Understand that writers and illustrators use lift-the-flap, cut-out, and pop-up features to make books fun to read.

RATIONALE

When you help children notice techniques writers and illustrators use to make their books fun to read, they can experiment with the same techniques in their own work.

ASSESS LEARNING

- Observe children's willingness to try different ways to make books fun to read.
- Look for evidence that children can use vocabulary such as *lift-the-flap*, *cut-out*, and *pop-up*.

MINILESSON

Use mentor texts to show children options for making books fun to read, such as lift-the-flap, cut-out, and pop-up features. Here is an example.

- Show the class writing from IW.21: Writing a Question-and-Answer Book.

  We can make some changes to this book to make it more fun to read. We could make flaps to hide the answers to the questions. Then the readers can lift up the flaps in the book to see the answers hiding underneath.

- Help the children understand how flaps are constructed by attaching a flap to the question-and-answer writing from IW.21 to hide the answer.

  Glue the flap onto the page like this. Lift it up to see what's underneath.

- Look at *The House That Jack Built* with children to help them notice the use of cut-outs, *Look Out!* or *Alligator Hide-and-Seek* to notice the fold-out pages, or any other books from your classroom library that have special features. Talk about how the feature makes the book fun to read.

Have a Try

Invite children to talk with a partner about pop-ups.

▶ Display a pop-up illustration in a book or on the prepared chart.

> **Turn and talk to your partner about what you notice about this illustration. What do you think it's called?**

Summarize and Apply

Write the principle at the top of the chart. Read it to children. Help children summarize what they have learned. Remind them to think about including special features in their own books.

> **What are some ways that authors and illustrators make their books fun to read?**
>
> **You can do the same things in your own books. Today during writing time, try doing one of the things we talked about—lift-the-flap, cut-outs, or pop-ups—in your own book. I will help you if you need help.**

Confer

▶ During independent writing, move around the room to confer briefly with as many individual children as time allows. Sit side by side with them and invite them to talk about making their books fun to read. Use prompts such as the following if needed.

- *Would you like to try adding flaps, cut-outs, or pop-ups to your book?*
- *What will you cover with the flaps?*
- *What do you want to pop up?*
- *What materials do you need to make that?*

Share

Following independent writing, gather children in the meeting area to share what they did to make their books fun to read.

> **Who would like to share something you did today to make your book fun to read?**

WML3
DRW.U3.WML3

Writing Minilesson Principle
Use found objects to create art for books.

You Will Need

- a familiar book with illustrations made with found objects, such as *Snowballs* by Lois Ehlert, from Text Set: Lois Ehlert: Bringing Color and Texture to Life
- chart paper prepared with an outline of a bird
- a collection of found objects such as feathers, twigs, buttons, leaves, and string
- glue stick

Academic Language/ Important Vocabulary

- found object
- art
- book
- illustrator

Continuum Connection

- Try out techniques other writers and illustrators used (p. 249)
- Understand that writers try to make their writing and drawings interesting and informative (p. 249)
- Create drawings that are related to the written text and increase readers' understanding and enjoyment (p. 249)

GOAL

Understand that writers and illustrators use different art materials and objects they have found to make pictures interesting.

RATIONALE

When you help children notice how illustrators use found objects in their art, they can experiment with the same technique in their own artwork.

ASSESS LEARNING

- Observe children's willingness to try different ways to make books fun to read.
- Look for evidence that children can use vocabulary such as *found object*, *art*, *book*, and *illustrator*.

MINILESSON

Use a mentor text to show children ideas for using found objects in drawings. Then demonstrate using found objects to create artwork. Here is an example.

- Show several pages from *Snowballs*. Stop on pages 14–15.

   What do you notice about the illustrations in this book?

   Lois Ehlert used collage and found objects to make the illustrations. Found objects are any objects that you can find, either indoors or outdoors. She put together pieces of paper and found objects to make a picture. Then she took a photo of the picture. What found objects did she use for this picture?

   What did she use for the snowman's mouth? For his eyes? For his nose?

- Point out the found objects available in the art center.
- Demonstrate how to make a picture using found objects. Display the outline of a bird that you prepared before class.

   I made this drawing of a bird and now I want to decorate it with found objects I have found. First, I'm going to glue feathers to the bird. Then, I'm going to use these twigs to make the bird's legs.

Have a Try

Invite children to talk to a partner about how to make the bird's eyes.

▶ Show a few different found objects, such as buttons, leaves, and string.

> Now, I want to give my bird an eye. What object should I use for the eye? Turn and talk to your partner about this.

▶ After children turn and talk, ask a few children to share their ideas. Demonstrate gluing a button (or another round object) to the bird picture to make an eye.

Summarize and Apply

Write the principle at the top of the chart. Read it to children. Help children summarize what they learned and remind them to think about using found objects to create art for their books.

> Today during writing time, try creating an illustration for your book using found objects.

Use found objects to create art for books.

Confer

▶ During independent writing, move around the room to confer briefly with as many individual children as time allows. Sit side by side with them and invite them to talk about making their pictures interesting. Use prompts such as the following if needed.

- *What is going to be in your picture?*
- *How could you use found objects to make that?*
- *Let's look at the objects we have. Do you see anything that you want to use?*
- *What could you use to make the person's arms? Look for something that is long and thin like an arm is.*

Share

Following independent writing, gather children in the meeting area to share how they used found objects in their drawings.

> Who would like to share a picture you made using found objects?

> What objects did you use to make that?

Section 5: Drawing

Assessment

After you have taught the minilessons in this umbrella, observe children as they draw, write, and talk about their drawing and writing. Use *The Literacy Continuum* (Fountas and Pinnell 2017) to notice, teach for, and support children's learning as you observe their attempts at writing and illustrating.

▶ What is the evidence of new understandings children have developed related to making pictures interesting?

- Are children using different techniques (e.g., lift-the-flap, cut-out, pop-up) to make their books interesting?
- Do they use found objects and collage to create art for their books?
- Do they understand and use vocabulary such as *illustration*, *illustrator*, *shape*, and *color*?

▶ In what other ways, beyond the scope of this umbrella, are children ready to expand their bookmaking techniques?

- Are they attempting to write stories?
- Are they beginning to write how-to and other nonfiction books?
- Are they making book covers and including text features?

Use your observations to determine the next umbrella you will teach. You may also consult Suggested Sequence of Lessons (pp. 483–494) for guidance.

EXTENSIONS FOR MAKING PICTURES INTERESTING

▶ Invite children to use the techniques they have learned to make a front or back cover for a book.

▶ Teach children how to use torn paper and collage to create a border around a page or illustration or on a cover.

▶ Invite children to create a watercolor painting and then tear or cut the painting into pieces or shapes to use in a collage.

▶ Invite children to experiment with other materials, such as transparent or vellum paper, aluminum foil, and found items like leaves, shells, discarded maps, pages from books, or recycled objects.

Minilessons in This Umbrella

WML1 Use photographs in your nonfiction book.

WML2 Look at pictures in books and draw some of the same details.

WML3 Trace pictures for your nonfiction book.

Before Teaching Umbrella 4 Minilessons

Read aloud a variety of engaging nonfiction books about different topics and give children plenty of opportunities to experiment with creating their own nonfiction books. Choose nonfiction books that include photographs and different styles of illustration. Use the following books from one of the *Fountas & Pinnell Classroom*™ *Interactive Read-Aloud Collection* text sets, or choose nonfiction books from the classroom library.

Exploring Nonfiction

I Love Our Earth by Bill Martin Jr. and Michael Sampson

How to Hide a Butterfly & Other Insects by Ruth Heller

As you read and enjoy these texts together, help children

- notice whether each book has photographs or illustrations,

- look closely at the pictures and share details that they notice, and

- discuss how the pictures help them better understand the book's topic.

Exploring Nonfiction

Writing Minilesson Principle
Use photographs in your nonfiction book.

You Will Need

- a familiar nonfiction book with photographs, such as *I Love Our Earth* by Bill Martin Jr. and Michael Sampson, from Text Set: Exploring Nonfiction

- a page from a nonfiction book that contains a photograph, or chart paper prepared with a photograph and text; cover the photograph

- a collection of other photographs (e.g., taken yourself, printed from the internet, or cut out from magazines)

- glue stick

- marker

Academic Language/ Important Vocabulary

- nonfiction
- photograph
- author

Continuum Connection

- Understand that pictures can accompany the writing to help readers understand the information (p. 244)

- Understand that a writer of a factual text uses words and illustrations to make it interesting to readers (p. 245)

- Understand that writers of nonfiction (factual) texts have many ways to show facts: e.g., labels, drawings, photos (p. 245)

GOAL

Understand that photographs make books interesting and help readers understand more about a topic.

RATIONALE

When children understand why and how authors use photographs in nonfiction books, they learn to study them for details and begin to use them in their own books.

ASSESS LEARNING

- Observe whether children can distinguish between a drawing and a photograph.

- Look for evidence that children understand that drawings and photographs in a nonfiction book are related to the text.

- Look for evidence that children can use vocabulary such as *nonfiction*, *photograph*, and *author*.

MINILESSON

Use a mentor text to engage children in an inquiry around photographs in nonfiction books. If you don't have a suitable nonfiction book to share, find a photograph about something that interests the children in your class and write a simple sentence to go with it. Here is an example.

- Show the cover of *I Love Our Earth* and read the title. Show several pages.

  What do you notice about the pictures in this nonfiction book? How were they made?

  This book has photographs. Some nonfiction books have drawings and some have photographs. What's the difference between a drawing and a photograph?

  Why do you think the authors decided to use photographs in their book?

  Authors use photographs, especially in nonfiction books, to help you understand what the book is about.

Have a Try

Invite children to talk to a partner about how the text and photograph in a nonfiction book are related.

▶ Show the covered photograph from a nonfiction book (or the one that you have prepared). Read the text aloud.

What do you think the hidden photograph shows? Turn and tell your partner.

▶ After children turn and talk, invite a few children to share their predictions. Reveal the photograph and talk about how it helps explain the text.

Summarize and Apply

Help children summarize what they learned about photographs. Remind them to think about using photographs in their nonfiction books.

What did you learn today about using photographs in nonfiction books?

▶ Write the principle on the chart and read it aloud.

Today during writing time, start working on a nonfiction book or continue one you have already started. Look to see if there are some pages that could use a photograph. We can look online and print out photographs.

Use photographs in your nonfiction book.

An apple is a fruit.

Confer

▶ During independent writing, move around the room to confer briefly with as many individual children as time allows. Sit side by side with them and invite them to talk about illustrating their nonfiction books. Use prompts such as the following if needed.

- *Let's talk about this page of your book.*
- *Why did you choose that photograph?*
- *What will that photograph help people learn about _____?*

Share

Following independent writing, gather children in the meeting area to share their nonfiction books. As needed, support children's oral language by providing a sentence frame, such as *I chose this photograph because _____.*

Who used a photograph in your nonfiction book? Tell about that.

Writing Minilesson Principle
Look at pictures in books and draw some of the same details.

Illustrating Nonfiction

You Will Need

- a familiar nonfiction book with detailed illustrations, such as *How to Hide a Butterfly & Other Insects* by Ruth Heller, from Text Set: Exploring Nonfiction
- chart paper and markers

Academic Language/ Important Vocabulary

- nonfiction
- drawing
- detail

Continuum Connection

- Understand that a writer of a factual text uses words and illustrations to make it interesting to readers (p. 245)
- Create drawings that employ careful attention to color or detail (p. 249)
- Create drawings that are related to the written text and increase readers' understanding and enjoyment (p. 249)

GOAL

Look at pictures to learn details to add to your own drawings.

RATIONALE

When children look closely at other illustrators' drawings and copy some of the details they see, they develop their observational skills and create richer, more informational illustrations for their nonfiction books.

ASSESS LEARNING

- Notice how children choose the details to put in their drawings.
- Look for evidence that children can use vocabulary such as *nonfiction*, *drawing*, and *detail*.

MINILESSON

Demonstrate looking closely at a picture in a nonfiction book and drawing some of the same details in your own drawing. Here is an example.

- Show the cover of *How to Hide a Butterfly & Other Insects* and read the title.

  I just read this great nonfiction book about butterflies and now I want to write my own book about butterflies. First, I will draw a picture of a butterfly. I want to make sure my butterfly looks real, so I'm going to look closely at the picture on the cover of the book and draw what I see.

- On chart paper, draw a picture of a butterfly similar to the one on the cover of *How to Hide a Butterfly & Other Insects*. Think aloud as you try to make each part of the butterfly look like the butterfly on the cover.

  I see that the butterfly has a long, skinny body, so I'm going to give my butterfly a body just like that. Now I'm going to add small, round eyes like the butterfly on the cover has.

- Stop before adding certain details (like the antennas).

Have a Try

Invite children to talk to a partner about what else to add to the drawing.

> What else should I add to my drawing of a butterfly? Look closely at the butterfly on the book cover. Do you see any details that are missing from my drawing? Turn and talk to your partner about this.

▶ After children turn and talk, invite a few children to share. Complete the drawing using the children's suggestions.

Summarize and Apply

Help children summarize what they learned today. Remind children that they can look at pictures in books to get ideas for their own drawings.

> What did you learn about drawing pictures for nonfiction books?

▶ Write the principle at the top of the chart.

> Today during writing time, start making a nonfiction book or continue working on one you have already started. You can look at pictures in books and draw some of the same details in your own drawings. Bring your book to share when we meet.

Look at pictures in books and draw some of the same details.

Confer

▶ During independent writing, move around the room to confer briefly with as many individual children as time allows. Sit side by side with them and invite them to talk about illustrating their nonfiction books. Use prompts such as the following if needed.

- *Talk about your book.*
- *What do you want to draw on this page?*
- *What details do you notice in that picture? Can you draw some of the same details in your own drawing?*

Share

Following independent writing, gather children in the meeting area to share their books.

> Who would like to share a drawing from your nonfiction book?

> How did you know what details to draw in your picture?

Writing Minilesson Principle
Trace pictures for your nonfiction book.

Illustrating Nonfiction

You Will Need

▸ a familiar nonfiction book with detailed illustrations, such as *How to Hide a Butterfly & Other Insects* by Ruth Heller, from Text Set: Exploring Nonfiction

▸ tracing paper

▸ clothespins, paper clips, or tape

▸ colored pencils

▸ chart paper and markers

▸ To download the following online resource for this lesson, visit **resources.fountasandpinnell.com**:

  ■ chart art [optional]

Academic Language/ Important Vocabulary

▸ nonfiction

▸ trace

▸ tracing paper

▸ picture

Continuum Connection

▸ Understand that pictures can accompany the writing to help readers understand the information (p. 244)

▸ Create drawings that employ careful attention to color or detail (p. 249)

▸ Create drawings that are related to the written text and increase readers' understanding and enjoyment (p. 249)

GOAL

Understand that tracing pictures can help you illustrate your book and show detailed information.

RATIONALE

When children understand that they can trace pictures in books, they are able to produce more detailed and accurate drawings than they could freehand. This gives them the confidence to continue developing their drawing skills. Tracing also helps children strengthen their fine motor skills.

ASSESS LEARNING

▸ Observe children's ability to trace a picture.

▸ Look for evidence that children can use vocabulary such as *nonfiction*, *trace*, *tracing paper*, and *picture*.

MINILESSON

Demonstrate tracing an illustration in a nonfiction book and engage children in a discussion about tracing. Here is an example.

▸ Show the cover of *How to Hide a Butterfly & Other Insects* and read the title. Turn to page 14 and show the illustration.

> I want to draw a picture of a praying mantis for a nonfiction book I'm working on. I want my praying mantis to look real, but I'm not sure that I can draw a praying mantis without help. I'm going to show you a way to draw a picture of something that seems very hard to draw. Watch what I do.

▸ Demonstrate attaching a piece of tracing paper with clothespins or paper clips or very lightly applied tape to the book (or to the downloadable art attached to chart paper). Then demonstrate tracing the main lines of the praying mantis.

> What did you notice about how I drew the praying mantis?

> I used tracing paper to trace the praying mantis in the book. Did I trace every detail of the praying mantis?

> When you trace, you don't have to trace every detail. Just trace the main parts of the picture. You can add more details later.

Have a Try

Invite children to talk about tracing a drawing.

> What materials did I use to trace the picture? Turn and tell your partner.

▶ Ask several children to share what they noticed. Record their responses on the chart.

> How can I finish my drawing?

▶ Encourage children to notice that you can fill it in with color.

Summarize and Apply

Help children summarize what they learned today. Remind them that they can trace pictures for their nonfiction books.

> How can you draw a picture that has a lot of details?

▶ Write the principle at the top of the chart and read it aloud.

> Today during writing time, try tracing a picture for your nonfiction book. You can look for a picture to use in any of the nonfiction books in our classroom library.

Trace pictures for your nonfiction book.

- Tracing paper
- Clips
- Pencil

Confer

▶ During independent writing, move around the room to confer briefly with as many individual children as time allows. Sit side by side with them and invite them to talk about illustrating their nonfiction books. Use prompts such as the following if needed.

- *What is this page about?*
- *What kind of drawing would help the reader?*
- *Show how you can attach the tracing paper to the book.*
- *What should you do now that you have finished tracing?*

Share

Following independent writing, gather children in the meeting area to share their books.

> Who would like to share the nonfiction book you are working on?

> Did anyone trace a picture?

Section 5: Drawing

Assessment

After you have taught the minilessons in this umbrella, observe children as they write, draw, and talk about their writing and drawing. Use *The Literacy Continuum* (Fountas and Pinnell 2017) to notice, teach for, and support children's learning as you observe their attempts at writing and illustrating.

▶ What evidence do you have of new understandings children have developed related to illustrating nonfiction?

  • Do children include photographs in their nonfiction books?

  • Do they use pictures in nonfiction books to get ideas for their own drawings?

  • Do they trace pictures for their nonfiction books?

  • Do they understand and use vocabulary such as *nonfiction*, *photograph*, *detail*, and *trace*?

▶ In what other ways, beyond the scope of this umbrella, are children working on nonfiction books?

  • Are they attempting to write different kinds of nonfiction books?

  • Are they trying to add text and organizational features to their nonfiction books?

Use your observations to determine the next umbrella you will teach. You may also consult Suggested Sequence of Lessons (pp. 483–494) for guidance.

EXTENSIONS FOR ILLUSTRATING NONFICTION

▶ Assist children with finding photographs for their nonfiction books. They might look online, take their own photographs, or bring photographs from home.

▶ Help children write captions for the photographs in their nonfiction books.

▶ Discuss other types of graphics in nonfiction books (e.g., maps, diagrams, charts). Invite children to include these types of images in their own books.

Section 6 | Exploring Early Writing

CHILDREN ARE EAGER to experiment with writing. The minilessons in this section will help you build on that curiosity and enthusiasm. By learning about these early writing concepts, children will develop ways of expressing themselves through writing.

6 Exploring Early Writing

Minilessons in This Umbrella

WML1   Notice the pictures and words on a page.

WML2   Trace your name.

WML3   Find the first and last letter in a word.

WML4   Write the words you say.

WML5   Leave a space before you write the next word.

WML6   Start your writing on the left.

Before Teaching Umbrella 1 Minilessons

Enjoy shared reading with the children using enlarged texts, such as poetry charts and big books, so that the print is easy to see. As you read, use a long, thin pointer to help children follow along and note the directionality of print from left to right and top to bottom.

Before teaching this umbrella, teach IW.1: Making a Name Chart to familiarize children with their own names and each other's names and IW.5: Making an ABC Book to reinforce the concept of a letter and a word. It is not necessary to teach these lessons consecutively. Teach them when you observe that the children are ready to learn the concepts. Some of the minilessons in this umbrella are best applied during word study or in the writing center during independent literacy work or choice time (p. 77).

Use the following texts from *Fountas & Pinnell Classroom™ Interactive Read-Aloud Collection* and *Shared Reading Collection*, plus interactive writing lessons, or choose books from the classroom that can be used to demonstrate the umbrella's concepts.

Interactive Read-Aloud Collection
Taking Care of Each Other: Family

Do Like Kyla by Angela Johnson

Shared Reading Collection

The Sleepover by Judith E. Nayer

School Days by Carlos Perez

Interactive Writing Lessons

IW.5: Making an ABC Book

As you read and enjoy these texts together, help children

- take turns using a thin pointer to point under the words as you read,

- find the first and last letter in a word, and

- notice the space between words and that writing starts on the left.

Interactive Read-Aloud
Family

Shared Reading

Interactive Writing

Section 6: Exploring Early Writing

WML1

EWR.U1.WML1

Writing Minilesson Principle
Notice the pictures and words on a page.

Learning Early Concepts of Print

You Will Need

▸ a familiar text with clearly connected print and illustrations, such as *Do Like Kyla* by Angela Johnson, from Text Set: Taking Care of Each Other: Family

▸ chart paper prepared with a page from IW.5: Making an ABC Book

▸ markers

▸ two cut-out arrows, one labeled *Picture* and one labeled *Words*

▸ tape or glue stick

Academic Language / Important Vocabulary

▸ words

▸ pictures

▸ illustrations

▸ match

Continuum Connection

▸ Understand that layout of print and illustrations is important in conveying the meaning of a text (p. 247)

▸ Understand that print and pictures can be placed in a variety of places on the page within a book (p. 247)

▸ Distinguish and talk about the differences between pictures and print (p. 365)

GOAL

Distinguish between pictures and print and understand that they are related.

RATIONALE

When you teach children to notice the placement of words and illustrations on a page it helps them understand that print contains a message and that the message is connected to the illustrations.

ASSESS LEARNING

▸ Observe children as they look at the pages of a book. Can they distinguish between illustrations and print?

▸ Notice whether they discuss the relationship between the pictures and words on a page.

▸ Observe for evidence that children can use vocabulary such as *words*, *pictures*, *illustrations*, and *match*.

MINILESSON

Share a familiar book with the children, such as *Do Like Kyla* by Angela Johnson, to help them to understand the connection between print and pictures. Here is an example lesson.

▸ Display *Do Like Kyla* and turn to page 5. Point to the picture.

> This is a picture.

> What do you notice about the picture on this page?

> Kyla and her sister are sitting in front of the mirror braiding their hair.

▸ Point under the words.

> These are the words.

> I will read the words while you listen. What do you notice about the picture and the words?

▸ Point under the words as you read the page. Allow time for discussion.

> The words tell what is happening on the page. The words match what is happening in the picture.

> What do you notice about the words? Where are they on the page?

> On this page, the words are on the bottom and the picture is on the top.

▸ Repeat this process for pages 7–8.

> Who would like to come up and point to the picture and the words?

Have a Try

Invite children to work with a partner to distinguish between the words and the picture from a piece of interactive writing the class created, such as the ABC book written in IW.5.

> Look at the chart. Where are the words and where is the picture on this page of our ABC book? Turn and talk to your partner about that.

▶ Ask a volunteer to place the two arrows on the chart.

Summarize and Apply

Write the principle at the top of the chart paper. Read it to the children. Then invite them to draw and write during independent writing time.

> When you read, it's important to read the words and look at the pictures.

> During writing time, you can make your own book about something you know a lot about or something that happened to you. Remember to make the words match the pictures.

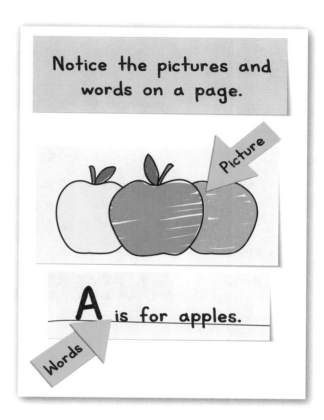

Notice the pictures and words on a page.

Picture

A is for apples.

Words

Confer

▶ During independent writing, move around the room to confer briefly with as many individual children as time allows. Sit side by side with them and invite them to talk about what they will include in the illustrations and what the words will be. Use prompts like the ones below as needed.

- *What do you want to tell about that?*
- *You can draw the pictures to show what happened.*
- *What else can you add to your picture?*
- *Think about how you want to draw that.*
- *Think about the words you want to write to tell what is happening in the picture.*

Share

Following independent writing, gather children in the meeting area to share their writing.

> Who would like to share what you wrote and drew today during writing time?

Learning Early Concepts of Print

You Will Need

- chart paper with your name written on it; a dot on each letter shows where to start the letter
- markers
- a name card for each child with the name written in black marker; a dot on each letter shows where to begin tracing
- To download the following online resource for this lesson, visit **resources.fountasandpinnell.com**:
  - Verbal Path for Letter Formation

Academic Language / Important Vocabulary

- trace
- name
- letters

Continuum Connection

- Write one's own name with a capital letter at the beginning (p. 247)
- Notice capital letters in names (p. 247)
- Write one's first name with all letters in accurate sequence (p. 365)
- Use letters from one's name to represent it or to write a message (p. 365)
- Use efficient and consistent motions to form letters in manuscript print with writing tools (p. 365)

GOAL

Trace the letters in one's name.

RATIONALE

Working with letters kinesthetically supports children's print awareness/ability to look at print. When children learn to trace the letters with a finger, it helps them remember and internalize the distinctive features of each letter and reinforces that a name is a word.

ASSESS LEARNING

- Notice whether children use the verbal path while tracing the letters in their names.
- Observe whether children form the letters in their names accurately and efficiently.
- Look for evidence that children can use vocabulary such as *trace*, *name*, and *letters*.

MINILESSON

Children can apply this lesson in the writing center during independent literacy work or choice time. Demonstrate for children how to trace letters using the Verbal Path for Letter Formation. Here is an example lesson.

- Display the chart paper with your name on it.

  Whose name is this?

  This is my name! My name, Mrs. Miller, has two parts: *Mrs.* and *Miller*. I am going to show you how to trace the letters in my name so that you will know how to trace the letters in your name. When you trace the letters in your name, you learn to write your name.

- Demonstrate how to trace the letters in your name, using your finger and verbal-path language.

  What do you notice I do as I trace each letter?

  I put my finger on the dot to begin making each letter. I say the directions to help me make the letter. To make the *M*, pull down, slant down, slant up, pull down.

- Hold up one of the children's name cards.

  Whose name is this? This is Manuel's name.

- Invite the child to come up and trace the letters in his name as you say the verbal path. (You might need to guide the child's hand.) The other children can practice the letters in the air. Repeat this process using several other name cards.

The Writing Minilessons Book, Kindergarten

Have a Try

Invite children to practice tracing the letters in their names with a partner. Remind them to begin each letter at the dot and to use verbal-path language.

▶ Give children their name cards.

> You can trace the letters in your name while your partner writes your name in the air.

▶ Invite a few pairs to demonstrate for the class.

Summarize and Apply

Talk about the principle and invite the children to practice tracing their names.

> When you trace the letters in your name, you start at the dot and move a finger over the letters while you say the words that help you remember how to make each letter correctly.

> If you want to practice tracing your name, I will be in the writing center to help you find your name card and practice tracing your name.

> Trace your name.

> Mrs. Miller

Confer

▶ During independent literacy work or choice time, observe children as they practice tracing their names on their name cards. You may want to model this first, and some may need support—place your hand atop theirs as they trace the letters. Use prompts like the ones below as needed.

- *Put your finger on the dot to start tracing the letter.*
- *Listen to how I say the words that help me.*
- *You know how to start it.*
- *Hold the marker (pencil) like this.*

Share

Following independent literacy work or choice time, gather children in the meeting area to share what they did.

> Who practiced tracing your name today? Show how you traced the letters in your name.

Writing Minilesson Principle
Find the first and last letter in a word.

Learning Early Concepts of Print

You Will Need

- chart paper prepared with several simple words
- marker
- highlighter or highlighter tape
- a name card for each child
- To download the following online resource for this lesson, visit **resources.fountasandpinnell.com**:
  - chart art (optional)

Academic Language / Important Vocabulary

- letter
- word
- name
- first
- last
- beginning

Continuum Connection

- Locate the first and last letters of words in continuous text (p.365)
- Understand and talk about the concept of a letter (p. 365)
- Recognize and talk about the sequence of letters in a word (p. 365)

GOAL

Find the first and last letter in a word.

RATIONALE

When you teach children that *first* and *last* have specific meanings when applied to print, they begin to understand the importance of letter sequence in words.

ASSESS LEARNING

- Notice if children point to the first and last letter in a word.
- Observe children to see if they can locate (and identify) the first and last letters in their names.
- Look for evidence that children can use vocabulary such as *letter*, *word*, *name*, *first*, *last*, and *beginning*.

MINILESSON

You might want to use this lesson just before independent literacy work or choice time, when children might be working in the word study center. To help children think about the minilesson principle, engage them in locating the first and last letter of several words. Here is an example.

- Display the prepared chart. Point to the first word.

  This is the word *sun*.

  What is the first letter in *sun*?

  It's an *s*. The first letter is on the left. It is at the beginning of the word.

- Highlight (or have a child highlight) the first letter.

  What is the last letter in *sun*?

  It's an *n*. The last letter is on the right. It is at the end of the word.

- Highlight (or have a child highlight) the last letter.

  Watch and listen as I run my finger under the word and say it.

- Repeat this process with several other words.

The Writing Minilessons Book, Kindergarten

Have a Try

Invite children to work with a partner to find the first and last letters in their names.

▶ Give each child a name card.

> Work with your partner to find the first and last letter in each of your names. What are the letters? Show your partner.

▶ Circulate among the pairs of children to see whether they can point to the first and last letter in their names.

Summarize and Apply

Write the principle on the chart. Read it to children. Then invite them to come to the word study center to highlight the first and last letter in their names.

> I will be in the word study center to help you as you highlight the first and last letters of your name. Remember, the first letter is on the left and the last letter is on the right.

Confer

▶ During independent literacy work or choice time, observe children as they highlight the first and last letters in their names or in another word. Use the following prompts as needed.

- *Point to the first (last) letter of your name.*
- *Point to the first (last) letter of the word.*
- *What is that letter?*

Share

Following independent literacy work or choice time, gather children in the meeting area. Invite individual children to share their work.

> Who highlighted the first and last letters in your name today? Would you like to share your name card with the class?

Writing Minilesson Principle
Write the words you say.

Learning Early Concepts
of Print

You Will Need

- pocket chart
- markers
- blank word cards
- blank sentence strip
- drawing materials (paper, colored pencils, markers, etc.)

Academic Language / Important Vocabulary

- words
- sounds
- sentence

Continuum Connection

- Use spaces between words to help readers understand the writing (p. 247)
- Place word in lines, starting left to right, top to bottom (p. 247)
- Understand and demonstrate that one spoken word matches one group of letters (p. 365)
- Understand and talk about the concept of a word (p. 365)

GOAL

Understand that what you say can be put into writing.

RATIONALE

When you teach children to rehearse a sentence before they write it, they learn to isolate and identify the words they hear in the sentence. Making the connection between a spoken word, the group of letters it represents, and how to transform that into written language is key for both writing and reading and will be valuable as children compose and write sentences.

ASSESS LEARNING

- Observe children's ability to verbally rehearse what they are going to write.
- Notice if children leave spaces between the words they write.
- Observe for evidence that children can use vocabulary such as *words*, *sounds*, and *sentence*.

MINILESSON

Demonstrate for children how to rehearse a sentence before writing it. Use a pocket chart to display the sentences that are generated. Have some blank word cards available so that you can record the separate words in each sentence. Here is an example.

> We use words to make sentences.

- Generate ideas with the children.

> We can talk about what we like to do. Then we can write the words that we say.
>
> Let's talk today about some of the things that you like to do with your friends.

- Choose one idea, using the children's own language.

> You said, "We like to play on the playground." Say the sentence with me.
>
> Let's count the words in the sentence. (Raise one finger for each word.)
>
> There are seven words in the sentence. We can write those words on these cards.
>
> What is the first word in our sentence? The first word is *We*.

- Record *We* on a blank card and place it in the pocket chart. Repeat that part of the sentence and pause for the children to supply the next word. Repeat this process for the whole sentence.

> I am leaving space between the end of one word and the beginning of the next word.

- When you are finished writing the sentence, reread it slowly.
- Repeat this process for one or two more sentences.

Have a Try

Invite children to work with a partner to form a sentence, rehearse it aloud, and count the words.

> Turn and talk about something else you like to do with your friends. How many words are in your sentence?

▶ After time to discuss, invite a volunteer to come up and say the sentence aloud while you record the words and add them to the pocket chart.

Summarize and Apply

Write the principle on a sentence strip and place it in the top row of the pocket chart. Read it to children and then invite them to write more sentences on blank cards.

> We talked about how you can write the words that you say. When you are writing today, think about something else you like to do with a friend. Say the sentence aloud, count the words, and then write the words on blank cards. You can draw a picture to go with your sentence.

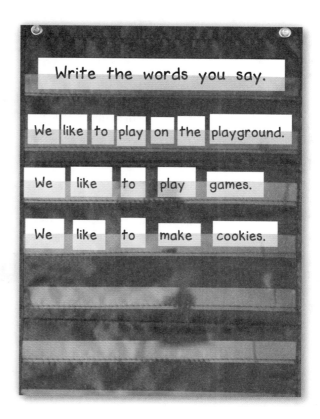

Confer

▶ During independent writing, move around the room to confer briefly with as many individual children as time allows. Sit side by side with them and invite them to talk about what they will write. Use prompts like the ones below as needed.

- *Think about what you want to tell about that.*
- *Think about the words you want to write to tell what is happening.*
- *Count the words that you want to write.*
- *You can draw the pictures to show what happened.*

Share

Following independent writing, gather children in the meeting area. Invite individual children to share their writing and drawing.

> Who would like to show us your sentence? You can put your word cards in the pocket chart.

WML5

EWR.U1.WML5

Writing Minilesson Principle
Leave a space before you write the next word.

Learning Early Concepts of Print

You Will Need

- a familiar enlarged text, such as *The Sleepover* by Judith E. Nayer, from *Shared Reading Collection*
- chart paper and markers
- To download the following online resource for this lesson, visit **resources.fountasandpinnell.com**:
  - chart art (optional)

Academic Language / Important Vocabulary

- words
- space
- sentence

Continuum Connection

- Use spaces between words to help readers understand the writing (p. 247)
- Understand word boundaries and leave space between words most of the time (p. 248)

GOAL

Understand that writers leave a space between words.

RATIONALE

When you teach children to record their ideas and compose sentences with proper spacing, they learn to understand word boundaries as well as make their writing accessible to the reader.

ASSESS LEARNING

- Observe children's writing to see whether they leave a good space between words.
- Notice if children can point under each word as they read.
- Observe for evidence that children can use vocabulary such as *words*, *space*, and *sentence*.

MINILESSON

To help children think about the minilesson principle, use an enlarged text to help them notice the spaces between words. You can use shared writing or interactive writing in this lesson. Here is an example.

- Show and read page 2 of *The Sleepover*. Point under each word as you read it.

  Let's count the words in the first sentence.

- Raise a finger for each word.

  There are four words. How do you know?

- Guide children to notice that there is always a space between two words.

  After you write a word, leave a space before you write the next word.

- Count the words in another sentence on the page.

- Help children compose a simple sentence.

  Jake packed a lot of things for his sleepover. What would you pack?

  We could write *Sam packed a blanket.* How many words is that?

  What is the first word?

- Write the word *Sam* on chart paper.

  Notice what I do before I write the word *packed*.

- Put two fingers on the paper to hold a space and then write the next word.

  What did you notice?

  I left a space before I wrote the next word so it is easier to read.

- Repeat this process to complete the sentence. Then point under each word as you reread the sentence slowly with the children.

Have a Try

Repeat the process with another item to bring to a sleepover.

▶ Invite children to turn and talk to a partner about ideas. After discussion, invite a child to come up and use two fingers to indicate the space before the next word as you write the sentence.

> Who can point to the spaces between the words in this sentence?

Summarize and Apply

Write the principle on the chart. Read it to the children. Then remind them to look for the space between words as they read and to leave space between words when they write.

> Why is it a good idea to leave a space before you write the next word?

> If you read today, look for spaces between the words. If you do some writing today, be sure to leave a space before you write the next word.

Leave a space before you write the next word.

Sam   packed   a   blanket.

Xavier   took   his   pillow.

Confer

▶ During independent writing, move around the room to confer briefly with as many individual children as time allows. Sit side by side with them and invite them to talk about leaving space between words. Use prompts like the following as needed.

- *Where will you start the next word?*
- *Put the next word here.*
- *Leave a space to help your reader.*
- *Put your finger on a place where you left a good space.*

Share

Following independent writing, gather children in the meeting area to share their writing.

> Who would like to share the writing you did today?

> Point to where you started your writing. What did you do after that word?

Writing Minilesson Principle
Start your writing on the left.

Learning Early Concepts of Print

You Will Need

- a familiar enlarged text, such as *School Days* by Carlos Perez, from *Shared Reading Collection*
- long, thin pointer (optional)
- chart paper and markers
- To download the online resource for this lesson, visit **resources.fountasandpinnell.com**:
  - chart art (optional)

Academic Language / Important Vocabulary

- write
- right
- left
- start
- begin

Continuum Connection

- Place words in lines, starting left to right, top to bottom (p. 247)
- Write left to right in lines (p. 248)

GOAL

Understand that writers start on the left side of the paper and move to the right.

RATIONALE

When you teach children the concept of directionality, it supports their understanding of how print works. This helps children begin to track print from left to right when reading and also write letters in words and sentences in proper sequence.

ASSESS LEARNING

- Observe children when they write to see if they begin at the left and move to the right.
- Notice if children can point to the words from left to right as they read.
- Observe for evidence that children can use vocabulary such as *write*, *right*, *left*, *start*, and *begin*.

MINILESSON

To help children think about the minilesson principle, use an enlarged text to help them notice that the writing starts on the left and moves to the right. Use your finger or a long, thin pointer with no distracting things on the pointing end (for example, no balls). You can use shared writing or interactive writing in this lesson, asking several children to contribute high-frequency words or letters for easy-to-hear sounds. Here is an example.

- Show and read page 2 of *School Days*. Point under each word as you read it.

  As I read, where did I start my pointer and where did I move after that?

- Guide children to notice you started on the left and moved to the right.

  I started on the left and moved to the right. When I got to the end of the line, I went back to the left to read the next line.

  When we write, we do the same thing.

- Help children compose a simple sentence about what a bus driver does. Write the sentences on chart paper in two lines.

  I will write this sentence: *A bus driver picks up children. He drives them safely to school.* Notice where I start my writing and where I move after that.

  What did you notice?

  I started on the left and moved to the right. When I ran out of room, I went back to the left and started writing the next line.

Have a Try

Repeat this process with another sentence or two about school.

▶ Invite children to turn and talk to a partner about where they should begin writing. After a brief discussion, invite a few to share.

> Who can point to where I will begin writing?
> Where do I start the next sentence?

Summarize and Apply

Write the principle on the chart. Read it to the children. Then remind them that when they are writing their own books they need to think first about where to start and then which way to move.

▶ Ask a child to use the pointer or a finger to show how the text on the chart moves from left to right.

> Remember to start writing on the left and then move to the right.

Start your writing on the left.

A bus driver picks up children.
He drives them safely to school.

This is our school.
It is made of brick.
It has lots of windows.

Confer

▶ During independent writing, move around the room to confer briefly with as many individual children as time allows. Sit side by side with them as they write, and notice if they are writing the letters in words and the words in sentences from left to right. Use prompts such as the following as needed.

- *Start here.*
- *Write here next.*
- *Put the next letter here.*
- *Put the next word here.*

Share

Following independent writing, gather children in the meeting area. Invite individual children to share anything they have written.

> Point to where you started your writing and which way you moved after that.

Assessment

After you have taught the minilessons in this umbrella, observe children as they draw, write, and talk about their writing. Use the behaviors and understandings in *The Literacy Continuum* (Fountas and Pinnell 2017) to notice, teach for, and support children's learning as you observe their attempts at drawing and writing.

▶ What evidence do you have that children are beginning to develop early concepts of print?

- Are children making connections between the pictures and words on a page?
- Can they trace the letters in their names, starting at the right point on each letter? Are they using approximated writing to begin writing their names?
- Do they understand that what they say can be put into writing?
- Can they find the first and last letter in a word and listen for the sounds?
- Do they leave a space between words?
- Do they start their writing on the left side of the paper and move to the right?
- What evidence is there that children can use vocabulary such as *word, pictures, illustrations, match, trace, name, letters, first, last, beginning, space, sentence, write, right, left,* and *start*?

Use your observations to determine the next umbrella to teach. You may also consult Suggested Sequence of Lessons (pp. 483–494) for guidance.

EXTENSIONS FOR LEARNING EARLY CONCEPTS OF PRINT

▶ Create name puzzles. Place each letter from a child's name on a small, cut-out square. Place all the squares in a sealable bag. Show children how to put the squares together to make their names.

▶ Encourage children to trace their names in sand or salt on a tray or cookie sheet.

▶ During interactive writing, show children where to start writing on the page and point out the spaces between the words. Likewise, during shared reading, highlight how the print starts on the left.

▶ Record children telling their stories. Play the recording, pausing every so often, so that children can connect their spoken words to their writing.

▶ Have children say a name slowly to listen for the first sound. Then say one word that starts with the same sound and letter as the name and one that doesn't. Ask children to identify which word starts with the same sound as the name [e.g., *Sam: sun, moon*].

▶ Have children point out the first and last letters of words during shared reading.

Minilessons in This Umbrella

WML1 Hold your marker and paper to do your best writing.

WML2 Use direction words to help you write letters.

WML3 Use the name chart to help you write the letters in your name.

Before Teaching Umbrella 2 Minilessons

The lessons in this umbrella are designed to expose children to the specific motor movements for writing the letters of the alphabet, helping them become more effective and efficient writers. Repeat WML2 as often as needed to teach children how to write letters not discussed in the lesson. Online resources such as Alphabet Linking Chart and Verbal Path for Letter Formation provide the information needed to teach how to form all the letters.

   Because you will want to be responsive in your teaching, it is not necessary to teach the lessons consecutively; instead, teach them when your observations of children indicate a readiness for a particular lesson. Although we recommend using the verbal path to help children form letters, use the prompts sparingly. Children need time to experiment with making marks on paper without any constraints at the initial writing stage. Blank unlined paper is recommended so that children have enough space to make their marks.

WML1

Writing Minilesson Principle
Hold your marker and paper to do your best writing.

Introducing Handwriting

You Will Need

- markers (one per child)
- a sheet of paper for demonstration
- document camera (if available)
- chart paper and markers
- To download the following online resource for this lesson, visit **resources.fountasandpinnell.com**:
  - chart art (optional)

Academic Language/ Important Vocabulary

- writing
- paper
- marker
- finger
- slanted

Continuum Connection

- Hold pen or pencil with satisfactory grip (p. 248)
- Use a preferred hand consistently for writing (p. 248)

GOAL

Hold writing tool and paper efficiently, consistently using a preferred hand for writing.

RATIONALE

Learning how to hold a writing tool and paper properly is the first step in learning how to form efficient, legible letters. When children are comfortable holding a marker and paper, they are better equipped to produce writing that communicates their message to the reader.

ASSESS LEARNING

- Notice children's writing and drawing behaviors.
- Notice whether children hold the writing tool and paper effectively and efficiently.
- Look for evidence that children can use vocabulary such as *writing*, *paper*, *marker*, *finger*, and *slanted*.

MINILESSON

Prior to teaching this lesson, provide children with opportunities to try out different writing tools and types of paper. For this lesson, use the writing tool of your choice, although washable markers are recommended to avoid erasures or torn paper. All of children's efforts should be visible. Encourage children to use the preferred hand when they write.

> Watch carefully to see how I pick up the marker.

- Demonstrate picking up the marker off of a table, ensuring children have a clear view of your hand, the marker, and the paper. If available, use a document camera.

> What did you notice about my hand and fingers as I picked up the marker?

> Now I am going to write. Watch how I hold the marker and paper.

- Hold a sheet of paper at an angle against an easel/whiteboard or use a document camera. Write on the paper. With your other hand, point to each finger as you talk about it.

- Use these or similar prompts as you model and discuss the way you are writing:
  - *What do you notice about how I hold the marker? I use my thumb and pointer finger. The marker is resting against my middle finger.*
  - *What do you notice about how I hold the paper? I hold the paper down with one hand and hold my marker in the other hand. I slant the paper a little bit.*

- Demonstrate holding the paper vertically, slanted to the left, and slanted to the right. Explain that it may take some practice for each child to find the most comfortable way to hold the paper as well as the hand that works best for writing.

Have a Try

Invite children to practice using the proper grip when holding a marker.

▶ Hand a marker to each child. Invite children to practice picking up the marker and holding it with the proper grip. Observe children as they practice and assist as needed.

Summarize and Apply

Write the principle on the chart and read it to the children. Summarize the learning and remind children to think about how they hold a marker and paper when they write.

> What did you learn about holding a marker and paper when you write?

▶ Guide the conversation as needed. On chart paper, briefly sketch children's ideas to help them remember how to hold hands, fingers, paper, and marker.

> Today when you write, practice holding the writing tools and paper in the way you learned. I will help you hold your paper and marker so you can do your best writing.

Hold your marker and paper to do your best writing.

Confer

▶ During independent writing, move around the room to confer briefly with as many individual children as time allows. Sit side by side with them and invite them to talk about how they are doing their best writing. Use the following prompts as needed.

- *Show me how to pick up the marker.*
- *Which fingers should you use to hold the marker?*
- *Show me how you write your name.*
- *Remember to hold the marker with your thumb, pointer finger, and middle finger.*

Share

Following independent writing, gather children in the meeting area. Ask a few children to share their experiences.

> How did you hold your marker (paper)?

WML2

EWR.U2.WML2

Writing Minilesson Principle
Use direction words to help you write letters.

Introducing Handwriting

You Will Need

- chart paper and markers
- To download the following online resources for this lesson, visit **resources.fountasandpinnell.com**:
  - Alphabet Linking Chart
  - Verbal Path for Letter Formation
  - Letters Made in Similar Ways

Academic Language/ Important Vocabulary

- writing
- direction words
- letter

Continuum Connection

- Hold pen or pencil with satisfactory grip (p. 248)
- Use a preferred hand consistently for writing (p. 248)
- Write left to right in lines (p. 248)
- Form upper- and lowercase letters efficiently/proportionately in manuscript print (p. 248)
- Recognize and point to the distinctive features of letter forms (p. 365)
- Recognize letters and state their names (p. 365)

GOAL

Follow the verbal path to form letters efficiently.

RATIONALE

When you say direction words (the verbal path) for a letter, you describe the process of forming that letter out loud as you are writing it. This helps children understand how to form the letter in an efficient way. Use the structure of this lesson whenever you teach children to write a new letter.

ASSESS LEARNING

- Observe children when they write letters.
- Notice how well children follow verbal directions for forming a letter.
- Look for evidence that children can use vocabulary such as *writing*, *direction words*, and *letter*.

MINILESSON

Prior to teaching this lesson, provide children with opportunities to try out different writing tools and paper. To help children think about the writing minilesson principle, model how to use the verbal path and help them form a short letter and a tall letter (e.g., lowercase *c* and *l*). Here is an example.

> Today, we are going to make the letter *c* and the letter *l*. The letter *c* is a short letter and the letter *l* is a tall letter.

- Point to the lowercase *c* on the ABC chart.

  > The letter *c* is at the beginning of words like *cat*, *cup*, and *cap*. Listen to the direction words that help make the letter *c*: pull back and around. Watch me make the letter *c*.

- Use a black marker to write a large letter *c* on chart paper as you say the verbal path.

- Invite several volunteers to come up and write the letter *c* over your writing, using different marker colors, making a rainbow letter. Have the other children make the letter *c* in the air using their fingers, repeating the verbal path as they practice.

- Point to the lowercase *l* on the ABC chart.

  > The letter *l* is at the beginning of words like *lion*, *leaf*, and *lamp*. To make the letter *l*, pull down. Watch me make the letter *l*.

- Repeat the process you used for writing the letter *c*.

Have a Try

Invite children to practice making the lowercase letters *c* and *l* with a partner.

> Turn and talk to your partner about the way you make the letters *c* and *l*. As you practice with your finger in the air and on the carpet, say the words that help you make the letters.

▶ As needed, assist with the verbal path language for lowercase *c* (pull back and around) and *l* (pull down).

Summarize and Apply

Write the principle on the chart and read it to the children. Summarize the learning and remind children to think about the verbal path when they write.

> We practiced making the letters *c* and *l*. Today when you are working on your books, think about how to write the short letter *c* and the tall letter *l*.

▶ Introduce making rainbow letters during choice time.

> We made rainbow letters today. Today during choice time, you can also make rainbow letters to practice writing *c* and *l*.

Use direction words to help you write letters.

Confer

▶ During choice time, move around the room to confer briefly with as many individual children as time allows. Sit side by side with them and invite them to talk about making letters. Use the following suggestions as needed to support letter formation.

- *Can you use your finger to trace the rainbow letters we made?*
- *Is this a short letter or a tall letter?*
- *What direction words can help you write the letter* c*?*

Share

Following choice time, gather children in the meeting area. Ask a few children to share their experiences.

> How did you make the letter *c* today?

> How did you make the letter *l* today?

Writing Minilesson Principle
Use the name chart to help you write the letters in your name.

Introducing Handwriting

You Will Need

- name chart (see IW.1: Making a Name Chart)
- a name card for each child (optional–in a pocket chart)
- chart paper and markers
- To download the following resource for this online lesson, visit **resources.fountasandpinnell.com**:
  - Verbal Path for Letter Formation

Academic Language/ Important Vocabulary

- name
- letter
- top
- left
- right

Continuum Connection

- Recognize and point to one's name (p. 365)
- Use letters from one's name to represent it or to write a message (p. 365)
- Write one's first name with all letters in accurate sequence (p. 365)
- Understand and talk about the concept of a letter (p. 365)
- Understand and talk about the concept of a word (p. 365)

GOAL

Use a name chart to write some of the letters in your name.

RATIONALE

Teaching children to use a name chart to write their names helps them learn to recognize letters and understand that words are made up of individual letters.

It is helpful to post the name chart that you created together in IW.1: Making a Name Chart. It is also helpful to have a pocket chart with each child's name on a separate card so children can take the name cards to a table to practice and compare the letters to the letters in other words.

ASSESS LEARNING

- Observe children as they write their names and notice how they form the letters.
- Notice whether children are using the name chart to help them write their names.
- Observe whether children can legibly write some of the letters in their names.
- Look for evidence that children can use vocabulary such as *name*, *letter*, *top*, *left*, and *right*.

MINILESSON

Prior to teaching this lesson, provide children with opportunities to try out different writing tools and paper for writing their names. To engage children in writing the letters in their names, help them use the name chart from IW.1: Making a Name Chart and the language of the verbal path. Here is an example.

> What do you notice about the name chart?

> You can use the name chart to help write the letters in your name. We can practice writing Drew's name (choose a child's name with just a few letters).

- Point to *Drew* on the name chart.

> *Drew* is a word. It is made up of four letters.

- Point to and count the letters, asking children to join in.

> The first letter in Drew's name is *D*. I will write the letter *D*. To make *D*, pull down, up, around.

- Have children make a *D* in the air while you write it on chart paper, leaving room to add the principle later.

> The next letter in *Drew* is *r*. I will write the letter *r* close to the *D* and to the right of it. To make the letter *r*, pull down, up, and over.

- Have children make an *r* in the air while you write it on chart paper next to the *D*. Continue for the remaining letter(s) in the child's name. Then read the name with children as you point under the name. You might choose to have Drew come up and trace the letters with his finger.

The Writing Minilessons Book, Kindergarten

Have a Try

Invite children to practice forming the letters in another name.

▶ Point to another name on the name chart (e.g., *Eva*).

> Now let's try writing Eva's name.

▶ Give verbal path instructions for the letters and invite children to write the name in the air and on the carpet while you write it on the chart paper. You might choose to have Eva trace her name with her finger. Repeat for one more name.

Summarize and Apply

Write the principle on the chart and read it to the children. Summarize the learning and remind children to use the name chart to help them write their names.

> Today you used the name chart to help you write the letters in names. When you are working on your writing, write your name on your paper. If you need your name card to help you, feel free to go and get it. Remember to return it when you are finished.

▶ Make sure children know how to get and return their name cards to the proper place.

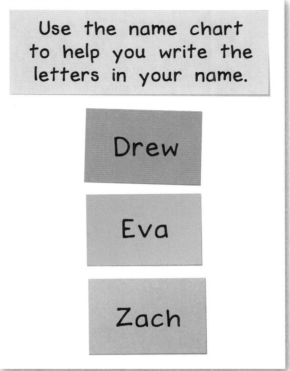

> Use the name chart to help you write the letters in your name.
>
> Drew
>
> Eva
>
> Zach

Confer

▶ During independent writing, move around the room to confer briefly with as many individual children as time allows. Sit side by side with them and invite them to talk about writing their names. Use the following prompts as needed.

- *Let's look at the name chart. What is the first letter in your name?*
- *Think about how to write the letter* E.
- *Remember to write the second letter in your name to the right of the first letter.*

Share

Following independent writing, gather children in the meeting area. Ask a few children to share their experiences writing their names.

> Who practiced writing your name today? Tell about that.
>
> Did you use the name chart to help you?

Assessment

After you have taught the minilessons in this umbrella, observe children as they begin writing letters. Use *The Literacy Continuum* (Fountas and Pinnell 2017) to notice, teach for, and support children's learning as you observe their attempts at reading and writing.

> ▶ What evidence do you have that children understand how to use drawing and writing tools?
>
> • Do children hold the marker and paper in a way that helps them write efficiently and comfortably?
>
> • Are they using direction words (the verbal path) to help them write letters?
>
> • Are they able to write some or all of the letters in their name, using the name chart for reference as needed?
>
> • Do they understand and use vocabulary such as *writing*, *paper*, *marker*, *finger*, *slanted*, *letter*, *direction words*, *name*, *top*, *left*, and *right*?
>
> ▶ In what ways, beyond the scope of this umbrella, are children showing readiness for writing?
>
> • Do children show an interest in writing for a variety of purposes?
>
> • Do they enjoy sharing their writing with others?

Use your observations to determine the next umbrella you will teach. You may also consult Suggested Sequence of Lessons (pp. 483–494) for guidance.

EXTENSIONS FOR INTRODUCING HANDWRITING

▶ Use WML2 and the verbal path to help children learn to write other letters.

▶ Revisit the online resource Letters Made in Similar Ways (see WML2) to help children practice forming other letters.

▶ Have children use the name chart to write the names of classmates or other words.

▶ Provide stencils or plastic forms to have children trace letters.

▶ Have children sort magnetic letters, both short and tall, so they think about the proper sizing of letters.

Minilessons in This Umbrella

WML1 Say words slowly and listen for the first sound.

WML2 Listen for all the sounds in a word.

WML3 Break apart words to help you write them.

WML4 Write words that you know quickly.

WML5 Use what you know about words to write new words.

Interactive Writing

Before Teaching Umbrella 3 Minilessons

This umbrella is designed to support children in learning how to write words to develop their independence in writing. Use interactive writing and shared writing to provide a scaffold for children to go from sound to symbol.

To build a strong foundation for teaching this umbrella, children should have experienced some interactive writing lessons, especially IW.6: Making Labels for the Classroom and IW.11: Writing from a Picture. Children will also benefit from familiarity with letter-sound relationships and some work with phonograms.

As you teach these lessons, refer to classroom resources, such as a word wall, ABC chart, and/or name chart, as well as items from each child's writing folder, such as a smaller ABC chart, a smaller name chart, and/or a personal word list.

Interactive Writing Lessons

IW.6: Making Labels for the Classroom

IW.11: Writing from a Picture

As you read and enjoy texts together, especially shared reading texts,

- use a pointer to help children follow along with the text as you read it,

- have children clap the syllables in a word, and

- ask children to point out words that they know.

WML1

EWR.U3.WML1

Writing Minilesson Principle
Say words slowly and listen for the first sound.

You Will Need

- a bin of categorized books from the classroom library
- name chart
- ABC chart
- word cards for labels
- chart paper and markers
- tape
- To download the following online resources for this lesson, visit **resources.fountasandpinnell.com**:
  - Verbal Path for Letter Formation
  - chart art (optional)

Academic Language / Important Vocabulary

- word
- sound
- letter
- slowly
- first

Continuum Connection

- Say words slowly to hear a sound and write a letter that represents it (p. 248)
- Write some words with consonant letters appropriate for sounds in words (beginning and ending) (p. 248)
- Recognize and use beginning consonant sounds and the letters that represent them: *b, c, d, f, g, h, j, k, l, m, n, p, qu, r, s, t, v, w, y, z* (p. 365)

GOAL

Say words slowly and listen for the first sound.

RATIONALE

When you teach children to say words slowly, they learn to isolate and identify the sounds they hear. Making the connection between a letter and the sound it represents is key for both writing and reading.

ASSESS LEARNING

- Observe children's ability to say a word slowly and listen for the first sound.
- Notice if children can identify the letter that goes with a sound.
- Observe for evidence that children can use vocabulary such as *word, sound, letter, slowly,* and *first*.

MINILESSON

To help children think about the minilesson principle, use their prior experience with making labels (IW.6). Here is an example.

> Let's label some of the book bins in our library.

- Display a bin from the classroom library with books that are sorted by category.

> What can I write on the label so that you know what all these books are about?

- Direct children to select a representative word (e.g., *farm*). Say the word aloud slowly, emphasizing the first sound.

> Let's say the word *farm* together slowly to listen for the first sound.
>
> What sound do you hear first?
>
> The first sound is /f/. What is the letter that goes with that sound?

- Point to *f* on the ABC chart or name chart. Use the Verbal Path for Letter Formation to describe how to form the first letter in the word. Write the letter on a label taped lightly to the chart.

> To make an *f*, pull back, down, and cross.

- Write the rest of the word.
- Repeat the process for a few more book bin labels. You might also want to ask children to illustrate the label on the bin after the lesson.

Have a Try

Invite children to work with a partner to listen for and identify the letter for the first sound in another word.

> What label could we put on this book bin?

> Turn and talk to your partner about the sound you hear first and the letter that stands for that sound.

▶ Add the word to a label on the chart.

▶ Leave the labels on the chart, or have children place them on the appropriate bins.

Summarize and Apply

Summarize the learning. Invite children to write more labels for book bins during independent writing.

> When you want to write a word, say it slowly and listen for the first sound. That will help you know what letter to write.

▶ Write the principle at the top of the chart.

> When you write a word, make sure to say it slowly to listen for the first sound in the word before you write it.

Say words slowly and listen for the first sound.

farm

school

bugs

Confer

▶ During independent writing, move around the room to confer briefly with as many individual children as time allows. Sit side by side with them and talk about how to write words. Use the following prompts as needed.

  • *You can say the word slowly and listen for the first sound (model).*

  • *What do you hear first? What letter goes with that sound?*

  • *You can think about the first sound and write the letter.*

Share

Following independent writing, gather children in the meeting area. Invite individual children to share their writing. Support children's oral language by providing a sentence frame: *The first letter in _____ is _____ .*

> Who would like to share your writing?

> Can you point to the first letter in a word? How did you know what letter to write?

Writing Minilesson Principle
Listen for all the sounds in a word.

Learning How to Write Words

You Will Need

- pocket chart
- name chart
- ABC chart
- picture cards of words that have easy-to-hear sounds
- word cards
- tape
- sentence strip
- To download the online resources for this lesson, visit **resources.fountasandpinnell.com**:
  - Verbal Path for Letter Formation
  - chart art (optional)

Academic Language / Important Vocabulary

- sounds
- listen
- word
- letter
- slowly

Continuum Connection

- Say words slowly to hear a sound and write a letter that represents it (p. 248)
- Write some words with consonant letters appropriate for sounds in words (beginning and ending) (p. 248)
- Attempt unknown words through sound analysis (p. 248)

GOAL

Say words slowly and listen for the first, middle, and ending sounds.

RATIONALE

When you teach children to say words slowly, they learn to isolate and identify the sounds they hear. Making the connection between a letter and the sound it represents is key for both writing and reading.

ASSESS LEARNING

- Observe children's ability to say a word slowly; listen for the first, middle, and ending sounds; and identify the letters that go with the sounds.
- Watch children as they write words to be sure they attend to the whole word.
- Observe for evidence that children can use vocabulary such as *sounds, listen, word, letter,* and *slowly*.

MINILESSON

To help children think about the minilesson principle, use picture cards of words with easily identifiable sounds throughout. Here is an example.

- Display a picture card and place it in a pocket chart (e.g., *pig*).

  Look at this picture. What is this?

- For each of the three sounds in *pig* (/p/, /i/, /g/), have children say the word slowly to listen for the sound, identify the letter, and write the letter following the verbal path directions.

  Let's say the word *pig* together slowly to listen for the first sound.

  What sound do you hear first in *pig*?

  The first sound is /p/. What letter goes with that sound?

- Point to *p* on the ABC chart or name chart. Use the verbal path to tell how to form the letter *p*. Write on a word card taped lightly to the easel.

  To make a *p*, pull down, up, and around.

- Complete the word *pig* by having children say the word again to listen for and identify the sounds and letter names for *i* and *g*. Use the verbal path to guide letter formation. Children can write the letters in the air.

- Read the word as you run your finger underneath it and emphasize all of the letter sounds. Place the card in the pocket chart.

  I wrote the word *pig* by saying it slowly and listening for all the sounds.

- Repeat this process using additional picture cards (e.g., *cap* and *nest*).

Have a Try

Repeat the process with more words. Invite children to work with a partner to listen for and identify the letters for the sounds they hear.

> Say the word *frog* slowly with your partner. Turn and talk about the sounds you hear and the letters that stand for those sounds.

▶ Invite volunteers to share what sounds they hear, guiding them to think about the sounds in the correct order. Record what the children say. Check the word by running your finger underneath the letters as they say the sounds.

Summarize and Apply

Summarize the learning. Remind children to listen for all the sounds in a word they want to write.

▶ Write the principle on a sentence strip and place it in the pocket chart.

> When you write a word, make sure to say it slowly to listen for the sounds. Write the letters for the sounds you hear in the order you hear them. Bring your writing to share when we meet later.

Listen for all the sounds in a word.

pig

cap

nest

frog

Confer

▶ During independent writing, move around the room to confer briefly with as many individual children as time allows. Sit side by side with them and invite them to talk about writing words. Use the following prompts as needed to support their ability to say a word slowly to listen for the predominant sounds.

- *You can say the word slowly and listen for the sounds you hear [model].*
- *What do you hear first [next, after that]?*
- *You can think about the sound and write the letter.*

Share

Following independent writing, gather children in the meeting area. Invite individual children to share their writing. Support children's oral language by providing a sentence frame: *I wrote the word _____ .*

> Who would like to share what you wrote today?

> How did you know what letters to write?

WML3

Writing Minilesson Principle
Break apart words to help you write them.

Learning How to Write Words

You Will Need

- pocket chart
- picture cards of words that have one or two syllables
- blank word cards
- tape
- sentence strip
- To download the following online resource for this lesson, visit **resources.fountasandpinnell.com**:
  - chart art (optional)

Academic Language / Important Vocabulary

- parts
- word
- syllable
- clap

Continuum Connection

- Hear, say, clap, and identify syllables in one- or two-syllable words: e.g., *big, frog, gold*; *lit/tle, mon/key, sil/ver* (p. 366)
- Understand and talk about the concept of a syllable (p. 366)

GOAL

Clap syllables and listen for sounds in each part to help write words.

RATIONALE

Hearing the syllables in words helps children learn how to break multisyllable words into parts that can be represented by letters.

ASSESS LEARNING

- Observe children's ability to say and clap syllables in words.
- Look for evidence that children can use vocabulary such as *parts*, *word*, *syllable*, and *clap*.

MINILESSON

To help children think about the minilesson principle, use picture cards representing words with easily identifiable syllable breaks. Here is an example.

> Today you are going to learn how to listen for parts of a word to help you write it.

- Display a picture card of a two-syllable word and place it in a pocket chart (e.g., *rabbit*).

  > Look at this picture. What is this?

  > When you say a word, you can clap the parts you hear. Each part is called a syllable. Say and clap *rab-bit*. How many parts do you hear in the word *rabbit*?

- Invite children to say the parts of the word slowly, focusing on one part at a time, as you record the letters on a word card taped lightly to the easel. Then place the card in the pocket chart.

- Repeat this process for additional two-syllable picture cards (e.g., *mitten* and *spider*).

Have a Try

Invite children to work with a partner to clap the parts of some additional two-syllable words.

> Say the word *tiger* with your partner and clap the syllables you hear. Turn and talk about how many parts you hear.

◗ Invite volunteers to clap the parts of *ti-ger*. Write *tiger* on a word card and place it in the pocket chart.

Summarize and Apply

Summarize the learning. Then remind children to break apart words into syllables to help them write words that have more than one syllable.

◗ Write the principle on a sentence strip and place it in the pocket chart.

> When you write a word that has more than one syllable, clap the syllables to help you hear all the parts. Bring your writing to share when we meet later.

Confer

◗ During independent writing, move around the room to confer briefly with as many individual children as time allows. Sit side by side with them and invite them to talk about writing words. Use prompts like the ones below as needed.

- Listen for the parts.
- Clap the parts you hear.
- You can say the part slowly and listen for the sounds you hear (model).
- You can think about the sound and write the letter.

Share

Following independent writing, gather children in the meeting area. Invite individual children to share their writing.

> Who would like to share your writing?

> Can you point to a word you wrote that has more than one part, or syllable?

> How did you know how to write that word?

Learning How to Write Words

You Will Need

- chart paper prepared with a piece of class writing with familiar high-frequency words, such as that from IW.11: Writing from a Picture
- highlighter or highlighter tape
- several word cards prepared with familiar high-frequency words (e.g., *go, my, out, see*)
- markers
- To download the following online resource for this lesson, visit **resources.fountasandpinnell.com**:
  - High-Frequency Word List

Academic Language / Important Vocabulary

- word
- quickly
- write
- spell

Continuum Connection

- Spell approximately twenty-five high-frequency words conventionally (p. 248)
- Recognize and use high-frequency words with one, two, or three letters: e.g., *a, I, in, is, of, to, and, the* (p. 366)
- Spell known words quickly (p. 366)

GOAL

Write known high-frequency words quickly and accurately.

RATIONALE

When you teach children to write high-frequency words quickly and accurately, they can share their thoughts in writing more fluently and begin to use these words as anchors to monitor and check their writing and reading. It also allows them more time to devote to unknown words, often by connecting new words to the familiar words using the beginning letter, sound, or part.

ASSESS LEARNING

- Observe children's ability to write high-frequency words quickly and accurately.
- Notice if children refer to resources around the room (such as the word wall) to help write high-frequency words.
- Observe for evidence that children can use vocabulary such as *word, quickly, write,* and *spell*.

MINILESSON

To help children think about the minilesson principle, identify high-frequency words in a piece of class interactive writing, such as that from IW.11: Writing from a Picture. If you do not have a class word wall, skip that part of the lesson.

- Display a piece of writing that the class wrote together.

  > Remember when we wrote about a picture? We wrote about the slide.

- Read the page aloud while pointing under the words.

  > You know some of the words that we wrote because they are on our word wall and you see them in the books that we read. You might even have them on your personal word list.

- Help a volunteer highlight the words he knows well (e.g., *the, likes, to*).

  > Who would like to come up and highlight the words you know?

  > Who can point to these highlighted words on the word wall?

- Invite children to write the high-frequency words in the air or on the carpet.

  > When you wrote these words, you were able to write them quickly because you know them. You didn't need to spend a lot of time thinking about how to write them.

  > Let's practice writing these words together in the air or on the carpet in front of you.

  > When you do your own writing and you write a word that you have seen and used a lot, remember to write it quickly.

Have a Try

Invite children to practice writing words they know quickly.

▶ Display one of the prepared word cards (e.g., *go*).

What word is this?

What are the letters in *go*?

▶ Ask a volunteer to write *go* on a clean sheet of chart paper. Remind her to write quickly but keep it legible. The other children can practice writing the word in the air or on the carpet.

▶ Repeat for the other word cards.

Summarize and Apply

Summarize the learning. Remind children to write the words they know quickly when they write.

Today, when you work on your writing, you can write words that you know quickly. Bring your writing to share after writing time. You can let us know how you wrote some words you knew.

Quinn plays on the playground.

Quinn likes to slide.

Confer

▶ During independent writing, move around the room to confer briefly with as many individual children as time allows. Sit side by side with them and invite them to talk about writing the words they know. Use prompts like the ones below as needed.

• *What are you going to write about today?*

• *Read this page aloud. Is there a word that you were able to write quickly?*

• *Find the word _____ on the word wall.*

• *You know this word. You can write it quickly.*

Share

Following independent writing, gather children in the meeting area. Invite individual children to share their writing.

Who would like to share your writing?

Is there a word that you could write quickly?

Writing Minilesson Principle

Use what you know about words to write new words.

Learning How to Write Words

You Will Need

- chart paper and markers
- To download the following online resource for this lesson, visit **resources.fountasandpinnell.com**:
  - High-Frequency Word List

Academic Language / Important Vocabulary

- letter
- word
- sound

Continuum Connection

- Use simple resources to help in spelling words or check on spelling words (word walls, personal word lists) (p. 248)
- Use known words to help spell an unknown word (p. 366)
- Use letter-sound relationships to help spell an unknown word (p. 366)

GOAL

Use knowledge of known words to write unknown words.

RATIONALE

Teaching children to read and write every individual word would be a huge, time-consuming, and impossible task. Fortunately that is not necessary. A more efficient approach is to teach children to use what they know (known words or parts of words, such as a letter, a cluster of letters, or a phonogram pattern) to understand something new. This method equips them with tools to solve new words when they read and write.

ASSESS LEARNING

- Notice if children refer to resources around the room (such as the word wall) to help write new words.
- Observe children's ability to use what they know about a word to write unknown words.
- Look for evidence that children can use vocabulary such as *letter*, *word*, and *sound*.

MINILESSON

To help children think about the minilesson principle, choose words that children know well (from the word wall if you have one) and demonstrate using them to spell new words. Here is an example.

- Write the word *at* on chart paper.

    This is a word that you know. Say it with me slowly: *at*.

- Write the word *cat* on the chart directly below *at*.

    What do you notice about these two words?

    How do you think I knew how to write *cat*?

- Point under the letters as you guide children to understand that *at* and *cat* have the same ending sounds, so you were able to use the word *at* to write *cat*.

    How can you figure out how to write *sat*?

Have a Try

Invite children to talk to a partner about using the word *day* to write other words.

> This is *day*. Turn and talk to your partner. How can you use *day* to spell *say*?

▶ Ask a volunteer to spell the word. Write it on the chart. Repeat with the word *play*.

Summarize and Apply

Help children summarize the lesson. Remind children to use what they know about words to write new words.

> What is something you can do to help you write new words?

▶ Write the principle at the top of the chart. Read it aloud.

> Today during writing time, think about words you already know to help you write new words. Bring your writing to share when we meet later.

Use what you know about words to write new words.

at	day
cat	say
sat	play

Confer

▶ During independent writing, move around the room to confer briefly with as many individual children as time allows. Sit side by side with them and invite them to talk about writing words. Use the following prompts as needed.

- *What can you do if you don't know how to write a word?*
- *Do you know a word that starts like that?*
- *Do you know a word that sounds like this one?*
- *Is that like a word you know?*

Share

Following independent writing, gather children in the meeting area. Invite individual children to share their writing.

> Who would like to share your writing?

> Can you point to a new word you wrote? How did you know what letters to write?

Assessment

After you have taught the minilessons in this umbrella, observe children as they draw, write, and talk about their writing. Use the behaviors and understandings in *The Literacy Continuum* (Fountas and Pinnell 2017) to notice, teach for, and support children's learning as you observe their attempts at drawing and writing.

▶ What evidence do you have that children are beginning to learn how to write words?

- Are children saying words slowly and listening for the first sound?
- Are they listening for the individual sounds in a word in sequence?
- Do they break apart words when they attempt to write multisyllable words?
- Do they write words that they know quickly?
- Can they use what they know about words to write new words?
- Do they understand and use vocabulary such as *letter*, *word*, and *sound*?

▶ In what other ways, beyond the scope of this umbrella, are the children learning how to write words?

- Would they benefit from learning how to use classroom resources to write words?
- Are they ready to learn when to use capital letters?

Use your observations to determine the next umbrella to teach. You may also consult Suggested Sequence of Lessons (pp. 483–494) for guidance.

EXTENSIONS FOR LEARNING HOW TO WRITE WORDS

▶ To help children listen for sounds, use an audio device and have them record and then listen to several easy-to-hear sounds.

▶ Continue to use interactive writing to demonstrate slowly articulating unknown words and writing predominant sounds in sequence (beginning, middle, and end).

▶ Place games in the word work center to practice recognizing and writing high-frequency words, understanding syllables, or building words from a phonogram (e.g., *an, can, man, pan, ran*).

▶ As children read, support them by pointing out known parts of words.

Minilessons in This Umbrella

WML1 Use the name chart and ABC chart to help you write words.

WML2 Use the word wall to help you write words.

WML3 Use your own word list to help you write words.

Before Teaching Umbrella 4 Minilessons

The goal of this umbrella is to help children learn how to use a variety of resources to help themselves write new words. These lessons use the text and example from IW.19: Making a Story Map Mural, so if you wish to use that example be sure to teach the lesson beforehand. However, this is only one possibility. You could also choose to write simple sentences about another book or about anything.

Before teaching the first two minilessons, children should already be familiar with the name chart, ABC chart, and word wall. WML3 shows children how to use the personal word list (available in online resources) as another resource for writing. When you confer with children, suggest words to add to their personal word lists. The words should be ones that children are learning and use frequently in their writing. The lists are stored in their writing folders (see MGT.U2.WML3). Write a few easy high-frequency words (e.g., *a*, *at*, *go*, *me*, *it*) on the word list prior to attaching it to their folders. Writing conferences are a good time to work with children to add words to their word lists.

Interactive Read-Aloud Collection

Exploring Animal Tales

The Three Billy Goats Gruff by P. C. Asbjørnsen and J. E. Moe

Interactive Writing Lessons

IW.19: Making a Story Map Mural

Interactive Read-Aloud
Animal Tales

Interactive Writing

Section 6: Exploring Early Writing

Writing Minilesson Principle
Use the name chart and ABC chart to help you write words.

Using Classroom Resources to Write Words

You Will Need

- a familiar book, such as *The Three Billy Goats Gruff* by P. C. Asbjørnsen and J. E. Moe, from Text Set: Exploring Animal Tales
- class writing from IW.19: Making a Story Map Mural
- name chart
- chart paper and markers
- To download the following online resources for this lesson, visit **resources.fountasandpinnell.com**:
  - Alphabet Linking Chart
  - chart art (optional)

Academic Language / Important Vocabulary

- writing
- word
- sound
- name chart
- letter
- ABC chart

Continuum Connection

- Say words slowly to hear a sound and write a letter that represents it (p. 248)
- Use one's name to learn about words and to make connections to words and to other names (p. 365)
- Hear and say the beginning phoneme in a word: e.g., *sun*, /s/ (p. 365)
- Use the initial letter in a name to make connections to other words: e.g., *Max*, *Maria*, *make*, *home*, *from* (p. 366)
- Use the initial letter in a name to read and write other words: e.g., *Tom*, *toy*, *town*, *stop*, *cat* (p. 366)

GOAL

Use the name chart and ABC chart as resources to help write words.

RATIONALE

When children learn to use classroom resources for writing, they become independent problem solvers who are responsible for their own writing because they can find solutions on their own.

ASSESS LEARNING

- Notice evidence that children understand that the name chart and ABC chart are two classroom resources they can use for writing.
- Observe whether children are using classroom resources to write words.
- Look for evidence that children can use vocabulary such as *writing*, *sound*, *letter*, *word*, *name chart*, and *ABC chart*.

MINILESSON

Prior to teaching this lesson, make sure children are familiar with the name chart and ABC chart. Provide a lesson in which you model how to use the name chart and ABC chart to help with writing. Here is an example.

- Show the cover of *The Three Billy Goats Gruff* and the story map from IW.19.

  Today, we can write more about the billy goats.

- Work with children to plan a sentence that summarizes pages 5–6 and model how to use the name chart and ABC chart to help write beginning sounds.

  Let's say our sentence together: *The little Billy Goat Gruff crossed the bridge.*

- Say each word as you write *The little*. Then pause. Accentuate /b/ when you say *Billy*.

  What is the next word in our sentence?

  Say *Billy*. **Billy starts with /b/. What do you see on the ABC chart that begins with the same sound?**

  What letter do you see with *bear*?

- Write the word *Billy*. Repeat the process for *Goat* and *Gruff*.

  The next word is *crossed*. **I know that** *Carlos* **begins with the same sound as the first sound in** *crossed*. **I can look at the name chart to help me write the first letter in** *crossed*.

- Write *crossed the*. Pause and have children reread the words written so far, pointing under each as you read with them.

Have a Try

Invite children to turn and talk about using the name chart and ABC chart.

> The next word we will write is *bridge*. With a partner, use the name chart or ABC chart to help you decide what letter is first in *bridge*.

▶ After time for partners to talk, ask a volunteer to share. Follow the child's suggestions in using the classroom resource. Then write the letter and finish writing the word.

Summarize and Apply

Help children summarize the lesson. Remind children to use the name chart and ABC chart when they write.

> Where can you look to think about the sounds that go with a letter?

> Where can you look to know what a letter looks like?

▶ Write the principle on the top of the chart.

> During writing time, use the name chart and ABC chart to help you write words.

Use the name chart and ABC chart to help you write words.

The little Billy Goat Gruff crossed the bridge.

Confer

▶ During independent writing, move around the room to confer briefly with as many individual children as time allows. Sit side by side with them and invite them to talk about using classroom resources to write words. Use the following prompts as needed.

- *Say the word slowly and listen for the first sound. What letter goes with that sound?*
- *How can the ABC chart (name chart) help you write the first letter?*
- *What name do you see on the name chart that can help you write this word?*

Share

Following independent writing, gather children in the meeting area. Ask children to share their experiences using the name chart and ABC chart.

> Who used the name chart or ABC chart for writing today? Tell about that.

WML2

Writing Minilesson Principle
Use the word wall to help you write words.

Using Classroom Resources to Write Words

You Will Need

- a familiar book, such as *The Three Billy Goats Gruff* by P. C. Asbjørnsen and J. E. Moe, from Text Set: Exploring Animal Tales
- word wall
- chart paper and markers
- To download the following online resource for this lesson, visit **resources.fountasandpinnell.com**:
  - chart art (optional)

Academic Language / Important Vocabulary

- writing
- sound
- letter
- word
- word wall

Continuum Connection

- Use simple resources to help in spelling words or check on spelling (word walls, personal word lists) (p. 248)

GOAL

Understand that the word wall can help you write some words quickly and easily.

RATIONALE

When children learn to use a word wall as one resource for writing, they make the connection that their knowledge of some words can help them write unfamiliar words. It can also help them learn to write high-frequency words quickly.

ASSESS LEARNING

- ▶ Notice evidence that children understand that a word wall can help them with writing.
- ▶ Observe whether children are using classroom resources such as the word wall for writing.
- ▶ Look for evidence that children can use vocabulary such as *writing*, *sound*, *letter*, *word*, and *word wall.*

MINILESSON

Prior to teaching this lesson, a word wall should be set up and functioning in the classroom. This minilesson builds on the previous minilesson to help children become familiar with using classroom resources when they write. Here is an example.

> Today, we can write another sentence about the billy goats.

▶ Show the cover of *The Three Billy Goats Gruff*. Work with children to plan a sentence that summarizes pages 7–8. Use the sentence to model how to use the word wall to help write words.

> Let's say our sentence together: *Then the troll shouted, "Who is going over my bridge?"*
>
> The first word in our sentence is *Then*. Sometimes the word that you want to write is on the word wall. Other times you can use other words on the word wall to help you write a word.

▶ Say *Then* slowly, emphasizing the first sound. Have children repeat it with you.

> The first sound in the word *Then* sounds like the first sound in the word *that*. Who can find *that* on the word wall?
>
> What letters are at the beginning of *that*?

▶ Write *Th*. Say *Then* slowly again, stressing the last part, *en*.

> The last part of *then* sounds like the last part of *hen*.

▶ Write *en*. Continue writing the sentence, pausing before any words that connect to a word on the word wall. Model how to slowly articulate the word and make connections to words on the word wall.

Have a Try

Invite children to turn and talk about using the word wall for a word they don't know how to write.

> Find a word on the word wall that could help you write the word *cat*. Tell your partner.

▶ After time for a brief discussion, ask volunteers to share a word from the word wall they could use to write *cat*, such as *can* or *at*.

Summarize and Apply

Help children summarize the lesson. Remind children to use the word wall when they write to help them write new words as needed.

> Where can you look to help you write words you don't know how to write?

▶ Write the principle at the top of the chart and read it aloud.

> During writing time, you can use the word wall to help you write words. You can use a whole word or part of a word to write a new word.

Use the word wall to help you write words.

Then the troll shouted, "Who is going over my bridge?"

Confer

▶ During independent writing, move around the room to confer briefly with as many individual children as time allows. Sit side by side with them and invite them to talk about using the word wall. Use the following prompts as needed.

- *Look at the word wall. What word can help you write what comes next?*
- *How can the word wall help you when you write?*
- *What word sounds like that at the beginning [end]?*

Share

Following independent writing, gather children in the meeting area to share how they used the word wall.

> Who used the word wall to write a new word today? Tell about that.

> Did anyone do anything else to help write a word?

Writing Minilesson Principle
Use your own word list to help you write words.

You Will Need

- a familiar book, such as *The Three Billy Goats Gruff* by P. C. Asbjørnsen and J. E. Moe, from Text Set: Exploring Animal Tales

- a personal word list with a few words on it, including words you will use in the lesson [e.g., *got, cat, that*]

- chart paper and markers

- highlighter tape

- children's writing folders with their personal word list inside

- To download the following online resources for this lesson, visit **resources.fountasandpinnell.com**:

  - My Words

  - chart art [optional]

Academic Language / Important Vocabulary

- writing

- personal word list

Continuum Connection

- Use simple resources to help in spelling words or check on spelling [word walls, personal word lists] [p. 248]

GOAL

Understand what a personal word list is and how to use it.

RATIONALE

When children learn to create and use a personal word list, they understand that the words they learn can be used again and again in their writing, and they learn how to keep track of words so they can refer to them as needed. If children have writing folders, the personal word lists can be fastened inside along with other reference tools.

ASSESS LEARNING

- Notice evidence that children understand how to refer to a personal word list.

- Look for evidence that children are creating and using personal word lists.

- Observe for evidence that children can use vocabulary such as *writing* and *personal word list*.

MINILESSON

To help children think about the minilesson principle, demonstrate how to use a personal word list as a resource for writing. Here is an example.

- Ahead of time, prepare a sample word list on chart paper. Include several words that will be used in the model writing you will do during this lesson.

- Post the word list side by side with a blank piece of chart paper.

  We can continue writing about the billy goats.

- Work with children to plan sentences that summarize pages 9–10 of *The Three Billy Goats Gruff*.

  Let's say our sentences together. *The little goat said, "I am not fat! You do not want to eat me! A bigger goat is right behind me!"*

- Model using your word list to write any words that are connected to words on your list. For example, write the first few words in the sentence. Stop when you get to the word *not*.

  The next word is *not*. Say it slowly. The word *not* rhymes with the word *got*, which is on my word list.

- Point to the word *got* on the chart.

  What part of the word *got* can help you write *not*?

- Continue in this way as you write the rest of the sentence. Make connections to additional words, such as the word *fat*. You could connect it to the word *at*.

  You can use your word list to help you write words.

Have a Try

Invite children to turn and talk about their personal word lists.

> Read two words on your personal word list to your partner.

Summarize and Apply

Write the principle at the top of the chart and summarize the lesson. Remind children that they can use their personal word lists during writing time.

> Today you learned how to use a word list to help you write a word. When we talk about your writing, I'll suggest some words for you to add to your personal word list. Your word list will always be in your writing folder so you can find it.

Confer

▸ During independent writing, move around the room to confer briefly with as many individual children as time allows. Sit side by side with them and invite them to talk about using their personal word lists. Use the following prompts as needed.

- *What are you going to write about today?*
- *What words do you have on your word list so far?*
- *What new word would you like to add to your word list?*
- *Which word on your list will help you write this new word?*
- *Show me where you will keep your word list when you are finished writing today.*

Share

Following independent writing, gather children in the meeting area to share their writing.

> Who would like to share what you wrote today?

> Did you use your word list to help you know how to write a word?

> Did anyone look anywhere else to get help to write a new word?

Use your own word list to help you write words.

The little goat said,
"I am not fat!
You do not want to eat me!
A bigger goat is right behind me!"

Assessment

After you have taught the minilessons in this umbrella, observe children as they write. Use *The Literacy Continuum* (Fountas and Pinnell 2017) to notice, teach for, and support children's learning as you observe their attempts at reading and writing.

▶ What evidence do you have of new understandings children have developed related to using classroom resources for writing?

- Are children using the name chart and ABC chart to help them write new words?

- Do you notice children using the word wall as they write?

- Has each child added words to a personal word list?

- Do they understand how to use a personal word list to write words?

- What evidence is there that children can use vocabulary such as *writing*, *sound*, *letter*, *name chart*, *ABC chart*, *word*, *word wall*, and *word list*?

▶ In what ways, beyond the scope of this umbrella, are children using classroom resources?

- Do they use the name chart to help write capital letters?

Use your observations to determine the next umbrella you will teach. You may also consult Suggested Sequence of Lessons (pp. 483–494) for guidance.

EXTENSIONS FOR USING CLASSROOM RESOURCES TO WRITE WORDS

▶ As you use shared reading books and other big books with children, from time to time have them make connections between the words they see and the name chart or ABC chart.

▶ Use the word wall in a variety of ways throughout the day (e.g., "I spy a word that begins with *t* and has two letters. What is it?").

▶ Encourage children to add content words to their personal word lists, such as after completing a science project or after attending a field trip.

Minilessons in This Umbrella

WML1 Notice the difference between uppercase and lowercase letters.

WML2 Capitalize the first letter of your name.

WML3 Capitalize the first letter of the first word in a sentence.

Before Teaching Umbrella 5 Minilessons

In this umbrella about using capital letters, please use the term that is more familiar to the children in your class, either *capital* or *uppercase*.

Before teaching this umbrella, ensure that the children have a good understanding of the difference between letters, words, and sentences and understand the concept of *first* in relation to words and sentences (first letter in a word, first word in a sentence).

Read and discuss simple books that the children will enjoy. Use the following texts from *Fountas & Pinnell Classroom™ Shared Reading Collection* and the class writing from IW.8: Making a Class Big Book. You can also choose any books from the classroom library that illustrate how capital letters are used.

Shared Reading Collection

Kate's Party by Jane Simon

Stars by Catherine Friend

Stripes by Catherine Friend

Spots by Judy Kentor Schmauss

Interactive Writing Lessons

IW.8: Making a Class Big Book

As you read and enjoy these texts together, help children

- identify and talk about different letters,

- notice names in the text, and

- identify the first letter in a word and the first word in a sentence.

Shared Reading

Interactive Writing

Section 6: Exploring Early Writing

WML1

EWR.U5.WML1

Writing Minilesson Principle
Notice the difference between uppercase and lowercase letters.

Using Capital Letters

You Will Need

- pairs of uppercase and lowercase magnetic letters
- magnetic board
- chart paper prepared with a chart that has three sections and labels for *Uppercase* and *Lowercase*
- markers
- three sticky notes: two labeled *Tall*, one labeled *Short*
- To download the following online resources for this lesson, visit **resources.fountasandpinnell.com**:
  - ABC Chart
  - Verbal Path for Letter Formation

Academic Language/ Important Vocabulary

- uppercase (capital)
- lowercase (small)
- letter

Continuum Connection

- Recognize and point to the distinctive features of letter forms (p. 365)
- Recognize and point to uppercase letters and lowercase letters: e.g., *B, b* (p. 365)
- Distinguish and talk about the differences between the uppercase and lowercase forms of a letter (p. 365)

GOAL

Notice the difference between uppercase and lowercase letters.

RATIONALE

Before children can begin using uppercase and lowercase letters correctly in their own writing, they must first learn to recognize and differentiate between the uppercase and lowercase form of each letter. Use the terms (*uppercase* or *capital*; *lowercase or small*) that you prefer.

ASSESS LEARNING

- Look for evidence that children understand the idea of tall and short lowercase letters.
- Notice whether children can identify uppercase and lowercase letters and talk about their differences.
- Observe for evidence that children can use vocabulary such as *uppercase (capital)*, *lowercase (small)*, and *letter*.

MINILESSON

This lesson uses magnetic letters on a magnetic board (a cookie tray works) to demonstrate uppercase and lowercase letters, but you could have children identify letters in an alphabet book or ABC chart. Here is an example.

- Place a variety of uppercase and lowercase magnetic letters at the top of a magnetic board. Make sure you have the uppercase and lowercase version of each letter, including *Bb* and *Cc*. Pull down *B* and *b*.

  What do you notice about these two letters?

- Help children notice that they are the same letter, one is uppercase and one is lowercase, *B* and *b* are about the same height, and they look different.

- Write *B* in the *Uppercase* column and *b* in the *Lowercase* column.

- Pull down *C* and *c*.

  What do you notice about these two letters?

- Help children notice that they are the same letter, one is uppercase and one is lowercase, *C* is taller than *c*, and they otherwise look the same.

- On the prepared chart, write *C* partway down the *Uppercase* column and *c* opposite it in the lower half of the *Lowercase* column.

- Continue identifying and describing a few more pairs of letters.

  What do you notice about where I wrote the lowercase letters?

  I wrote the tall lowercase letters together, and I wrote the short lowercase letters together.

- Add (or have a child add) the sticky notes for *Tall* and *Short* to the chart.

Have a Try

Invite children to talk with a partner about the uppercase letters.

> On our chart, we have some lowercase letters that are tall and some that are short. Look at the uppercase letters on the chart. Turn and talk to your partner about what you notice.

▶ Guide children to understand that all uppercase letters are tall. Add the sticky note for *Tall* to the chart.

Summarize and Apply

Summarize the learning and remind children to think about uppercase and lowercase letters when they write.

> What did you learn today about uppercase and lowercase letters?

> Today during writing time, remember to make the tall letters tall and the short letters short. You can use the ABC chart to help you remember how to make each letter.

Uppercase Letters	Lowercase Letters
B	b
D	d
F	f
H	h
C	c
E	e
M	m
S	s

Tall (uppercase column)

Tall (lowercase column)

Short (lowercase column)

Confer

▶ During independent writing, move around the room to confer briefly with as many individual children as time allows. Sit side by side with them and invite them to talk about how to write letters. Use prompts such as the following to remind them about using uppercase and lowercase letters.

- *Let's look at the ABC chart. Find the uppercase A.*
- *Can you write an uppercase A?*
- *To make a lowercase a, pull back, around, up, and down.*
- *How is the lowercase a different from the uppercase A?*

Share

Following independent writing, gather children in the meeting area to share their writing.

> Give a thumbs up if you practiced writing uppercase and lowercase letters today.

> Who would like to share what you wrote today? Did you use any uppercase letters?

Writing Minilesson Principle
Capitalize the first letter of your name.

Using Capital Letters

You Will Need

- your class's name chart
- the class-created text from IW.8: Making a Class Big Book
- a familiar book that contains people's names, such as *Kate's Party* by Jane Simon, from *Shared Reading Collection*
- chart paper and markers
- highlighter

Academic Language/ Important Vocabulary

- capitalize
- uppercase (capital)
- letter
- name

Continuum Connection

- Demonstrate knowledge of the use of upper- and lowercase letters of the alphabet (p. 247)
- Write one's own name with a capital letter at the beginning (p. 247)
- Show awareness of the position of capital letters at the beginning of some words (p. 247)
- Use a capital letter at the beginning of a familiar proper noun (p. 247)
- Understand and talk about the concepts of first and last in written language (p. 365)

GOAL

Understand that names begin with capital letters.

RATIONALE

When you help children notice that people's names are always capitalized, they begin to understand that certain types of words need to be capitalized. Later, they will learn that all proper nouns are capitalized. Use the term, *uppercase* or *capital*, that you prefer.

ASSESS LEARNING

- Observe whether children capitalize the first letter of their names.
- Notice evidence that children can use vocabulary such as *capitalize*, *uppercase* (capital), *letter*, and *name*.

MINILESSON

To help children think about the minilesson principle, use the name chart and books with names in them. Here is an example.

- Show the class name chart. Point to the first letter of several names.

    What do you notice about the first letter of all the names?

    They are all uppercase.

- Write a few of the names on chart paper, highlighting the first letter.
- Show the class-created text from IW.8: Making a Class Big Book. Read one page aloud.

    What do you notice about the *A* in Alex's name?

- Add the name to the chart.
- Show *Kate's Party*. Read page 2 aloud.

    What do you notice about the names *Lily*, *Rob*, *Jack*, and *Pat*?

- Add the names to the chart.

    What are you noticing about the letters in a person's name?

Have a Try

Invite children to talk to a partner about how they would write their own names.

> **Turn and talk to your partner about how you would write the first letter of your name.**

Summarize and Apply

Help children summarize the learning and remind them to capitalize the first letter of names.

> **What kind of letter should you write at the beginning of someone's name?**

▶ Write the principle on the chart.

> **When you write an uppercase letter in a name, you capitalize it. Say it with me: *capitalize*. During writing time today, be sure to write your name on your work. Remember to capitalize the first letter.**

> ### Capitalize the first letter of your name.
>
> | | |
> |---|---|
> | Connor | Lily |
> | Gabriel | Rob |
> | Mia | Jack |
> | Alex | Pat |

Section 6: Exploring Early Writing

Confer

▶ During independent writing, move around the room to confer briefly with as many individual children as time allows. Sit side by side with them and invite them to talk about using uppercase letters. Use prompts such as the following as needed.

- *Remember to write your name on your paper.*
- *What is the first letter of your name?*
- *How should you write the first letter? Should it be uppercase or lowercase?*
- *Look at the name chart to help you remember how to write your name.*

Share

Following independent writing, gather children in the meeting area to share their writing.

> **Give a thumbs up if you wrote your name on your paper today.**
>
> **How did you write the first letter?**

Writing Minilesson Principle
Capitalize the first letter of the first word in a sentence.

Using Capital Letters

You Will Need

- familiar books with only one sentence per page, such as *Stars* and *Stripes* by Catherine Friend and *Spots* by Judy Kentor Schmauss, from *Shared Reading Collection*
- chart paper and markers
- highlighter

Academic Language/ Important Vocabulary

- capitalize
- uppercase (capital)
- letter
- word
- sentence

Continuum Connection

- Locate a capital letter at the beginning of a sentence during shared or interactive writing or in a piece of dictated writing (p. 247)
- Understand and talk about the concepts of first and last in written language (p. 365)
- Locate the first and last letters of words in continuous text (p. 365)

GOAL

Understand that a sentence begins with a capital letter.

RATIONALE

When children notice that sentences in books begin with uppercase (capital) letters, they will understand that they, too, should capitalize the first word in a sentence in their own writing. Children should have a solid understanding of the concepts of *first*, *letter*, *word*, and *sentence* before this lesson is taught. Use the term, *uppercase* or *capital*, that you prefer.

ASSESS LEARNING

- Observe whether children begin sentences with capital letters.
- Notice evidence that children can use vocabulary such as *capitalize*, *uppercase (capital)*, *letter*, *word*, *and sentence*.

MINILESSON

Use mentor texts to help children notice that sentences begin with capital letters.

- Show the cover of *Stars* and read the title. Read page 2. Point to the *Y* in *You*.

  What do you notice about the first letter of the first word in this sentence?

- Read page 16.

  What do you notice about the first letter of this sentence?

- Repeat with a page in *Stripes* and a page in *Spots*.

- Decide on a simple sentence to write.

  I am going to write the sentence *Lunch will be in ten minutes*. What letter is at the beginning of *Lunch*?

  Lunch begins with *L*. Should I write an uppercase or a lowercase letter?

- Highlight the first letter or invite a child to highlight it.

  What are you noticing about the first letter of a sentence?

Have a Try

Invite children to talk to a partner about a sentence to write and about how to write the first letter in the sentence.

> Turn and talk to your partner about a sentence we could write on the chart. What kind of letter would go at the beginning?

▶ Write several of the sentences on the chart. Highlight the first letter in each sentence.

Summarize and Apply

Help children summarize the learning and remind them to capitalize the first letter in a sentence.

> What kind of letter do you write at the beginning of a sentence?

▶ Write the principle on the chart and read it aloud.

> When you write a letter for the first word in a sentence, you capitalize it. Say it with me: *capitalize*. Remember to capitalize the first letter of the first word in every sentence you write.

Capitalize the first letter of the first word in a sentence.

Lunch will be in ten minutes.

Tomorrow is Yasmin's birthday!

Nik has a new baby brother.

Last week we got a fish.

Confer

▶ During independent writing, move around the room to confer briefly with as many individual children as time allows. Sit side by side with them and invite them to talk about using capital letters. Use prompts such as the following as needed.

- *What are you going to write on this page?*
- *What's the first word in your sentence?*
- *What's the first letter in that word?*
- *How should you write that letter? Should it be uppercase or lowercase?*

Share

Following independent writing, gather children in the meeting area to share their writing.

> Who would like to share a sentence you wrote today?

> How did you write the first letter in that sentence? Did you make it uppercase or lowercase?

Assessment

After you have taught the minilessons in this umbrella, observe children as they write and talk about their writing. Use *The Literacy Continuum* (Fountas and Pinnell 2017) to notice, teach for, and support children's learning as you observe their attempts at drawing and writing.

▶ What evidence do you have of new understandings children have developed related to using capital letters?

- Do children understand the difference between uppercase and lowercase letters?
- Do they capitalize the first letter in a person's name?
- Do they capitalize the first letter of the first word in a sentence?
- What evidence is there that children can use vocabulary such as *uppercase*, *lowercase*, and *capitalize*?

▶ In what other ways, beyond the scope of this umbrella, are children ready to expand their writing skills?

- Are they noticing different types of punctuation?

Use your observations to determine the next umbrella you will teach. You may also consult Suggested Sequence of Lessons (pp. 483–494) for guidance.

EXTENSIONS FOR USING CAPITAL LETTERS

▶ Encourage children to reread their writing to make sure they have used capital letters correctly. (See WPS.U5: Proofreading Writing.)

▶ Help children notice that all proper nouns begin with capital letters, not just the names of people (names of places, schools, companies, etc.).

▶ Teach children that the word *I* is always capitalized.

▶ If children make a finished copy of their writing on a computer, teach them how to use the Shift key to make capital letters.

Minilessons in This Umbrella

WML1 Use a period to end a sentence.

WML2 Use a question mark to end a question.

WML3 Use an exclamation point to show something exciting or surprising.

Before Teaching Umbrella 6 Minilessons

Prior to teaching these minilessons, make sure children have had experiences reading and discussing books with a variety of punctuation marks, including periods, question marks, and exclamation points. Class-made books from lessons in the Interactive Writing section that you have taught can serve as mentor texts for these lessons (e.g., IW.12: Making a Counting Book). You may also choose the following from *Fountas & Pinnell Classroom™ Interactive Read-Aloud Collection* and *Shared Reading Collection*, or you might use other texts from the classroom library. It is recommended that you include big books in the lessons so that children can clearly see and identify the punctuation marks.

Interactive Read-Aloud Collection
Exploring Animal Tales

The Little Red Hen by Paul Galdone

The Three Little Pigs by Patricia Seibert

The Three Billy Goats Gruff by P. C. Asbjørnsen and J. E. Moe

Shared Reading Collection

Goldy by Athena Tsatsaronis

Morning on the Farm by Jane Simon

Smash! Crash! by Catherine Friend

Interactive Writing Lessons

IW.12: Making a Counting Book

As you read and enjoy these texts together, help children

- notice punctuation marks in text, and

- notice the way your voice changes when you read a sentence that ends with a period, a question mark, or an exclamation point.

Interactive Read-Aloud
Exploring Animal Tales

Shared Reading

Interactive Writing

Section 6: Exploring Early Writing

WML1
EWR.U6.WML1

Writing Minilesson Principle
Use a period to end a sentence.

Learning About Punctuation

You Will Need

- a familiar book with short sentences ending in periods, such as the following:
  - *Goldy* by Athena Tsatsaronis, from *Shared Reading Collection*
- class-made book from IW.12: Making a Counting Book
- highlighter or highlighter tape (optional)
- chart paper prepared with several simple sentences without periods at the end
- markers
- To download the following online resource for this lesson, visit **resources.fountasandpinnell.com**:
  - chart art (optional)

Academic Language / Important Vocabulary

- writing
- sentence
- period

Continuum Connection

- Notice the use of punctuation marks in books and try them out in one's own writing (p. 247)
- Use periods, exclamation marks, and question marks as end marks (p. 247)

GOAL

Understand that writers put a period at the end of a statement to help the reader understand the message.

RATIONALE

When children recognize how periods at the end of sentences convey meaning, they learn to use punctuation to interpret a writer's intention and begin adding periods to the end of the sentences they write.

ASSESS LEARNING

- Notice evidence that children understand the significance of a period at the end of a sentence.
- Observe whether children are beginning to add periods to the end of sentences when they write.
- Notice evidence that children can use vocabulary such as *writing*, *sentence*, and *period*.

MINILESSON

To help children understand the meaning of a period at the end of a sentence and help them use periods in their own writing, provide a brief interactive lesson. Here is an example.

- Show page 4 of *Goldy* and read the sentence, making sure your voice goes down and stops after the period.

  What do you notice at the end of this sentence?

- As children identify the period, point underneath it.

  Why do you think the author decided to add a period at the end of the sentence?

- Guide the conversation, helping them recognize that the period shows the end of a sentence, or one complete idea.

- Show the class-made book from IW.12 and read the first sentence.

  Who would like to come and point to (highlight) the period in this sentence?

- Have children reread the sentence with you, pointing under each word and the period as you read.

  When you read a sentence, your voice goes down at the end. This is how you can tell where to put a period.

Have a Try

Invite children to turn and talk about periods at the end of sentences.

▶ Show the prepared chart. Point under the first sentence as you read it aloud.

> Who can add a period to this sentence?

▶ Continue in the same manner for the other sentences.

Summarize and Apply

Help children summarize the lesson. Remind children to make sure they add periods to the sentences they write.

> Where does the period go in a sentence?

▶ Write the principle at the top of the chart.

> Writers add a period at the end of a sentence to show where the sentence ends. During writing time, make sure you put a period at the end of each sentence. Bring your writing to share when we meet later.

> Use a period to end a sentence.

> Today is sunny.

> It is Monday.

> Tomorrow it will rain.

Confer

▶ During independent writing, move around the room to confer briefly with as many individual children as time allows. Sit side by side with them and invite them to talk about using punctuation in their writing. Use the following prompts as needed.

> • *What sentence will you write on this page?*

> • *I will point to the end of your sentence, and you can write a period there. Then we can read the sentence together.*

> • *How does a period help the reader understand what you write?*

Share

Following independent writing, gather children in the meeting area to share their writing.

> Who would like to share what you wrote today?

> Tell about how you decided where to put the period in this sentence.

WML2
EWR.U6.WML2

Writing Minilesson Principle
Use a question mark to end a question.

Learning About Punctuation

You Will Need

- several familiar books that have sentences ending in question marks, such as the following:
  - *The Little Red Hen* by Paul Galdone, from Text Set: Exploring Animal Tales
  - *Goldy* by Athena Tsatsaronis and *Morning on the Farm* by Jane Simon, from *Shared Reading Collection*
- chart paper and markers
- highlighter tape (optional)

Academic Language / Important Vocabulary

- writing
- question
- question mark

Continuum Connection

- Notice the use of punctuation marks in books and try them out in one's own writing (p. 247)
- Use periods, exclamation marks, and question marks as end marks (p. 247)

GOAL

Understand that writers put a question mark at the end of a question to show that something is being asked.

RATIONALE

When children recognize that question marks at the end of sentences convey meaning, they learn that they can make questions in their own writing by adding question marks to show the reader that something is being asked.

ASSESS LEARNING

- Notice evidence that children understand that a question mark indicates that something is being asked.
- Observe whether children try using question marks in their own writing.
- Notice evidence that children can use vocabulary such as *writing*, *question*, and *question mark*.

MINILESSON

To help children notice and identify questions and to help them use question marks in their own writing, provide a brief interactive lesson. Here is an example.

- Show the cover of *The Little Red Hen*.

  Do you remember in *The Little Red Hen* how the hen keeps asking the other animals to help? Listen as I read a few things she says.

- Read page 12. Ask children to read the question with you, emphasizing the way your voice goes up at the end.

- Repeat with the question on page 32.

  What do you notice about these sentences?

- Guide the conversation to help children notice that each sentence is a question, so it ends in a question mark. Have children use a finger to make a question mark in the air. You might have children put highlighter tape on the question marks.

- Continue reading the questions and having children identify the question marks on page 11 of *Goldy* and page 3 of *Morning on the Farm*.

Have a Try

Invite children to add question marks at the end of sentences.

> What is a question we could write?

▶ Write the question on chart paper.

> Who can add a question mark to this sentence?

▶ Read the sentence together, emphasizing how the voice rises at the end of a question. Then write several more sentences to which children add question marks.

Summarize and Apply

Help children summarize the lesson. During writing time, remind children to add question marks to the questions they write.

> When do you use a question mark?

▶ Write the principle at the top of the chart.

> Writers add a question mark at the end of a sentence to show that they are asking something. During writing time, add question marks to the end of questions you write. Bring your writing to share when we meet later.

> **Use a question mark to end a question.**
>
> What is for lunch today?
>
> How are you?
>
> How old are you?
>
> Where is your coat?

Confer

▶ During independent writing, move around the room to confer briefly with as many individual children as time allows. Sit side by side with them and invite them to talk about using punctuation in their writing. Use the following prompts as needed.

- *What are you writing about today?*
- *What question could you ask?*
- *Where will you put the question mark?*
- *I will draw a question mark at the end lightly. You can trace over it.*

Share

Following independent writing, gather children in the meeting area to share their writing.

> Who would like to share your writing?

> Did you write a question? Read it.

Writing Minilesson Principle
Use an exclamation point to show something exciting or surprising.

Learning About Punctuation

You Will Need

- several familiar books that have exclamation points, such as the following:
  - *The Three Little Pigs* by Patricia Seibert and *The Three Billy Goats Gruff* by P. C. Asbjørnsen and J. E. Moe, from Text Set: Exploring Animal Tales
  - *Smash! Crash!* by Catherine Friend, from *Shared Reading Collection*
- chart paper and markers
- highlighter tape (optional)

Academic Language / Important Vocabulary

- writing
- exclamation point
- exciting
- surprising

Continuum Connection

- Notice the use of punctuation marks in books and try them out in one's own writing (p. 247)
- Use periods, exclamation marks, and question marks as end marks (p. 247)

GOAL

Understand that writers put an exclamation point at the end of a sentence to show something exciting or surprising.

RATIONALE

When children recognize that exclamation points convey meaning, they learn that they can show emphasis in their own writing by adding exclamation points to the end of sentences.

ASSESS LEARNING

- Look for evidence that children understand that an exclamation point signifies something exciting or surprising.
- Observe whether children are trying to use exclamation points in their own writing.
- Notice evidence that children can use vocabulary such as *writing*, *exclamation point*, *exciting*, and *surprising*.

MINILESSON

To help children notice, identify, and use exclamation points, provide a brief interactive lesson. Here is an example.

> Listen as I read the conversation between the pigs and the wolf.

- Show pictures as you read sentences with exclamation points on pages 18–20 of *The Three Little Pigs*. As you do, point under the words and exclamation points on the chart.

> What do you notice about the sentences?

- Guide children to notice the exclamation points and talk about why the writer uses them. If you wish, add highlighter tape to the exclamation points.

> The writer put exclamation points at the end of each of these sentences. The exclamation point helps you know that these characters are using strong voices that show something is exciting or surprising. Let's read the words like the characters. I'll be the wolf and you be the pigs.

- As you read and role-play, encourage children to use a strong voice.
- Show pages 5 and 6 of *The Three Billy Goats Gruff*.

> The goat crossing the bridge makes this sound: *Trip, trap! Trip, trap!* Why do you think the writer added exclamation points to the end?

- After a brief discussion, have children stand up and *trip, trap* like the goat, using a strong voice to say the words as they do. If you wish, add highlighter tape to the exclamation points.

Have a Try

Invite children to add exclamation points to sentences.

> What exciting sentence could we write?

▶ Write the sentence on chart paper.

> Who can add an exclamation point to this sentence?

▶ Read the sentence together as you point under the words. Emphasize using a strong voice. Repeat with several more sentences.

Summarize and Apply

Help children summarize the lesson. During writing time, remind children to add exclamation points to show excitement or surprise.

> When do you use an exclamation point?

▶ Write the principle at the top of the chart.

> When you are writing, look for words or sentences that tell something exciting or surprising. Write an exclamation point at the end of those words or sentences.

Use an exclamation point to show something exciting or surprising.

I lost a tooth!

Oh, no, it's raining!

Kaboom!

Confer

▶ During independent writing, move around the room to confer briefly with as many individual children as time allows. Sit side by side with them and invite them to talk about using punctuation in their writing. Use the following prompts as needed.

- *What are you writing about today?*
- *Is there a sentence about something exciting or surprising?*
- *Where will you put the exclamation point?*
- *I will draw an exclamation point at the end lightly. You can trace over it.*

Share

Following independent writing, gather children in the meeting area to talk about their writing.

> Who would like to share what you wrote today?

> Do you have any exciting or surprising sentences? Did you put an exclamation point at the end?

Assessment

After you have taught the minilessons in this umbrella, observe children as they write. Use *The Literacy Continuum* (Fountas and Pinnell 2017) to notice, teach for, and support children's learning as you observe their attempts at reading and writing.

▶ What evidence do you have of new understandings children have developed related to punctuation?

- Do children understand the use of periods, question marks, and exclamation points?

- What evidence is there that children can use vocabulary related to punctuation, such as *writing*, *sentence*, *period*, *question*, *question mark*, *exclamation point*, *exciting*, and *surprising*?

▶ In what ways, beyond the scope of this umbrella, are children understanding the purpose of punctuation?

- Do they show an interest in using a variety of punctuation in their own writing?

Use your observations to determine the next umbrella you will teach. You may also consult Suggested Sequence of Lessons (pp. 483–494) for guidance.

EXTENSIONS FOR LEARNING ABOUT PUNCTUATION

▶ Teach minilessons that relate to punctuation marks that children notice while reading. If you use *The Reading Minilessons Book, Kindergarten* (Fountas and Pinnell 2019), see SAS.U3: Maintaining Fluency.

▶ Make a survey for the morning question and have children add the question marks each day. (See IW.13: Taking a Survey.)

▶ Working with small groups, write the same sentence three times (e.g., *That dog is mine*), each with a different punctuation mark at the end. Read the sentences. Then have children talk in the small group about how the sentence changes meaning depending on which punctuation mark is used.

▶ As you read with children, encourage them to notice periods, question marks, and exclamation points and talk about the writer's intention in choosing each type of end mark.

Minilessons in This Umbrella

WML1 Draw and write when you play market.

WML2 Draw and write when you play blocks.

WML3 Draw and write when you play post office.

WML4 Draw and write when you play restaurant.

Before Teaching Umbrella 7 Minilessons

These minilessons demonstrate how play can inspire drawing and writing, so we recommend that you teach a lesson before you send the children off to play and work in the classroom centers rather than before independent writing time.

These lessons are not meant to be taught consecutively; instead, teach each lesson when you convert the play corner into a new setting (e.g., store, post office, restaurant). Use children's background knowledge, picture books, and class-made books to generate ideas for children to draw and write as they play. Some suggestions from *Fountas & Pinnell Classroom™ Interactive Read-Aloud Collection* text sets and class-created writing from interactive writing lessons are below.

Interactive Read-Aloud Collection

Letters at Work: The Alphabet

On Market Street by Arnold Lobel

Living and Working Together: Community

My Steps by Sally Derby

Lola at the Library by Anna McQuinn

Grace Lin: Exploring Family and Culture

Dim Sum for Everyone!

Interactive Writing Lessons

IW.4: Making a Menu

IW.7: Writing a Thank You Card

IW.16: Making Signs

IW.23: Writing a Letter About a Book

Interactive Read-Aloud
The Alphabet

Community

Grace Lin

Interactive Writing

WML1

Writing Minilesson Principle
Draw and write when you play market.

Learning to Draw and Write Through Play

You Will Need

- a familiar book that relates to a market, such as *On Market Street* by Arnold Lobel, from Text Set: Letters at Work: The Alphabet
- the class menu from IW.4: Making a Menu
- chart paper and markers
- To download the following online resource for this lesson, visit **resources.fountasandpinnell.com**:
  - chart art (optional)

Academic Language / Important Vocabulary

- draw
- write
- play
- store
- market
- groceries

Continuum Connection

- Draw and write, extracting ideas from particular environments: e.g., restaurants, house, shops, doctor's office (p. 248)
- Engage in dramatic play (p. 331)
- Engage in dramatic dialogue in play or role-playing contexts (p. 331)
- Recognize and name letters in the environment (signs, labels, etc.) (p. 365)

GOAL

Use background experience and knowledge of environmental print to think of ways to draw and write when playing market or store.

RATIONALE

When children incorporate drawing and writing into play, they learn that writing is used for everyday purposes, such as creating signs at a grocery store or making a shopping list.

ASSESS LEARNING

- Observe whether children are talking about ways people use drawing and writing at a store.
- Look for evidence that children are drawing and writing as they play store.
- Observe for evidence that children can use vocabulary such as *draw*, *write*, *play*, *store*, *market*, and *groceries*.

MINILESSON

Before teaching this lesson, share books about supermarkets or stores and convert the play corner into a store by adding props (e.g., pretend food, food containers, cash register, play money, shopping baskets, grocery bags, boxes, scale). Also teach IW.4: Making a Menu. Teach a lesson to help children think about what they can draw and write as they play store. Here is an example.

- Show a few pages with items you find in a market from *On Market Street*.

  What are some things you might see at the store when you go shopping for food?

- Have children use their prior experiences to describe shopping at a grocery store. Guide the children to talk about items they see and some different words for a market (e.g., store, supermarket, grocery store).

- Show the menu from IW.4.

  Here is the menu we made for the restaurant at a market. What other drawings and words do you see in a store?

- Record children's ideas on chart paper. Support the conversation to help children think of multiple ways they might see drawing and writing on a visit to the supermarket (e.g., produce names, prices, departments, store hours, shopping lists).

Have a Try

Invite children to turn and talk about drawing and writing when playing store.

> Turn and talk to your partner about what you might draw and write when you play in the market.

▶ Ask a few volunteers to share. Add new ideas to the chart.

Summarize and Apply

Summarize the lesson. Remind children that they can write and draw when they play.

▶ Write the principle on the chart and read it aloud.

> Remember that you can draw and write when you play. If you play in the market today, you might make some signs or write a shopping list. If you play in another center, you might also want to do some drawing and writing.

Confer

▶ During choice time, move around the room to confer briefly with as many individual children as time allows. Sit side by side with them and invite them to talk about what they are writing or could write when they play. Use the following prompts as needed.

- *How will people know if the store is open? You could make a sign.*
- *What would a sign for these grocery items look like?*
- *What can you add to your shopping list?*

Share

Invite children to the meeting area to share their drawing and writing.

> What did you draw and write today?

> Did anyone do some drawing and writing for the market?

Writing Minilesson Principle
Draw and write when you play blocks.

You Will Need

- several books about communities, such as the following from Text Set: Living and Working Together: Community
  - *My Steps* by Sally Derby
  - *Lola at the Library* by Anna McQuinn
- the class writing from IW.16: Making Signs
- chart paper and markers
- To download the following online resource for this lesson, visit **resources.fountasandpinnell.com**:
  - chart art (optional)

Academic Language / Important Vocabulary

- neighborhood
- town
- city
- blocks

Continuum Connection

- Draw and write, extracting ideas from particular environments: e.g., restaurants, house, shops, doctor's office (p. 248)
- Engage in dramatic play (p. 331)
- Engage in dramatic dialogue in play or role-playing contexts (p. 331)
- Recognize and name letters in the environment (signs, labels, etc.) (p. 365)

GOAL

Use background experience and knowledge of environmental print to think of ways to draw and write when playing blocks.

RATIONALE

By infusing drawing and writing when they build imaginary towns, children can experiment with how drawing and writing is used in the real world.

ASSESS LEARNING

- Look for evidence that children are thinking and talking about ways people use drawing and writing in a town or city.
- Notice whether children draw and write when they play with blocks.
- Observe for evidence that children can use vocabulary such as *neighborhood*, *town*, *city*, and *blocks*.

MINILESSON

This minilesson uses a neighborhood as a context for building with blocks, but any setting could be used. Before the lesson, share books about communities, neighborhoods, and buildings. Add props to the block area that could be used in a town or city, such as figures of people and toy cars. You might also take a walk around the neighborhood and/or teach IW.16: Making Signs. Here is a sample lesson to help children think about what they can draw and write as they build with blocks.

- Show a few pages from *My Steps* and *Lola at the Library* and the class-made signs from IW.16.

  > The people in these books are outside in their communities. They might see many buildings and signs like these signs we made. What are some of the things people might see when they walk or drive around their neighborhoods? (What did we see when we walked around the neighborhood?)

- Support the conversation, guiding children to brainstorm several buildings, landmarks, and signs in the area around the school or their homes. Extend their thinking to talk about what they might see in a city or town.

  > You have been using blocks to make buildings and things you see in the neighborhood. Think about what words and drawings you might add in the city or town you are building.

- Encourage children to express their ideas, and support the conversation so they understand there are many uses for drawings and words (e.g., to identify and label buildings, make street signs, indicate construction, warn of a railroad crossing). Record their ideas on chart paper.

Have a Try

▶ Invite children to talk to a partner about drawing and writing while using blocks.

> Turn and talk to your partner about what you might draw and write when you make things in the neighborhood with blocks.

▶ Ask several volunteers to share. Add new ideas to the chart.

Summarize and Apply

Summarize the learning. Remind children that they can write and draw when they play.

▶ Write the principle on the chart and read it aloud.

> Remember that you can draw and write when you play. If you play with blocks today, you can make signs or you can write about what you made. If you play in another center, you might also want to do some drawing and writing.

Confer

▶ During choice time, move around the room to confer briefly with as many individual children as time allows. Sit side by side with them and invite them to talk about what they are writing or could write when they play. Use the following prompts as needed to encourage drawing and writing.

- *Talk about each place you made. You can label all the places.*
- *What things do people do in this building? You can draw and write about that.*
- *You made a town from blocks. You can make a sign for each place.*

Share

Invite children to the meeting area to share their drawing and writing.

> Who would like to share the drawing and writing you did today?

> Did anyone draw and write when you played with blocks? Tell about that.

WML3

EWR.U7.WML3

Writing Minilesson Principle
Draw and write when you play post office.

Learning to Draw and Write Through Play

You Will Need

- several examples of letters, possibly made by the children, as in these lessons:
  - EWR.U8: Writing a Friendly Letter
  - IW.7: Writing a Thank You Card
  - IW.23: Writing a Letter About a Book
- chart paper and markers
- To download the following online resource for this lesson, visit **resources.fountasandpinnell.com**:
  - chart art (optional)

Academic Language / Important Vocabulary

- draw
- write
- play
- post office

Continuum Connection

- Draw and write, extracting ideas from particular environments: e.g., restaurants, house, shops, doctor's office (p. 248)
- Engage in dramatic play (p. 331)
- Engage in dramatic dialogue in play or role-playing contexts (p. 331)
- Recognize and name letters in the environment (signs, labels, etc.) (p. 365)

GOAL

Use background experience and knowledge of environmental print to think of ways to draw and write when playing post office.

RATIONALE

Through play, children learn that writing is an important part of everyday life. Playing post office provides numerous natural opportunities for children to explore drawing and writing and to learn vocabulary related to the post office.

ASSESS LEARNING

- Look for evidence that children think about ways people use drawing and writing at the post office.
- Observe whether children draw and write as they play post office.
- Observe for evidence that children can use vocabulary such as *draw*, *write*, *play*, and *post office*.

MINILESSON

The play corner can be transformed into a post office at any time by adding props (e.g., note cards, envelopes, boxes, tape, scales, mailboxes), but it is especially meaningful after children have learned to write letters. (See EWR.U8: Writing a Friendly Letter; IW.7: Writing a Thank You Card; IW.23: Writing a Letter About a Book). Before teaching this lesson, share books about the post office and letters. If possible, visit a post office. Here is an example to help children think about what to draw and write as they play post office.

- Show a few examples of letters, preferably ones that the class has made.

  If you wanted to mail a letter to someone, what would you need to do?

- Support the conversation by placing one of the letters in an envelope, addressing the envelope, adding a stamp, taking it to the play corner post office, and putting it in the mailbox.

  Sometimes we write letters, notes, and invitations and mail them at the post office. Have you ever been to a post office? What do you know about the post office?

  What are some words and pictures you might see at a post office?

- Guide children to understand that there are many examples of pictures and writing in the post office and that they have a purpose (e.g., letters, labels for packages, stamps, names on mailboxes, name tags on postal workers). Record their ideas on chart paper.

Have a Try

▶ Invite children to talk to a partner about drawing and writing while playing post office.

> **What can you draw and write when you play post office? Turn and talk about that.**

▶ Ask several volunteers to share. Add new ideas to the chart.

Summarize and Apply

Summarize the lesson. Remind children that they can write and draw when they play.

▶ Write the principle on the chart and read it aloud.

> **Remember that you can draw and write when you play. If you play post office today, you could make any of the ideas on the chart or something else. If you play in another center, you might also want to do some drawing and writing.**

Confer

▶ During choice time, move around the room to confer briefly with as many individual children as time allows. Sit side by side with them and invite them to talk about what they are writing or what they could write when they play. Use the following prompts as needed to encourage drawing and writing.

- *What will you write on the label for this package?*
- *You can write some letters when you play post office. Who will you write to? What will you say?*
- *When you walk into the post office, what pictures and words do you see?*

Share

Invite children to the meeting area to share their drawing and writing.

> **Who would like to share the drawing and writing you did today?**

> **Did anyone draw and write at the post office? Tell about that.**

WML 4

EWR.U7.WML4

Writing Minilesson Principle
Draw and write when you play restaurant.

Learning to Draw and Write Through Play

You Will Need

- a familiar book that shows a restaurant, such as *Dim Sum for Everyone!* by Grace Lin, from Text Set: Grace Lin: Exploring Family and Culture
- the menu from IW.4: Making a Menu
- chart paper and markers
- To download the following online resource for this lesson, visit **resources.fountasandpinnell.com**:
  - chart art (optional)

Academic Language / Important Vocabulary

- draw
- write
- play
- restaurant
- food
- order

Continuum Connection

- Draw and write, extracting ideas from particular environments: e.g., restaurants, house, shops, doctor's office (p. 248)
- Engage in dramatic play (p. 331)
- Engage in dramatic dialogue in play or role-playing contexts (p. 331)
- Recognize and name letters in the environment (signs, labels, etc.) (p. 365)

GOAL

Use background experience and knowledge of environmental print to think of ways to draw and write when playing restaurant.

RATIONALE

Some children have background information related to restaurants and can make connections as they play. When you guide them to include drawing and writing when they play restaurant, they learn to use drawing and writing for real-world purposes.

ASSESS LEARNING

- Observe whether children are talking about ways people use drawing and writing related to restaurants.
- Look for evidence that children draw and write as they play restaurant.
- Observe for evidence that children can use vocabulary such as *draw*, *write*, *play*, *restaurant*, *food*, and *order*.

MINILESSON

Prior to teaching this lesson, share books about restaurants and transform the play corner into a restaurant by adding props (e.g., dining tables and chairs, tableware, menus, play food, order pads, play money, chef's clothing). Also teach IW.4: Making a Menu. Teach a lesson to help children think about what they can draw and write as they play restaurant. Here is an example.

- Show several pages from *Dim Sum for Everyone!*

   This family is enjoying eating at a restaurant. Have you ever been to a restaurant? What do you know about going out to eat at a restaurant?

- Show the class-made menu from IW.4.

   What kinds of food do you like to order from a menu?

   Where else can you see words and pictures at a restaurant?

- As children respond, make a list on chart paper of their ideas. Guide the conversation so children discuss the many instances when writing and drawing are used in restaurants (e.g., hours of operation, order pads, reservations list, name tags for employees, shopping list).

Have a Try

Invite children to talk to a partner about drawing and writing while playing restaurant.

> Turn and talk to your partner about what you might draw and write when you play restaurant.

▶ Ask a few volunteers to share. Add new ideas to the chart.

Summarize and Apply

Summarize the lesson. Remind children that they can write and draw when they play.

▶ Write the principle on the chart and read it aloud.

> Remember that you can draw and write when you play. If you play restaurant today, you could make any of the ideas on the chart or something else. If you play in another center, you might also want to do some drawing and writing.

Draw and write when you play restaurant.

Labels

Hours — OPEN 11:30 A.M. – 8:00 P.M.

Menu — MENU Eggs and Toast Pancakes Oatmeal

Order pad — Order

Confer

▶ During choice time, move around the room to confer briefly with as many individual children as time allows. Sit side by side with them and invite them to talk about what they are writing or could write when they play. Use the following prompts as needed to encourage drawing and writing.

- *What will you draw and write on the menu for your restaurant?*
- *What type of food do you cook at this restaurant? You can make labels for the food.*
- *How will you remember what people order? You can make a list of the food they want to eat.*

Share

Invite children to the meeting area to share their drawing and writing.

> Who would like to share the drawing and writing you did today?

> Did anyone draw and write at the restaurant today? Tell about that.

Assessment

After you have taught the minilessons in this umbrella, observe children as they draw and write during play. Use *The Literacy Continuum* (Fountas and Pinnell 2017) to notice, teach for, and support children's learning as you observe their attempts at drawing and writing.

> ▶ What evidence do you have of new understandings children have developed related to drawing and writing through play?
>   - Are children thinking of ideas to draw or write when they play?
>   - Are they making attempts at writing letters and words?
>   - Do they draw and write independently while playing?
>   - Are they using vocabulary such as *store*, *neighborhood*, *city*, *town*, *blocks*, *post office*, and *restaurant*?

Use your observations to determine the next umbrella you will teach. You may also consult Suggested Sequence of Lessons (pp. 483–494) for guidance.

EXTENSIONS FOR LEARNING TO DRAW AND WRITE THROUGH PLAY

▶ When you see evidence that children are ready for a change in the play corner, transform the area into a new setting, such as a bakery or a veterinary hospital. Talk with them using new vocabulary related to each environment.

▶ Introduce seasonal fun (as appropriate to your setting) into the play corner by converting it into a winter wonderland, a spring garden, or a summer beach setting. As children play, they might write about either their imaginary play or the real-life things they do during each season.

▶ Have children draw and write in the classroom library. Arrange it so they can check out books. Children can write about the books they read or role-play the part of librarian and write book recommendations.

▶ When the children are using blocks, provide clipboards and graph paper so they can make blueprints to plan what to build. When the block cities or towns are finished, you can take pictures so that children can make a how-to book to explain how they constructed the city or town.

▶ Encourage children to write about other things they do during play on the playground, in other areas of the school, or outside of school.

Minilessons in This Umbrella

WML1 Write a letter to someone.

WML2 Write your name and the name of the person you are writing to in a letter.

WML3 Write important information in a letter.

Interactive Read-Aloud
Lois Ehlert

Interactive Writing

Before Teaching Umbrella 8 Minilessons

Prior to teaching these minilessons, teach both IW.7: Writing a Thank You Card and IW.23: Writing a Letter About a Book. You will use the class-made letters from those interactive writing lessons for this umbrella. If you are using *The Reading Minilessons Book, Kindergarten* (Fountas and Pinnell 2019), it would also be helpful to teach WAR.U6.RML4 (Write a letter to share your thinking about a book). You may choose the following from *Fountas & Pinnell Classroom™ Interactive Read-Aloud Collection*, or you might use other texts that have examples of letters.

Interactive Read-Aloud Collection

Lois Ehlert: Bringing Color and Texture to Life

Mole's Hill: A Woodland Tale by Lois Ehlert

Interactive Writing Lessons

IW.7: Writing a Thank You Card

IW.23: Writing a Letter About a Book

As you read and enjoy these mentor texts together, help children

- notice details in the letters, and
- notice the different reasons why people write letters.

Writing Minilesson Principle
Write a letter to someone.

You Will Need

- several mentor texts that show a sample letter, such as the following:
  - *Mole's Hill* by Lois Ehlert, from Text Set: Lois Ehlert: Bringing Color and Texture to Life
  - class letter from IW.7: Writing a Thank You Card
  - class letter from IW.23: Writing a Letter About a Book
- chart paper and markers
- To download the following online resource for this lesson, visit **resources.fountasandpinnell.com**:
  - chart art (optional)

Academic Language / Important Vocabulary

- friendly letter
- invite
- thanks
- information
- opinion

Continuum Connection

- Understand that written communication can be used for different purposes: e.g., to give information, to invite, to give thanks (p. 244)
- Write with a specific purpose in mind (p. 244)
- Write notes, cards, invitations, and emails to others (p. 244)

GOAL

Understand the reasons people write letters.

RATIONALE

When children understand why people write letters, they begin to think about what they could write in a letter and to understand that they can write with purpose and authenticity.

ASSESS LEARNING

- Notice evidence that children realize that letters can be written for a variety of purposes.
- Observe for evidence that children can use vocabulary such as *friendly letter*, *invite*, *thanks*, *information*, and *opinion*.

MINILESSON

Prior to teaching this lesson, provide experiences for children to engage with a variety of types of letters. To help them plan and begin writing letters independently, provide a brief lesson to think about why people write friendly letters. Here is an example.

- Review pages 7–8 of *Mole's Hill*.

  Think about this letter that Fox writes to Mole. Turn and talk about why you think Fox wrote the letter.

- After time for a brief discussion, guide children in a conversation to ensure they understand Fox's purpose. Then restate the reason for the letter along with a definition of *friendly letter*.

  This letter is an invitation. Fox and friends are inviting Mole to a meeting at the maple tree.

- Begin a list on chart paper of reasons why people write letters.
- Revisit the letter from IW.7: Writing a Thank You Card.

  What is the reason that this letter was written?

- Add to the list.
- Continue with several other letter examples, adding to the list as children identify other reasons for writing letters.

  When you write to someone you know, you might tell something about yourself or ask how the person is doing. The letter is called a friendly letter.

Have a Try

Invite children to turn and talk about an idea they have for writing a letter.

> Think about why you might write a letter. Turn and tell your partner.

▸ After time for discussion, ask a few children to share. Add new ideas to the chart.

Summarize and Apply

Write the principle on the top of the chart. Have children choose an idea and begin writing a letter during independent writing time.

> During writing time, choose a reason for writing a letter. You may also begin writing if you are ready. Look back at the chart if you need ideas. Bring your writing to share when we meet later.

Write a letter to someone.

- Invite to an event

- Say thank you

- Tell some news about yourself

- Ask how your friend is

- Share an opinion

- Give information

- Email to say hi

Confer

▸ During independent writing, move around the room to confer briefly with as many individual children as time allows. Sit side by side with them and invite them to talk about their letters. Use the following prompts as needed.

- *What is your letter about?*
- *What would you like to say in your letter?*
- *Let's look at the chart for some ideas.*

Share

Following independent writing, gather children in the meeting area to share their letters.

> Who would like to share what you wrote today?

> How did you decide what to write?

Section 6: Exploring Early Writing

Write your name and the name of the person you are writing to in a letter.

Writing a Friendly Letter

You Will Need

- several mentor texts that show a sample letter, such as the following:
  - *Mole's Hill* by Lois Ehlert, from Text Set: Lois Ehlert: Bringing Color and Texture to Life
  - class letter from IW.7: Writing a Thank You Card
  - class letter from IW.23: Writing a Letter About a Book
- projector (optional)
- highlighter tape

Academic Language / Important Vocabulary

- friendly letter
- name

Continuum Connection

- Understand that the sender and the receiver must be clearly shown (p. 244)
- Understand how to learn about writing notes, cards, and invitations by noticing the characteristics of examples (p. 244)

GOAL

Understand that the sender and receiver must be clearly shown in a letter.

RATIONALE

When children learn how to write friendly letters by looking at examples, they will include important details in the letters they write, such as the names of the sender and receiver.

ASSESS LEARNING

- Notice evidence that children understand that both the sender's name and the receiver's name must be included in a friendly letter.
- Observe whether children are including the names of the sender and the receiver in the letters they write.
- Look for evidence that children can use vocabulary such as *friendly letter* and *name*.

MINILESSON

To help children understand that letters include the names of both the sender and the receiver, provide a brief interactive lesson that uses model letters. Here is an example.

- Show pages 7–8 of *Mole's Hill*. Read the greeting, pointing under each word as you do.

  > This letter from Fox to Mole starts with *Dear Mole.* Why do you think Fox started the letter in this way?

- Read and point to the signature line.

  > Fox ends this letter by writing *Fox Skunk Raccoon.* Why do you think Fox ends the letter in this way?

- Engage children in a conversation to help them identify that the letter opens by telling the person to whom the letter is written. It closes with the person the letter is from.

- Show the class letter from IW.7.

  > What do you notice about the way this letter begins and ends?

- Use highlighter tape to assist children in noticing that the receiver's name is at the beginning and the sender's name is at the end. Help them recognize where each name is placed on the page.

- Repeat with the class letter from IW.23.

Have a Try

Invite children to turn and talk about including names in a friendly letter.

> Turn and talk about what names you will include in the friendly letter you are writing.

▶ After time for a brief discussion, ask a few children to share whose names they will include. Ask them to identify where they will write the names on the page.

Summarize and Apply

Summarize the lesson. Have children include their name and the name of the person they are writing to in the friendly letter they are working on.

> During writing time, write a friendly letter. Write the name of the person you are writing to at the beginning. Write your name at the end. Bring your letter to share when we meet later.

Write your name and the name of the person you are writing to in a letter.

Dear Ms. Adamu,

Thank you for helping us learn to paint and draw. It was fun to paint the pictures for the pumpkin party.

From,

Mr. Sousa's Class

Confer

▶ During independent writing, move around the room to confer briefly with as many individual children as time allows. Sit side by side with them and invite them to talk about their letters. Use the following prompts as needed.

- *Show me where you will write your name on your letter.*
- *Whom are you writing to? Where will that name go?*
- *Why is it important to include names in your friendly letter?*

Share

Following independent writing, gather children in the meeting area.

▶ Ask children to share their experiences writing friendly letters.

> Whose names did you include in your friendly letter? Show where you wrote the names on the page.

Writing Minilesson Principle
Write important information in a letter.

Writing a Friendly Letter

You Will Need

- several mentor texts that show a sample letter, such as the following:
  - *Mole's Hill* by Lois Ehlert, from Text Set: Lois Ehlert: Bringing Color and Texture to Life
  - class letter from IW.7: Writing a Thank You Card
  - class letter from IW.23: Writing a Letter About a Book
- highlighter tape

Academic Language / Important Vocabulary

- friendly letter
- important
- information

Continuum Connection

- Include important information in the communication (p. 244)
- Understand how to learn about writing notes, cards, and invitations by noticing the characteristics of examples (p. 244)

GOAL

Understand that you write important information in a letter.

RATIONALE

When children learn to include important information in a friendly letter, they will think about a letter's purpose and include important details as they write their own friendly letters.

ASSESS LEARNING

- Notice evidence that children understand that friendly letters include important details.
- Observe whether children add relevant details to their friendly letters.
- Look for evidence that children can use vocabulary such as *friendly letter*, *important*, and *information*.

MINILESSON

To help children understand that letters include important information, provide a brief interactive lesson that uses model letters. Here is an example.

- Show pages 7–8 of *Mole's Hill*. Revisit the body of the letter.

  > Fox wrote his letter to invite his friends to meet. What important information did Fox include in this letter he wrote to Mole?

  > What if Fox forgot to write where his friends should meet?

- Engage children in a conversation to help them recognize that Fox wrote a letter to invite his friends to meet and included important information, including where and when to meet.

- Show and revisit the class letter from IW.7.

  > We wrote a letter to thank Ms. Adamu. What important information did we put in the letter?

- As children discuss, add highlighter tape to key words. This will help children identify and recognize the important information that is included in the letter.

Have a Try

Invite children to turn and talk about including important information in a friendly letter.

▶ Show and revisit the class letter from IW.23.

Turn and talk about what important information is included in this letter.

▶ After time for a brief discussion, ask a few volunteers to share ideas. Use highlighter tape to emphasize important information.

Summarize and Apply

Summarize the lesson. Remind children to include important information in the friendly letters they are working on.

During writing time, you can work on your friendly letter. Think about the important information you want to write in your letter. Bring your letter to share when we meet later.

> Write important information in a letter.
>
> Dear Ms. Adamu,
>
> Thank you for helping us learn to paint and draw. It was fun to paint the pictures for the pumpkin party.
>
> From,
>
> Mr. Sousa's Class

Confer

▶ During independent writing, move around the room to confer briefly with as many individual children as time allows. Sit side by side with them and invite them to talk about their letters. Use the following prompts as needed.

- *What are you writing about in your letter?*
- *What information would you like to include in your friendly letter?*
- *Let's talk about what words you can use to write the important information.*
- *Reread your letter to be sure that you gave all the information.*

Share

Following independent writing, gather children in the meeting area. Ask several children to share what their friendly letters are about.

What important information did you write in your friendly letter?

Assessment

After you have taught the minilessons in this umbrella, observe children as they write letters. Use *The Literacy Continuum* (Fountas and Pinnell 2017) to notice, teach for, and support children's learning as you observe their attempts at reading and writing.

▶ What evidence do you have of new understandings children have developed related to writing friendly letters?

- Do they understand reasons for letter writing?

- Are they including names in the letters they write?

- Do children include important information in friendly letters?

- What evidence is there that children can use vocabulary related to writing a friendly letter, such as *friendly letter*, *invite*, *thanks*, *information*, *opinion*, and *important*?

▶ In what ways, beyond the scope of this umbrella, are children engaging in purposeful writing?

- Do they show an interest in writing notes and making cards?

- Are they thinking about different ways to share their thoughts and express their opinions when they write to others?

Use your observations to determine the next umbrella you will teach. You may also consult Suggested Sequence of Lessons (pp. 483–494) for guidance.

EXTENSIONS FOR WRITING A FRIENDLY LETTER

▶ In small groups, engage children in the interactive writing of a thank you letter to a member of the school staff.

▶ Children can write letters to families to invite them to an upcoming class event.

▶ Have children write a letter to another class to share their opinion about a book.

▶ Use a small journal to write notes in letter format back and forth to individual students.

▶ Assist as children write an email to a family member.

Writing Process

CHILDREN LEARN TO write by writing. As they write, they engage in some aspect of the writing process. They plan what to write, make a draft and make changes to improve it, check their work to be sure others can read it, and publish it by sharing it with an audience. Not all aspects of the writing process will happen at one time, and they won't always happen in the same order. Writers tend to move back and forth. But over time, each writer will experience the full writing process. The lessons in this section will help you guide the children in your class through the writing process.

7   Writing Process

Planning and Rehearsing

Drafting and Revising

Editing and Proofreading

Publishing

Minilessons in This Umbrella

WML1 Get ideas from things you collect.

WML2 Look at the class story charts.

WML3 Get ideas from other writers.

WML4 Go back to ideas you love.

Before Teaching Umbrella 1 Minilessons

We recommend teaching STR.U1: Storytelling before teaching these minilessons. You do not need to teach the minilessons in this umbrella consecutively. Rather, they can be used whenever you feel the children need some writing inspiration.

Give children plenty of opportunities to write and draw freely and without constraints. Read and discuss simple books from a variety of genres that the children will enjoy. Use the following texts from *Fountas & Pinnell Classroom™ Interactive Read-Aloud Collection*, or choose books from your classroom library.

Interactive Read-Aloud Collection

Eric Carle: Exploring the Natural World

From Head to Toe

Does a Kangaroo Have a Mother, Too?

"Slowly, Slowly, Slowly," said the Sloth

Have You Seen My Cat?

The Mixed-Up Chameleon

Interactive Writing Lessons

IW.20: Writing an Alternative Ending

As you read and enjoy books together, help children

- discuss, whenever possible, how the author got the idea for the book (using the author's note, if applicable),

- notice when an author writes repeatedly about the same topic, idea, or characters, and

- talk about their own ideas for writing about a similar topic or theme.

Interactive Read-Aloud
Eric Carle

Interactive Writing

Writing Minilesson Principle
Get ideas from things you collect.

Getting Ideas for Writing

You Will Need

- several interesting objects
- Me Box for each child (see STR.U1.WML4) or objects to write about
- chart paper and markers

Academic Language/ Important Vocabulary

- idea
- collect
- writing

Continuum Connection

- Generate and expand ideas through talk with peers and teacher (p. 248)
- Understand that writers gather information for their writing: e.g., objects, books, photos, sticky notes, etc. (p. 248)
- Observe carefully before writing about a person, animal, object, place, action (p. 248)

GOAL

Understand that writers can get ideas from collected objects that are connected to important ideas or memories.

RATIONALE

When children learn that they can get ideas for writing from collected objects, they are likely to write about things that are meaningful and important to them. They will therefore have the motivation and confidence to continue their writing journey.

ASSESS LEARNING

- Notice whether children get ideas for their writing from collected objects.
- Look at children's drawing and writing. What details about the objects do they include?
- Observe for evidence that children can use vocabulary such as *idea*, *collect*, and *writing*.

MINILESSON

To help children think about the minilesson principle, demonstrate writing about an object. Here is an example.

- Show several objects that are meaningful to you.

  I remember a story about each of these objects. I bet these objects can give me a lot of ideas for my writing.

- Pick up one of the objects (for example, a dried flower, a second-place ribbon, a knickknack). Look at it carefully. Then discuss your ideas for writing about it.

  Here's a dried flower from my grandmother's garden. I could write a poem about what it looks like, or I could write about the colors in the garden. It also makes me remember planting flowers with her. I'm going to write about that.

- Describe what you are thinking as you write a little story about planting flowers.

Have a Try

Invite children to talk to a partner about their ideas for writing.

> Look at the objects in your Me Box. You told stories about some of them. You can write the stories that you tell. What ideas do they give you for writing? Turn and talk to your partner to share your ideas.

> ▶ After children turn and talk, invite a few children to share their ideas with the class.

Summarize and Apply

Write the principle at the top of the chart. Read it to children. Summarize the learning and remind children to think about objects they collect to get ideas for writing.

> Today during writing time, try writing about one of the objects in your Me Box, or you could write about a different object. For example, there might be a special object that you have collected. Bring your writing to share when we meet later.

Get ideas from things you collect.

When I was a young girl, I helped my grandmother in her garden.

We planted beautiful roses and lilies.

It was so much fun to see things grow!

Confer

> ▶ During independent writing, move around the room to confer briefly with as many individual children as time allows. Sit side by side with them and invite them to talk about their ideas for writing. Use prompts such as the following if needed.

> • *What object would you like to write about?*
> • *What ideas does that object give you?*
> • *What does it make you think about?*
> • *Do you have any special memories of a _____ ?*

Share

Following independent writing, gather children in the meeting area to share their writing.

> What object did you write about today?

> What did you write about it?

Getting Ideas for Writing

You Will Need

- the charts created for STR.U1: Storytelling
- sticky notes
- markers
- the principle for this minilesson written on a strip of paper
- glue stick or tape

Academic Language/ Important Vocabulary

- story
- story chart
- idea
- writing

Continuum Connection

- Understand that writers may tell stories from their own lives (p. 244)
- Generate and expand ideas through talk with peers and teacher (p. 248)
- Understand that writers get help from other writers (p. 248)
- Think of what to work on next as a writer (p. 249)

GOAL

Understand that writers write stories that they have told and can get ideas from other people's stories.

RATIONALE

When children understand that they can write stories they have already told orally and get ideas from other people's stories, they have a greater repertoire of ideas to draw from for their writing.

ASSESS LEARNING

- Notice whether children get ideas from stories they have told or heard orally.
- Look at children's drawing and writing. Do they reflect the stories children have told?
- Observe for evidence that children can use vocabulary such as *story*, *story chart*, *idea*, and *writing*.

MINILESSON

Demonstrate how to use the class story charts (created for Telling Stories U1: Storytelling) to get ideas for writing.

- Display one of the story charts your class created.

    You can look at the story charts we made to get ideas for stories you can write. You can write down stories you have told aloud. Kinsley told us a story about playing the piano. She can write a book about that story, too!

    You can also get ideas from other people's stories. Your story doesn't have to be exactly the same. For example, Giana told a story about bathing her dog. That gives me an idea to write a story about a little girl who helps give her baby sister a bath.

Have a Try

Invite children to talk to a partner about their ideas for writing.

▶ Display another one of the story charts. (The example shown here is from STR.U1.WML4.) Read the story ideas aloud.

> **What ideas for writing do these stories give you? Turn and talk to your partner about your ideas.**

▶ After children turn and talk, invite a few children to share their ideas. Write them on sticky notes and add them to the chart.

Summarize and Apply

Attach the new principle over the old one. Read it to children. Summarize the learning and remind them to look at the class story charts to get ideas for writing.

> **During writing time today, you can look at the class story charts to get ideas for your writing.**
> **You can write down a story that you've told before, or you can get ideas from other people's stories.**

> Look at the class story charts.
>
> Carlos won an award.   A story about winning a race
>
> Yon found a penny.   A story about finding a hidden treasure
>
> Spencer saw an elephant at the zoo.
> A story about an elephant
>
> Rosa found a feather on a hike.
> A story about a pet bird

Confer

▶ During independent writing, move around the room to confer briefly with as many individual children as time allows. Sit side by side with them and invite them to talk about their story ideas. Use prompts such as the following if needed.

- *Let's look at the class story charts together.*
- *What ideas do the charts give you?*
- *Do you want to write down your story about _____?*
- *What does _____'s story make you think about? Has something similar ever happened to you?*

Share

Following independent writing, gather children in the meeting area.

> **Did anyone get an idea for writing from the class story charts today?**

Getting Ideas for Writing

You Will Need

- the text created during IW.20: Writing an Alternative Ending
- a few teacher- or child-created examples of books that were inspired in some way by another book (e.g., same topic or theme, same characters, same style)
- a book that you read aloud very recently
- chart paper and markers
- To download the online resource for this lesson, visit **resources.fountasandpinnell.com**:
  - chart art (optional)

Academic Language/ Important Vocabulary

- idea
- writer
- ending

Continuum Connection

- Understand that writers get help from other writers (p. 248)
- Understand that writers can learn how to write from other writers (p. 249)

GOAL

Understand that writers get ideas from other writers.

RATIONALE

When children understand the myriad of ways that writers can be inspired by other authors, they find it easier to decide what to write about and expand their writing to produce more complex texts.

ASSESS LEARNING

- Listen to children talk about their ideas for writing. Do they mention things that writers do that they can try in their own writing?
- Observe for evidence that children can use vocabulary such as *idea*, *writer*, and *ending*.

MINILESSON

Use mentor texts to engage children in a discussion about getting ideas from other writers and the various ways that writers can be inspired by each other.

- Show the class-created text from IW.20: Writing an Alternative Ending. Read it aloud.

   Where did we get the idea to write this?

   We got the idea from a story we read. We decided to write a different ending to the story. This is one way that you can get ideas for your writing from other writers.

- Start a list on chart paper of different ways to get ideas from other writers.
- Show one of the teacher- or child-created example books you selected (for example, a book about the same topic as a book your class read). Explain where you got the idea for the book, or ask the child who wrote it to explain.

   Books you read can give you ideas for your own stories. That's another way to get ideas from other writers.

- Add to the chart.
- Continue in a similar manner with a couple of other examples.

Have a Try

Invite children to talk to a partner about their ideas for writing.

▶ Show a book that you read aloud very recently. Briefly review the pages.

> What ideas does this book give you for your own writing? Turn and talk to your partner about your ideas.

▶ After children turn and talk, ask several children to share their ideas. Add to the chart if they suggest new ways of being inspired by an author.

Summarize and Apply

Write the principle at the top of the chart. Read it to children. Summarize the learning and remind them to think about books they have read when they are deciding what to write about.

> Today you noticed that you can get ideas from other writers in lots of different ways. When you are deciding what to write about today, think about books you have read. What ideas can you get from those books?

Get ideas from other writers.

- Write a different ending.

- Write about the same topic.

- Write about the same characters.

- Write in the same way.

- Make the pictures the same way.

Confer

▶ During independent writing, move around the room to confer briefly with as many individual children as time allows. Sit side by side with them and invite them to talk about their ideas for writing. Use prompts such as the following as needed.

- *What are you going to write about?*
- *What ideas does your favorite book give you for your own writing?*
- *Could you write a story that has the same characters doing something different?*
- *Is there something on the chart that makes you think of something in your own life?*

Share

Following independent writing, gather children in the meeting area.

> Did anyone get an idea for your writing from another writer?

> What did you write about? Where did you get that idea?

WML 4

WPS.U1.WML4

Writing Minilesson Principle
Go back to ideas you love.

Getting Ideas for Writing

You Will Need

- several familiar books by the same author, such as those in Text Set: Eric Carle: Exploring the Natural World
- a simple text you have written, such as the text created for WML1
- chart paper and markers

Academic Language/ Important Vocabulary

- writing
- idea

Continuum Connection

- Generate and expand ideas through talk with peers and teacher (p. 248)
- Look for ideas and topics in personal experiences, shared through talk (p. 248)
- Have ideas to tell, write, and draw about (p. 249)

GOAL

Understand that writers often return to the same idea or topic for different writing pieces.

RATIONALE

When children understand that they can write about the same idea or topic many times in different ways, they will find it easy to think of things to write about and will be motivated and excited to continue writing about their favorite topics.

ASSESS LEARNING

- Notice whether children write more than once about an idea or a topic.
- Observe for evidence that children can use vocabulary such as *writing* and *idea*.

MINILESSON

Use several books by the same author to demonstrate that authors can write about the same idea more than once.

- Show several books by Eric Carle (or another familiar author). Read the titles.

  We have read lots of books by Eric Carle. When you read a lot of books by the same person, you learn what he likes to write about. What do you think Eric Carle likes to write about?

  Eric Carle likes to write about animals. He has written lots of books about animals.

- Display the chart created for WML1 or another simple text you have written. Read it aloud.

  Remember when I wrote this? What did I write about?

  I love writing about flowers. I'm going to write something new now. Watch what I do.

- Talk about your thinking as you write another simple text about another aspect of the same topic. Read it aloud.

  How is this example the same as what I wrote before?

  How is it different?

  I wrote about flowers again because I love them. But instead of writing about planting flowers with my grandmother, I wrote about how to plant a flower. If there is something you love, you can write about it in different ways.

Have a Try

Invite children to talk to a partner about their ideas for writing.

> Think about something you've written about. What did you write about it? Could you write about it again in a different way? Turn and talk to your partner about your ideas.

Summarize and Apply

Write the principle at the top of the chart. Read it to children. Summarize the learning and remind children that they can return to ideas they love writing about.

> Today during writing time, you might want to go back to an idea you've written about before. You can write about the same idea or topic in a different way.

Confer

▶ During independent writing, move around the room to confer briefly with as many individual children as time allows. Sit side by side with them and invite them to talk about their ideas for writing. Use prompts such as the following as needed.

- *Let's look at some books you've already written.*
- *What did you write about in that book?*
- *Do you want to write about that again?*
- *How could you write about that idea in a different way?*

Share

Following independent writing, gather children in the meeting area to share their writing.

> Did anyone write about something you've written about before?

> What did you write this time?

Get ideas from things you collect

When I was a young girl, I helped my grandmother in her garden.
We planted beautiful roses and lilies.
It was so much fun to see things grow!

Go back to ideas you love.

How to Plant a Flower

1. Dig a hole.
2. Put a seed in the hole.
3. Cover the seed with dirt.
4. Water the seed.

Assessment

After you have taught the minilessons in this umbrella, observe children as they draw and write. Use the behaviors and understandings in *The Literacy Continuum* (Fountas and Pinnell 2017) to notice, teach for, and support children's learning as you observe their attempts at reading and writing.

▶ What evidence do you have of new understandings children have developed related to getting ideas for writing?

- Can children independently think of ideas for writing?
- Do they get ideas from things they collect?
- Do they look at the class story charts to get ideas for writing?
- Do they get ideas from other writers?
- Do they return to their favorite ideas or topics?
- What evidence is there that children can use vocabulary such as *idea*, *writing*, and *story*?

▶ In what other ways, beyond the scope of this umbrella, are children ready to expand their writing and illustrating skills?

- Are they ready to learn about revising (adding, reorganizing) their writing?
- Do they need support in drawing pictures?

Use your observations to determine the next umbrella you will teach. You may also consult Suggested Sequence of Lessons (pp. 483–494) for guidance.

EXTENSIONS FOR GETTING IDEAS FOR WRITING

▶ In the books you read aloud, look to see if the authors reveal where they got their ideas (for example, in an author's note). If so, share this information with the children.

▶ Invite children to bring in objects from home and use them as inspiration for writing.

▶ After reading aloud a book, invite children to write their own text that is inspired in some way by the book, for example, the same story with a different ending, the same characters in a different situation, or the same writing or illustration style.

Minilessons in This Umbrella

WML1 Add details to your drawings.

WML2 Use a caret to add a word.

WML3 Add a page to give more information.

Before Teaching Umbrella 2 Minilessons

Teaching these minilessons helps children progress in the writing process by expanding ideas for revising their writing. It is not necessary to teach these lessons consecutively. Instead, you might choose to teach them throughout the year as needed because revision is a high-level concept and children will need multiple exposures to these lessons.

Model the revising process for children so they understand how to look back at their work to find areas for improvement. Use a variety of picture books as examples to highlight how authors include only information that fits and to show that authors write their stories or information in an order that makes sense. Some suggestions from *Fountas & Pinnell Classroom™ Interactive Read-Aloud Collection* and *Shared Reading Collection*, plus interactive writing lessons, are below. You can also choose books from the classroom library that the children will enjoy.

Interactive Read-Aloud Collection

Living and Working Together: Community

My Steps by Sally Derby

Shared Reading Collection

City Kid, Country Kid by David Andrews

Interactive Writing Lessons

IW.8: Making a Class Big Book

IW.14: Writing About a Class Memory

As you read and enjoy these texts together, help children

- notice and talk about details in the illustrations,
- notice descriptive language, and
- discuss how the story evolves over the course of the book.

Interactive Read-Aloud
Community

Shared Reading

Interactive Writing

Adding to Writing

You Will Need

- a familiar picture book with detailed illustrations, such as *City Kid, Country Kid* by David Andrews, from *Shared Reading Collection*
- books the children have made
- chart paper and markers
- To download the following online resource, visit **resources.fountasandpinnell.com**:
  - chart art (optional)

Academic Language/ Important Vocabulary

- detail
- add
- illustration
- drawing

Continuum Connection

- Review a drawing to revise by adding (or deleting) information (p. 249)
- Add or remove details from drawings to plan, draft, revise work (p. 249)
- Add details to a drawing to give more information to the reader and to make the writing more interesting (p. 249)

GOAL

Understand that details in a drawing are important.

RATIONALE

By observing and discussing details in pictures, children learn that the details make a difference in what the reader understands about a story. Children learn that the details in their own pictures matter and that it is a good idea to look closely at them to decide if more details are needed.

ASSESS LEARNING

- Listen to children as they talk about their drawings. Do the drawings reflect what they say?
- Notice whether children are willing to revise (add details to) their drawings.
- Observe for evidence that children can use vocabulary such as *detail*, *add*, *illustration*, and *drawing*.

MINILESSON

To help children think about the minilesson principle, use a familiar picture book to engage children in a discussion about details in illustrations. Here is an example.

- Show the cover of *City Kid, Country Kid* and read the title. Show the illustration on page 2.

  Where does Luke live?

  What can you tell about the place where he lives?

  Luke lives in a big, noisy city with people, cars, and tall buildings. We know this because of the details in the picture. A detail is a small part of something.

- Turn to page 3.

  What details do you see in the illustration? What do they tell you?

  The illustration shows farm animals, so Rita lives in the country. Look at the words in the illustration. They are the sounds of the cows and the chickens that wake Rita in the morning.

- Turn to page 12.

  What is the weather like?

  What kinds of details do illustrators draw in their pictures to help you understand the story?

- Record children's responses on chart paper.

Have a Try

Invite children to talk to a partner about their own drawings.

▶ Have children look at a book they have already written or are currently working on.

> Look at your pictures. What details could you add to help people understand more about the story? Turn and talk to your partner about this.

Summarize and Apply

Summarize the learning and remind children to add details to their drawings.

▶ Write the principle at the top of the chart. Read it aloud.

> You talked to your partner about the details you could add to your drawings. Today during writing time, try to add some of the details you talked about. Bring your drawing to share when we meet later.

Add details to your drawings.

- Where
- Characters
- Sounds — Moo!
- Weather

Confer

▶ During independent writing, move around the room to confer briefly with as many individual children as time allows. Sit side by side with them and invite them to talk about adding details to their drawings. Use prompts such as the following as needed.

- *What did you draw on this page?*
- *What details could you add to help people learn more about that?*
- *Is there something in your story that you could add to your drawing?*
- *When you told me your story, you said _____. Can you draw that?*

Share

Following independent writing, gather children in the meeting area to share their drawings.

> Who would like to share the details you added to a drawing?

> Why did you add those details?

Writing Minilesson Principle
Use a caret to add a word.

Adding to Writing

You Will Need

- a familiar picture book with examples of descriptive language, such as *My Steps* by Sally Derby, from Text Set: Living and Working Together: Community

- the class writing from IW.14: Writing About a Class Memory

- books the children have made

- chart paper and markers

Academic Language/ Important Vocabulary

- caret
- add
- revising

Continuum Connection

- Add letters, words, phrases, or sentences using a caret, a strip of paper, or a sticky note (p. 249)

- Add words, phrases, or sentences to provide more information to readers (p. 249)

- Add words, phrases, or sentences to make the writing more interesting or exciting for readers (p. 249)

GOAL

Understand that writers can use a caret to add words as a way to make the writing more interesting or exciting.

RATIONALE

When children reread their writing and think about how their writing could be better, they are thinking like a writer. Teaching children to add or change words in their books is a revision strategy they will use as writers.

ASSESS LEARNING

- Notice whether children can elaborate on their stories orally and then transfer the oral elaboration to writing.

- Observe whether children understand how to use a caret to revise their writing.

- Look for evidence that children can use vocabulary such as *caret*, *add*, and *revising*.

MINILESSON

To help children think about the minilesson principle, demonstrate how to use a caret to revise a sentence. You might also teach children to use a strip of paper (a spider leg) to add words. Here is an example.

- Show the cover of *My Steps* and read the title. Read pages 11–12 aloud.

  What words does the author use to tell about the steps?

  The author uses *shady, cool, hard*, and *smooth*.

  How does the girl feel when she lies on the top step?

  The author wrote *shivery-cool*. I like that. That's more interesting than saying she felt cold. The words *shivery-cool* help me imagine how she feels.

  When you write books, reread what you wrote and think about revising it. When you add or change words to make your writing more interesting, you are revising.

- Display the class writing from IW.14: Writing About a Class Memory. Read it aloud, pointing under each word as you read it.

  What words could you add to this to make the writing more interesting?

  What is a word that tells about the park?

- Demonstrate how to use a caret to add words to the writing, following the children's suggestions.

  This little mark is called a caret. It points to where you want to add a word.

- Show children how to add a word to describe the flowers.

Have a Try

Invite children to talk to a partner about their own writing.

▶ Have children look at a book they have already written or are currently working on.

Read the words in your book. What word could you add to make your writing more interesting? Turn and talk to your partner about this.

Summarize and Apply

Summarize the learning. Remind children to use a caret when they add words to their writing.

You talked to your partner about what words you could add to your book to make your writing more interesting. How will you add a word to your writing?

Today during writing time, add some of the words you talked about. Remember to use a caret to show where the new words go.

Section 7: Writing Process

Confer

▶ During independent writing, move around the room to confer briefly with as many individual children as time allows. Sit side by side with them and invite them to talk about adding words to their writing. Use prompts such as the following as needed.

- *Tell what you wrote about on this page.*
- *Where will you put the caret to add the word?*
- *What could you say about the _____? What did it look (sound, smell, feel, taste) like?*
- *You added the word _____. That helps me imagine what it was like.*

Share

Following independent writing, gather children in the meeting area to share their writing.

Who would like to share the words you added to your book today?

Why did you add those words? What do they help people understand?

WML3

WPS.U2.WML3

Writing Minilesson Principle
Add a page to give more information.

Adding to Writing

You Will Need

- class writing from IW.8: Making a Class Big Book
- paper to match IW.8
- books the children have made or are working on
- chart paper and markers

Academic Language/ Important Vocabulary

- page
- information
- revise
- book

Continuum Connection

- Add pages to a book or booklet (p. 249)
- Add words, phrases, or sentences to provide more information to readers (p. 249)
- Add words, phrases, or sentences to make the writing more interesting or exciting for readers (p. 249)

GOAL

Add pages to a book to give more information to readers.

RATIONALE

When children reread their writing and think about what information to add to help the reader understand more about the topic or story, they learn to make their writing more complete. Teaching children to give more information by adding pages to their books is a revision strategy they will use as writers.

ASSESS LEARNING

- Notice whether children can elaborate on the content of their books orally and then transfer the oral elaboration to writing.
- Observe whether children add pages to give more information in their books.
- Observe for evidence that children can use vocabulary such as *page*, *information*, *add*, *revise*, and *book*.

MINILESSON

Use a piece of class writing to engage children in an inquiry around revising a book by adding pages. Discuss what additional information might be added to give more information to the reader. Here is an example.

- Discuss how writers revise to add more information on a new page. Display the class writing from IW.8: Making a Class Big Book.

  Writers go back to their writing many times to make parts of their books clearer or more interesting. They can use a caret to add words. Sometimes they have so much to add that they need a whole new page. You can add a page to your writing, too.

  Let's look at what we wrote about our class in this book. As I read part of what we wrote, think about what else the reader might be wondering about our class.

- Read a few pages and discuss adding a page. Prompt children's thinking if necessary. Possible ideas include a page about yourself, a class pet, what the class does in school, a child new to the class since the book was written, or an aide who works with the class.

- Following the children's suggestions, write on paper that matches the original writing and is attached to the easel. Then talk about where in the book the page should be added—beginning, middle, or end.

Have a Try

Invite children to talk to a partner about adding a page to their own books.

▶ Give children a book they have already written or are currently working on.

> Look at your book. Could you add a page to your book? What could you write about on it? Turn and talk to your partner about this.

Summarize and Apply

Summarize the learning. Remind children to look at their books and think about whether their readers need more information.

▶ Write the principle at the top of the chart.

> You talked to your partner about adding a page to your book. Today during writing time, work on your book. Think about if you need to add a page to give more information.

▶ Show children where they can get paper to add to their books. Explain that you will help them take out the staples in their books and then staple the pages back together.

> Add a page to give more information.

> Freddy the fish lives in Room 12.
> Freddy likes to swim and eat fish food.

Confer

▶ During independent writing, move around the room to confer briefly with as many individual children as time allows. Sit side by side with them and invite them to talk about adding pages to their books. Use prompts such as the following as needed.

  • *What are you going to write about on the next page in your book?*

  • *What happens after that? Can you add a page about that?*

  • *What else might your reader want to know? Write that on a new page and add that to your book.*

Share

Following independent writing, gather children in the meeting area to share their writing.

> Who added a page to your book today?

> How did you decide what to write about on the new page?

Assessment

After you have taught the minilessons in this umbrella, observe children as they draw, write, and talk about their writing. Use the behaviors and understandings in *The Literacy Continuum* (Fountas and Pinnell 2017) to notice, teach for, and support children's learning as you observe their attempts at drawing and writing.

▶ What evidence do you have of new understandings children have developed related to adding to writing?

- Do children understand that they can revise their books to make them better?
- What kinds of details do they add to their drawings to give more information?
- Do they use carets to add words to their writing?
- Are they willing to revise their books by adding pages to give more information?
- Are they using vocabulary such as *add*, *detail*, *page*, *book*, and *information*?

▶ In what other ways, beyond the scope of this umbrella, are the children showing an interest in drawing and writing?

- Are they trying to make their drawings more interesting?
- Are they ready to choose a piece of writing to celebrate?

Use your observations to determine what you will teach next. You may also consult Suggested Sequence of Lessons (pp. 483–494) for guidance.

EXTENSIONS FOR ADDING TO WRITING

▶ When you read aloud to the children, stop to examine an illustration and discuss the details that the illustrator chose to include. Details might include the expression on a character's face, a color, or items that show the setting (e.g., couch and chair in a living room).

▶ Gather together a guided writing group of several children who would benefit from support in adding to their writing.

▶ Teach children how to use a strip of paper (a spider leg) or sticky note to add words to their writing as an alternative or in addition to a caret.

▶ Teach children how to delete and/or replace words in their books.

Minilessons in This Umbrella

WML1 Cross out a word that does not fit or make sense.

WML2 Take out a page that does not fit or make sense.

WML3 Read your writing to make sure the order makes sense.

Before Teaching Umbrella 3 Minilessons

Children are not always willing to change their writing when they are finished, but teaching these minilessons helps them progress in the writing process by expanding ideas for revising their writing. Teach these lessons when you see that children are ready for them. It is not necessary to teach the lessons consecutively; instead, you might teach them throughout the year as needed because revision is a high-level concept and children will need multiple exposures to these lessons.

As you read aloud and enjoy books together, help children notice that all the pages are about the story or topic. Highlight how authors include only information that fits and make sure that their stories and information are presented in an order that makes sense. Use examples of your own writing to model the revising process for children so they understand how to look back at their writing to find areas for improvement.

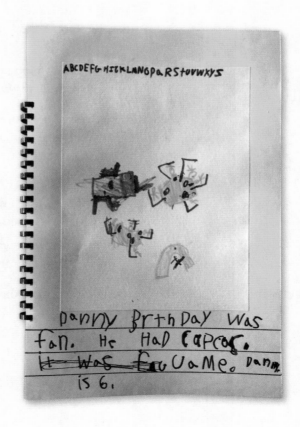

WML1
WPS.U3.WML1

Writing Minilesson Principle
Cross out a word that does not fit or make sense.

Deleting and Reorganizing Writing

You Will Need

- chart paper prepared with two pages of a book that have words that do not fit with the story
- marker
- To download the online resource for this lesson, visit **resources.fountasandpinnell.com**:
  - chart art (optional)

Academic Language / Important Vocabulary

- writing
- reread
- makes sense
- cross out
- fit
- fix

Continuum Connection

- Reread writing to be sure the meaning is clear (p. 249)
- Delete words or sentences that do not make sense (p. 249)
- Cross out words or sentences with pencil or marker (p. 249)
- Cross out to change a text (p. 249)
- Delete text to better express meaning and make more logical (p. 249)

GOAL

Understand that writers cross out words or sentences that do not fit or make sense.

RATIONALE

When children learn to look back at their writing and take out parts that do not fit, they learn that writers make changes to their writing to help readers understand it.

ASSESS LEARNING

- Look for evidence that children reread their writing to determine whether it makes sense.
- Observe whether children are willing to reread their writing and make changes.
- Look for evidence that children can use vocabulary such as *writing*, *reread*, *makes sense*, *cross out*, *fit*, and *fix*.

MINILESSON

To help children think about the minilesson principle, engage them in a lesson that helps them reread their writing to determine if there are parts that do not make sense. Here is an example.

- Ahead of time, prepare two pages of a book. Each page should have a word that does not make sense. Attach the pages to chart paper so that everyone can see them.

  I went swimming and I wrote a story about it. Can you help me check to make sure all the words in my story make sense?

- Read the first page of the story to the children as you point under each word. Have them listen for any words that don't make sense. (This will help children reread their writing to check for words that do not make sense.)

  Did all the words make sense?

  You noticed that I wrote a word that doesn't belong in the sentence. What do you think I should do?

  Sometimes when you reread your writing, you find that there is a word that doesn't belong. If that happens, you can cross out the word.

- Show how to cross out (not erase) the word that doesn't belong.

Have a Try

Invite children to turn and talk about whether there are any words that do not make sense.

▶ Show and read the second page of the story as you point under each word.

> Are there any words on this page of the book that do not make sense? How can I fix that?

▶ After time for a brief discussion, ask volunteers to make suggestions. Ask a volunteer to cross out the part that does not fit or make sense.

Summarize and Apply

Summarize the lesson. Remind children to check their writing for words that do not make sense.

> What did we talk about today?

▶ Write the principle at the top of the chart. Read it aloud.

> During writing time, read each page in your book to make sure all the words make sense. Bring your writing to share when we meet later.

Confer

▶ During independent writing, move around the room to confer briefly with as many individual children as time allows. Sit side by side with them and invite them to talk about what to do with words in their writing that do not fit or make sense. Use the following prompts as needed.

- *Read the words on this page. Do they all fit with your story?*
- *How can you fix a part of your writing that does not make sense?*
- *What did you notice when you reread your writing?*

Share

Following independent writing, gather children in the meeting area to share their writing.

> Who would like to share your writing?

> Did anyone find words in your writing that did not make sense? Share how you fixed it.

Section 7: Writing Process

Writing Minilesson Principle
Take out a page that does not fit or make sense.

Deleting and Reorganizing Writing

You Will Need

- chart paper prepared with four pages of a story, including one page that does not fit with the story
- children's writing
- marker
- To download the online resource for this lesson, visit **resources.fountasandpinnell.com**:
  - chart art (optional)

Academic Language / Important Vocabulary

- take out
- remove
- pages
- fit
- makes sense

Continuum Connection

- Reread writing to be sure the meaning is clear (p. 249)
- Delete pages when information is not needed (p. 249)
- Remove pages from a book or booklet (p. 249)

GOAL

Understand that writers revise their writing by removing pages that do not fit or make sense.

RATIONALE

When children understand that writers make sure each page of their writing communicates their ideas clearly, they learn to revise their own writing and delete pages with language, an idea, or a picture that does not make sense.

ASSESS LEARNING

- Look for evidence that children can determine if each page in their books fits with the other pages.
- Observe whether children understand how to remove pages of their own writing that do not make sense.
- Look for evidence that children can use vocabulary such as *take out*, *remove*, *pages*, *fit*, and *makes sense*.

MINILESSON

To help children think about the minilesson principle, engage them in a lesson that helps them look back at their own writing to determine if there are pages that do not make sense. Here is an example.

- Ahead of time, prepare four pages of a book, each on a separate piece of paper. One of the pages should not make sense with the other pages. Attach the four pages to chart paper so that everyone can see them.

  I went hiking. Here's a story I wrote about it. Can you help me check to make sure all the pages belong in my story?

- Read the story to the children. Have them listen for any part that doesn't make sense.

  Did all the pages fit in my story?

  You noticed that I wrote a page about seeing a snake at the zoo. That page isn't about my hike, is it? This page doesn't fit with my story. What do you think I should do?

  Sometimes when you make a book, you might find that one of the pages doesn't fit with the rest of your story. In case that happens, I will show you how to remove the staples so that you can take that page out of your book.

- Remove the page from the chart.

  I am going to save this page because sometime I could write a story about when I went to the zoo!

The Writing Minilessons Book, Kindergarten

Have a Try

Invite children to turn and talk about how to fix a page in a book that does not fit.

▶ Give children a book they have made.

> Take a look at your book. Do all the pages fit with what you wrote about? Is there a page that doesn't fit? Turn and talk to your partner about that.

Summarize and Apply

Summarize the lesson. Remind children to reread their writing and remove pages that do not make sense.

> What did we talk about today?

▶ Write the principle at the top of the chart. Read it aloud.

> During writing time, look at each page in your book to make sure it fits with the whole book. I will help you remove the page if you find one.

Confer

▶ During independent writing, move around the room to confer briefly with as many individual children as time allows. Sit side by side with them and invite them to talk about what to do if pages in their books don't make sense. Use the following prompts as needed.

- *As you reread your book, point under each word. Do all the pages make sense?*
- *How can you fix a page that does not fit with the other pages?*
- *You can make a new book with the page you took out. What will the new book be about?*

Share

Following independent writing, gather children in the meeting area to share their writing.

> Who would like to share your writing?

> Did anyone take out a page that did not make sense? Tell about that.

WML3

WPS.U3.WML3

Writing Minilesson Principle
Read your writing to make sure the order makes sense.

Deleting and Reorganizing Writing

You Will Need

- chart paper prepared with four pages of a book, the last page out of order
- marker
- To download the online resource for this lesson, visit **resources.fountasandpinnell.com**:
  - chart art (optional)

Academic Language / Important Vocabulary

- writing
- makes sense
- order

Continuum Connection

- Reread writing to be sure the meaning is clear (p. 249)
- Rearrange and revise writing to better express meaning or make the text more logical (reorder drawings, reorder pages, cut and paste) (p. 249)

GOAL

Understand that writers reread their writing to be sure the order makes sense.

RATIONALE

When children are able to revise their own writing by rereading it to check if the order makes sense, they begin to see themselves as writers who have responsibility for communicating clearly and meaningfully.

ASSESS LEARNING

- Look for evidence that children reread their own writing to determine if the order makes sense.
- Observe whether children understand that the sequence of events is important.
- Look for evidence that children can use vocabulary such as *writing*, *makes sense*, and *order*.

MINILESSON

To help children think about the minilesson principle, engage them in a lesson that helps them review their own writing to determine if there are pages that are out of order. Here is an example.

- Ahead of time, prepare four pages of a book, each on a separate piece of paper. The last page should be out of order. Attach the four pages to chart paper so that everyone can see them.

  Here's a story I wrote about our trip to the science museum. Can you help me check to make sure I told about our trip in the right order?

- Read what you wrote aloud. Have them listen for any part that is out of order.

  Did I tell about our trip in the right order?

  You noticed that the last page is out of order. We ate lunch before we left the museum and went back to school. What do you think I should do?

  Sometimes when you make a book, you write a page that is out of order. If that happens, I will show you how to remove the staples so that you can move the page to the right place in your book.

- Swap the last two pages on the chart.

- Support a conversation about why the story does not make sense when the pages are out of order.

Have a Try

Invite children to turn and talk about how to fix a page in a book that is out of order.

▶ Give children a book they have made.

> Take a look at your book. Are the pages in the right order? Turn and talk about that with your partner.

Summarize and Apply

Summarize the lesson. Remind children to reread their writing and reorder pages that are out of order.

> What did we talk about today?

▶ Write the principle at the top of the chart. Read it aloud.

> During writing time, look at each page in your book to make sure all the pages are in order. I will help you fix the pages if you find one out of order.

Read your writing to make sure the order makes sense.

We took the bus to the science museum.

The first thing we saw was the dinosaur exhibit.

When she got back to school, Ella noticed she left her coat at the museum.

We ate lunch in the cafeteria at the museum.

Confer

▶ During independent writing, move around the room to confer briefly with as many individual children as time allows. Sit side by side with them and invite them to talk about the order of the pages in their books. Use the following prompts as needed.

- *Did you reread your book? Does the order make sense?*
- *How can you fix the order of the pages?*
- *What happens first in your story? next? last?*

Share

Following independent writing, gather children in the meeting area to share their writing.

> Who would like to share your writing?

> Did anyone find a page that was out of order? Tell about that.

Assessment

After you have taught the minilessons in this umbrella, observe children as they draw, write, and talk about their writing. Use *The Literacy Continuum* (Fountas and Pinnell 2017) to notice, teach for, and support children's learning as you observe their attempts at drawing and writing.

▶ What evidence do you have of new understandings children have developed related to drafting and revising writing?

  • Are children rereading their writing and taking out words that do not fit?

  • Can they recognize pages in their writing that do not make sense?

  • Do they reread their writing to determine whether the order makes sense and reorder as necessary?

  • Do they understand and use vocabulary such as *writing*, *words*, *pages*, *reread*, *makes sense*, *order*, *fix*, and *fit*?

▶ In what ways, beyond the scope of this umbrella, are children taking part in the writing process?

  • Do they think about ways to make their writing interesting?

  • Are they showing a desire to celebrate their writing?

Use your observations to determine the next umbrella you will teach. You may also consult Suggested Sequence of Lessons (pp. 483–494) for guidance.

EXTENSIONS FOR DELETING AND REORGANIZING WRITING

▶ Demonstrate ways children can use a page they take out of one book to make a new book.

▶ Model how to add pages in the middle of books to add missing information.

▶ Show children how to use a staple remover and stapler safely to delete or reorder pages in their books. Alternatively, you can have children show you which pages to delete or reorder and use the tools yourself.

Minilessons in This Umbrella

WML1 Make the beginning of your book interesting.

WML2 Choose your words carefully.

WML3 Use repeating words.

WML4 Make the ending of your book interesting.

Before Teaching Umbrella 4 Minilessons

We recommend teaching WPS.U2: Adding to Writing before teaching this umbrella. You do not need to teach the minilessons in this umbrella consecutively; rather, teach them based on your observations of children's writing needs and their appropriateness at a particular point in time.

Use the following books from *Fountas & Pinnell Classroom™ Interactive Read-Aloud Collection* text sets, or choose books from the classroom library that have clear examples of interesting writing.

Learning How to Be Yourself

Harold Finds a Voice by Courtney Dicmas

Three Hens and a Peacock by Lester L. Laminack

Understanding Feelings

When Sophie Gets Angry—Really, Really Angry . . . by Molly Bang

Tough Boris by Mem Fox

Rhythm and Rhyme: Joyful Language

Sleepy Bears by Mem Fox

When It Starts to Snow by Phillis Gershator

The Doorbell Rang by Pat Hutchins

Mary Wore Her Red Dress and Henry Wore His Green Sneakers by Merle Peek

As you read and enjoy these texts together, help children

- notice how each story begins and ends,

- talk about the decisions authors make when they write a book, and

- notice features such as descriptive language and repetition.

Be Yourself

Understanding Feelings

Joyful Language

WML1
WPS.U4.WML1

Writing Minilesson Principle
Make the beginning of your book interesting.

Making Writing Interesting

You Will Need

- a few familiar fiction books with examples of different kinds of beginnings, such as the following:
  - *Three Hens and a Peacock* by Lester L. Laminack, from Text Set: Learning How to Be Yourself
  - *The Doorbell Rang* by Pat Hutchins and *When It Starts to Snow* by Phillis Gershator, from Text Set: Rhythm and Rhyme: Joyful Language
- chart paper and markers
- To download the online resource for this lesson, visit **resources.fountasandpinnell.com**:
  - chart art (optional)

Academic Language/ Important Vocabulary

- book
- story
- beginning
- interesting
- author

Continuum Connection

- Tell a story or give information in an interesting way (p. 247)
- Try out techniques other writers and illustrators used (p. 249)
- Add words, phrases, or sentences to make the writing more interesting or exciting for readers (p. 249)

GOAL

Understand that writers can add words, phrases, or sentences to the beginning of one's writing to make it more interesting or exciting for the readers.

RATIONALE

When children notice the variety of ways that published authors begin their books, they understand that they can use the same, or similar, techniques in their own writing. They learn to craft interesting beginnings that attract and engage the reader.

ASSESS LEARNING

- Look for evidence that children notice that authors begin their books in different ways.
- Notice whether children experiment with different ways of beginning their books.
- Observe for evidence that children can use vocabulary such as *book*, *story*, *beginning*, *interesting*, and *author*.

MINILESSON

Use mentor texts to engage children in an inquiry around different ways to make story beginnings interesting. Here is an example.

- Show the cover of *Three Hens and a Peacock*. Read the title. Read pages 1–2.

  How does the author begin his story?

- Record children's responses on chart paper.

  The author begins by telling about the setting and the characters. The setting is where the story happens. Where does this story happen?

- Show the cover of *The Doorbell Rang* and read the title. Read page 1.

  How does the author of this story begin her book?

  She begins by telling what the characters are saying. Sometimes authors give you a bit of information at the start of the story so you know what to expect. Other times, the author goes right into the story.

- Add to the chart.
- Show the cover of *When It Starts to Snow* and read the title. Read page 1.

  How does the author make the beginning of this book interesting?

  The author asks questions. You can think about these questions before you read the rest of the story.

- Add to the chart.

Have a Try

Invite children to talk to a partner about how to begin a story.

▶ Ask children to help you write a couple of opening sentences for a story about a recent shared class experience (e.g., a fire drill).

> **Let's write the first sentence of a story about yesterday's fire drill. How could we make the beginning of our book interesting? Turn and talk to your partner about how we could start our story.**

▶ After children turn and talk, ask several pairs to share their ideas. Write a title and several of their ideas on chart paper.

Summarize and Apply

Write the principle at the top of the chart. Read it to children. Summarize the learning and remind children to think about how to make the beginning of their books interesting.

> **On the chart, you see some different ways that an author can make the beginning of a book interesting. When you write today, try to make the beginning of your book interesting. You might try something we talked about.**

Make the beginning of your book interesting.

- •Tell about the setting/characters.

- •Tell what the characters are saying.

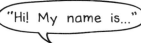

"Hi! My name is..."

- •Ask questions.

Fire Drill!

Ring, ring, ring!

"What's that noise?" asked Sam.

Confer

▶ During independent writing, move around the room to confer briefly with as many individual children as time allows. Sit side by side with them and invite them to talk about beginning their books in an interesting way. Use prompts such as the following as needed.

- • *What are you going to write about today?*
- • *How could you begin your book in an interesting way?*
- • *You could start by telling about where the story happens.*
- • *Could you ask a question to begin your book?*

Share

Following independent writing, gather children in the meeting area to talk about their writing.

> **Who would like to share your writing?**

> **What did you try to make the beginning of your story interesting?**

Section 7: Writing Process

WML2
WPS.U4.WML2

Choose your words carefully.

Making Writing Interesting

You Will Need

- a couple of familiar books with examples of descriptive language, such as the following:
  - *When Sophie Gets Angry– Really, Really Angry . . .* by Molly Bang, from Text Set: Understanding Feelings
  - *Sleepy Bears* by Mem Fox, from Text Set: Rhythm and Rhyme: Joyful Language
- a photo of a familiar place (such as a playground or local business)
- chart paper and markers
- To download the following online resource, visit **resources.fountasandpinnell.com**:
  - chart art (optional)

Academic Language/ Important Vocabulary

- word
- describe
- author

Continuum Connection

- Begin to be aware that the language of books is different in some ways from talk (p. 246)
- Tell a story or give information in an interesting way (p. 247)
- Observe carefully before writing about a person, animal, object, place, action (p. 248)
- Try out techniques other writers and illustrators used (p. 249)
- Add words, phrases, or sentences to make the writing more interesting or exciting for readers (p. 249)

GOAL

Generate words to describe objects, people, and places, and learn how to add descriptive words to writing.

RATIONALE

When you teach children to notice and use descriptive language, they observe things more carefully. They begin to understand that the words they choose to use have a meaningful impact on the reader's understanding.

ASSESS LEARNING

- Observe children as they write to see whether they try techniques other writers or illustrators have used.
- Notice whether they attempt to use descriptive words in their writing.
- Observe for evidence that children can use vocabulary such as *word*, *describe*, and *author*.

MINILESSON

To help children think about the minilesson principle, use familiar books to engage them in a discussion around descriptive language. Here is an example.

- Show the cover of *When Sophie Gets Angry* and read the title. Read page 9.

  Can someone really roar a "red, red roar"?

- Read page 11.

  Is Sophie really a "volcano, ready to explode"?

  Why do you think the author uses these words to describe, or tell about, Sophie?

  When I imagine Sophie as being like a volcano, ready to explode, or a roaring lion, I understand that the author wants me to know that Sophie is very, very angry.

- Show the cover of *Sleepy Bears*. Read page 10.

  Think about how the author describes the circus. What sounds could you hear at this circus?

  What could you see at this circus?

  The author carefully chooses her words so you can picture in your mind what it's like to be at this circus.

- Show a photo of a familiar place, such as a playground or local business. Ask children what they could see, hear, and smell at the place. Encourage them to use descriptive words. Record their responses on chart paper.

Have a Try

Invite children to talk to a partner about their ideas for writing about the place.

> Let's write a few sentences about the playground. What could we write to help people imagine being at the playground? Turn and talk to your partner about your ideas. Choose your words carefully.

▶ After children turn and talk, invite several pairs to share their ideas. Write a few sentences about the place, using the children's suggestions.

Summarize and Apply

Write the principle at the top of the chart. Help children summarize what they learned. Remind children to choose their words carefully when they write.

> Why do authors choose their words carefully?

> During writing time today, remember to choose your words carefully. When you choose your words carefully, you help people make a picture in their minds.

Confer

▶ During independent writing, move around the room to confer briefly with as many individual children as time allows. Sit side by side with them and invite them to talk about choosing their words carefully. Use prompts such as the following if needed.

- *Talk more about your writing.*
- *What is the _____ like? What words could help people make a picture in their minds?*
- *What color is the _____?*
- *How big is the _____?*
- *What does the _____ feel (sound, taste, smell, look) like?*

Share

Following independent writing, gather children in the meeting area to share their writing.

> Who would like to read aloud what you wrote?

> What words did you use to describe something?

Choose your words carefully.

See	Hear	Smell
• Leafy tree	• Bouncing ball	• Spicy pizza
• Silver slide	• Bird singing	
• Empty swings	• Loud shouting	

The Playground

Two boys are playing basketball.

One boy shouts, "Give me the ball!"

The other boy is bouncing the ball.

A bird is singing in the leafy tree.

Making Writing Interesting

You Will Need

- a couple of familiar books with examples of repetition, such as the following from Text Set: Rhythm and Rhyme: Joyful Language:
  - *Mary Wore Her Red Dress and Henry Wore His Green Sneakers* by Merle Peek
  - *The Doorbell Rang* by Pat Hutchins
- chart paper prepared with a partially written text containing repeating words (see example on the following page)
- markers
- To download the following online resource for this lesson, visit **resources.fountasandpinnell.com**:
  - chart art (optional)

Academic Language/ Important Vocabulary

- repeating
- word
- sentence
- author

Continuum Connection

- Tell a story or give information in an interesting way (p. 247)
- Try out techniques other writers and illustrators used (p. 249)
- Add words, phrases, or sentences to make the writing more interesting or exciting for readers (p. 249)

GOAL

Understand that writers sometimes repeat words, phrases, and sentence structures to make their writing interesting.

RATIONALE

When children notice how authors use repeating words, phrases, and sentence structures, they are more likely to try this technique in their own writing or in the stories they tell. Repetition can be used to add interest or rhythm to writing or to emphasize an important point.

ASSESS LEARNING

- Notice whether children attempt to use repetition in their writing.
- Observe for evidence that children can use vocabulary such as *repeating*, *word*, *sentence*, and *author*.

MINILESSON

Use familiar books to engage children in an inquiry around repetition. Here is an example.

- Show the cover of *Mary Wore Her Red Dress and Henry Wore His Green Sneakers* and read the title. Read pages 1–6.

  What do you notice about the words in this book? How are they the same on each page? How are they different?

  The words are almost the same on every page. The only things that change are the name of the character, the type of clothing, and the color of the clothing. Why do you think the author repeats the same type of sentence on each page?

  The words in this book come from a song. Songs often have repeating words or sentences. Repeating words give the song a rhythm and make it fun and easy to sing.

- Show the cover of *The Doorbell Rang* and read the title. Read pages 3, 7, and 11.

  What words do you hear again and again?

  Why do you think the author repeats the sentence "'No one makes cookies like Grandma,' said Ma as the doorbell rang"? What happens at the end of the book?

  Sometimes authors using repeating words to show that an idea is important. In this book, the repeated sentence is important because it gives you a clue about how the story is going to end.

Have a Try

Invite children to help you write a text with repeating words.

> I started writing a song that has repeating words. Can you help me finish it?

▶ Read the song aloud. Point out the blank spaces that need words. Invite children to talk to a partner about what words should go in the spaces.

▶ Complete the text using the children's suggestions. Read the whole text aloud.

Summarize and Apply

Write the principle at the top of the chart. Read it to children. Summarize the learning and remind children to think about using repeating words in their own writing.

> You noticed that authors sometimes use repeating words to make their books more fun to read or to show that an idea is important. Today during writing time, you may want to try using repeating words in your own writing.

Use repeating words.

Four little monkeys sit on a branch.
One jumps off. Now there are three!

Three little monkeys sit on a branch.
One jumps off. Now there are two!

Two little monkeys sit on a branch.
One jumps off. Now there is one!

Confer

▶ During independent writing, move around the room to confer briefly with as many individual children as time allows. Sit side by side with them and invite them to talk about using repeating words. Use prompts such as the following if needed.

- *Which words could you repeat in your book?*
- *What might that character say again and again?*
- *You repeated the sentence _____. That tells me that this is an important idea.*
- *Why did you decide to repeat those words?*

Share

Following independent writing, gather children in the meeting area to share their writing.

> Did anyone use repeating words in your writing today?
>
> What words did you repeat?
>
> Why did you repeat those words?

WML4
WPS.U4.WML4

Writing Minilesson Principle
Make the ending of your book interesting.

Making Writing Interesting

You Will Need

- a few familiar fiction books with examples of different kinds of endings, such as the following:

  - *Harold Finds a Voice* by Courtney Dicmas, from Text Set: Learning How to Be Yourself

  - *When Sophie Gets Angry–Really, Really Angry . . .* by Molly Bang and *Tough Boris* by Mem Fox, from Text Set: Understanding Feelings

- books the children have made

- chart paper and markers

- To download the following online resource for this lesson, visit **resources.fountasandpinnell.com**:

  - chart art (optional)

Academic Language/ Important Vocabulary

- book
- story
- ending
- interesting
- author

Continuum Connection

- Tell a story or give information in an interesting way (p. 247)

- Add words, phrases, or sentences to make the writing more interesting or exciting for readers (p. 249)

- Try out techniques other writers and illustrators used (p. 249)

GOAL

Understand that writers can add words, phrases, or sentences to the end of their writing to make it more interesting or exciting for the readers.

RATIONALE

When children notice the variety of different ways that published authors end their books, they understand that they can create the same kinds of endings in their own writing. They learn to craft interesting endings that provide a sense of closure.

ASSESS LEARNING

- Notice whether children experiment with different ways of ending their books.

- Observe for evidence that children can use vocabulary such as *book*, *story*, *ending*, *interesting*, and *author*.

MINILESSON

Use mentor texts to engage children in an inquiry around different ways to make story endings interesting. Here is an example.

- Show the cover of *Harold Finds a Voice* and read the title. Read the final page of the book.

  How does the author of this story end her book?

  Harold finds his voice and learns that his own voice makes him happiest of all. Sometimes authors end their books by telling what a character learned.

- Record the response on chart paper.

- Show the cover of *When Sophie Gets Angry*. Read the title and then read the last page.

  How does this story end?

  Sophie is not angry anymore because she took the time to calm down in a special place. Sometimes authors end their books by showing how a problem is solved, or fixed.

- Add to the chart.

- Show the cover of *Tough Boris* and read the title. Read the last two pages.

  What makes the ending of this book interesting? What do you learn at the end?

  At the end of this book, you learn that the person telling the story is the young boy in the pictures. Sometimes authors end their books with a surprise!

- Add to the chart.

Have a Try

Invite children to share their own writing with a partner.

▶ Have children look at a book they're currently working on (or have recently finished).

> Look at your book. How can you make the ending of your book interesting? Turn and talk to your partner about your ideas.

Summarize and Apply

Write the principle at the top of the chart. Read it to children. Summarize the learning and remind children to think about how to make the ending of their books interesting.

> Today you noticed some different ways that authors make the endings of their books interesting. Then you talked with a partner about your ideas for making the ending of your own book interesting. During writing time today, try making the ending of your book interesting by using an idea on our list. Bring your writing to share when we meet later.

> **Make the ending of your book interesting.**
>
> • Tell what the character learned.
>
> • Tell how the problem is solved.
>
> • End with a surprise.

Confer

▶ During independent writing, move around the room to confer briefly with as many individual children as time allows. Sit side by side with them and invite them to talk about ending their books in an interesting way. Use prompts such as the following as needed.

- *What is your book about?*
- *How could you make the ending of your book interesting?*
- *Could you tell what the character learned?*
- *Do you want to tell how the problem is solved?*

Share

Following independent writing, gather children in the meeting area to share their writing.

> Who would like to share the ending of your book?

> How did you make it interesting?

Assessment

After you have taught the minilessons in this umbrella, observe children as they draw, write, and talk about their writing. Use the behaviors and understandings in *The Literacy Continuum* (Fountas and Pinnell 2017) to notice, teach for, and support children's attempts at drawing and writing.

▌ What evidence do you have of new understandings children have developed related to making writing interesting?

- Do children notice and talk about interesting examples of author's craft?
- Are they willing to try techniques they have seen other writers use?
- Do they use descriptive language or repeating words in their writing?
- Do they experiment with writing different kinds of beginnings and endings?
- Do children understand and use vocabulary such as *interesting*, *beginning*, *ending*, *describe*, and *repeating*?

▌ In what other ways, beyond the scope of this umbrella, are children ready to develop their writing?

- Are they ready to learn how to revise their writing?
- Are they ready to learn how to proofread their writing?

Use your observations to determine the next umbrella you will teach. You may also consult Suggested Sequence of Lessons (pp. 483–494) for guidance.

EXTENSIONS FOR MAKING WRITING INTERESTING

▌ Continue to help children notice interesting examples of author's craft during interactive read-aloud and shared reading. Teach minilessons about specific techniques that they notice (e.g., onomatopoeia, interesting uses of punctuation, different types of print).

▌ Use interactive writing to make a counting book with a repeating sentence pattern. (See IW.12: Making a Counting Book.)

▌ Encourage children to write an alternative ending to a familiar book. (See IW.20: Writing an Alternative Ending.)

▌ After reading aloud a book, ask children to offer their opinions, supported with evidence, about how the author began or ended the book.

Minilessons in This Umbrella

WML1 Check the spaces between your words.

WML2 Check your letters to make sure they are easy to read

WML3 Check to make sure you wrote the words you know correctly.

Before Teaching Umbrella 5 Minilessons

The goal of this umbrella is to help children understand how to check their own work. Before teaching these lessons, make sure children have had many experiences writing and reading their work. It would be helpful to teach minilessons about early concepts of print (EWR.U1) and handwriting (EWR.U2) as well as writing process (WPS.U1–WPS.U4). After children complete the minilessons in this umbrella, you may want to add the Checklist for Writing (download from **resources. fountasandpinnell.com**) to their writing folders to help them edit and proofread their work.

Use a variety of mentor texts as examples to highlight that authors edit and proofread their own work. Include samples of class-made writing as well as examples from *Fountas & Pinnell Classroom™ Shared Reading Collection*. Some suggestions are below.

Shared Reading Collection

Counting on the Farm by Tess Fletcher

Ten Big Elephants by Susan F. Rank

Interactive Writing Lessons

IW.7: Writing a Thank You Card

IW.10: Writing a Color Poem

IW.12: Making a Counting Book

Shared Reading

Interactive Writing

Section 7: Writing Process

Writing Minilesson Principle
Check the spaces between your words.

Proofreading Writing

You Will Need

▸ several familiar books that show clear spacing between words, such as the following:

  ■ *Counting on the Farm* by Tess Fletcher and *Ten Big Elephants* by Susan F. Rank, from *Shared Reading Collection*

▸ class writing from IW.12: Making a Counting Book or other class writing

▸ chart paper and markers

▸ highlighter tape (optional)

▸ children's writing (one per child or pair of children)

Academic Language / Important Vocabulary

▸ writing

▸ check

▸ spaces

▸ between

▸ words

Continuum Connection

▸ Use spaces between words to help readers understand the writing (p. 247)

▸ Understand that the better the spelling and space between words, the easier it is for the reader to read it (p. 249)

▸ Cross out to change a text (p. 249)

GOAL

Reread writing to check for spaces between words so the reader can understand the message.

RATIONALE

When children learn that to check their work by checking for spaces between words, they understand that how their writing looks matters to the reader. They also gain independence and ownership over their own writing.

ASSESS LEARNING

▸ Look for evidence that children understand that they can check their writing.

▸ Observe whether children are proofreading work by checking for spaces between words.

▸ Look for evidence that children can use vocabulary such as *writing*, *check*, *spaces*, *between*, and *words*.

MINILESSON

To help children learn to proofread (check) their work, provide examples of mentor texts with proper spacing. Model the steps to fix writing when the words are written too closely together. Here is an example.

▸ Show sentences from several familiar books, such as *Counting on the Farm* and *Ten Big Elephants*.

  Take a look at the words as I read them. How can you tell where one word ends and the next word begins?

▸ Guide the conversation to help children notice the spaces between words. Emphasize the spaces with highlighter tape or ask two or three children to point to the spaces.

▸ Show the class-made writing from IW.12: Making a Counting Book and read the text.

  Are there spaces between the words we wrote in this book? Who can point to one?

  How do spaces between words help the reader?

  When you do your own writing, make sure you leave spaces between the words so that your reader will understand what you wrote. You need to check your writing to make sure other people can read it.

▸ Begin a checklist on chart paper by writing the minilesson principle. Show children how to make a check mark in the box after they check their writing.

Have a Try

Invite children to turn and talk about spaces in their writing.

▶ Give children a sample of their writing (or one sample per pair).

> Turn and tell your partner if there are any words that need better spaces between them and how you could fix the problem.

▶ Guide children to understand that they should cross out the words that are not properly spaced and rewrite them clearly above.

▶ Save the chart for WML2.

Summarize and Apply

Summarize the lesson. Remind children to check word spacing when they proofread their writing.

> During writing time, check for spaces between words by reading what you have written. Bring your writing to share when we meet later.

Checklist for Writing

☑ Check the spaces between your words.

will go

~~willgo~~

Confer

▶ During independent writing, move around the room to confer briefly with as many individual children as time allows. Sit side by side with them and invite them to talk about checking their writing. You might wish to have children start using the Checklist for Writing now or wait until after WML3. Use the following prompts as needed.

- *Show how to use your finger to check if there is space between each word.*
- *Read this sentence. Is there a space between all the words?*
- *How can you fix these two words that are too close together?*
- *Did you check your writing and put a check mark in the box?*

Share

Following independent writing, gather children in the meeting area. Have them bring their writing from today.

> Who would like to share your writing?

> Did anyone fix the spaces between words in your writing? Show what you did.

Writing Minilesson Principle
Check your letters to make sure they are easy to read.

Proofreading Writing

You Will Need

- class-made book from IW.10: Writing a Color Poem or other class writing
- chart from WML1
- markers
- children's writing (one per child or pair of children)

Academic Language / Important Vocabulary

- writing
- check
- letters

Continuum Connection

- Form upper- and lowercase letters efficiently in manuscript print (p. 248)
- Form upper- and lowercase letters proportionately in manuscript print (p. 248)
- Cross out to change a text (p. 249)
- Check and correct letter formation or orientation (p. 249)

GOAL

Reread writing to check for correct letter formation and orientation so the reader can understand the message.

RATIONALE

Asking children to proofread their writing gives them a reason to attend to the details of conveying a message in writing. If their letters are not clear, the reader will not understand the message.

ASSESS LEARNING

- Notice evidence that children proofread their work.
- Observe whether children check for correct letter formation and orientation when rereading their work.
- Look for evidence that children can use vocabulary such as *writing*, *check*, and *letters*.

MINILESSON

To help children learn to proofread their work, provide examples of mentor texts with proper letter formation and orientation. Model the steps to fix writing when letters are not formed properly. Here is an example.

- Show the class writing from IW.10: Writing a Color Poem.

  How does the way the letters are written help you read this?

- Guide the conversation to help children notice that the letters are written so that they are easy to read and they go from left to right.

  When you do your own writing, make your letters the best that you can so that your readers will understand what you wrote. When you check your writing, make sure that your letters are clear and easy to read.

- Add the minilesson principle to the checklist you began in WML1.

- Make sure children understand to cross out (not erase) the word and then rewrite it above.

Have a Try

Invite children to turn and talk about how to correct letters that are improperly formed.

▶ Give children a sample of their writing (or one sample per pair).

> Look at the writing. Turn and tell your partner about any letters that should be fixed and how you can fix them.

▶ Guide children to understand that they should cross out the word that has a letter that could be made better and rewrite it clearly above.

▶ Save the chart for WML3.

Summarize and Apply

Summarize the lesson. Remind children to proofread their writing.

> Check your writing to make sure your letters are easy to read. Neatly cross out the letters that need to be fixed and write them above.

> During writing time, read your writing to make sure that you have written each letter so it is easy to read.

Checklist for Writing

☑ Check the spaces between your words.

will go
~~willgo~~

☑ Check your letters to make sure they are easy to read.

S
~~Sun~~ un

Confer

▶ During independent writing, move around the room to confer briefly with as many individual children as time allows. Sit side by side with them and invite them to talk about checking their writing. You might want children to use the Checklist for Writing now or wait until after WML3. Use the following prompts as needed.

- *Look at your writing. Are there any letters that you need to write better?*
- *Where can you look to know how to make a letter?*
- *How can you fix this letter?*
- *Did you put a check mark on your Checklist for Writing?*

Share

Following independent writing, gather children in the meeting area. Have them bring their writing from today.

> Who would like to share your writing?

> Did you fix any letters after you read your writing? Show what you did.

Writing Minilesson Principle
Check to make sure you wrote the words you know correctly.

Proofreading Writing

You Will Need

- several familiar books with commonly used words, such as the following:
  - *Ten Big Elephants* by Susan F. Rank, from *Shared Reading Collection*
- class-made book from IW.7: Writing a Thank You Card
- chart from WML2
- markers
- To download the online resources for this lesson, visit **resources.fountasandpinnell.com**:
  - Checklist for Writing
  - High-Frequency Word List

Academic Language / Important Vocabulary

- writing
- check
- words
- spelling

Continuum Connection

- Understand that a writer uses what is known to spell words (p. 249)
- Understand that the better the spelling and space between words, the easier it is for the reader to read it (p. 249)
- Edit for spelling errors by making another attempt (p. 249)
- Notice words that do not look right and spell by saying them slowly to represent as much of the word as possible (p. 249)
- Cross out to change a text (p. 249)

GOAL

Reread writing to check for correct spelling so the reader can understand the message.

RATIONALE

When children learn to proofread by checking for misspelled words, they understand that it is the writer's responsibility to spell words they know correctly.

ASSESS LEARNING

- Notice evidence that children make sure that the words they know are spelled correctly.
- Observe whether children understand that it is the writer's responsibility to proofread for spelling.
- Look for evidence that children can use vocabulary such as *writing*, *check*, *words*, and *spelling*.

MINILESSON

To help children learn to proofread their work, display mentor texts with examples of proper spellings of words that the children know. Model how to fix writing when words they know are spelled incorrectly. Here is an example.

- Show the cover of *Ten Big Elephants*. Read the title and page 16.

  Can you point to a word you know on this page?

- Guide the conversation to help children notice the correct spelling.

  You know the words *in* and *the*. Notice that they are always spelled the same way. That's how you know what those words are.

- Show the class-made writing from IW.7: Writing a Thank You Card.

  Are there words you know? Who can point to one?

- Guide the conversation to help children understand that words are spelled the same way all the time and readers recognize that.

  It's important to write the words you know correctly so that your reader will understand what you wrote. When you check your writing and find a word that you think is not written correctly, where can you look to find out?

- Remind children to look at the word wall, personal word list, or another source of words that may be available.

- Add the minilesson principle to the checklist from WML2.

- Make sure children cross out (not erase) the word and then rewrite it above.

The Writing Minilessons Book, Kindergarten

Have a Try

Invite children to turn and talk about how to correct spelling.

▶ Give children a sample of their writing (or one sample per pair).

> Look at the writing. Turn and tell your partner about a word you know that needs to be fixed. How can you fix it?

▶ Guide children to understand that they should cross out the word and rewrite it clearly above.

Summarize and Apply

Summarize the lesson. Remind children to proofread their writing and to check off the items on the checklist as they do them.

> Today you learned to check your writing to make sure the words you know are spelled correctly. During writing time, check for spelling by reading what you have written.

Confer

▶ During independent writing, move around the room to confer briefly with as many individual children as time allows. Sit side by side with them and invite them to talk about checking their writing. You might want to have children use the Checklist for Writing. Use the following prompts as needed.

- *Read this sentence to make sure the words you know are spelled correctly.*
- *What do you notice about this sentence?*
- *How can you fix the spelling of this word?*
- *Did you put a check mark on your Checklist for Writing?*

Share

Following independent writing, gather children in the meeting area. Have them bring their writing from today.

> Who would like to share your writing?

> Did you have to fix any words in your writing? Show what you did.

Checklist for Writing

☑ Check the spaces between your words. — will go / ~~willgo~~

☑ Check your letters to make sure they are easy to read. — s ~~sun~~

☑ Check to make sure you wrote the words you know correctly. — like / ~~lik~~

Assessment

After you have taught the minilessons in this umbrella, observe children as they write. Use *The Literacy Continuum* (Fountas and Pinnell 2017) to notice, teach for, and support children's learning as you observe their attempts at reading and writing.

- ❱ What evidence do you have of new understandings children have developed related to proofreading?
  - Are children checking for spaces between words and correcting errors by crossing out and rewriting?
  - Is there evidence that they can proofread to make sure that they have made letters easy to read by using their best handwriting?
  - Do they proofread to make sure that the words they know are spelled correctly?
  - Do they understand and use vocabulary such as *writing*, *check*, *spaces*, *between*, *words*, *letters*, and *spelling*?
- ❱ In what ways, beyond the scope of this umbrella, are children taking part in the writing process?
  - Do they reread their work to add and delete information?

Use your observations to determine the next umbrella you will teach. You may also consult Suggested Sequence of Lessons (pp. 483–494) for guidance.

EXTENSIONS FOR PROOFREADING WRITING

- ❱ Have children add other things to check to the Checklist for Writing, such as correct use of capitalization and punctuation.

- ❱ Gather together a guided writing group of several children who need support in a specific area of writing.

- ❱ Revisit WPS.U5.WML3 when working with classroom resources (see EWR.U4). The children could use the name chart, the word wall, and their personal word lists to help with proofreading.

Minilessons in This Umbrella

WML1 Get ready to share a book or poem you want to celebrate.

WML2 Make your book or poem ready for others to read.

WML3 Celebrate something new you tried.

Before Teaching Umbrella 6 Minilessons

We recommend teaching U1: Getting Started with Making Books and U2: Expanding Bookmaking, both in the Making Books section, before teaching the minilessons in this umbrella. It would also be helpful to make a book yourself to use for demonstrating this umbrella's principles.

The purpose of the minilessons in this umbrella is to prepare children to choose pieces they are proud of to share with an audience. Some ways that children can share their books include reading them aloud to the whole class or a small group, inviting the children's families to a class celebration, or sharing with another classroom or grade level. Some children might occasionally enjoy typing their work on a computer, with an adult's help, to create a more polished product. However, we recommend that this process be reserved for special occasions, as children's work should generally speak for itself. We want children's writing to look like children's writing!

As you read aloud and enjoy books together, help children

- be aware of how you read aloud to them (look at them, speak so they can understand), and

- talk about how authors make their books ready for others to read.

Celebrating Writing

You Will Need

- a book that you have made as an example
- chart paper and markers
- To download the online resource for this lesson, visit **resources.fountasandpinnell.com**:
  - chart art (optional)

Academic Language/ Important Vocabulary

- book
- poem
- celebrate
- share
- read

Continuum Connection

- Select best pieces of writing from own collection (p. 249)
- Share a text with peers by reading it aloud to the class (p. 249)
- When finished with a piece of writing, talk about it to others (p. 249)

GOAL

Choose books to celebrate and prepare to share with an audience.

RATIONALE

Before children can share their work with an audience, they must first choose which piece to share and then practice sharing it. This lesson helps them think about the criteria they can use to evaluate their work. When children think carefully about which pieces to share, they are more likely to share work that they are truly proud of and confident about.

ASSESS LEARNING

- Listen to children's reasons for choosing pieces to celebrate.
- Notice whether children read their work aloud in a consistent way each time.
- Look for evidence that children can use vocabulary such as *book*, *poem*, *celebrate*, *share*, and *read*.

MINILESSON

To help children think about the minilesson principle, share why you have chosen to celebrate a particular book and help them generate a list of criteria for evaluating pieces to share. Here is an example.

> You have been working very hard at writing books and poems. Sometimes you might want to celebrate some writing that you're proud of by sharing it.

- Display the book that you prepared before class.

> Here's a book that I wrote and illustrated. I'm very proud of it! I worked hard to make it, and I checked my writing carefully to make sure that it shows my best work. I also made sure that the pictures and the words match. It's about something important to me, and I think other people will like it.
>
> What did you notice about how I chose this book?

- Use children's responses to begin a list of how to get ready for sharing a piece of writing.

> Now that I've chosen to share this book, I need to get ready to share it. I will get ready by practicing reading it aloud. Watch how I read it.

- Read a few pages of the book aloud.

> What happened on these pages?
>
> If I were to read these pages to you again tomorrow, would the same things happen?
>
> The words and the pictures mean the same things each time I share my book. To get ready to share your book, practice reading it the same way each time.

Have a Try

Invite children to talk to a partner about a book to celebrate.

> Think about the books or poems you have written lately. Which one would you like to share? Why? Turn and talk to your partner about that.

> Now talk about how you will get ready to share it.

Summarize and Apply

Write the principle at the top of the chart. Read it to children. Summarize the learning and invite children to get ready to share a book or poem they want to celebrate.

> Today you learned about how to get ready to share a book or poem you want to celebrate. During writing time today, you will have a chance to think more about which book or poem you'd like to share and to practice sharing it.

Get ready to share a book or poem you want to celebrate.

- Choose something you are proud of.

- Check your writing.

~~dg~~ dog

- Make sure the pictures and the words match.

My hat is blue.

- Practice reading it the same way each time.

Confer

▶ During independent writing, move around the room to confer briefly with as many individual children as time allows. Sit side by side with them and invite them to talk about sharing a book or poem. Use prompts such as the following as needed.

- *Which book did you work on the hardest?*
- *What do you like most about this poem?*
- *Tell why you chose this book to share.*
- *How should your voice sound when you share?*

Share

Following independent writing, gather children in the meeting area to share their writing. As needed, support children's oral language by providing a sentence frame, such as *I chose this book (poem) because _____.*

> Who would like to share a book or poem you made?

> Why did you choose this book [poem]?

> Remember to read it the same way you did the last time you read it.

Writing Minilesson Principle

Make your book or poem ready for others to read.

Celebrating Writing

You Will Need

- an example book that has been typed and printed and has a cardboard cover
- a typed poem that has been framed or mounted
- chart paper and markers
- To download the online resource for this lesson, visit **resources.fountasandpinnell.com**:
  - chart art (optional)

Academic Language/ Important Vocabulary

- type
- computer
- label
- cover
- title
- author

Continuum Connection

- Select a poem, story, or informational book to publish in a variety of appropriate ways: e.g., typed/printed, framed and mounted, or otherwise displayed (p. 249)
- When finished with a piece of writing, talk about it to others (p. 249)

GOAL

Learn different ways to "publish" a piece of writing and make it accessible to others.

RATIONALE

When you teach children different ways to make their writing accessible to others, they begin to understand that writing is a process that may involve several steps beyond just writing the words and drawing the pictures. They also begin to conceptualize the idea of writing not just for themselves but also for an audience.

ASSESS LEARNING

- Observe what children do to make their books and poems ready for others to read.
- Notice whether children experiment with different ways of making their writing accessible to others (e.g., typing their books, adding a cover, framing or mounting a poem).
- Look for evidence that children can use vocabulary such as *type*, *computer*, *label*, *cover*, *title*, and *author*.

MINILESSON

To help children think about the minilesson principle, engage them in a discussion about different ways to make their books and poems ready for other people to read. Here is an example.

- Display the example book you prepared before class and draw attention to the cardboard cover. Add to the chart as you discuss each way of getting work ready to share.

  What do you notice about my book?

  I put a cardboard cover on my book so that it won't tear easily.

  What did I write on the cover?

  The cover helps readers know what the book is about and who wrote it.

  What could I add to the pictures in my book to help readers get more information?

  I could add labels to my pictures.

- Display the framed or mounted poem.

  What do you notice about how I got my poem ready for others to read?

  I put my poem on a piece of construction paper to make it look nice.

  What do you notice about the words in my poem? How did I write them?

- Talk about how typing the words makes them easier for others to read.

  When I typed my poem, I had to think about where on the page to put the words and where to put the picture.

The Writing Minilessons Book, Kindergarten

Have a Try

Invite children to talk to a partner about how they would like to make their books and poems ready for others to read.

> Think about a book or poem that you would like to celebrate. How would you like to get it ready for others to read? Talk to your partner about what you would do.

Summarize and Apply

Write the principle at the top of the chart. Read it to children. Summarize the learning and remind children to think about different ways of making their books or poems ready for others to read.

> We talked about different things you can do to make your books and poems ready for others to read. Today during writing time, you will have the chance to get one of your books or poems ready.

Make your book or poem ready for others to read.

- Add a cover.

To the Moon!
Mr. Edwards

- Write the title and author.

- Add labels to the pictures.

The Sun

- Type it.

- Frame it.

Section 7: Writing Process

Confer

▶ During independent writing, move around the room to confer briefly with as many individual children as time allows. Sit side by side with them and invite them to talk about how they will make their book or poem ready for others to read. Use prompts such as the following as needed.

- *What would you like to do to get your book/poem ready for people to read?*
- *Would you like to type your poem?*
- *Where would you like to put the words on the page? Where would you like to put the picture?*
- *What can you write on the cover of your book?*

Share

Following independent writing, gather children in the meeting area to talk about getting books ready to read.

> Tell what you did to get your book (poem) ready for others to read.

Writing Minilesson Principle
Celebrate something new you tried.

Celebrating Writing

You Will Need

- several examples of children's work that show something new the writer tried (e.g., speech bubbles, repeating words, use of different art materials)
- chart paper and markers

Academic Language/ Important Vocabulary

- celebrate
- book
- poem

Continuum Connection

- Self-evaluate writing and talk about what is good about it and what techniques were used (p. 249)

GOAL

Identify and celebrate trying new writing techniques.

RATIONALE

Encouraging children to share the new things they have tried in their writing makes it more likely that other children will try similar things. Identifying the risks children have taken in their writing makes that writing worth celebrating.

ASSESS LEARNING

- Observe children's attempts at trying something new in their writing and illustrating.
- Notice whether children identify and celebrate new writing or illustrating techniques they have tried.
- Look for evidence that children can use vocabulary such as *celebrate*, *book*, and *poem*.

MINILESSON

To help children think about the minilesson principle, engage them in talking about trying new things in their writing and illustrating. Here is an example.

- Display one of the examples of children's work that you selected before class.

    _____ worked hard to write this poem. She tried something new in this poem. What did you try, _____?

    _____ used repeating words in her poem.

- Record the example on chart paper.
- Continue sharing examples of new things that children tried in their writing and illustrating. Add words and sketches to the chart to represent them.

Have a Try

Invite children to talk to a partner about something new they have tried in their writing or illustrating.

> Turn and talk to your partner about something new you have tried in your writing or pictures.

▶ After a brief time, ask several volunteers to share with the class. Add any new ideas to the chart.

Summarize and Apply

Write the principle at the top of the chart. Read it to children. Summarize the learning and remind children to celebrate new techniques they have tried.

> Today during writing time, I would like you to spend some more time thinking about new things you have tried in your writing or drawing. If you are proud of something new you tried in a book, you might want to choose that book to celebrate and share when we meet together.

Confer

▶ During independent writing, move around the room to confer briefly with as many individual children as time allows. Sit side by side with them and invite them to talk about their reasons for choosing a piece of writing to share. Use prompts such as the following if needed.

- *What new thing did you try in your book/poem? How do you feel about that?*
- *You tried speech bubbles for the first time. Would you like to celebrate this book?*

Share

Following independent writing, gather children in the meeting area to share the new things they tried in their books.

> Who would like to share something new you tried in your book (poem)?

Section 7: Writing Process

Assessment

After you have taught the minilessons in this umbrella, observe children as they draw, write, and talk about their writing. Use the behaviors and understandings in *The Literacy Continuum* (Fountas and Pinnell 2017) to notice, teach for, and support children's attempts at drawing and writing.

▶ What evidence do you have of new understandings children have developed related to celebrating writing?

- Do children celebrate books and poems they have made with an audience?

- Are they able to read their writing the same way each time?

- How do they make their books and poems ready for others to read?

- Have they tried new writing and illustrating techniques and then talked about what they tried?

- Do they understand and use vocabulary such as *book*, *poem*, *share*, and *celebrate*?

▶ In what other ways, beyond the scope of this umbrella, are children exploring the writing process?

- Are they revising, editing, and proofreading their writing?

Use your observations to determine the next umbrella you will teach. You may also consult Suggested Sequence of Lessons (pp. 483–494) for guidance.

EXTENSIONS FOR CELEBRATING WRITING

▶ Help children identify and talk about different text features in published books (e.g., title page, dedication, table of contents, author page). Invite them to add the same features to their own books.

▶ Dedicate a section of the classroom library or area of the school (e.g., hallway or lobby) to display and celebrate children's own books.

▶ Help children create a class anthology that includes selected pieces from every child in the class.

Appendix:
Suggested Sequence of Lessons

The Suggested Sequence of Lessons is also available in the Fountas & Pinnell Online Resources site (**resources.fountasandpinnell.com**).

Suggested Sequence of Lessons

This sequence shows when you might teach the interactive writing lessons and writing minilessons across the year. It also aligns these lessons with the texts from *Fountas & Pinnell Classroom™ Shared Reading Collection* and *Interactive Read-Aloud Collection*, as well as the reading minilesson umbrellas from *The Reading Minilessons Book, Kindergarten*. You do not need these other resources to teach the lessons in this book, but this comprehensive sequence helps you see how all these pieces can fit together and think about how you might organize reading and writing across the year. Note that the number of days refers to approximately how long it will take to teach the lessons. It does not indicate how long your students might spend applying new ideas or experimenting with new kinds of writing.

Suggested Sequence of Lessons

Months	Texts from *Fountas & Pinnell Classroom™ Shared Reading Collection*	Text Sets from *Fountas & Pinnell Classroom™ Interactive Read-Aloud Collection*	Reading Minilessons (RML) Sequence from *The Reading Minilessons Book, Kindergarten*	Interactive Writing (IW) Lessons*	Writing Minilesson (WML) Umbrellas	Teaching Suggestions for Extending Learning
Months 1 & 2	The Itsy Bitsy Spider Wiggles: Poems to Make You Wiggle Your Fingers and Toes School Days	Sharing Stories and Songs: Nursery Rhymes Learning and Playing Together: School	MGT.U1: Working Together in the Classroom MGT.U2: Using the Classroom Library for Independent Reading (RML1–RML5)	**IW.1: Making a Name Chart (1 day)** **IW.2: Writing About Our Classroom (1 day)** **IW.3: Creating a Job Chart (1–2 days)**	**MGT.U1: Working Together in the Classroom (8 days)**	If you are using *The Reading Minilessons Book, Kindergarten*, you do not need to teach MGT.U1. Both RML and WML establish the same routines. However, be sure to take time to build community in your classroom by asking children to draw and write about themselves as they practice these new routines. The opening page of the writing minilessons umbrella MGT.U1 provides specific suggestions. IW.2 can be taught as a culminating activity.

*Interactive writing lessons can be taught on the same day as a writing minilesson or in place of a writing minilesson.

Key
MGT: Management   STR: Telling Stories   MBK: Making Books   DRW: Drawing
EWR: Exploring Early Writing   WPS: Writing Process

Months	Texts from *Fountas & Pinnell Classroom™ Shared Reading Collection*	Text Sets from *Fountas & Pinnell Classroom™ Interactive Read-Aloud Collection*	Reading Minilessons (RML) Sequence from *The Reading Minilessons Book, Kindergarten*	Interactive Writing (IW) Lessons*	Writing Minilesson (WML) Umbrellas	Teaching Suggestions for Extending Learning
Months 1 & 2 (cont.)	City ABCs Country ABCs The Sleepover	Letters at Work: The Alphabet	LA.U1: Thinking and Talking About Books	**IW.4: Making a Menu (1 day)**	**EWR.U7 Learning to Draw and Write Through Play, WML1 (1 day)**	Teach IW.4 shortly before EWR.U7. Together IW.4 and ERW.U7.WML1 show children how writing can be part of their daily play. Invite them to write for the play corner during both choice time and independent writing.
				IW.5: Making an ABC Book (1 day)		After reading several ABC books together, teach IW.5. Children can work on finishing the class ABC book during independent writing. You can also invite them to make their own ABC books in the writing center.
			MGT.U3: Engaging in Classroom Literacy Work, RML1–RML5, RML10	**IW.6: Making Labels for the Classroom (1–2 days)**	**MGT.U3: Learning About Choice Time, WML1–WML5 (5 days)**	Note that the writing center and word work center are introduced in both reading minilessons (MGT.U3) and writing minilessons (MGT.U3). It is not necessary to do both. The routines are the same whether children engage in an activity during literacy work time or choice time. Teach the first five minilessons early in the year to make choice time options open and accessible. Add more centers over time.
	Look Out! Coco Steps Out	Taking Care of Each Other: Family		**IW.7: Writing a Thank You Card (1 day)**		
					STR.U1: Storytelling, WML1–WML2 (2 days)	Teach the minilessons in STR.U1 over time so that children have more time to tell stories. Continue inviting children to tell stories as you teach MGT.U4, EWR.U1, and STR.U2.

Months	Texts from *Fountas & Pinnell Classroom™ Shared Reading Collection*	Text Sets from *Fountas & Pinnell Classroom™ Interactive Read-Aloud Collection*	Reading Minilessons (RML) Sequence from *The Reading Minilessons Book, Kindergarten*	Interactive Writing (IW) Lessons*	Writing Minilesson (WML) Umbrellas	Teaching Suggestions for Extending Learning
Months 1 & 2 (cont.)	Hand in Hand: Poems About Friends A Big Bear in the Little Woods The Right Tools By the Light of the Moon	The Importance of Friendship	LA.U14: Understanding Characters in Stories	IW.8: Making a Class Big Book (3–5 days)	**MGT.U4: Using Drawing and Writing Tools (4 days)**	When you teach this umbrella, children may be engaged in a variety of writing activities during independent writing. They may be telling stories, drawing their stories, making labels for the classroom (IW.6), or making their own cards (IW.7). Teach all four lessons in MGT.U4, or wait to teach WML4 until after you introduce bookmaking.
					EWR.U1: Learning Early Concepts of Print, WML1–WML4 (4 days)	Teach the lessons in EWR.U1 over time. It is helpful for children to begin to learn the letters in their own names and their classmates' names so they can use this knowledge to make connections to words they are learning. IW.8: Making a Class Big Book reinforces learning classmates' names.
					MGT.U3: Learning About Choice Time, WML6–WML9 (4 days)	Introduce the next four centers once children have control over the routines of choice time.
					EWR.U2: Introducing Handwriting (3 days)	Repeat any of these lessons to teach different letters and as children learn more about writing.
					DRW.U1: Making a Self-Portrait (2 days)	Teach DRW.U1 before making a class big book so you can use children's self-portraits in the class big book.
					MBK.U1: Getting Started with Making Books (5 days)	Invite and encourage children to make books about anything they want. Suggest that they draw (and write) some of the stories they have been sharing orally. The class writing from IW.5 and IW.8 can be used to model bookmaking.

Months	Texts from *Fountas & Pinnell Classroom™ Shared Reading Collection*	Text Sets from *Fountas & Pinnell Classroom™ Interactive Read-Aloud Collection*	Reading Minilessons (RML) Sequence from *The Reading Minilessons Book, Kindergarten*	Interactive Writing (IW) Lessons*	Writing Minilesson (WML) Umbrellas	Teaching Suggestions for Extending Learning
Months 1 & 2 (cont.)					**STR.U1: Storytelling, WML3–WML4 (2 days)**	Teach and revisit the lessons in STR.U1 across the year whenever your class needs a new avenue for exploring writing ideas. You may want to carve out a space during morning meeting, before writing time, or in a choice/literacy center for children to tell stories. When they tell their stories, they are rehearsing for writing. Help them see that they can write the stories they tell.
					DRW.U2: Learning to Draw (6 days)	The six lessons in DRW.U2 support children in making representational drawings as well as in learning new drawing techniques.
Months 3 & 4	Spots	Noticing the Way the World Looks: Colors	WAR.U1: Introducing a Reader's Notebook	IW.9: Making a Color Chart (1 day)	**MGT.U2: Establishing Independent Writing (7 days)**	Once children are comfortable with the routine of making books at an established time of day, it will be easy to establish the routines of independent writing. Introduce this umbrella earlier in the year if your children are ready. We suggest introducing it after they have had time to experiment with bookmaking so they understand how to use their time during independent writing.
	Stars					
	Stripes			IW.10: Writing a Color Poem (1 day)		
	Hearts					
	A Rainbow of Fruit					
	The Orange Butterfly: A Story in Pictures	Exploring Pictures: Wordless Books				
			LA.U17: Using Pictures in a Book to Tell the Story		**STR.U2: Acting Out Stories, WML1 (1 day)**	As children practice telling stories from pictures and acting out stories, they learn more about story structure.

Months	Texts from *Fountas & Pinnell Classroom™ Shared Reading Collection*	Text Sets from *Fountas & Pinnell Classroom™ Interactive Read-Aloud Collection*	Reading Minilessons (RML) Sequence from *The Reading Minilessons Book, Kindergarten*	Interactive Writing (IW) Lessons*	Writing Minilesson (WML) Umbrellas	Teaching Suggestions for Extending Learning
Months 3 & 4 (cont.)	One Summer Day: A Story in Pictures			IW.11: Writing from a Picture (1 day)	WPS.U1: Getting Ideas for Writing, WML1–WML2 (2 days)	If you are teaching reading minilessons, the lessons in WAR.U1– which ask children to write about themselves, their families, and their friends–can be revisited as another way to get ideas for writing. Teach or revisit WPS.U1 whenever children need support generating ideas.
	Counting on the Farm	Numbers at Work: Counting	LA.U5: Getting Started with Book Clubs	IW.12: Making a Counting Book (3–5 days)	EWR.U3: Learning How to Write Words (5 days)	In EWR.U3, children learn how to transfer the behaviors they have learned in interactive writing to their independent writing. Invite them to write their own counting books or to write from pictures to apply this new learning.
	Ten Big Elephants			IW.13: Taking a Survey (1–2 days)		
	Ten in the Bed					
	Kate's Party		MGT.U3: Engaging in Classroom Literacy Work, RML6–RML9, revisit RML10		EWR.U1: Learning Early Concepts of Print, WML5–WML6 (2 days)	These two minilessons help children think about leaving space between words and starting their writing on the left. In writing conferences, draw their attention to effective use of space.
	City Kid, Country Kid	The Importance of Kindness			MBK.U2: Expanding Bookmaking (5 days)	The lessons in this umbrella offer children more ways to apply what they are learning about writing words. Teach lessons only when children are ready.
		Eric Carle: Exploring the Natural World			EWR.U5: Using Capital Letters (3 days)	Introduce EWR.U5 when the majority of children are writing most letters. You might choose to teach only the first two lessons now and leave the third for later depending on your class. This umbrella will support children in remembering to capitalize the first letter of their names.
			LA.U3: Studying Authors and Illustrators		DRW.U3: Making Pictures Interesting, WML1 (1 day)	LA.U3 pairs well with DRW.U3. Both are designed to help children study techniques used by writers and illustrators, including by Eric Carle, whose books are mentor texts in DRW.U3.WML1. Teach the lessons in DRW.U3 over time to limit the materials needed at one time.

Months	Texts from *Fountas & Pinnell Classroom™ Shared Reading Collection*	Text Sets from *Fountas & Pinnell Classroom™ Interactive Read-Aloud Collection*	Reading Minilessons (RML) Sequence from *The Reading Minilessons Book, Kindergarten*	Interactive Writing (IW) Lessons*	Writing Minilesson (WML) Umbrellas	Teaching Suggestions for Extending Learning
Months 3 & 4 (cont.)					**WPS.U6: Celebrating Writing (1–3 days)**	Repeat this umbrella throughout the year to give children plenty of opportunities to celebrate and "publish" their writing for others. You do not have to teach the lessons consecutively. Pick and choose depending on your goals for the class.
Months 5 & 6	Not Quite Right	The Place You Call Home	WAR.U2: Using a Reader's Notebook	**IW.14: Writing About a Class Memory (1–2 days)** **IW.15: Writing About Our Creations (2–3 days)**	**STR.U3: Learning How to Tell Stories (3 days)**	STR.U3 is a nice way to continue storytelling while teaching children how to present to an audience. This umbrella builds on the experience of celebrating writing with an audience and further develops oral language. Storytelling will also help children generate ideas for writing memory books (MBK.U3).
	The Dog Park Coming Around the Mountain	Living and Working Together: Community		**IW.16: Making Signs (1 day)**	**EWR.U7: Learning to Draw and Write Through Play, WML2 (1 day)**	The minilessons in EWR.U7 can be taught at any time to infuse writing into play. However, it is helpful to have taught IW.15 and IW.16 before introducing this minilesson.
	Sticky A Bear and His Honey	Exploring Fiction and Nonfiction		**IW.17: Labeling a Map (1–2 days)**	**MBK.U3: Making Memory Books (5 days)**	Teach IW.14 and use the class writing as a mentor text in MBK.U3. If you are using the text sets from *Fountas & Pinnell Classroom™ Interactive Read-Aloud Collection*, note that some of these lessons use books from the end of the year according to the sequence. We encourage you to read them now and later. Students will benefit from listening to these stories more than once.
	Fly Away Bouncing Balls Spin, Spin, Spin		LA.U6: Studying Fiction and Nonfiction		**WPS.U2: Adding to Writing (3 days)**	This umbrella provides a simple introduction to what it means to revise writing by adding details. Children can apply these lessons to the memory books they are working on or to any other writing they want to improve.

Months	Texts from *Fountas & Pinnell Classroom™ Shared Reading Collection*	Text Sets from *Fountas & Pinnell Classroom™ Interactive Read-Aloud Collection*	Reading Minilessons (RML) Sequence from *The Reading Minilessons Book, Kindergarten*	Interactive Writing (IW) Lessons*	Writing Minilesson (WML) Umbrellas	Teaching Suggestions for Extending Learning
Months 5 & 6 (cont.)	Rolling Slip and Slide Playing Basketball On the Go A Scary Story: A Story for Two Voices Smash! Crash! Morning on the Farm Crunch: A Story for Two Voices Goldy	Having Fun with Language Exploring Animal Tales	SAS.U1: Searching for and Using Meaning, Language, and Visual Information WAR.U3: Introducing Writing About Reading in a Reader's Notebook	IW.18: **Writing a How-to Book (3–5 days)**	**WPS.U3: Deleting and Reorganizing Writing (3 days)**	In WPS.U3, children learn another way to revise. Invite them to apply the minilessons in this umbrella to the memory books they are making.
					Revisit **WPS.U6: Celebrating Writing (1 day)**	Revisit any of the minilessons in WPS.U6 to celebrate writing. For example, ask children to share one of their favorite memory books or tell about a risk they took as they tried out parts of the writing process (WPS.U2, WPS.U5).
					MBK.U4: Making How-to Books (4 days)	After children study the difference between fiction and nonfiction (LA.U6), invite them to write a nonfiction how-to book. We recommend teaching IW.18 before MBK.U4 so the class writing can serve as a mentor text. If you are using *Fountas & Pinnell Classroom™ Interactive Read-Aloud Collection*, note that this umbrella uses a few books that come later in the sequence. However, you do not need to read them ahead of time for children to understand the minilessons.
					WPS.U5: Proofreading Writing (3 days)	WPS.U5 provides a simple introduction to editing. Invite children to apply these lessons to their writing (e.g., a how-to book). This umbrella also reinforces the behaviors and understandings taught in the reading minilessons in SAS.U1.
					EWR.U6: Learning About Punctuation (3 days)	After teaching these minilessons, invite children to extend their proofreading and editing to include checking for punctuation.
					Revisit **WPS.U6: Celebrating Writing (1 day)**	Use any of the minilessons in WPS.U6 to help children "publish" and celebrate their writing. Invite them to share their favorite how-to books.

Months	Texts from *Fountas & Pinnell Classroom™ Shared Reading Collection*	Text Sets from *Fountas & Pinnell Classroom™ Interactive Read-Aloud Collection*	Reading Minilessons (RML) Sequence from *The Reading Minilessons Book, Kindergarten*	Interactive Writing (IW) Lessons*	Writing Minilesson (WML) Umbrellas	Teaching Suggestions for Extending Learning
Months 5 & 6 (cont.)				**IW.19: Making a Story Map Mural (1–2 days)**	**STR.U2: Acting Out Stories, WML2 (1 day)**	STR.U2.WML2 and IW.19 develop children's understanding of story structure. IW.19 also offers a high level of support for writing about reading. The reading minilessons in WAR.U3 also help children develop ways to write about reading.
			LA.U7: Studying Animal Tales		**EWR.U4: Using Classroom Resources to Write Words (3 days)**	At this point in the year, most kindergartners begin to expand their writing. They need ways to write unfamiliar words on their own. This umbrella offers children generative ways to spell new words.
Months 7 & 8	The Big Race: An Aesop Fable	Sharing Stories: Folktales	SAS.U2: Monitoring and Self-Correcting	**IW.20: Writing an Alternative Ending (1 day)**	**WPS.U1: Getting Ideas for Writing, WML3–WML4 (2 days)**	These minilessons offer children ways to get ideas for their writing. Invite them to not only choose their topic but also the type of writing they want to do.
	The Sleeping Giant				**STR.U2: Acting Out Stories, WML3 (1 day)**	Children love to act out familiar folktales with puppets. STR.U2.WML3 continues to develop children's understanding of important story elements. Invite them to build on IW.20 by acting out alternative endings and then writing them or vice versa.
	Mondo					
	Molly's Leash					
	Animal Masks					
	Alligator Hide-and-Seek	Sharing the Earth: Animals	LA.U4: Giving a Book Talk	**IW.21: Writing a Question-and-Answer Book (3–5 days)**	**DRW.U3: Making Pictures Interesting, WML2 (1 day)**	We recommend teaching the minilessons in this umbrella over the course of the year to allow children time to experiment with different materials and techniques. Use the class writing from IW.21 as a mentor text for adding interesting features, like flaps, to books.
	Up in the Cloud Forest					
	In the Arctic				Revisit as needed: **WPS.U2 Adding to Writing, WPS.U3 Deleting and Reorganizing Writing (1–3 days)**	Children can apply these minilessons to any kind of writing, such as variations on folktales or question-and-answer books (based on IW.20 and IW.21).
	In the Outback					

Months	Texts from *Fountas & Pinnell Classroom™ Shared Reading Collection*	Text Sets from *Fountas & Pinnell Classroom™ Interactive Read-Aloud Collection*	Reading Minilessons (RML) Sequence from *The Reading Minilessons Book, Kindergarten*	Interactive Writing (IW) Lessons*	Writing Minilesson (WML) Umbrellas	Teaching Suggestions for Extending Learning
Months 7 & 8 (cont.)		Lois Ehlert: Bringing Color and Texture to Life	WAR.U6: Writing Opinions About Books	IW.22: Writing Scientific Observations (1 day)	Revisit WPS.U6: Celebrating Writing (1 day)	Provide opportunities throughout the year to celebrate writing. Revisit any lesson in WPS.U6 that meets children's needs. Even as children celebrate their writing, use interactive writing to introduce new ways to write, such as IW.22. This interactive writing lesson can be taught at any time of the year and revisited for several different scientific observations.
			LA.U3: Studying Authors and Illustrators		DRW.U3: Making Pictures Interesting, WML3 (1 day)	This minilesson uses the work of Lois Ehlert to inspire children to use found objects in their drawings. They can revisit books they have made to apply this minilesson or try it on new pieces of writing.
		Learning How to Be Yourself	LA.U15: Getting to Know the Characters in Stories	IW.23: Writing a Letter About a Book (1 day)	EWR.U8: Writing a Friendly Letter (3 days)	EWR.U8 builds on learning started in IW.23 as well as in the reading minilessons in WAR.U6. Letters are a wonderful way to invite children to write about their reading.
		Understanding Feelings			EWR.U7: Learning to Draw and Write Through Play, WML3 (1 day)	EWR.U7 builds on the work done in IW.23 and EWR.U8. When you change your play corner into a post office, you create a space for children to engage not only in letter writing but in all kinds of functional writing.
					Revisit MBK.U3: Making Memory Books (4 days)	If time allows, revisit MBK.U3. Revisiting this umbrella gives children the opportunity to expand their writing and try out some of the new understandings they have learned.
			LA.U12: Thinking About Where Stories Happen		Revisit DRW.U2: Learning to Draw, WML3 (1 day)	As children become more aware of their surroundings and learn about story settings (e.g., from the reading minilessons in LA.U12), you see them start to experiment with writing about where their stories take place. Revisit DRW.U2.WML3 to remind them about adding details to the backgrounds of their pictures.

Months	Texts from *Fountas & Pinnell Classroom™ Shared Reading Collection*	Text Sets from *Fountas & Pinnell Classroom™ Interactive Read-Aloud Collection*	Reading Minilessons (RML) Sequence from *The Reading Minilessons Book, Kindergarten*	Interactive Writing (IW) Lessons*	Writing Minilesson (WML) Umbrellas	Teaching Suggestions for Extending Learning
Months 7 & 8 (cont.)			SAS.U3: Maintaining Fluency		Revisit as needed: **MBK.U2: Expanding Bookmaking (1–2 days)**	Consider repeating MBK.U2 with different mentor texts. Connect WML1 and WML3 to what children know about drawing backgrounds by suggesting that they label their backgrounds and write about them.
			WAR.U4: Writing About Fiction Books in a Reader's Notebook		Revisit as needed: **EWR.U6: Learning About Punctuation (1–3 days)**	This might be a good time of the year to revisit punctuation, especially if the class is studying how to read punctuation (e.g., SAS.U3 reading minilessons). At this point, children will have more control over their writing and can make decisions about how they want those sentences to be read. They begin to notice that authors make important choices about punctuation.
Months 9 & 10	The Log Up, Down, and Around Scream for Ice Cream Fuzzy and Buzzy Jump and Hop: Poems to Make You Move Dancing in the Mud The Wheels on the Bike Miss Mary Mack Giggles: Poems to Make You Laugh	Exploring Nonfiction Rhythm and Rhyme: Joyful Language	LA.U9: Learning About Nonfiction Books	**IW.24: Writing an All-About Book (2–4 days)** **IW.25: Innovating on a Text (1 day)**	Revisit as needed: **EWR.U3: Learning How to Write Words** and **EWR.U4: Using Classroom Resources to Write Words (1–3 days)**	As children learn more about nonfiction books, they will write more nonfiction. Revisit lessons that will help them write more complex vocabulary.
					MBK.U5: Making All-About Books (4 days)	MBK.U5 builds on the experiences children have had with nonfiction books across the year. If you are using reading minilessons, it will be helpful to have taught LA.U9. Also teach IW.24 ahead of MBK.U5 so you can use the class writing as a mentor text.

Months	Texts from *Fountas & Pinnell Classroom™ Shared Reading Collection*	Text Sets from *Fountas & Pinnell Classroom™ Interactive Read-Aloud Collection*	Reading Minilessons (RML) Sequence from *The Reading Minilessons Book, Kindergarten*	Interactive Writing (IW) Lessons*	Writing Minilesson (WML) Umbrellas	Teaching Suggestions for Extending Learning
Months 9 & 10 (cont.)		Grace Lin: Exploring Family and Culture	LA.U18: Looking Closely at Illustrations		**DRW.U4: Illustrating Nonfiction (3 days)**	DRW.U4 builds on an illustration study of fiction and nonfiction that you might be working on through reading minilessons (LA.U18 and LA.U10). It can also stand on its own based on all of the discussions you have had about illustrations across the year. Children are becoming more aware of illustrator's craft and the decisions that illustrators make. Invite them to apply the minilessons in DRW.U4 to the all-about books they are working on or to any other piece of nonfiction they have written.
			LA.U10: Learning Information from Illustrations/ Graphics			
			WAR.U5: Writing About Nonfiction Books in a Reader's Notebook		Revisit as needed: **WPS.U2: Adding to Writing** or **WPS.U3: Deleting and Reorganizing Writing (1–4 days)**	Repeat minilessons to help children add to, reorganize, or omit unnecessary details from their writing. They can apply these minilessons to the all-about books they may be writing. If you are teaching the reading minilessons in LA.U11, you might see children experimenting with features like sidebars or tables of contents in their own writing. In later grades, children will experience writing minilessons about nonfiction text features. For now, encourage children to experiment and have fun trying the things they see in books.
			LA.U11: Using Text Features to Gain Information			
		Celebrating Differences	LA.U13: Understanding How Stories Work		**EWR.U7: Learning to Draw and Write Through Play, WML4 (1 day)**	EWR.U7.WML4 helps children think about opportunities to draw and write while playing restaurant. In this lesson, we recommend turning the play corner into a restaurant as part of a study of family, food, and culture. Through play, children learn about their classmates and celebrate similarities and differences.
	My Little Rooster					
	The Stuck Truck				Revisit as needed: **STR.U1: Storytelling** or **WPS.U1: Getting Ideas for Writing (2–5 days)**	If children need new ideas to fuel their writing, revisit STR.U1 or WPS.U1. They will have a new set of stories to tell and new ways to think about the minilesson principles. Use new examples in the lessons when possible. Invite children to choose any type of writing that fits their purpose.
	The House that Jack Built	Using Patterns: Cumulative Tales				
	The Old Lady Who Swallowed a Fly		LA.U16: Understanding Character Change			

Months	Texts from *Fountas & Pinnell Classroom™ Shared Reading Collection*	Text Sets from *Fountas & Pinnell Classroom™ Interactive Read-Aloud Collection*	Reading Minilessons (RML) Sequence from *The Reading Minilessons Book, Kindergarten*	Interactive Writing (IW) Lessons*	Writing Minilesson (WML) Umbrellas	Teaching Suggestions for Extending Learning
Months 9 & 10 (cont.)	Pitter Patter Splish, Splash		LA.U8: Thinking About the Author's Message		**WPS.U4: Making Writing Interesting (3 days)**	Teach the minilessons in this umbrella any time you think your students are ready. We have placed it at the end of the year so children can bring their experiences with a variety of texts to this study.
			LA.U2: Noticing How Authors Tell Their Stories		**WPS.U6: Celebrating Writing (1–3 days)**	End the year with a final writing celebration!

Glossary

active learning experience A meaningful experience, such as reading and talking about books, making something, or going somewhere, prior to interactive writing.

all-about book A nonfiction book that tells about only one subject or topic.

alphabet book/ABC book A book that helps children develop the concept and sequence of the alphabet by pairing alphabet letters with pictures of people, animals, or objects with labels related to the letters.

alphabet linking chart A chart containing upper- and lowercase letters of the alphabet paired with pictures representing words beginning with each letter (a, *apple*, for example).

assessment A means for gathering information or data that reveals what learners control, partially control, or do not yet control consistently.

audience The readers of a text. Often a writer crafts a text with a particular audience in mind.

behaviors Actions that are observable as children read or write.

bold / boldface Type that is heavier and darker than usual, often used for emphasis.

book and print features (as text characteristics) The physical attributes of a text (for example, font, layout, and length).

character An individual, usually a person or animal, in a text.

choice time An essential part of the preschool learning experience in which children make their own decisions regarding which activities to do.

chronological sequence An underlying structural pattern used especially in nonfiction texts to describe a series of events in the order they happened in time.

compose Think about the message and how to say it.

concepts of print Basic understandings related to how written language or print is organized and used—how it works.

construct Write the message that has been composed together; includes sharing the pen.

conventions In writing, formal usage that has become customary in written language. Grammar, usage, capitalization, punctuation, spelling, handwriting, and text layout are categories of writing conventions.

counting book A book that teaches counting in which the structure follows numeric progression.

craft In writing, how an individual piece of writing is shaped. Elements of craft are organization, idea development, language use, word choice, and voice.

dialogue Spoken words, usually set off with quotation marks in text.

directionality The orientation of print (in the English language, from left to right).

directions (how-to) Part of a procedural nonfiction text that shows the steps involved in performing a task. A set of directions may include diagrams or drawings with labels.

drafting and revising The process of getting ideas down on paper and shaping them to convey the writer's message.

drawing In writing, creating a rough image (i.e, a drawing) of a person, place, thing, or idea to capture, work with, and render the writer's ideas.

editing and proofreading The process of polishing the final draft of a written composition to prepare it for publication.

elements of fiction Important elements of fiction include narrator, characters, plot, setting, theme, and style.

elements of poetry Important elements of poetry include figurative language, imagery, personification, rhythm, rhyme, repetition, alliteration, assonance, consonance, onomatopoeia, and aspects of layout.

English learners People whose native language is not English and who are acquiring English as an additional language.

family, friends, and school story A contemporary realistic text focused on the everyday experiences of children of a variety of ages, including relationships with family and friends and experiences at school.

fiction Invented, imaginative prose or poetry that tells a story. Fiction texts can be organized into the categories realism and fantasy. Along with nonfiction, fiction is one of two basic genres of literature.

figurative language An element of a writer's style, figurative language changes or goes beyond literal meaning. Two common types of figurative language are metaphor (a direct comparison) and simile (a comparison that uses *like* or *as*).

font In printed text, the collection of type (letters) in a particular style.

form A kind of text that is characterized by particular elements. Mystery, for example, is a form of writing within the realistic fiction genre. Another term for form is *subgenre*.

friendly letter In writing, a functional nonfiction text usually addressed to friends or family that may take the form of notes, letters, invitations, or email.

functional text A nonfiction text intended to accomplish a practical task, for example, labels, lists, letters, and directions with steps (how-to).

genre A category of written text that is characterized by a particular style, form, or content.

graphic feature In fiction texts, graphic features are usually illustrations. In nonfiction texts, graphic features include photographs, paintings and drawings, captions, charts, diagrams, tables and graphs, maps, and timelines.

high-frequency words Words that occur often in spoken and written language (for example, *the*).

illustration Graphic representation of important content (for example, art, photos, maps, graphs, charts) in a fiction or nonfiction text.

independent writing A text written by children independently with teacher support as needed.

informational text A nonfiction text in which a purpose is to inform or give facts about a topic. Informational texts include the following genres: biography, autobiography, memoir, and narrative nonfiction, as well as expository texts, procedural texts, and persuasive texts.

innovate on a text Change the ending, the series of events, the characters, or the setting of a familiar text.

interactive read-aloud An instructional context in which students are actively listening and responding to an oral reading of a text.

interactive writing A teaching context in which the teacher and students cooperatively plan, compose, and write a group text; both teacher and students act as scribes (in turn).

italic (italics) A styling of type that is characterized by slanted letters.

label A written word or phrase that names the content of an illustration.

layout The way the print and illustrations are arranged on a page.

learning zone The level at which it is most productive to aim one's teaching for each student (the zone of proximal development).

lowercase letter A small letterform that is usually different from its corresponding capital or uppercase form.

main idea The central underlying idea, concept, or message that the author conveys in a nonfiction text. See also *message*.

memory story A story about something experienced personally.

mentor texts Books or other texts that serve as examples of excellent writing. Mentor texts are read and reread to provide models for literature discussion and student writing.

message An important idea that an author conveys in a fiction or nonfiction text. See also *main idea*.

modeled writing An instructional technique in which a teacher demonstrates the process of composing a particular genre, making the process explicit for students.

nonfiction Prose or poetry that provides factual information. According to their structures, nonfiction texts can be organized into the categories of narrative and nonnarrative. Along with fiction, nonfiction is one of the two basic genres of literature.

organization The arrangement of ideas in a text according to a logical structure, either narrative or nonnarrative. Another term for organization is *text structure*.

organizational tools and sources of information A design feature of nonfiction texts. Organizational tools and sources of information help a reader process and understand nonfiction texts. Examples include tables of contents, headings, indexes, glossaries, appendices, author bios, and references.

picture book An illustrated fiction or nonfiction text in which pictures work with the text to tell a story or provide information.

planning and rehearsing The process of collecting, working with, and selecting ideas for a written composition.

plot The events, action, conflict, and resolution of a story presented in a certain order in a fiction text. A simple plot progresses chronologically from start to end, whereas more complex plots may shift back and forth in time.

poetry Compact, metrical writing characterized by imagination and artistry and imbued with intense meaning. Along with prose, poetry is one of the two broad categories into which all literature can be divided.

principle A generalization that is predictable. It is the key idea that children will learn and be invited to apply.

print feature In nonfiction texts, features that include the color, size, style, and font of type, as well as various aspects of layout.

procedural text A nonfiction text that explains how to do something. Procedural texts are almost always organized in temporal sequence and take the form of directions (or how-to texts) or descriptions of a process.

prompt A question, direction, or statement designed to encourage the child to say more about a topic.

publishing The process of making the final draft of a written composition public.

punctuation Marks used in written text to clarify meaning and separate structural units. The comma and the period are common punctuation marks.

purpose A writer's overall intention in creating a text, or a reader's overall intention in reading a text. To tell a story is one example of a writer's purpose, and to be entertained is one example of a reader's purpose.

question and answer A structural pattern used especially in nonfiction texts to organize information in a series of questions with responses. Question-and-answer texts may be based on a verbal or written interview or on frequently arising or logical questions about a topic.

repetition Repeated words or phrases that help create rhythm and emphasis in poetry or prose.

rhyme The repetition of vowel and consonant sounds in the stressed and unstressed syllables of words in verse, especially at the ends of lines.

rhythm The regular or ordered repetition of stressed and unstressed syllables in poetry, other writing, or speech.

sequence See *chronological sequence* and *temporal sequence*.

setting The place and time in which a fiction text or biographical text takes place.

share the pen At points selected by the teacher for instructional value, individual children take over or "share the pen" with the teacher.

shared reading An instructional context in which the teacher involves a group of students in the reading of a particular big book to introduce aspects of literacy (such as print conventions), develop reading strategies (such as decoding or predicting), and teach vocabulary.

shared writing An instructional context in which the teacher involves a group of students in the composing of a coherent text together. The teacher writes while scaffolding children's language and ideas.

sidebar Information that is additional to the main text, placed alongside the text and sometimes set off from the main text in a box.

speech bubble A shape, often rounded, containing the words a character says in a cartoon or other text. Another term for *speech bubble* is *speech balloon*.

story A series of events in narrative form, either fiction or nonfiction.

story map A representation of the sequence of events from a text using drawings or writing.

style The way a writer chooses and arranges words to create a meaningful text. Aspects of style include sentence length, word choice, and the use of figurative language and symbolism.

survey Asking a question and recording the responses.

syllable A minimal unit of sequential speech sounds composed of a vowel sound or a consonant-vowel combination. A syllable always contains a vowel or vowel-like speech sound (e.g., *pen/ny*).

temporal sequence An underlying structural pattern used especially in nonfiction texts to describe the sequence in which something always or usually occurs, such as the steps in a process or a life cycle. See also *procedural text*.

text structure The overall architecture or organization of a piece of writing. Another term for text structure is *organization*.

thought bubble A shape, often rounded, containing the words (or sometimes an image that suggests one or more words) a character thinks in a cartoon or other text. Another term for *thought bubble* is *thought balloon*.

tools As text characteristics, parts of a text designed to help the reader access or better understand it (tables of contents, glossaries, headings). In writing, references that support the writing process (dictionary, thesaurus).

topic The subject of a piece of writing.

uppercase letter A large letterform that is usually different from its corresponding lowercase form. Another term for *uppercase letter* is *capital letter*.

verbal path Language prompts paired with motor movements to help children learn to form letters correctly.

viewing self as writer Having attitudes and using practices that support a student in becoming a lifelong writer.

word boundaries The space that appears before the first letter and after the last letter of a word and that defines the letter or letters as a word. It is important for young readers to learn to recognize word boundaries.

wordless picture book A form in which a story is told exclusively with pictures.

writers' workshop A classroom structure that begins with a whole-group minilesson; continues with independent writing, individual conferences, and small-group instruction; and ends with a whole-group share.

writing Children engaging in the writing process and producing pieces of their own writing in many genres.

writing about reading Children responding to reading a text by writing and sometimes drawing.

writing process Key phases of creating a piece of writing: planning and rehearsing, drafting and revising, editing and proofreading, and publishing.

Credits

Cover image from *Baa Baa Black Sheep* written and illustrated by Iza Trapani. Copyright © Charlesbridge Publishing, Inc. All rights reserved. Used with permission of Charlesbridge Publishing, Inc. www.charlesbridge.com.

Cover image from *B Is for Bulldozer: A Construction ABC* by June Sobel. Text copyright © 2003 by June Sobel. Illustrations copyright © 2003 by Melissa Iwai. Reprinted by permission of Houghton Mifflin Harcourt Trade Publishing.

Cover image from *Building a House* by Byron Barton. Copyright © 1981 by Byron Barton. Used by permission of HarperCollins Publishers.

Cover image from *The Bus for Us*, written and illustrated by Suzanne Bloom. Copyright © by Suzanne Bloom. Published by Boyds Mills Press. Used by permission.

Cover image from *Do Like Kyla* by Angela Johnson. Jacket illustration copyright © 1990 by James E. Ransome. Scholastic Inc./Orchard Books. Used by permission.

Cover image from *Does a Kangaroo Have a Mother, Too?* by Eric Carle. Cover art copyright © 2000 by Eric Carle. Used by permission of HarperCollins Publishers.

Cover image from *The Doorbell Rang* by Pat Hutchins. Copyright © 1986 by Pat Hutchins. Used by permission of HarperCollins Publishers.

Cover image from *Elizabeti's Doll* by Stephanie Stuve-Bodeen, illustrated by Christy Hale. Copyright © 2002 Stephanie Stuve-Bodeen and Christy Hale. Permission arranged with Lee & Low Books, Inc., New York, NY 10016.

Cover image from *Flower Garden* by Eve Bunting. Text copyright © 1994 by Eve Bunting. Illustrations copyright © 1994 by Kathryn Hewitt. Reprinted by permission of Houghton Mifflin Harcourt Trade Publishing.

Cover image from *From Head to Toe* by Eric Carle. Cover art copyright © 1997 by Eric Carle. Used by permission of HarperCollins Publishers.

Cover image from *A Fruit Is a Suitcase for Seeds* by Jean Richards, illustrated by Anca Hariton. Text copyright © 2002 by Jean Richards. Illustration copyright © 2002 by Anca Hariton. Reprinted with the permission of Millbrook Press, a division of Lerner Publishing Group, Inc. All rights reserved. No part of this excerpt may be used or reproduced in any manner whatsoever without the prior written permission of Lerner Publishing Group, Inc.

Cover image from *The Gingerbread Boy* by Paul Galdone. Copyright © 1975 by Paul Galdone. Reprinted by permission of Houghton Mifflin Harcourt Trade Publishing.

Cover image from *Good Morning, Chick* by Mirra Ginsburg, illustrated by Byron Burton. Copyright © 1989. Used by permission of HarperCollins Publishers.

Cover image from *Harold Finds a Voice*. © 2013 Courtney Dicmas. Reproduced by permission of Child's Play (International) Ltd.

Cover image from *Hats, Hats, Hats* by Ann Morris, illustrated by Ken Heyman. Text copyright © 1989 by Ann Morris. Art copyright © 1989 by Ken Heyman. Used by permission of HarperCollins Publishers, and Ken Heyman.

Works Cited

Clay, Marie M. 1975. *What Did I Write? Beginning Writing Behaviour*. Portsmouth, NH: Heinemann.

Fountas, Irene C., and Gay Su Pinnell. 2019. *The Reading Minilessons Book, Kindergarten*. Portsmouth, NH: Heinemann.

———. 2018. *Fountas & Pinnell Classroom™ Interactive Read-Aloud Collection*. Portsmouth, NH: Heinemann.

———. 2018. *Fountas & Pinnell Classroom™ Shared Reading Collection*. Portsmouth, NH: Heinemann.

———. 2018. *The Literacy Quick Guide: A Reference Tool for Responsive Literacy Teaching*. Portsmouth, NH: Heinemann.

———. 2017. *Fountas & Pinnell Literacy Continuum: A Tool for Assessment, Planning, and Teaching*. Portsmouth, NH: Heinemann.

———. 2017. *Guided Reading: Responsive Teaching Across the Grades*, 2nd ed. Portsmouth, NH: Heinemann.

———. 2017. *Phonics, Spelling, and Word Study System, for Kindergarten*. Portsmouth, NH: Heinemann.

Gardner-Neblett, Nicole. "The Conversation." September 2015. https://theconversation.com/why-storytelling-skills-matter-for-african-american-kids-46844.

Glover, Matt. 2009. *Engaging Young Writers, Preschool–Grade 1*. Portsmouth, NH: Heinemann.

Hoberman, Mary Ann. 2007. *A House Is a House for Me*. New York: Penguin Young Readers Group.

Johnston, Peter, Kathy Champeau, Andrea Hartwig, Sarah Helmer, Merry Komar, Tara Krueger, and Laurie McCarthy. 2020. *Engaging Literate Minds: Developing Children's Social, Emotional, and Intellectual Lives, K–3*. Portsmouth, NH: Stenhouse.

Masurel, Claire. 2001. *Two Homes*. Somerville, MA: Candlewick.

McCarrier, Andrea, Irene C. Fountas, and Gay Su Pinnell. 2000. *Interactive Writing: How Language and Literacy Come Together, K–2*. Portsmouth, NH: Heinemann.

Morris, Ann. 1992. *Houses and Homes*. New York: HarperCollins.

Ray, Katie Wood, and Matt Glover. 2008. *Already Ready: Nurturing Writers in Preschool and Kindergarten*. Portsmouth, NH: Heinemann.

ck, Lauren B., and Catherine E. Snow. 2009. *Speaking and Listening for hool Through Third Grade*. Revised Edition. University of Pittsburgh National Center on Education and the Economy. Published under New Standards® trademark is owned by the University of The National Center on Education and the Economy at NW, Suite 500 West, Washington, DC, 20004, USA.

9. *Mind in Society: The Development of Higher cal Processes*. Cambridge, MA: Harvard University Press.

Works Cited

Clay, Marie M. 1975. *What Did I Write? Beginning Writing Behaviour*. Portsmouth, NH: Heinemann.

Fountas, Irene C., and Gay Su Pinnell. 2019. *The Reading Minilessons Book, Kindergarten*. Portsmouth, NH: Heinemann.

———. 2018. *Fountas & Pinnell Classroom™ Interactive Read-Aloud Collection*. Portsmouth, NH: Heinemann.

———. 2018. *Fountas & Pinnell Classroom™ Shared Reading Collection*. Portsmouth, NH: Heinemann.

———. 2018. *The Literacy Quick Guide: A Reference Tool for Responsive Literacy Teaching*. Portsmouth, NH: Heinemann.

———. 2017. *Fountas & Pinnell Literacy Continuum: A Tool for Assessment, Planning, and Teaching*. Portsmouth, NH: Heinemann.

———. 2017. *Guided Reading: Responsive Teaching Across the Grades*, 2nd ed. Portsmouth, NH: Heinemann.

———. 2017. *Phonics, Spelling, and Word Study System, for Kindergarten*. Portsmouth, NH: Heinemann.

Gardner-Neblett, Nicole. "The Conversation." September 2015. https://theconversation.com/why-storytelling-skills-matter-for-african-american-kids-46844.

Glover, Matt. 2009. *Engaging Young Writers, Preschool–Grade 1*. Portsmouth, NH: Heinemann.

Hoberman, Mary Ann. 2007. *A House Is a House for Me*. New York: Penguin Young Readers Group.

Johnston, Peter, Kathy Champeau, Andrea Hartwig, Sarah Helmer, Merry Komar, Tara Krueger, and Laurie McCarthy. 2020. *Engaging Literate Minds: Developing Children's Social, Emotional, and Intellectual Lives, K–3*. Portsmouth, NH: Stenhouse.

Masurel, Claire. 2001. *Two Homes*. Somerville, MA: Candlewick.

McCarrier, Andrea, Irene C. Fountas, and Gay Su Pinnell. 2000. *Interactive Writing: How Language and Literacy Come Together, K–2*. Portsmouth, NH: Heinemann.

Morris, Ann. 1992. *Houses and Homes*. New York: HarperCollins.

Ray, Katie Wood, and Matt Glover. 2008. *Already Ready: Nurturing Writers in Preschool and Kindergarten*. Portsmouth, NH: Heinemann.

Resnick, Lauren B., and Catherine E. Snow. 2009. *Speaking and Listening for Preschool Through Third Grade*. Revised Edition. University of Pittsburgh and The National Center on Education and the Economy. Published under license. The New Standards® trademark is owned by the University of Pittsburgh and The National Center on Education and the Economy at 555 13th Street NW, Suite 500 West, Washington, DC, 20004, USA.

Vygotsky, Lev. 1979. *Mind in Society: The Development of Higher Psychological Processes*. Cambridge, MA: Harvard University Press.